FILM FESTIVALS
CINEMA AND CULTURAL EXCHANGE

LEGENDA

LEGENDA is the Modern Humanities Research Association's book imprint for new research in the Humanities. Founded in 1995 by Malcolm Bowie and others within the University of Oxford, Legenda has always been a collaborative publishing enterprise, directly governed by scholars. The Modern Humanities Research Association (MHRA) joined this collaboration in 1998, became half-owner in 2004, in partnership with Maney Publishing and then Routledge, and has since 2016 been sole owner. Titles range from medieval texts to contemporary cinema and form a widely comparative view of the modern humanities, including works on Arabic, Catalan, English, French, German, Greek, Italian, Portuguese, Russian, Spanish, and Yiddish literature. Editorial boards and committees of more than 60 leading academic specialists work in collaboration with bodies such as the Society for French Studies, the British Comparative Literature Association and the Association of Hispanists of Great Britain & Ireland.

The MHRA encourages and promotes advanced study and research in the field of the modern humanities, especially modern European languages and literature, including English, and also cinema. It aims to break down the barriers between scholars working in different disciplines and to maintain the unity of humanistic scholarship. The Association fulfils this purpose through the publication of journals, bibliographies, monographs, critical editions, and the MHRA Style Guide, and by making grants in support of research. Membership is open to all who work in the Humanities, whether independent or in a University post, and the participation of younger colleagues entering the field is especially welcomed.

ALSO PUBLISHED BY THE ASSOCIATION

Critical Texts
Tudor and Stuart Translations • *New Translations* • *European Translations*
MHRA Library of Medieval Welsh Literature

MHRA Bibliographies
Publications of the Modern Humanities Research Association

The Annual Bibliography of English Language & Literature
Austrian Studies
Modern Language Review
Portuguese Studies
The Slavonic and East European Review
Working Papers in the Humanities
The Yearbook of English Studies

www.mhra.org.uk
www.legendabooks.com

STUDIES IN HISPANIC AND LUSOPHONE CULTURES

Studies in Hispanic and Lusophone Cultures are selected and edited by the Association of Hispanists of Great Britain & Ireland. The series seeks to publish the best new research in all areas of the literature, thought, history, culture, film, and languages of Spain, Spanish America, and the Portuguese-speaking world.

The Association of Hispanists of Great Britain & Ireland is a professional association which represents a very diverse discipline, in terms of both geographical coverage and objects of study. Its website showcases new work by members, and publicises jobs, conferences and grants in the field.

Founding Editor
Trevor Dadson

Editorial Committee
Chair: Professor Catherine Davies (University of London)
Professor Stephanie Dennison (University of Leeds)
Professor Sally Faulkner (University of Exeter)
Professor Andrew Ginger
(New College of Humanities at Northeastern University)
Professor James Mandrell (Brandeis University, USA)
Professor Hilary Owen (University of Manchester/University of Oxford)
Professor Philip Swanson (University of Sheffield)
Professor Jonathan Thacker (Exeter College, University of Oxford)

Managing Editor
Dr Graham Nelson
41 Wellington Square, Oxford OX1 2JF, UK

www.legendabooks.com/series/shlc

STUDIES IN HISPANIC AND LUSOPHONE CULTURES

1. *Unamuno's Theory of the Novel*, by C. A. Longhurst
2. *Pessoa's Geometry of the Abyss: Modernity and the* Book of Disquiet, by Paulo de Medeiros
3. *Artifice and Invention in the Spanish Golden Age*, edited by Stephen Boyd and Terence O'Reilly
4. *The Latin American Short Story at its Limits: Fragmentation, Hybridity and Intermediality*, by Lucy Bell
5. *Spanish New York Narratives 1898–1936: Modernisation, Otherness and Nation*, by David Miranda-Barreiro
6. *The Art of Ana Clavel: Ghosts, Urinals, Dolls, Shadows and Outlaw Desires*, by Jane Elizabeth Lavery
7. *Alejo Carpentier and the Musical Text*, by Katia Chornik
8. *Britain, Spain and the Treaty of Utrecht 1713-2013*, edited by Trevor J. Dadson and J. H. Elliott
9. *Books and Periodicals in Brazil 1768-1930: A Transatlantic Perspective*, edited by Ana Cláudia Suriani da Silva and Sandra Guardini Vasconcelos
10. *Lisbon Revisited: Urban Masculinities in Twentieth-Century Portuguese Fiction*, by Rhian Atkin
11. *Urban Space, Identity and Postmodernity in 1980s Spain: Rethinking the Movida*, by Maite Usoz de la Fuente
12. *Santería, Vodou and Resistance in Caribbean Literature: Daughters of the Spirits*, by Paul Humphrey
13. *Reprojecting the City: Urban Space and Dissident Sexualities in Recent Latin American Cinema*, by Benedict Hoff
14. *Rethinking Juan Rulfo's Creative World: Prose, Photography, Film*, edited by Dylan Brennan and Nuala Finnegan
15. *The Last Days of Humanism: A Reappraisal of Quevedo's Thought*, by Alfonso Rey
16. *Catalan Narrative 1875-2015*, edited by Jordi Larios and Montserrat Lunati
17. *Islamic Culture in Spain to 1614: Essays and Studies*, by L. P. Harvey
18. *Film Festivals: Cinema and Cultural Exchange*, by Mar Diestro-Dópido
19. *St Teresa of Avila: Her Writings and Life*, edited by Terence O'Reilly, Colin Thompson and Lesley Twomey
20. *(Un)veiling Bodies: A Trajectory of Chilean Post-Dictatorship Documentary*, by Elizabeth Ramírez-Soto

Film Festivals

Cinema and Cultural Exchange

❖

Mar Diestro-Dópido

l

LEGENDA

Studies in Hispanic and Lusophone Cultures 18
Modern Humanities Research Association
2021

*Published by Legenda
an imprint of the Modern Humanities Research Association
Salisbury House, Station Road, Cambridge* CB1 2LA

*ISBN 978-1-78188-705-9 (HB)
ISBN 978-1-78188-399-0 (PB)*

First published 2021

All rights reserved. No part of this publication may be reproduced or disseminated or transmitted in any form or by any means, electronic, mechanical, photocopying, recording or otherwise, or stored in any retrieval system, or otherwise used in any manner whatsoever without written permission of the copyright owner, except in accordance with the provisions of the Copyright, Designs and Patents Act 1988, or under the terms of a licence permitting restricted copying issued in the UK by the Copyright Licensing Agency Ltd, Saffron House, 6–10 Kirby Street, London EC1N 8TS, *England, or in the USA by the Copyright Clearance Center, 222 Rosewood Drive, Danvers MA 01923. Application for the written permission of the copyright owner to reproduce any part of this publication must be made by email to legenda@mhra.org.uk.*

Disclaimer: Statements of fact and opinion contained in this book are those of the author and not of the editors or the Modern Humanities Research Association. The publisher makes no representation, express or implied, in respect of the accuracy of the material in this book and cannot accept any legal responsibility or liability for any errors or omissions that may be made.

Trademark notice: Product or corporate names may be trademarks or registered trademarks, and are used only for identification and explanation without intent to infringe.

© *Modern Humanities Research Association 2021*

Copy-Editor: Dr Ellen Jones

CONTENTS
❖

Acknowledgements	x
Notes on Referencing and Formatting	xii
Introduction: 'History doesn't record reality but constructs it as the object of its discourse'	1
Film Criticism and Academia	1
Three Amigos: Contextualising the Film Festival	3
Avoiding a Definition of Festival	8
In the Beginning...	12
Cinephilia and FIPRESCI	15
Glamour	18
The Market, the Industry and the Transnational	20
FIAPF	23
1 BAFICI, Buenos Aires Festival Internacional de Cine Independiente: The Festival As International Platform	33
Introduction	34
Establishing a Context for BAFICI: A Wind of Change	34
BAFICI: The New Face of Independent Cinema	39
Buenos Aires Lab (BAL): Investing in New Argentine Cinema (NAC)	56
National Identity, BAFICI and the New Argentine Cinema	60
BAFICI and Historical Memory	67
Impact and Success: The Legacy of BAFICI	72
2 Festival de San Sebastián/Donostia Zinemaldia/International Film Festival: A Film Festival of Contrasts	87
Introduction	88
Concocting the San Sebastián Film Festival; 1953–1955	88
Taking Film Seriously: The Tenure of Antonio de Zulueta, the Influence of José María García Escudero and the Promotion of the New(er) Spanish Cinema; 1956–1964	95
Every Cloud Has its Silver Lining; 1965–1975	102
The Road to Freedom; San Sebastián During the Transition; 1975–1980	105
Rethinking the Festival; 1980s and 1990s	108
The Old, the New and the Rediscovered; San Sebastián's Commitment to Film Preservation	114
Renewing the Festival; The National and the Local	117
Looking In and Looking Out	128
Back to the Future	130

3 The BFI London Film Festival: A Public Festival of Festivals 141
    Introduction 142
    Once Upon a Time. The LFF's Origins 146
    The LFF and British Cinema 151
    The 'Festival of Festivals' Debate 159
    The Eternal Dichotomy: Culture vs. Entertainment 167
    Funding, the Future and Contextualising the LFF's Programme 178

   Conclusion: The End of Festivals? 194

   Bibliography 204

   Index 222

A mi familia
Para Nerea

ACKNOWLEDGEMENTS

❖

The list of people I have to thank for this book never stops. Rather, it keeps on growing in number, like the festivals that populate these pages. But it would have never come into existence without the truly generous funding from the Arts and Humanities Research Council Collaborative Doctoral Award. Likewise, it would have not been published in its current book form without the prize to the best doctoral thesis I was awarded by the Association of Hispanists of Great Britain and Ireland in 2015.

Further financial support was received from the BFI London Film Festival and Queen Mary University of London's Central Research Fund and School of English and Drama, which proved as crucial as the professional and economic backup from London's Research Department at the Royal Central School of Speech and Drama, who provided the time and economic means I needed to finish this fascinating project, and to get it out to the public. I thank them for continuing to believing in it.

The following is one of those endless lists of wonderful people who in one way or another, directly or indirectly, contributed to this book.

First of all, my most sincere gratitude to my main supervisors: Professor Maria M. Delgado, Royal Central School of Speech and Drama (at the time, Queen Mary University of London), and Sandra Hebron, former Artistic Director of the BFI London Film Festival. Thanks also to my secondary supervisors: Dr Sue Harris, Queen Mary University of London, and Helen De Witt, Programmer and former Festivals Producer (2004–2013), BFI London Film Festival.

In Argentina: Mariano Martín Kairuz, Sergio Wolf, Eloísa Solaas and the International Press Department at BAFICI. Quintín, Flavia, Fernando Martín Peña, Andrés Di Tella, Diego Lerer, Celina Murga, Juan Villegas, Javier Portafuz, Cecilia Sosa and Agustín Masaedo.

In Spain: Diego Galán, Mikel Olaciregui, Javier Rebordinos, José Ángel Herrero Velarde, aka 'El Notario', Pere Portabella, José María Prado and the staff at the Filmoteca Española, Gemma Beltrán and San Sebastián's press department, the Filmoteca Vasca, Jaime Pena, Chema de la Peña, Miguel Marías, Reyes Martínez, Álvaro Arroba, Manuel Asín, Carlos F. Heredero, José María de Orbe, José Luis Cienfuegos.

In the UK: Anne-Marie Flynn, Michael Hayden, Sarah Lutton, Professor Ian Christie, Geoffrey Nowell-Smith, Tony Rayns, Richard Porton, Andrei Plakhov, Libby Saxton, Rob Winter, Joana Granero and the London Spanish Festival staff, Carmen Brieva and the Spanish Embassy's Cultural Office staff, my colleagues at *Sight & Sound*, the BFI Reuben library staff, BFI London Film Festival staff and

Press Department, the staff at Queen Mary University of London, and the Royal School of Speech and Drama's Research Department. Also thank you to Kieron Corless.

Thanks also to all the 'angels', as referred to in BAFICI; i.e. all of those who have welcomed me at each of the festivals I have attended, and to every one of my friends who has ever asked the question: 'how's your PhD/book going?' and meant it.

And to LuisJa, for all the music.

★ ★ ★ ★

Above all, I do want to dedicate this book to my parents and my sister, who regardless of circumstances and challenges, refuse to ever stop believing and supporting me, no matter how farfetched my projects seem.

And to my daughter, Nerea (& P.), for having accompanied me on this journey every single step of the way.

Thank you for always being there.

M.D.D., London, March 2021

NOTES ON REFERENCING AND FORMATTING

❖

All translations from Spanish are mine unless otherwise indicated.

Where interviews were conducted in Spanish this is specified in the list of interviews at the beginning of each chapter.

Spanish-language films are named first in Spanish then in English the first time they are mentioned, but only in English (if available) thereafter; for example: *Cría cuervos/Raise Ravens* (1975) when first mentioned; *Raise Ravens* after that.

The same convention is used for Spanish-language organizations: Spanish and then English for the first mention, and English alone (if available) after that.

For all film festivals other than my three case studies, the English name is given.

INTRODUCTION

❖

*'History doesn't record reality but constructs it
as the object of its discourse'*[1]

Film Criticism and Academia

Even though film festivals are the focus of innumerable journalistic reports, historically there has been relatively little written on this topic in the world of academia — especially in comparison to other areas of film studies, such as national and world cinemas, genres, gender and sexuality, celebrity culture, or psychoanalysis. What is more, the existing academic work on film festivals has generally focused on the history or annual performance of a given film festival, more often than not used as the basis for the study of a particular new wave, national cinema or filmmaker. As such, studies have focused on the content, rather than the festival itself — what Thomas Elsaesser pointedly refers to as the 'missing link' in film studies[2] — as an institution and a cultural event.

This situation began shifting about two decades ago, and film festivals are steadily being established as a scholarly subject within Film Studies. This is being achieved not only through an increasing number and variety of academic publications, as well as conferences and workshops dedicated to the subject, but also through the organization of academic modules on film festivals, as well as on programming, or on how to use these events as pedagogical tools.[3]

Yet, in my view, the single most important reason for this shift into academic research on this subject is academic attendance at film festivals. I would argue this has been brought about as a result of two changes. Firstly the increase in the number of film festivals, in many varied locations, a direct consequence of which has inevitably been greater accessibility — many of the smaller and medium-sized film festivals are nothing like as hermetic as the majority of A-list or international festivals have been historically.

Secondly, the growth of local and medium-sized festivals has increased competition amongst them in terms of attendance and content (particularly the inclusion of premieres — international or otherwise) and highlighted the need for improvement in key areas such as audiences. What before was reserved and 'closed off' to critics and film professionals is now open to the public in many forms, from straightforward attendance to active participation via paid (front of house) or un-paid (volunteer) work. This 'opening' has given audiences around the world, and in particular academics, the chance to access the subject of their research more easily. As a film critic and academic, for me what is even more relevant is the access to the inner workings of these heterogeneous events that this entails, opening a door onto the complexities of the exchanges and trading — economic and cultural alike — that require the collaboration of the multiple actors involved in the running of festivals; funding bodies, corporate sponsors, filmmakers, programmers, etc., and the impact that these have on the film industry.

My own experience as film critic and occasional programme advisor, as well as film academic — and above all as a member of the audience — meant I embarked on this project in 2008 with the purpose of bringing together these multifarious ways of experiencing a festival. Since then, this cross-over approach within the academic research of film festivals seems to have captured the zeitgeist. Some of the most influential and seminal projects that have emerged in the late noughties in this field have applied this immersive type of research and a few have brought this film-professional/academic duality to the fore.

The setting up of the online Film Festival Research Network FFRN[4] by Marijke de Valck and Skadi Loist in 2008 is one example of such research. The Network's activities include academic conferences on the subject, as well as organizing regular meetings at film festivals. At Birkbeck, University of London, Dorota Ostrowska's module on Film Festivals offers students the chance to attend the Berlin Film Festival every year. Since 2011 the 'Film Festivals Research' group — part of the FFRN — has taken part in conferences and panels organized by the European Network for Cinema and Media Studies (NECS).

But it is the extensive work of Professor Dina Iordanova of The University of St Andrews in Scotland that has brought these two different research perspectives closest together. This disciplinary cross-over became a physical cross-over when Iordanova organized the first symposium on Film Festivals at St Andrews. Iordanova was also the guest editor of a dossier in the journal *Film Int.*, dedicated to film festivals in 2008,[5] as well as editor of the film festival series she has created under the rubric the Film Festival Yearbooks. In all her projects — conferences, journals and books — contributors comprise mainly academics but also film professionals (critics, programmers, festival directors) and their content includes both essays and interviews. Iordanova's reflections on this type of 'cross-over' approach (as film critic Jonathan Rosenbaum refers to it in his review of the Film Festival series[6]) were set out in her introduction to the first Film Festival Yearbook[7].

The addition of a perspective from the 'inside' has also been part of the approach that scholar Cindy Hing-Yuk Wong adopted in her 2012 book *Film Festivals: Culture, People, and Power on the Global Screen*[8] through her experience at the Hong Kong International Film Festival HKIFF with her brother (Asian film programmer and curator Jacob Wong) and husband (Gary McDonogh, English-language writer and editor of the festival published material from 2006–2008). Her (and Iordanova's) take on the subject is to give an all-inclusive, overarching view of all the different forces that drive, shape and structure film festivals around the world, providing a summary of theories and existing approaches, and therefore making her book, as I myself noted in my review,[9] an indispensable tool for film festival studies.

My own approach echoes Wong and Iordanova's to some extent, but, I would argue, it has one significant difference. This book builds in a further perspective; that of the film critic, i.e. an analytical point of view reflected in the festival coverage that is unique to this particular profession. Or to put it in other words, what Adam Nayman refers to when reviewing Iordanova et al.'s film festival series:[10] an 'on the ground' element, where immersive 'experience' is highlighted over the 'accumulation of data'[11] generated from my own personal experience as a critic, programme advisor and Film Studies academic.

This approach is not lacking in difficulties however, and has proved problematic at times, for despite the (comparatively small) amount of overlap outlined above, the cross-fertilization between academic researchers and film professionals still remains more of an illusion than a reality. One of the main obstacles I have encountered during my research is precisely the substantial gap that still exists between these two somewhat hermetically sealed worlds. Yet where access to a festival on one level can be acquired through purchasing tickets or getting accreditation (paid or unpaid), access to academia can only be via professional output and standing. Likewise, it became noticeable early on that my academic credentials were not going to be of actual help in getting me to talk to the 'insiders', the professionals working at these festivals.

Three Amigos

The ever-expanding film festival circuit makes the study of such events (now numbering in the thousands) crucial, yet fraught with difficulties — how to encompass such a range and diverse ecology? The answer appears to be to focus on a particular angle, be it a certain subject or theme — national cinemas, or the role of the market — or to build case studies of individual festivals by exploring their defining traits and aiming to account for the correspondences and differences between them in a way which may enhance our understanding of film festivals more generally. In this book I take the latter route, doing so via the use of three fascinating case studies. The Buenos Aires Festival Internacional de Cine Independiente/Buenos Aires Independent Film Festival, regularly referred to as BAFICI. The Festival de San Sebastián/San Sebastián Film Festival, known in Basque as Donostia Zinemaldia. And the BFI London Film Festival, the UK's largest film festival; in other words, a non-European, an A-list and a festival-of-festivals respectively.

BAFICI is an audience-driven festival dedicated to showcasing independent cinema, which first opened its doors in 1999. By way of contrast, the oldest festival of the three, San Sebastián, started in 1953 and is one of only fifteen A-list competitive film festivals recognized by FIAPF in the world. Last but not least, the BFI London Film Festival, in many ways brings together elements located in the previous two, as a self-defined 'festival of festivals' that started in 1957.

But how are these three particular festivals related to their national cinemas? In the case of BAFICI and San Sebastián, at the outset their impact was intrinsically linked, and mutually dependent on, the emergence of a new generation of filmmakers within their respective national cinemas. San Sebastián not only promotes Spanish-language (national and Latin American) cinema but also regional cinema through its dedication to programming Basque films. In contrast, the LFF has historically had a less close relationship with British cinema. Closer in essence to Rotterdam or Toronto, London, like its host city, is arguably a plural, eclectic, hybrid festival.

One element these three festivals do have in common, though, is their varying involvement with matters of production, distribution and exhibition, through their respective relationships with the film industry and the organization of their own production funds. These essentially economic transactions are situated within the international film festival circuit, a fact that highlights their transnational nature. Given that transnational spaces such as film festivals operate within a fully globalized economy, one of the elements that I do explore is the overarching economic relations that have recently been established by A-list and other international film festivals with their counterparts and film-makers in developing countries, through a variety of funding mechanisms set up to assist productions in the latter, and their mutually influential relations.

From the particular perspective of this book, two of these exchanges include BAFICI's (and to some extent the new Argentine filmmakers') relationship with Rotterdam International Film Festival's Hubert Bals Fund and the completion scheme Cine en Construcción/Films in Progress that San Sebastián in collaboration with the Cinélatino, Rencontres de Toulose, has been running since 2002, in order to help film-makers from Latin American countries raise enough funds in post-production to complete their films.

It could be argued that production programmes, such as BAFICI's BAL and San Sebastián's completion scheme, Films in Progress, actually have a homogenizing effect on film culture rather than producing a greater aesthetic variety, as is their stated goal. This issue not only proved to be vexing and truly divisive when raised with my interviewees, it also linked to another slippery concept, that of the 'festival film', or what scholar Tamara L. Falicov refers to as the 'construction of a globalized art-house aesthetic',[12] connecting in turn with the notion of cultural (neo)colonialism explored by scholars Julian Stringer, Thomas Elsaesser, Marijke De Valck and Bill Nichols, amongst others.[13]

Chapter 1 is therefore taken up with a non-western festival, the Buenos Aires Festival Internacional de Cine Independiente, aka BAFICI, the youngest festival of the three, which has been taking place in the city of Buenos Aires every April since 1999 and has run uninterruptedly for twenty-two years. There were two principal reasons why this festival was founded: the lack of art-house screening facilities in the city (and indeed the whole country), and the emergence of a new wave of Argentine filmmakers, which galvanized an already existent cinephile/critical scene to the point where three specialized magazines, in particular *El Amante Cine* and *Film* — and to a lesser extent the more industry oriented *Haciendo Cine* — were founded, and which further highlighted the need for a space in which to screen these new films.

Aside from a shared common language — Spanish — some of the issues dealt with in my chapter on BAFICI find their echo in the following chapter, focused on San Sebastián; for instance, the relationship between these festivals and the military dictatorships in their respective countries in the not too distant past (1983 in Argentina, 1975 in Spain). In both cases, the influence of those dictatorial regimes has shaped the way these two countries relate to historical and collective memory: to remembering, but also, to forgetting. The subject of identity becomes especially crucial in the case of San Sebastián, as it involves not only the charged interaction of the national (Spain) with the regional (the Basque Country), but also its international status. For this reason, amongst others, San Sebastián is a prime example of the malleability and versatility inherent in every festival, illustrated by its turbulent, sixty-eight-year political history. A survivor of the transition from the dictatorship to democracy, San Sebastián has been shaped at its core by the Basque issue, and the terrorist acts of the separatist political group Euskadi Ta Askatasuna, known as ETA.

In the case of BAFICI, these tensions are reflected in the carelessness initially displayed towards archiving the material generated by the event (hence the difficulty I experienced in tracing its 'official' history) during its first decade. Yet at the same time, BAFICI's famously thorough retrospectives demonstrate the importance it undeniably attached to the understanding of film history. BAFICI's tenth anniversary marked a U-turn in this attitude with a book, organized by the festival, telling its story from the perspective of the people involved from its inception. Its twentieth anniversary in 2018 was similarly celebrated, with another volume, *Otoños Porteños*. The literature published in partnership with the Festival is now stored and available online.

The San Sebastián Film Festival's dedicated relationship to film history echoes BAFICI's, and is most clearly reflected in the close relationship it has had from the outset with the Filmoteca Española/Spanish Cinemateque — the first ever retrospective took place at San Sebastián's second edition in 1954. Accompanying each retrospective since 1956 — and also in collaboration with the Cinemateque — the Festival publishes a book of essays. An indication of the Festival's constant dialogue with its own past is its commissioning of two books covering its history from its inception to 1977, as well as a complete TV series on its history, directed by Diego Galán and broadcast in 2010. A former director of the Festival, Galán also wrote his own history of the event in 2001.[14]

In the case of London, the literature produced by the Festival has mostly consisted of the catalogues that accompany the programme each year, bar a couple of booklets published to mark the Festival's twenty-fifth and fiftieth anniversaries.[15] Despite being part of the British Film Institute, or BFI, whose main function is to preserve and disseminate the UK's film heritage, retrospectives are not a feature of the LFF, although recently restored films from archives all over the world are shown at the Festival, in what was, up until the 2012 edition, a dedicated section. Yet the LFF is the only festival that can boast a public library solely dedicated to cinema, where all its own brochures and anniversary booklets are available and accessible on request. Set up twenty-two years before the Festival itself in 1935, the recently rechristened BFI Reuben Library was relocated in 2012 to the Southbank, birthplace of the Festival.

In addition to the already extensive press coverage that accompanies any substantial film festival, the evolving digital platforms and forums for cinephilia also inevitably impact debates about these three festivals, and festivals in general. The massive expansion in the number of film festivals worldwide has meant new constituencies developing a stake in these events, not least academics and students. In addition, bloggers and online magazines have become essential for the dissemination of writings about film festivals, focused not just on the films screened but also often on the quality or otherwise of the actual events.

Perhaps one of the most interesting subjects, at least from my perspective, was to also look at each festival's co-dependence and impact on their respective localities: a large urban centre in the case of BAFICI and the LFF, while San Sebastián's coastal location, more akin to Cannes or Venice, raises issues to do with tourism (cultural or otherwise). The fact that the end of summer event in San Sebastián was originally conceived of being either a fashion show or an international music festival — which incidentally would have preceded the Eurovision contest by four years — highlights notions of nation-branding that informed the European geopolitical landscape after World War II.

Linked to this nation-branding, and the accrual of value (cultural or otherwise) at film festivals in the form of awards, press coverage, international presence and red carpet events, is San Sebastián's initial struggle with FIAPF recognition. As I discuss further on in this introduction, the value of FIAPF and its festival categorization has been questioned recently. Where San Sebastián has hustled over the years to achieve and retain its A-list status, the LFF opted out in 2011, resigning its B-category status (non-competitive international film festival) awarded in 1958.

The value-addition supposedly signified by FIAPF's categorization leads me directly to the LFF. Its programme has always brought together the 'best films' from other international film festivals. These films were more often than not awarded prizes at those festivals, and the value of the films themselves was not only the award, but also their presence in these A-list festivals. In fact, for a long time, the festivals where these films had first shown (before playing at the LFF) were thoroughly specified and highlighted in the LFF's brochure.

As previously mentioned, in some ways the LFF is an amalgam of some of the themes that emerge in my discussions of BAFICI and San Sebastián. As an audience festival, the LFF's origins chime with those of BAFICI, since the rationale at its inception was to bring to the city those films that would have otherwise been unable to find distribution in the country. Its programming policy of focusing on the 'best of' other festivals would fill up a void in exhibition just as BAFICI did, and still does. They also share an incipient cinephilia accompanied by the funding of film magazines.

Linking the LFF to San Sebastián is an emphasis on red-carpet glamour — the sole protagonist of the LFF's 2011's edition advertising campaign[16] — even if San

Sebastián's carpet became a black one in 2010. The blurred, Janus-faced dichotomy between the more mediated and commercial content of San Sebastián and BAFICI-style art-house programming structures my discussion of the LFF in Chapter 3. Following on from my observations about San Sebastián, I look at the specific use of glamour that characterizes the LFF and the dialogue it establishes between cinema as art form and as entertainment.

There has been a great deal of discussion over the years about the 'breadth' and 'inclusiveness' of the LFF's programme, which some critics have regarded as lacking an editorial line. But others, such as Wlaschin in 1977, defended these aspects of the LFF early on, arguing that the role of a festival is to offer something for everyone and not just to cater for the 'cinema-buffs and the experimentally minded'.[17] The LFF's extensive programme is similar in scale to BAFICI's own (also an audience festival) and calls to mind the etymology of the word 'festival' as a 'feast' or 'celebration', as well as Bakhtin's notion of the carnival, whereby, a 'feast' (an essential trait of the carnival) is considered a 'primary human cultural form'.[18]

The current ubiquitous presence of industry-oriented events and markets at international film festivals is an issue that I deal with in all three festivals, as each has become directly involved in production in one way or another. Examples of industry events taking place at these festivals are the placement of 'Industry Offices' present in all of them, or industry-focused events such as San Sebastián's Europe-Latin America Co-production Forum, and the LFF's Production Finance Market in collaboration with Film London, all of which underline and to some extent reinforce the transnational nature of film festivals, both in financial and cultural terms alike.

In the case of the LFF, I also look at the way the Festival's promotion of British cinema has shifted during the years to a point where, as part of the rebranding of the BFI, British film acquired its own official competition status award at the Festival for best British newcomer in 2009,[19] the same year the Best Film award was also introduced. British film is also being 'aided' internationally by a new film fund dedicated to the promotion of UK films in the US,[20] and the targeting of China and Brazil as new markets. British film's presence at the main festival markets has also been beefed up under the umbrella phrase We Are UK Film at EFM Berlin,[21] FILMART Hong Kong,[22] Marché du Film[23] at Cannes, Toronto International Film Festival[24] and CineMart Rotterdam.[25]

It could be argued that all these funding and marketing strategies have at their core certain preoccupations regarding the consumption of cultural artefacts in general and film festivals in particular, most clearly evinced by a focus on the changing habits of film viewing registered by buzz words such as 'accessibility' and 'audience'. It is however beyond the scope of this book to address such matters in depth, as the inclusion of market studies and statistics would have steered my course towards economics, rather than ethnography and a more socially oriented approach.

However, a look at these three festivals' websites and their respective audience strategies (particularly numerous in the case of the BFI/LFF, as discussed in chapter 3) only serve to highlight the potential for a thorough comparative study of the actual impact of festivals on the screening facilities where they take place. In this regard, one particular area I explore in Chapter 1 is BAFICI's occupation, during its first fourteen years, of a shopping centre, or the use, discussed in chapter 3, by the LFF of an exhibition chain such as VUE. By contrast, San Sebastián only screens films in local cinemas and theatres. In some cases, it could be argued that the use of more prominent commercial locations sheds light on, or somehow 'reveals', the festival itself, which in turn might compel newcomers to the festival experience to sample other items in other venues (what Simon Fields refers to as the 'sandwich process').[26] The opposite is also true, as these more commercially oriented enterprises are also searching for new audiences, and can therefore benefit from the added buzz created by the festival, something I've experienced directly in my three case studies, especially in the case of the LFF, as discussed in chapter three.

The spaces in which this type of coexistence between high and low culture takes place have been identified by US journalist John Sebrook as *'nobrow'*.[27] This seemingly mutual beneficial interaction of a more commercially-oriented cinema, red carpet glamour and celebrities, together with art-house films and cult directors is therefore the focus of Chapter 3. Although cultural theories have been applied throughout this book as a way of framing my findings, in London and San Sebastián studies such as Guy Debord's 'The Society of the Spectacle'[28] and Theodor W. Adorno and Max Horkheimer, 'The Culture Industry: Enlightenment as Mass Deception'[29] acquire particular significance. The dialectic between film as entertainment and film as art is taking place at a time when the increasing number of industry events cropping up at festivals are changing the actual definition of these events — shifting their role from exhibition platforms, to markets. Or as Carlo Chatrian, artistic director of Berlin Film Festival (2019–), and former director of Locarno (2013–2018), has it (speaking of Toronto), as 'supermarkets'.[30]

Avoiding a Definition of Festival

A prolonged, recurrent social encounter that takes place at a particular time and place — an ephemeral live event that cannot, unlike film, be reproduced, and therefore unique — festivals can historically be traced back to cultural practices in ancient Greece. The largest of them all, the Panathenaea — origin of the Olympic Games — included poetic and musical competitions as part of the cultural events offered. The central events of the Dyonisia festival were the theatrical performance of tragedies and comedies. Celebratory in nature, these events also included an opening and closing and award ceremonies. From these Greek celebrations to world expositions, film weeks, religious pageants, folklore festivities, art fairs, festivals online, music festivals — they share basic traits common to all festivals, such as bringing together individuals to be part of particular artistic encounters. The massive number of film festivals taking place worldwide reflects the heterogeneity that exists in each individual event itself. For many of these film festivals are in reality, as festival director Diego Galán notes, film weeks, or film societies that cover what used to be done by film clubs, at their height during the 1960s and '70s.

The innately malleable nature of festivals (be it film or otherwise), i.e. their chameleonic capacity to balance and adapt to the demands of their various constituencies, allows for a large number of smaller and more specialized film festivals that more often than not serve as local or regional platforms and have no real input into the global market. The research study published by the British Art Festivals Association (BAFA) on art festivals in the UK in 2008, for example, sheds light on the actual impact that these festivals have on local communities,[31] their annual conference in 2012 was focused on the value of festivals as an integral part of society.[32]

Generally less interested in or dependent on premieres and the red carpet, such festivals cover a wide variety of subjects, often organized around or specializing in the work of a particular group, format, minority, film genre, nationality or ideology. There are festivals on different genres or issues such as the environment, horror, sci-fi, animation, human rights, adventure, sports, lesbian, gay and transgender issues, women, burlesque, Jewish people, etc. Cindy Hing-Yuk Wong's survey of this broad and diverse range of festivals points to their protean nature.

This idea was echoed by Hans Hurch, director of the Vienna International Film Festival (known as the Viennale) between 1997 and his sudden death in 2017, who believed the exercise of constructing a definition must emerge from the festival itself:

> The definition and self-definition of every festival has too many layers, their political and cultural tasks is [sic] much too contradictory, just like all the interests intertwined with it. The motives reach from political self-portrayal to touristic returns to the region, from corporate interests to cultural information, from commercial market-orientation to radical self-organisation, from regional development strategies to media events; motives which affect the work and the charm of a film festival. And these are only some terms and insufficient generalisations, which constantly intermingle with each other.[33]

A useful place to begin to try and establish a definition of film festivals that encompasses all these different elements is Alessandro Falassi's seminal work on the origin and meaning of these events. Particularly valuable in this regard is his study of the term festival itself, in his book's chapter 'Festival: Definition and Morphology', which looks at the origins of festivals and the etymology of the word, whose meanings include: fiesta, feast, solemn and celebration. Falassi identifies the basic units of every festival, what he refers to as 'oicotyes', i.e. the 'building blocks' of any given festival (be it religious, folklore, art, culture, food). These blocks, for Falassi, can all be considered ritual acts, or 'rites', for, as he explains, 'they happen within an exceptional frame of time and space, and their meaning is considered to go beyond their literal and explicit aspects'.[34]

A festival, therefore, has an autonomous duration and a spatial dimension, which is devoted to special activities, or rites, which Falassi identifies as follows (these rites find their contemporary echoes in film festivals, and I use them as an organizing structure to discuss the operation of film festivals, as included below).

Falassi's *rites of valorization* are 'the framing ritual' that opens the festival (which for religious events has been called sacralization) and which 'modifies the usual and daily function and meaning of time and space. [...] To serve as the theatre of the festive events an area is reclaimed, cleared, delimited, blessed, adorned, forbidden to normal activities'.[35] French film critic and theorist André Bazin, in his article 'The Festival Viewed as a Religious Order', famously likened festivals (and in particular Cannes) to a convent, a monastery governed by its own rituals, a liturgical celebration where even the press has to wear a uniform (the tuxedo) to the premieres.[36]

Falassi follows with the *rites of purification*, which are identified with the preparation of the space in which the festival is going to take place, as 'these rites of safeguard include various forms of benediction and procession of sacred objects around and through significant points of the festival space setting'.[37] At a film festival these can include film posters, banners around the city, or any other merchandise on display announcing the event; but primarily, the opening gala and its multi-media coverage.

The *rites of passage*, citing Arnold van Gennep's 1909 seminal work on ritual ceremonies,[38] is akin to Marijke de Valck's own theory in which she adapts van Gennep's rites to 'sites of passage' where she sees festivals' main 'function as the gateways to cultural legitimization'.[39] Or rather, all the steps that a film professional has to go through in order to be able to participate in a festival, to the actual screening of the film to an audience. To some extent this could also be applied to any festival attendant, the experience a transformative one in both those cases.

'Through symbolic inversion' Falassi's *rites of reversal* 'drastically represent the mutability of people, culture, and life itself. Significant terms which are in binary opposition in the 'normal' life of a culture are inverted'.[40] This approach relates to the notion of the festival circuit in itself, a distribution, exhibition and — increasingly — production platform operating as a counterweight to the mainstream. Falassi also mentions that 'sacred and profane spaces are used in reverse',[41] which can be seen as the use of shopping malls, museums, old churches, prisons, city squares, factories, and other spaces which are taken over by the festival for its duration. It is also important to note that, although these spaces' original roles are in most cases restored after the festival, their very presence in everyday function acts as trace or remnant of the festival itself.

Falassi's notion of the *rites of conspicuous display* alludes to the 'symbolic elements of the community' or 'sacred elements', which encompass film stars and cult directors, those who can be 'seen, touched, adored, or worshipped',[42] traditionally on the red carpet. Yet these encounters can also take place when guests circulate among the audience themselves, thereby 'enhancing the sense of communitas',[43] as academic Mikel Koven notes.

Albeit Falassi relates the *rites of conspicuous consumption* to food, they refer primarily to 'abundance' and 'excess', as they are 'made generously available, and solemnly consumed in various forms of feast, banquets, or symposia'.[44] In his report on the 2014 edition of FIDMarseille, critic and programmer Neil Young describes how 'film-festival bloat is reaching near-endemic proportions'.[45] Hundreds of films to choose from, events to attend, Q&As, workshops, the stars themselves crowding the red carpet, guests, press members and indeed audiences — the festival space is a constant buzz of consumption. For Simon Fields this experience is 'intoxicating', as some festivals such as Toronto become 'gargantuan',[46] leading to what could be referred to as 'cultural binging', or a 'filmathon', as trade journalist Steven Gaydos refers to the Canadian festival.[47]

In fact, this celebratory 'feast' of abundance and excess is an essential part of the pleasure of film festivals. For Pierre Bourdieu, cultural practices cannot be fully understood 'unless "culture", in the restricted, normative sense of ordinary usage, is brought back into "culture" in the anthropological sense, and the elaborated taste for the most refined objects is reconnected with the elementary taste for the flavours of food'.[48] And the feast is something that Russian literary theorist Mikhail Bakhtin sees as 'a primary human cultural form'. For the festival is directly related with the upside down world of Bakhtin's Carnival as it follows a 'peculiar logic' taking place in a given space and time, where 'all the symbols of the carnival idiom are filled with this pathos of change and renewal, with the sense of the gay relativity of prevailing truths and authorities'.[49] Everyday rules are suspended and there is 'a reversal of the normal patterns of cinema attendance'.[50] This is an idea explored further by Falassi:

> If we consider that the primary and most general function of the festival is to renounce and then to announce culture, to renew periodically the lifestream of a community by creating new energy, and to give sanction to its institutions, the symbolic means to achieve it is to represent the primordial chaos before creation, or a historical disorder before the establishment of the culture, society, or regime where the festival happens to take place.
>
> Such representation cannot be properly accomplished by reversal behavior or by rites of intensification alone, but only by the simultaneous presence in the same festival of all the basic behavioral modalities of daily social life, all modified — by distortion, inversion, stylization, or disguise — in such a way that they take on an especially meaningful symbolic character.[51]

Directly linked to the value bestowed by award ceremonies, the extolling of auteurs and stars or a new national wave of filmmakers, Falassi's *Ritual dramas* are 'usually staged at festival sites, as rites have a strong tie to myths. Their subject matter is often a creation myth, a foundation or migratory legend'.[52] A good example of this is the book that Argentine novelist César Aira wrote using as his inspiration his attendance as a jury member for BAFICI's 2010 edition. Although a fascinating character study on the festival crowd, the story centres on an imaginary festival's most cherished and main guest, an obscure filmmaker whose work has been recently re-discovered and changed his status from 'unknown' to cult. But more interesting, this figure is adored by some and considered the emperor's new clothes by others.

Both money and goods, as well as 'at more abstract and symbolic levels, information, ritual gifts or visits', characterize Falassi's *Rites of exchange*. Encounters are the foundation of any festival, its DNA. In my review of Cindy Hing-Yuk Wong's *Film Festivals: Culture, People, and Power on the Global Screen*, I note how she centres her work on festivals as sites where meetings take place between all kinds of people.[53] Janet Harbord also considers this the principle behind film cultures such as festivals, seeing the latter as 'sites of exchange', 'mixed spaces crossed by commercial interest, specialized film knowledge and tourist trajectories'. Harbord identifies festivals as film cultural discourses 'that come into being in transactions and exchanges, redefining limits and boundaries as they shift around one another'.[54] Indeed, from audiences to filmmakers, critics, producers, film stars, film agents, press, TV crews, projectionists, sales agents, ushers, front of house staff, distributors, festival directors, hotel staff, volunteers, businessmen and women, students, etc., art, film, culture and business get together in the same space for a given time to constitute the 'global community' that informs De Valck's work, and which she identifies as constituent of the majority of film festivals.[55]

The *rites of competition* refer to the 'various forms of contest and prize giving' included in festival competitions, whereby, 'by singling out its outstanding members and giving them prizes, the group implicitly reaffirms some of its most important values [...] In their symbolic aspect, festival competitions may be seen as a metaphor for the emergence and establishment of power'.[56] Although not every film festival has a competition, I would argue that the process of selection and the shaping of the festival's programme is in itself a form of competition. The former because of the actual inclusion at a given film festival; the latter based on the hierarchic division of the programme into sections such as galas, experimental work, or world cinema; the order of these sections; and the actual place where films are played (a shopping mall, a museum, etc.). Participation in a festival is also a means of adding value to the selected films — sometimes monetary value (i.e. cash prizes), but more importantly cultural value, as these films are not only exhibited under special circumstances, and prior to general release, but also covered by the press, fan sites, bloggers and Twitter and Instagram users.

The festival 'life cycle' that Falassi proposes concludes with the *rite of devalorization*, which is symmetrical to the opening rite and 'marks the end of the festival activities and the return to the normal spatial and temporal dimensions of daily life',[57] i.e. the closing gala with its consecration of old and new stars, now assimilated into the festival universe. The most valuable and enduring expression of this is the festival's logo used on the opening credits of any film awarded and/or selected at a given festival.

In the Beginning...

There is a gap of almost forty years between the inception of cinema in 1895[58] and the inauguration of the first ever film festival; it took a particular ideological stance, in this case Fascism, to make it happen. Under Italian dictator Benito Mussolini, the first Esposizione d'Arte Cinematografica came into being in 1932 as part of the eighteenth art exhibition known as the Venice Biennale. In its first edition, the Venice Film Festival attracted over 25,000 spectators, and there were no official awards — instead, an audience referendum was conducted.[59] But the volatile political situation in Europe in the 1930s and the Festival's programming favouring films from Italy and Germany — famously Renoir's *La grande illusion* (1937) was denied the top prize because of its pacifist subject matter[60] — soon generated a response. The Festival de Cannes was originally organized to take place in 1939 but was postponed, following the outbreak of World War II, until 1946.

However — as noted by Jesper Strandgaard Pedersen and Carmelo Mazza (citing Harbord, Elsaesser and De Valck) amongst many others who have written on the history of film festivals — it was the new political order shaping Europe after WWII that determined that the continent would become the cradle of the festival phenomenon,[61] even if the second festival in the world took place on the other side of the Iron Curtain, in Russia. The first Moscow International Film Festival was inaugurated in 1935, and had Sergei M. Eisenstein as the head of the jury, although it did not become a regular event until 1959.[62]

Back in Europe, the reestablishment of Cannes was followed by the founding of Locarno and Karlovy Vary the same year, 1946, Edinburgh in 1947, Berlin in 1951, San Sebastián in 1953, Valladolid in 1956 and London in 1957, whilst both the International Film Festival of India and Melbourne held their first editions in 1952; on the other side of the globe, the first ever Latin American film festival took place in 1951 in Punta del Este, Uruguay, followed by Montevideo, three years later, in 1954, when Mar del Plata also celebrated its first edition in Argentina. In Africa, the Panafrican Film and Television Festival of Ouagadougou was founded in 1969. Albeit quite markedly Eurocentric, the festival phenomenon had become global within twenty years.

The emergence of these international film festival events was also partly a response to the slow disappearance of what were known as cine-clubs. During the 1920s, as Lauren Rabinovitz illustrates, cine-clubs were 'critical to the development of a European avant-garde cinema', as they provided an 'institutional basis for production, exhibition and consumption'.[63] Their heyday occurred during the 1960s and '70s. It was only after the counter-cultural and militant movements that culminated in the 1968 protests in France (which famously closed down that year's Cannes Film Festival) that avant-garde cinema became a staple of many European film festivals.

In 1969, the year following its temporary closure, Cannes attempted to offer a more risqué and less commercial programme than the main competition, via a new sidebar to the festival. The Quinzaine des réalisateurs celebrated its first edition in 1969 as a showcase for the avant-garde and independent non-commercial cinema. This counter-cinema, as Elsaesser notes, would become the bread and butter of the numerous new festivals that started up in or around the 1970s, from Telluride (1973), Pesaro (1965), Toronto (1975) and Rotterdam (1972).[64] This would mark a new period in film festival history that De Valck identifies as being one in which the programmer rose to prominence, just as the rise of the auteur became the clear focus of festivals.[65] Previous to this period, the selection of films was made by Foreign Affairs ministers and diplomats, and mainly focused on national cinemas. In 1972, the first selection committee was inaugurated at Cannes.

Developing this, Elsaesser regards the international festival scene as a 'network (with nodes, flows and exchanges)'[66] that would really establish itself from the

1980s onwards, where what he defines as 'manifestations of post-national cinema' would screen and be given a European dimension, instead of a national one. He also suggests the festival as the historical 'missing link' in our understanding of European cinema, not just since 1945, but since the demise of the historical avant-garde in the 1930s.

Adopting the larger perspective of the whole circuit, Elsaesser takes up the argument where Julian Stringer left off by proposing the application of the following theories: the auto-poetic feedback loops as proposed by Niklas Luhmann, Manuel Castell's theory of the 'space of flows', the 'actor-network-theory' of Bruno Latour, and the theories of complex adaptive systems, centred on 'emergence', 'attractors' and 'self-organization',[67] all cited and developed in De Valck's referential work.

In an echo of this, for Dina Iordanova, 'festivals are a key node in the system of film marketing and distribution [and, I would add, increasingly they are also alternative aids to production] and an important factor in the context of cultural industries at large'.[68] Yet in her account of the various stakeholders pulling the strings at festivals, Ragan Rhyne sees film festivals not as one coherent circuit, but rather as an 'international cultural sector linked by a common economy of public and private subsidy'.[69]

Richard Porton's coverage of the festivals' workshop at St Andrews echoes Rhyne's argument. He notes that festivals are 'complex bureaucratic institutions'[70] which are dependent on the heterogeneous interests (economic, cultural, touristic, et al.) of local governments, private sponsors, and programmers, amongst others. The 'utopian possibilities' and the 'dystopian realities' Porton highlights in the title of his article form the bedrock of many of today's film festivals.

For Elsaesser, festivals encompass both, as he perceives them as '[t]he regular watering-holes for the world's film lovers, critics and journalists, as well as being the marketplaces for producers, directors, distributors, television acquisition heads, and studio bosses'.[71] For trading is, I would argue, the bedrock of film festivals. Interestingly, Elsaesser draws attention to how industrial cities such as Oberhausen — and in an interesting dialogue between industry and tourism, I would add San Sebastián — organized a film festival to add an element of cultural tourism to the city. It is the way cities — and before them, nations — trade in culture that leads me to Pierre Bourdieu's notion of cultural capital, a term that refers to non-financial (social in his case) assets that promote (social) mobility beyond economic means:

> Because the social conditions of its transmission and acquisition are more disguised than those of economic capital, it is predisposed to function as symbolic capital, i.e., to be unrecognized as capital and recognized as legitimate competence, as authority exerting an effect of (mis)recognition, e.g., [...] in all the markets in which economic capital is not fully recognized, whether in matters of culture, with the great art collections or great cultural foundations, or in social welfare, with the economy of generosity and the gift. Furthermore, the specifically symbolic logic of distinction additionally secures material and symbolic profits for the possessors of a large cultural capital.[72]

The concepts of 'transmission and acquisition' in Bourdieu's study are at the centre of Brian Moeran and Jesper Strangaard Pedersen's comprehensive study of the varied ways in which value is accrued at film festivals, amongst other creative industries.[73] Strangaard Pedersen's work with Steven Mezias, Silviya Svejenova and Carmelo Mazza look at the actual impact of European festivals on the film industry, seen as 'tournament rituals', Mezias et al. focus on film festivals as mediators between art and commerce.[74]

Finally, María Devesa Fernández's in-depth study of Seminci, celebrated since 1956 in Valladolid, the second oldest international film festival in Spain,[75] explores the economic impact of festivals on the actual locations where they are held. Her study crucially reveals the role that festivals have in educating audiences, and how the value of the cinephilic knowledge acquired at a film festival resides precisely in those audiences coming back for more in future editions. Also using Seminci as a case-study, this time in comparison to FICXixon, Núria Triana Toribio looks at the way these two Spanish festivals have survived down the years through the prism of their origins and relationships with their respective cities, Valladolid and Gijón.[76]

This cross-disciplinary and fast-forward introduction to the existing literature on festivals is certainly not exhaustive and it is far from including everything that has been written — and continues to be written — on these fascinating filmic ceremonies. But it does highlight the eclectic, myriad possible ways of exploring their multifaceted nature and signals key trends in the ways in which film festivals have been explored by academics, film critics and film professionals.

Cinephilia and FIPRESCI

Exploring the impact that festivals have on cinema historiography, Francesco Di Chiara and Valentina Re[77] identify four levels of possible inquiry: the programming criteria; publications; conferences, workshops, round tables and gatherings; as well as promotional materials. Di Chiara and Re look at the role played by media coverage in adding value to film festivals, but also its (debatable) influence on programming choices,[78] which for them could explain 'the anxiety about novelty and discovery that affects any festival'.[79]

Yet, festivals not only generate external written material in press coverage, academic and journalistic writing etc., but are themselves producers of written material. Of all these activities, the material published by festivals not only adds value to the event itself, but Di Chiara and Re also see this practice as an essential self-marketing tool, that helps create a sense of the festival's identity.[80] In this regard, in my opinion one of festivals' most overlooked aspects is their role as publishers. Furthermore, just as important as the academic material that already exists on these events, and the written texts produced by festivals themselves — monographs, essay collections, special issues, the festival diary — is the festival's own catalogue. It is in the catalogue that much of the festival's own interests and hierarchies are displayed, from its organization into countries, subjects or galas and competitions, to the particular order in which these are displayed.

The value of cinephiles' coverage of festivals cannot be underestimated, as film critic, programmer and former director of the Edinburgh Film Festival (2012–2014) Chris Fujiwara asserts: the 'film festival [i]s an institution that nourishes and shapes cinephilia'; thus, making the festival an object of study and criticism is an urgent task for Fujiwara.[81] In fact, the new accessibility generated by the exponential rise in the number of film festivals around the world has not only brought about the participation of academics in festivals, but has also had an impact on the emergence of a new cinephilia which mainly uses the Internet to disseminate its writings, and which in turn has a direct impact on the coverage of film festivals.[82]

Laurent Jullier and Jean-Marc Leveratto's chapter[83] relates to this by way of what they regard as the democratization of cinephilia by the access that the digital world has facilitated in the present[84] — and one which has inevitably caused essential changes in cinema viewing such as the use of small screens for individual viewing, and the lack of attendance at cinemas themselves. Susan Sontag famously pointed to the changes that cinephilia was already undergoing in the 1990s in her pessimistic essay, 'The Decay of Cinema',[85] where she declared that both cinema and cinephilia had died. The looming question is of course what form cinephilia takes *now* in the digital world compared to what it was *then* — aside from, as Adrian Martin puts it, the banal and indiscriminate (anybody can be a cinema lover[86]) 'love of film'. De Valck references Paul Willemen's seminal 'Through the Glass Darkly: Cinephilia Reconsidered'[87] to locate cinephilia in 'French cultural history and relate it specifically to the 1920s discourse on photogénie'[88]. For Willemen:

> the cinephiliac moment is located in the personal relationship of the viewer to the screen, when he/she discovers extra information — a gesture, body position, look, mise-en-scène etc. that was or was not choreographed for the spectator to see — that touches his/her subjectivity. The immersion of the spectator in the movie theatre is essential to Willemen's understanding of cinephilia.[89]

Jullier and Leveratto, as well as Fujiwara, refer to the timely dossier in the U.S. academic journal *Framework* in 2004, edited by Jonathan Buchsbaum and Elena Gorfinkel.[90] This dossier asked the question 'What is being fought for by today's cinephilia(s)?', which was answered in various ways by its contributors Laura Mulvey, James Quandt, Adrian Martin and Fujiwara himself, and elicited heated response from Jonathan Rosembaum, among others.[91]

As Adam Nayman notes in his review of Porton's *On Film Festivals*, former director of BAFICI Quintín proudly extols the cultivation of an 'atmosphere of film-critical solidarity' during his tenure, and asserts that one of his targets was to welcome to the Festival what he calls a 'nice mafia', 'a united front of critics, programmers and filmmakers with like-minded concepts of cinephilia who can act as a buttress against the encroachment of what Quintín refers to as 'body snatcher' cinephiles; in other words:

> one of those persons who appears agreeable and knowledgeable, but who turns out to regard cinema with the mentality of a Harvey Weinstein.[92]

Following on from Quintín's comment, in his review Nayman identifies a trait he finds common to all the chapters of *On Film Festivals*, which he describes as an attitude of 'us versus them', since many of the contributors are, what he refers to as,

> members — or at least affiliates — of Quintín's 'nice mafia', including Robert Koehler, Olaf Möller and Christoph Huber, all of whom happen to be

regular writers for the Canadian film magazine Cinema Scope (a.k.a. Mafia Headquarters).[93]

Robert Koehler's own take on the current relationship between festivals (at least in the Anglo-Saxon world) and cinephilia is suffused with despair. In a 2019 festival report he bitterly complains about the 'inescapable vortex of the Academy Awards' in relation to smaller, less cinephile-driven film festivals such as Palm Springs (and not so small, like Venice).[94] As such, Koehler identifies the most serious threat to the future of these festivals as 'their general and unexamined aversion to cinephilia, and an unwillingness to place cinephilia at the centre of festivals'[95] activities.

Koehler explains:

> The heart of the matter is an informed philosophy of cinephilia, a practice, an essential way of being and approach to cinema that either imbues a festival's programming, or doesn't. The construction and selection of any section immediately declares itself as, first of all, a critical statement, for film festival programming is always and forever in its first phase an act of criticism, and along with this a declaration of values, comprising two equally important components: those films that are included, and those films that are left out.[96]

In order to safeguard the professional interests of film critics and journalists as well as promote film culture, the Fédération Internationale de la Presse Cinématographique/International Federation of Film Critics (FIPRESCI) was founded in 1925 by a group of Belgian and French film critics, and by 1935 included professionals from fifteen different countries. During the 1946 edition of the Cannes Film Festival, British critic Dilys Powell presided over a FIPRESCI jury that presented an award for the first time, commencing a process the organization still follows today.[97] FIPRESCI's importance not only lies in its promotion and expansion of the idea of cinema 'as a means of artistic expression and cultural education',[98] but a FIPRESCI jury alongside the main jury at many film festivals is the organization's main activity for Honorary FIPRESCI president Andrei Plakhov. Film critic, historian and writer of a Russian-language book on the history of Russian film festivals published in 2006, he notes:

> FIPRESCI's activity is very important because it is the alternative to official juries, which have become more and more terrible everywhere. They always consist of celebrities or media people and never a single critic. In the golden age of Cannes, I would say that each year there was a critic on the jury. One year an international critic, the next one French. It was a rule. But now that's gone, it does not happen anymore. The same in Berlin and in Venice. Critics sit on sidebar juries, on the upcoming cinema say, but not on the main jury. That's why there are so many cases where the decisions handed down by the main juries are completely stupid, because when they consist of three actors and a producer of big films, and they sit in judgement on films by Sokurov or Tsai Ming-liang., nothing good happens.[99]

Cementing the link between the preservation of film criticism and that of film itself, I would like to draw attention to the role of archival material at film festivals, as there is no cinephilia without a comprehensive knowledge of film history, both past and present. Another of the varied roles of the film festival identified here is the active commitment of some festivals to the preservation of film itself, and by extension the festival's own relationship to film history — which takes us back to Di Chiara and Re's study of festivals' impact on historiography. In fact, the whole of the fifth volume of the *Film Festival Yearbook* is dedicated to the subject of archival film festivals.[100]

Julian Stringer also sees preservation as one of film festivals' key roles, and in linking it to cinephilia, notes that

> the ever-expanding globalised film festival circuit proves that cinephilia is alive and well and living in the international marketplace; [...] veritable museums of audio-visual culture [t]he international festival circuit now plays a significant role in the re-circulation and re-modification of 'old' and 'classic' movies.[101]

Using the LFF as his case study, Stringer looks at the revival of old Hollywood films that formed part of the festival's programme from 1981 to 2001 and argues that the choice of those particular films 'serves distinct institutional interests',[102] i.e. the BFI's own role as an organization dedicated to preservation. Interestingly, he argues that although festivals are avowedly committed to exhibiting non-Hollywood films, in fact once Hollywood films have been valued by different criteria, such as the difficulty of restoration, or their original costs, they become reinstated within the festival as alternative cinema — ie. archival material.

Perhaps the inclusion of these films over other restorations can be ascribed to the tastes of one particular programmer, but it nevertheless chimes with a more general welcoming of contemporary Hollywood films by the directors of the LFF (Sheila Whitaker and Adrian Wootton) during the period covered by Stringer. A tendency that beffitingly leads on to my next point; the presence — and deployment — of celebrities and glamour at film festivals.

Glamour

Glamour and the attendance of celebrities became an important part of film festivals from early on, peaking during the 1950s and '60s in the most visible event of all, Cannes. As Emilie Bickerton notes in her introduction to Bazin's 'The Festival Viewed as a Religious Order' essay on French Riviera's Festival de Cannes, at the time (1955) the festival circuit was relatively newly established and more importantly, 'it retained an independence from producers and the industry that no longer exists in today's hob-nobbing and glitz on the Croisette'.[103] For Bazin — as well as for some of the 1968 protesters, including Jean-Luc Godard and François Truffaut, who led the protests that shut down the festival that year[104] — 'these festivals were mostly humiliating spectacles, with cinema decking itself out as a whore for two weeks'.[105] Bazin's metaphor is echoed by Kenneth Turan when he describes attendance at Cannes as 'a fight in a brothel during a fire'.[106] In protest, Bazin had founded his own anti-Cannes festival in 1948, which ran for two editions, the 'Festival du Film Maudit', and in a previous article written in 1953 he had asked 'Why can't we have a serious geology?' of the cinematic art, rather than the 'flashy geography' on display at Cannes.[107]

For Richard Porton, the presence of celebrities at Cannes and other festivals is a vestige of 'the transformative power of ancient rituals' to provide pleasure.[108] It also calls to mind Tom Gunning's concept of early cinema as a 'cinema of attractions'.[109] For Gunning, opposed to the narrative-driven cinema that would later be established as the dominant practice in Hollywood, he suggests early cinema's main purpose was akin to the 'curiosity-arousing devices of the fairground'.[110] More relevant to this book, for Gunning, the term 'cinema of attractions' denotes 'early cinema's fascination with novelty and its foregrounding of the *act of display*'[111] (my italics). Unlike narrative, he continues, 'attractions have one basic temporality, that of the alternation of presence/absence that is embodied in the act of display. In this intense form of present tense, the attraction is displayed with the immediacy of a 'Here it is! Look at it.'[112]

It is Gunning's notion of the 'act of display' as the 'attraction' that I would argue links early cinema with the way audiences experience and consume film festivals. What is more, his concept can be applied as much (and more obviously) to the 'parade' that takes place during the celebrity presence on the red carpet and at gala events and premieres — or during the less glamour-oriented Q&As — as well as to the 'display' of the discovered work of a given filmmaker or national wave. The first instance echoes Bazin's own perspective on what he considered the predominance of glamour that characterized Cannes, particularly during the 1950s and '60s. The latter can be traced further back to those attractions featuring travelogues that precede cinema itself, in which exotic cultures were displayed to an audience. Laura Mulvey's seminal observations, in her essay 'Visual Pleasure and Narrative Cinema',[113] of who does the looking and who is looked at in cinema can certainly be applied to film festivals as well.

The somewhat blurred dichotomy that has defined cinema from its origins — as entertainment (Méliés) and art (the Lumiére brothers) — echoes observations by Stephen Mezias et al., who identify one of the defining traits of film festivals (and one that I discuss at length in relation to the BFI London Film Festival in Chapter 3), as 'mediators between art and commerce in the classification system of the cinema field'[114], as well as 'tournament rituals'[115], with the understanding that 'culture is acknowledged pluralistic, with fluid boundaries between the high and the popular'[116]. Mezias et al. also reference John Seabrook's celebrated *New Yorker* article in which he identifies these intermediate categories, 'the space between the familiar categories of high and low culture', as *nobrow.*[117]

Mezias et al.'s views on glamour at festivals, as well as Seabrook's notion of nobrow, echo Paul DiMaggio who, in 1992, stated that festivals play a role in bridging high and low culture, as they 'play with the boundaries between art and market, between the culture of the elite and the entertainments of the street'.[118] Christian Jungen dedicates his whole book to the tensions that arise through the presence of Hollywood at Cannes[119] and De Valck highlights what she calls the 'Miramaxization' or the use of 'festival exposure, marketing strategies, stars and controversies to promote 'quality' films with cross-over appeal to ensure their box-office success.[120] Former Rotterdam Festival director Simon Field has repeatedly drawn attention to the strategy of screening commercial cinema to help draw attention to the smaller, lesser known films that he deployed during his tenure at Rotterdam (and which he identifies as a Dutch practice), referred to as the 'sandwich process'.[121]

Poet and filmmaker Jean Cocteau's perception of Cannes was rather different to Bazin's. As the Festival's first ever jury president, he is cited on its website describing Cannes as 'an apolitical no-man's-land, a microcosm of what the world would be like if people could make direct contact with one another and speak the same language'.[122] Cocteau's statement could not be more different to Bazin's experience. I would contend that such a disparity in response actually demonstrates something shared by all festivals: that the endless permutations brought about by the plenitude of content at festivals means each attendee experiences their own personal festival — what Chris Fujiwara refers to as 'micro-festivals'[123] — as I noted in my report on the LFF in 2012.[124]

The Market, the Industry and the Transnational

Yet, festivals, as Cocteau earnestly puts it, are first and foremost exchanges, communal experiences. Jérôme Segal uses Falassi's 'time out of time' concept to refer to these events as sites 'where a blending of cultures takes place and a new common identity emerges'[125]. The possibilities of encounters, of new synergies, shape the innately transnational nature of these events. As the world economic order needs to find 'new strategies for executing corporate and political domination', Christian Fuchs notes that 'the restructuration of capitalism [...] is characterised by the emergence of transnational, networked spaces in the economic, political and cultural system', which have become 'more fluid and dynamic' as they have 'enlarged their borders to a transnational scale'[126].

Although in the past, as Stefano Odorico notes in his review of De Valck's book, festivals were 'often considered an occasion for celebrating national culture and identity,' nowadays, 'festivals aim for an international dimension and a direct effect on the market'.[127] For although festivals too are markets to some degree, and have their own fixed rules and hierarchies, they also form a counter-system to the dominant form of cinema. This mirrors Fuchs' definition of the global networks of capitalism as 'an antagonistic system; transnational networks are both spaces of domination and spaces of potential liberation from domination'.[128]

For Lucy Mazdon it is precisely the presence of a market at film festivals (she focuses on Cannes's Marché International du Film established in 1959) that makes a festival into a '*hybrid*' and a '*transnational*' space (her italics); she sees the integral element of these events as 'commerce on a global scale'.[129] She continues:

> cinema is crucial to the construction of the modern nation state. [...] Any attempt to construct a national cinema is essentially about carving a space in a broader international arena and cinema production, exhibition and reception inevitably involve negotiation of these inter- or trans-national relationships.[130]

Behind these transnational features lies the hunger for 'exoticism' that in Stringer's opinion dominates the programming of every film festival — accentuated now by the priority many medium and large festivals such as Toronto and Telluride place on premieres. Liz Czach, refers to Janet Staiger's notion of 'politics of selection' that she uses in her article 'The Politics of Film Canons' to draw attention at the influence that programming has in extolling a constructed version of national cinema.[131]

Recalling Bill Nichols study of the Iranian new wave, Elsaesser locates this sense of 'discovery'[132] — which itself recalls Gunning's ideas around 'attraction' and 'display' — particularly in the European festivals of the 1970s, which I would contend followed on from the nation-building that characterized the reconstruction of Europe after WWII. As De Valck notes, the political climate of the 1970s, in which decolonization movements figured large, ignited an interest in films from 'unfamiliar cinematic cultures, especially the ones sprouting from revolutions in Third World countries'[133] creating what she, and Stringer before her, refer to as cultural colonialism.[134]

In relation to this notion, Julian Stringer identifies a colonialist game of discovery that some film academics engage in, since

> so many of the non-Western films that Western audiences are likely to be familiar with emerged as festival entries, scholars tend to approach them through the nostalgic invocation of those moments when non-Western industries were 'discovered' — that is, discovered by Westerners — at major international competitions.

Stringer pursues this argument further by suggesting that these international cinemas do not get included within a World Cinema canon until they are (colonially) discovered by the West, again usually through these film festivals.[135]

Both De Valck and Wong (herself referencing De Valck) refer to the 'dogma of discovery'[136] with regard to festivals' role in discovering new waves, particularly in relation to the importance that the latter have acquired from the 1980s onwards. For me, the most welcome and distinctive element in Wong's book is her attention to questions of orientalism and cultural colonialism, which also serve to bring to the fore the inequalities of what is generally referred to as 'global' cinema. Her own research has been closely followed by monographs on Asian film festivals, such as SooJeong Ahn's book on the Pusan International Film Festival[137] and more recently, Chris Berry and Luke Robinson's *Chinese Film Festivals: Sites of Translation*.[138]

In this light, Mikel Koven's labelling of festival attendees of all stripes as 'cinematic tourists'[139] responds to what could be regarded as a species of on-site cultural post-tourism, not dissimilar to that experienced by attendees at a World Exhibition. Generally known as 'Expos', these exhibitions originally focused on science and technology; the first World Exhibition famously took place in London in 1851, entitled Great Exhibition of the Works of Industry of All Nations.[140] The precursor of the National Film Theatre (NFT), where the first ever edition of the London Film Festival was held in 1957, was the Telekinema, a state of the art cinema that formed part of the centenary of the first World Fair, the Great Exhibition that took place in 1951 at London's Southbank.

Yet these expository events that took place in the wake of WWII soon shifted into a focus on cultural exchange and nation branding, responding in part to the Cold War political landscape. This shift from a focus on technology to culture and national identity was further signalled in the West by the creation of the first Ministry of Culture by Charles De Gaulle's government in 1959. For Janet Harbord, citing Bordwell, Staiger and Thomson's 1985 study, this also responded to European efforts towards cultural and urban regeneration after WWII: the common ground on which these festivals were built.[141] Another aspect of nation-branding after WWII was the inception of events such as the Eurovision Song Contest, first held in 1956.

Bringing together the countries of the European Broadcasting Union in the service of a 'light entertainment programme', the target was an 'ambitious project to join many countries together in a wide-area international network'.[142] But the Eurovision Song Contest, not dissimilarly to film festivals, was also about constructing a certain definition of national identity, as well as making the local transnational by bringing it into an international sphere, in this case an abstract space where certain rules, rituals and awards are followed, and more importantly where the contestants bring an interpretation of their own nationality.[143]

I would insert an aside at this juncture about the ever so divisive notion of the 'festival film'. Whereas De Valck defines this festival film by its actual exhibition life, limited to being screened within the festival circuit,[144] in his contribution to *On Film Festivals*, James Quandt looks at the actual films themselves, and registers the emergence of

> an international arthouse-festival formula [...] *adagio* rhythms and oblique narrative; a tone of quietude and reticence, an aura of unexplained or unearned anguish; attenuated takes, long tracking or panning shots.[145] (Italics as per original text.)

Commenting on Quandt's chapter, Chris Fujiwara points out that 'films that obey this formula win awards and critical applause not because they do anything interesting, but merely because they do the same kind of thing that was liked before.'[146] Quandt further asks whether this 'uniform international aesthetic' has been 'nurtured by the festival circuit, and by such monetary bodies as Rotterdam's wholly admirable Hubert Bals Fund? And how can such films be considered discoveries when they conform to such a familiar style?'.[147]

Quintín's[148] opinion echoes Quandt's and Pere Portabella's,[149] amongst others, as it suggests the existence of what is debatably known as a 'festival film'; i.e., films with certain shared traits; a view also shared by Wong. A similar discussion is instigated by Tamara L. Falicov's extensive work on the actual mechanisms of film festival production funds such as Hubert Bals and San Sebastián's En Construcción, and their capacity to construct what she refers to as 'a globalized art-house aesthetic'.[150] Other works concerned with the increasing involvement of festivals in film production through various funding mechanisms include Mar Binimelis Adell on co-productions between Latin America and A-list film festivals.[151] Miriam Ross also adopts a critical stance when looking at the role of the Hubert Bals Fund in relation to Latin American films, uncovering an interest on the part of the former in creating easily recognisable national products.[152] Minerva Campos Rabadán further explores the implications of funding schemes such as Cine en Construcción in two of her works.[153] Certainly, in my experience, the mere mention of the term 'festival film' would visibly send a shudder down the spine of many of my interviewees, regardless of their opinion.

FIAPF

Moving from production funds to producers, I would like to end this contextualizing introduction with a discussion of perhaps the most controversial of collaborations taking place at film festivals; the problematic role of FIAPF, Fédération Internationale des Associations de Producteurs de Films/International Federation of Film Producers Associations.[154]

A non-profit organization with its headquarters located in Paris, FIAPF was established in 1933. On its official website, it defines its role as regulator of international film festivals. In the words of its current president, Luis Alberto Scalella, the FIAPF International Film Festival Regulations

> act as quality label for international film festivals that meet minimum standards regarding quality of reception, promotion, infrastructure and screenings. Through this approach, the international producers' community gathered within our Federation supports those festivals that commit to put the artistic and economic interests of the films first and to do so with competence and enthusiasm.[155]

The forty-eight current members of FIAPF are grouped under the following four divisions: competitive feature film festivals; or what has generally become known as the A-list; competitive specialized feature film festivals, aka the B-list; non-competitive feature film festivals, the C-list; documentary and short film festivals.

FIAPF's self-assigned role is to ensure the following: good year-round organizational resources; genuinely international selections of films and competition juries; good facilities for servicing international press correspondents; stringent measures to prevent theft or illegal copying of films; evidence of support from the local film industry; insurance of all film copies against loss, theft or damage; high standards for official publications and information management (catalogue, programmes, fliers).[156]

The (obvious) focus of FIAPF on the industry has prompted former director of BAFICI and film critic Quintín to refer to it as a 'rather bureaucratic organization scheme, Stalinist in effect, and one that signaled the transformation of state-run festivals into industry festivals', as they 'established hierarchies, rules and legitimacy requirements for festivals as well as systems for circulating films amongst them'.[157]

Although FIAPF's divisions have gone unchallenged for much of the organization's eighty-one-year history, they were disputed in 2003, together with FIAPF's overall role and influence. This was mainly due to two reasons. Firstly, because these categories are generally understood as hierarchical — hence A, B and C. Secondly, the pressure generated by the increasing number of film festivals and the competition for premieres, press and publicity this brings with it inevitably impacted on FIAPF. One of FIAPF's self-appointed tasks regarding film festivals is monitoring that they do not overlap. This was the source of the dispute between FIAPF and Montreal, as the festival director at the time, Serge Losique moved the festival dates without consulting FIAPF and ended up overlapping with Venice and Toronto. Losique's response to FIAPF was that Montreal 'did not want to be accredited by an association that has no real authority'.[158] In his coverage of the story, *Variety* critic Steven Gaydos poses the inevitable question:

> In today's fast-moving fest world, unrecognizable from the genteel scene of even 25 years ago, would anybody invent FIAPF if it didn't exist already?[159]

Gaydos refers to Toronto's then director Piers Handling, who recognized the need for a governing organization, which Toronto decided to join because it is 'very useful in settling disputes when some festivals started behaving in a wildcat way.'[160] In an interview in 2012, the director (2012–2015) of the Rome Film Festival, Marco Müller, also called for a confederation of festivals so that festivals become an autonomous and independent reality.[161]

A consequence of the Montreal dispute occurred the following year, when FIAPF, for the first time in over three decades, made public 'a new set of regulations and a series of statements and declarations in which it was reiterated that the categories are not a ranking'.[162] Lobbying, audiovisual laws, copyright issues, tax regulations and anti-piracy became the new foci. Charles Masters also reports that the then director general of FIAPF Bertrand Moullier had pointed out that the 'A-list category is in fact a misnomer because the list is purely descriptive of these events' competitive status and makes no qualitative distinction between them', adding that 'We are not scrapping anything — what we're doing is the reverse. We never did have a classification which distinguished between festivals of high impact'.[163]

Covering the news that festivals will have to make their data public, *Variety*'s John Hopewell asked in 2004:

> Once Fiapf [sic] begins to publish data of festivals, it could be just a further short step to begin to use them for a new classification of festivals.
> This could benefit some, but create challenges for others if they have not been screening a high number of world or international preems [sic] in the past.[164]

FIAPF's authority was also openly questioned in 2007 in the wake of Sundance's director Geoffrey Gilmore's accusations that the producers' organization was 'perpetuating mediocrity with its film festival policy, which is widely seen as a ranking system for international film festivals'.[165]

The response from FIAPF is reproduced in Liz Shackleton's coverage of this dispute for *Screen*:

> Geoffrey Gilmore bases all his criticisms on an alleged 'rating' system carried out by FIAPF: the current accreditation system definitively does not aim at ranking international film festivals. Accredited film festivals are categorised depending on their programming profile, not through some unilateral and subjective criteria about what constitutes quality.[166]

> Being accredited simply means that the international festival commits itself to implementing standards defined by FIAPF members as suppliers of films, such as clear procedures for submission and competition, strong concern regarding the security of screeners, prints and piracy in theatres.[167]

In fact, FIAPF has changed with the times. As Gilmore notes, the world is very different now and the prominence of some festivals over others is not reflected in their recognition by FIAPF, or indeed the latter's categories — as the aforementioned cases of San Sebastián and London illustrate. For the LFF and other B-list festivals, as former producer of the festival Helen De Witt notes,

> Remaining a member of FIAPF was just not good value for money, and that money could be deployed elsewhere for better value for the festival. And several years on, there has been no detrimental effect of leaving.[168]

Yet for San Sebastián, the historical juncture at which it received FIAPF's recognition is an important factor, as the total number of international festivals then was very low, making it a more exclusive club to belong to at a time when Franco's Spain was seeking international validation. The granting of A-list status to the Spanish festival in 1957 placed it on the same level as other international film festivals such as Berlin, Cannes or Venice, adding recognizable international value, legitimizing its international status and, more importantly, validating both, not only the festival, but also Franco's regime.[169]

The necessity for FIAPF to adapt and clarify its position in order to maintain its presence on the festival circuit is indicative of new circumstances; the booming numbers of film festivals of every shape and size. This ubiquity, particularly in terms of expansion outside the hitherto dominant Western world, has not only brought about new challenges that I deal with in the conclusion of this book, but also greater competition. Nowhere is this shift more evident than in the rise of specialized film festivals, exemplified by the case study chosen for Chapter 1, the Buenos Aires Festival de Cine Independiente, or BAFICI; a festival that both specializes in independent film and is most typical of a wider shift in critical perspective from Europe and the Western world to Latin America.

Notes to the Introduction

1. Francesco Di Chiara and Valentina Re, 'Film Festival/Film History: The Impact of Film Festivals on Cinema Historiography. *Il cinema ritrovato* and beyond', *Cinémas: revue d'études cinématographiques/Cinémas: Journal of Film Studies*, 21, 2–3 (2001), 131–51 (p. 139).
2. Thomas Elsaesser, 'Film Festival Networks: The New Topographies of Cinema in Europe', in *European Cinema: Face to Face with Hollywood* (Amsterdam: Amsterdam Univ. Press, 2005), pp. 82–107 (p. 83).
3. For a dossier on using film festivals as a pedagogical tool and examples of already existing modules, see Ger Zielinski, 'Dossier: Film Festival Pedagogy: Using the Film Festival in or as a Film Course', *Scope: An Online Journal of Film and Television Studies*, 26, February 2014, <www.nottingham.ac.uk/scope/documents/2014/february/zielinksi.pdf> [accessed 3 March 2020].
4. 'Film Festival Research Network', <http://www.filmfestivalresearch.org/> [accessed 3 March 2020].
5. 'Film Festivals Dossier', Special Issue of *Film International*, ed. by Dina Iordanova, 6, 4 (2008), 4–81.

6. Jonathan Rosenbaum's book review quoted in Michael Guillén, 'Film Festival Yearbook 2: Film Festivals and Imagined Communities', *The Evening Class*, 24 February 2010, <http://theeveningclass.blogspot.co.uk/2010_02_01_archive.html> [accessed 3 March 2020].
7. Dina Iordanova's website used to be available at <http://www.dinaview.com>; this is no longer the case.
8. Cindy Hing-Yuk Wong, *Film Festivals: Culture, People, and Power on the Global Screen* (New Brunswick, NJ: Rutgers University Press, 2011)
9. Mar Diestro-Dópido, 'Cindy Hing-Yuk Wong: Film Festivals: Culture, People, and Power on the Global Screen', *Journal of Cultural Economics*, 36, 4 (2012), 353–56.
10. Adam Nayman, 'Reviewed Works: *Dekalog 3: On Film Festivals* by Richard Porton; *Film Festival Yearbook 1: The Festival Circuit* by Dina Iordanova, Ragan Rhyne; *Film Festival Yearbook 2: Film Festivals and Imagined Communities* by Dina Iordanova, Ruby Cheung', *Cinéaste*, 35, 3 (Summer 2010), 62–63.
11. Adam Nayman, 'Reviewed Works: *Dekalog 3: On Film Festivals* by Richard Porton; *Film Festival Yearbook 1: The Festival Circuit* by Dina Iordanova, Ragan Rhyne; *Film Festival Yearbook 2: Film Festivals and Imagined Communities* by Dina Iordanova, Ruby Cheung', *Cinéaste*, 35, 3 (Summer 2010), 62–63. Nayman notes: 'One of the great strengths of the FFY publications (both edited by Dina Iordanova, with Ragan Rhyne and Ruby Cheung, respectively, as co-editors) is a general absence of any murky, self-parodically academic writing; the newness of film festival scholarship means that these writers are less inclined to use jargon as a theoretical crutch. Even more valuable is the series's commitment to the viewpoints of the 'on-the-ground' contingent — experienced travellers on the circuit whose observations resonate beyond the mere accumulation of data'.
12. Tamara L. Falicov, '"Cine en Construcción"/"Films in Progress": How Spanish and Latin American Film-Makers Negotiate the Construction of a Globalized Art-House Aesthetic', *Transnational Cinemas*, 4, 2 (2013), 253–71; see also, Tamara L. Falicov, 'Migrating from South to North: The Role of Film Festivals in Funding and Shaping Global South Film and Video', in *Locating Migrating Media* (Lanham, MD: Lexington Books, 2010), ed. by Greg Elmer, Charles H. Davis, Janine Marchessault and John McCullough, pp. 3–21; Tamara L. Falicov, '"The 'Festival Film": Film Festival Funds as Cultural Intermediaries', in *Film Festivals: History, Theory, Method, Practice*, ed. by Marijke de Valck, Brendan Kredell, and Skadi Loist (London, New York: Routledge, 2016) pp. 209–29.
13. Julian Stringer, 'Global Cities and the International Film Festival Economy', in *Cinema and the City: Film and Urban Societies in a Global Context*, ed. by Mark Shiel and Tony Fitzmaurice (London: Blackwell, 2001), pp. 134–44; Thomas Elsaesser, 'Film Festival Networks: The New Topographies of Cinema in Europe', in *European Cinema: Face to Face with Hollywood* (Amsterdam: Amsterdam University Press, 2005), pp. 82–107; Marijke De Valck, *Film Festivals: From European Geopolitics to Global Cinephilia* (Amsterdam: Amsterdam University Press, 2007); Bill Nichols, 'Global Image Consumption in the Age of Late Capitalism', *East-West Film Journal*, 8, 1 (1994), 68–85.
14. Diego Galán, *Jack Lemmon nunca cenó aquí* (Madrid: Plaza & Janés, 2001).
15. *Water Under the Bridge: 25 Years of the London Film Festival*, ed. by Martin Auty and Gillian Hartnoll (London: British Film Institute, 1981); *50/06. Lost and Found. Two Weeks in Autumn. International Visions*, ed. by Gareth Evans (BFI: The Times BFI 50th London Film Festival, 2006).
16. The cover of the Festival's 2011 brochure was a red carpet and the video accompanying it shows a camera following one as it covers the streets of London. 'The 55th BFI London Film Festival Trailer', YouTube, 13 October 2011, <https://www.youtube.com/watch?v=5n9JacMaKHE> [accessed 3 March 2020].
17. Ken Wlaschin, LFF brochure, 1977, p. 2.
18. Alessandro Falassi, *Time Out of Time: Essays on the Festival* (Albuquerque: University of New Mexico Press, 1987), pp.1–10; Mikhail Bakhtin, *Rabelais and His World*, trans. by Hélène Iswolsky (Bloomington: Indiana University Press, 1968, revised edition 1984), p. 11.
19. Note that the UK Film Talent Award introduced in 2004 precedes the Best British Award, although the former was not an official award.

20. Michael Rosser, 'BFI Launches US Distribution Fund', *Screen International*, 13 January 2014, <http://www.screendaily.com/news/bfi-launches-us-distribution-fund/5065271.article> [accessed 3 March 2020].
21. European Film Market Berlin, <https://www.efm-berlinale.de/en/HomePage.php> [accessed 3 March 2020].
22. Hong Kong International Film & TV Market, <http://www.hktdc.com/fair/hkfilmart-en/Hong-Kong-International-Film---TV-Market--FILMART-.html> [accessed 3 March 2020].
23. Marché du Film, <http://www.marchedufilm.com/en> [accessed 3 March 2020].
24. Toronto International Film Festival, <http://www.tiff.net/> [accessed 3 March 2020].
25. Rotterdam Cinemart, <http://www.filmfestivalrotterdam.com/en/cinemart/> [accessed 3 March 2020].
26. Simon Fields quoted in James Quandt, 'The Sandwich Process: Simon Field Talks about Polemics and Poetry at Film Festivals', in *Dekalog 3: On Film Festivals*, ed. by Richard Porton (London: Wallflower Press, 2009), pp. 53–80 (pp. 56–57)
27. John Seabrook, 'Nobrow Culture', *The New Yorker*, 20 September 1999, <http://www.booknoise.net/johnseabrook/stories/culture/nobrow/> [accessed 3 March 2020].
28. Guy Debord, 'The Society of the Spectacle', trans. by Black and Red in 1977, reproduced in *Marxists.com*, originally written in 1967, < https://www.marxists.org/reference/archive/debord/society.htm> [accessed 3 March 2020].
29. Theodor W. Adorno and Max Horkheimer, *Dialectic of Enlightenment* (London and New York: Verso Classics, 1979–1997, original published in 1944), pp. 120–67.
30. Julien Gester, 'Carlo Chatrian: A Locarno Nous Sommes en Dehors de la Logique de Supermarché', *Libération*, 6 August 2014, <http://next.liberation.fr/cinema/2014/08/06/a-locarno-nous-sommes-en-dehors-de-la-logique-de-supermarche_1076520> [accessed 3 March 2020].
31. Festivals Mean Business 3. A Survey of Arts Festivals in the UK. Produced for the British Arts Festivals Association by sam and the University of Brighton. Supported by the Arts Council of Wales. March 2008, <http://www.artsfestivals.co.uk/sites/default/files/FMB3%20Report%20FINAL3%20MAY%202008.pdf> [accessed 3 March 2020].
32. 'Exploring the Festival Model', *ArtsProfessional*, 7 February 2013, <https://www.artsprofessional.co.uk/magazine/262/feature/exploring-festival-model> [accessed 3 March 2020].
33. Hurch, Hans, 'The Film Festival as a Space of Experience', *Schnitt*, 54 (February 2009), 31-33
34. Alessandro Falassi, *Time Out of Time: Essays on the Festival* (Albuquerque: University of New Mexico Press, 1987), pp. 1–10.
35. Falassi, *Time Out of Time*, p. 3.
36. André Bazin, 'The Festival Viewed as a Religious Order', *Cahiers du Cinéma*, June 1955, trans. by Emilie Bickerton and reproduced in *Dekalog 3: On Film Festivals*, ed. by Richard Porton (London: Wallflower Press, 2009), pp. 13–19.
37. Falassi, *Time Out of Time*, p. 3.
38. Arnold van Gennep, *The Rites of Passage* (London: Routledge, 2004).
39. De Valck, *Film Festivals: From European Geopolitics to Global Cinephilia*, p. 37.
40. Falassi, *Time Out of Time*, p. 4.
41. Falassi, *Time Out of Time*, p. 4.
42. Falassi, *Time Out of Time*, p. 4.
43. Mikel Koven, 'Film Festivals as Spaces of Meaning: Researching Festival Audiences as Producers of Meaning', *From the Mind of Mikel. A University of Worcester Film Studies Blog*, 6 September 2013, <http://fromthemindofmikel.wordpress.com/2013/09/06/film-festivals-as-spaces-of-meaning-researching-festival-audiences-as-producers-of-meaning/> [accessed 4 March 2020].
44. Falassi, *Time Out of Time*, p. 4.
45. Neil Young, 'You, The Jury: The XXV FIDMarseille', in *Sight & Sound*, 24, 9 (2014), 20.
46. Simon Field in Quandt, p. 58.
47. Steven Gaydos, 'Battle Behind the Scenes' *Variety*, 24 August 2003, <https://variety.com/2003/scene/markets-festivals/battle-behind-the-scenes-1117891416/> [accessed 4 March 2020].
48. Pierre Bourdieu, *Distinction: A Social Critique of the Judgement of Taste*, trans. by Richard Nice (Oxford: Routledge, 2010), p. xxiv.

49. Mikhail Bakhtin, *Rabelais and his World*, p. 11.
50. Koven, 'Film Festivals as Spaces of Meaning: Researching Festival Audiences as Producers of Meaning'.
51. Falassi, *Time Out of Time*, p. 4.
52. Falassi, *Time Out of Time*, p. 5.
53. Cindy Hing-Yuk Wong, *Film Festivals: Culture, People, and Power on the Global Screen* (New Brunswick, NJ: Rutgers University Press, 2011); Mar Diestro-Dópido, 'Cindy Hing-Yuk Wong: Film Festivals: Culture, People, and Power on the Global Screen', *Journal of Cultural Economics*, 36, 4 (2012), 353–56.
54. Janet Harbord, *Film Cultures*, pp. 60–61.
55. De Valck, *Film Festivals: From European Geopolitics to Global Cinephilia*.
56. Falassi, *Time Out of Time*, p. 5.
57. Falassi, *Time Out of Time*, p. 5.
58. Although Thomas Edison and Eadweard Muybridge had been doing experiments in cinema previous to this date, their experiences involved a single spectator. This is the reason why 1895 is considered the birth of cinema, as the Lumière brother's cinematographe was the first collective show. For more information see Guy Austin, 'French Cinema from 1895 to 1968, a Brief Survey', in *Contemporary French Cinema: An Introduction* (Manchester: Manchester University Press, 1996, p. 1–17 (p. 1); Tom Gunning, ''Now You See It, Now You Don't': The Temporality of the Cinema of Attractions', in *The Silent Cinema Reader*, ed. by Lee Grieveson and Peter Krämer (New York: Routledge, 2004), pp. 41–50. See also Tom Gunning, 'The Cinema of Attractions Early Film, Its Spectator and the Avant-Garde' in *Early Cinema. Space. Frame. Time*, ed. by Thomas Elsaesser (London: British Film Institute, 2006), pp. 56–62.
59. For more information about both the Venice Film Festival and the Venice Biennale, see <http://www.labiennale.org/en/cinema/history/the30s.html?back=true> [accessed 4 March 2020].
60. Kenneth Turan, *Sundance to Sarajevo: Film Festivals and the World They Made* (Berkeley: University of California Press, 2002), p. 18.
61. All cited in Jesper Strandgaard Pedersen and Carmelo Mazza, 'International Film Festivals: For the Benefit of Whom?', *Culture Unbound. Journal of Current Cultural Research*, 3 (2011), 139–65 (p. 145).
62. Moscow International Film Festival, <http://36.moscowfilmfestival.ru/miff36/eng/page/?page=history> [accessed 4 March 2020].
63. Lauren Rabinovitz, *Points of Resistance: Women, Power & Politics in the New York Avant-garde Cinema, 1943–71* (Urbana and Chicago: University of Illinois Press, 2003), p. 39.
64. Elsaesser, 'Film Festival Networks: The New Topographies of Cinema in Europe', p. 100.
65. De Valck, *Film Festivals: From European Geopolitics to Global Cinephilia*.
66. Elsaesser, 'Film Festival Networks: The New Topographies of Cinema in Europe', p. 84.
67. Elsaesser, 'Film Festival Networks: The New Topographies of Cinema in Europe', p. 83.
68. 'Film Festivals', Special Issue of *Film International*, ed. by Dina Iordanova,. 6, 4 (2008), 4–81 (p. 4).
69. Ragan Rhyne, 'Film Festival Circuits and Stakeholders', in *Film Festival Yearbook 1: The Festival Circuit*, ed. by Dina Iordanova with Ragan Rhyne (St. Andrews: St. Andrews Film Studies, 2009), pp. 9–39. Rhyne's earlier doctoral thesis opens up the study of stakeholders in festivals to the Gay and Lesbian communities. See Ragan Rhyne, *Pink Dollars Gay and Lesbian Film Festivals and the Economy of Visibility* (unpublished doctoral thesis, New York University, 2007).
70. Richard Porton, 'The Festival Whirl. The Utopian Possibilities — and Dystopian Realities — of the Modern Film Festival', *Museum of the Moving Image*, 8 September 2009, <http://www.movingimagesource.us/articles/the-festival-whirl-20090908> [accessed 4 march 2020].
71. Elsaesser, 'Film Festival Networks: The New Topographies of Cinema in Europe', p. 84.
72. Pierre Bourdieu, 'The Forms of Capital', trans. by Richard Nice, in *Handbook of Theory and Research for the Sociology of Education*, ed. by J. Richardson (New York, Greenwood, 1986), pp. 241–58, <https://www.marxists.org/reference/subject/philosophy/works/fr/bourdieu-forms-capital.htm> [accessed 4 March 2020].
73. *Negotiating Values in the Creative Industries: Fairs, Festivals and Competitive Events*, ed. by Brian Moeran and Jesper Strandgaard Pederson (Cambridge: Cambridge University Press, 2011).

74. Stephen Mezias, Jesper Strandgaard Pedersen, Silviya Svejenova and Carmelo Mazza, 'Much Ado about Nothing? Untangling the Impact of European Premier Film Festivals' (Denmark: Copenhagen Business School, 2008), Creative Encounters Working Paper, <http://openarchive.cbs.dk/bitstream/handle/10398/7781/Creative%20Encounters%20Working%20Papers%2014.pdf?sequence=1> [accessed 4 March 2020].
75. María Devesa Fernández, *El impacto económico de los festivales culturales: el caso de la Semana Internacional de Cine de Valladolid* (Madrid: Fundación Autor, 2006).
76. Núria Triana Toribio, 'FICXixón and Seminci: Two Spanish Film Festivals at the End of the Festival Era', *Journal of Spanish Cultural Studies*, 12, 2 (2011), 217–36.
77. Francesco Di Chiara and Valentina Re, 'Film Festival/Film History: The Impact of Film Festivals on Cinema Historiography. *Il cinema ritrovato* and beyond', *Cinémas: revue d'études cinématographiques/Cinémas: Journal of Film Studies*, 21, 2–3 (2001), 131–51, <http://www.erudit.org/revue/cine/2011/v21/n2-3/1005587ar.html> [accessed 4 March 2020].
78. Di Chiara and Re, 'Film Festival/Film History', p. 144.
79. Di Chiara and Re, 'Film Festival/Film History', p. 144.
80. Di Chiara and Re, 'Film Festival/Film History', p. 135.
81. Chris Fujiwara, '*On Film Festivals*, edited by Richard Porton (London: Wallflower Press, 2009)', FIPRESCI *The International Federation of Film Critics*, 2010, <http://fipresci.hegenauer.co.uk/undercurrent/issue_0609/fujiwara_festivals.htm> [accessed 25 May 2020].
82. Some examples of film blogs include: Lumière, <http://www.elumiere.net/> [accessed 4 March 2020]; senses of cinema, <http://sensesofcinema.com/> [accessed 4 March 2020]; Jonathan Rosenbaum, <http://www.jonathanrosenbaum.com/?cat=5> [accessed 4 March 2020].
83. Laurent Jullier and Jean-Marc Leveratto, 'Cinephilia in the Digital Age', in *Audiences*, ed. by Ian Christie (Amsterdam: Amsterdam University Press, 2012), pp. 143–54.
84. Jullier and Leveratto, 'Cinephilia in the Digital Age', pp. 143–54.
85. Susan Sontag, 'The Decay of Cinema', *New York Times Magazine*, 25 February 1996.
86. Adrian Martin, 'Cinephilia as War Machine', *Framework: The Journal of Cinema and Media*, 50, 1 and 2 (2009), 221–25 (p. 221).
87. Paul Willemen, 'Through the Glass Darkly: Cinephilia Reconsidered', *Looks and Frictions* (London: British Film Institute, 1994), p. 231.
88. De Valck, *Film Festivals: From European Geopolitics to Global Cinephilia*, p. 183.
89. Paul Willemen in De Valck, *Film Festivals: From European Geopolitics to Global Cinephilia*, p. 183.
90. 'What's Being Fought by Today's Cinephilia(s)?', ed. by Jonathan Buchsbaum and Elena Gorfinkel, *Framework. The Journal of Cinema and Media*, 50 (2009).
91. Jonathan Rosenbaum, 'Reply to Cinephilia Survey', *Jonathan Rosenbaum*, 21 June 2009, <http://www.jonathanrosenbaum.net/2009/06/reply-to-cinephilia-survey/> [accessed 4 March 2020].
92. Quintín, 'The Festival Galaxy', in *Dekalog 3: On Film Festivals*, ed. by Richard Porton (London: Wallflower, 2009), pp. 38–52 (p. 50).
93. Nayman, 'Dekalog 3: On Film Festivals, Film Festival/Yearbook 1: The Festival Circuit/Film Festival Yearbook 2: Film Festivals and Imagined Communities'.
94. Robert Koehler, 'What the Palm Springs Film Festival Tells Us About the State of Cinema', *filmjourney.com*, 22 January 2019, <https://filmjourney.org/?p=3630> [accessed 4 March 2020].
95. Robert Koehler, 'Cinephilia and Film Festivals', in *Dekalog 3: On Film Festivals*, ed. Richard Porton (London: Wallflower, 2009), pp. 81–97 (p. 81).
96. Koehler, 'Cinephilia and Film Festivals', p. 82.
97. FIPRESCI, <http://www.fipresci.org/about/history.htm> [accessed 4 March 2020].
98. FIPRESCI.
99. Andrei Plakhov, interview with Mar Diestro-Dópido, London Russian Film Festival offices, 13 December 2011.
100. *Film Festival Yearbook 5: Archival Film Festivals*, ed. by Alex Marlow-Mann (St Andrews: St Andrews Film Studies, 2013).
101. Julian Stringer, 'Raiding the Archive: Film Festivals and the Revival of Classic Hollywood', in *Memory and Popular Film*, ed. by Paul Grainge (Manchester: Manchester University Press, 2003), pp. 81–96 (p. 82).

102. Stringer, 'Raiding the Archive', p. 84.
103. Emilie Bickerton, 'Introduction', in André Bazin, 'The Festival Viewed as a Religious Order', *Cahiers du Cinéma*, June 1955, trans. by Emilie Bickerton and reproduced in *Dekalog 3: On Film Festivals*, ed. by Richard Porton (London: Wallflower Press, 2009), pp. 13–19 (p. 13).
104. Damon Wise, 'Cannes 1968: The Year Jean-Luc Godard and François Truffaut Led Protests that Shut Down the Festival', *Deadline*, 18 May 2018, <https://deadline.com/2018/05/cannes-film-festival-1968-protests-anniversary-commentary-news-1202380606/> [accessed 4 March 2020].
105. Bickerton in André Bazin, 'The Festival Viewed as a Religious Order', p. 14.
106. Kenneth Turan, *Sundance to Sarajevo: Film Festivals and the World They Made* (Berkeley: University of California Press, 2002), p. 13.
107. Bickerton in André Bazin, 'The Festival Viewed as a Religious Order', p. 14.
108. *Dekalog 3: On Film Festivals*, ed. by Richard Porton (London: Wallflower Press, 2009), p. 3.
109. Tom Gunning, '"Now You See It, Now You Don't": The Temporality of the Cinema of Attractions' in *The Silent Cinema Reader*, ed. by Lee Grieveson and Peter Krämer (New York: Routledge, 2004), pp. 41–50. See also Tom Gunning, 'The Cinema of Attractions Early Film, its Spectator and the Avant-Garde', in *Early Cinema. Space. Frame. Time*, ed. by Thomas Elsaesser (London: British Film Institute, 2006), pp. 56–62.
110. Gunning, '"Now You See it, Now You Don't": The Temporality of the Cinema of Attractions', p. 42.
111. Gunning, '"Now You See it, Now You Don't": The Temporality of the Cinema of Attractions', p. 42.
112. Gunning, '"Now You See it, Now You Don't": The Temporality of the Cinema of Attractions', p. 44.
113. Laura Mulvey, *Visual and Other Pleasures* (Hampshire: Palgrave, 1989). See also John Berger, *Ways of Seeing* (London: British Broadcasting Corporation and Penguin Books, 1988) and Theodor W. Adorno, *The Culture Industry: Selected Essays on Mass Culture* (London: Routledge, 2001). The attention paid by film festivals to the phenomenon of stardom can be connected to the increasing interest in social aspects of the cinema. See for instance David Giles, *Illusions of Immortality: A Psychology of Fame and Celebrity* (New York: St. Martin's, 2000).
114. Stephen Mezias, Jesper Strandgaard Pedersen, Silviya Svejenova and Carmelo Mazza, 'Much Ado about Nothing? Untangling the Impact of European Premier Film Festivals', *Creative Encounters*, Working Papers 14 (Copenhagen Business School: Institut for Interkulturel Kommunikation og Ledelse, 2008), 1–31 (p. 4)
115. Stephen Mezias, et al., 'Much Ado about Nothing? Untangling the Impact of European Premier Film Festivals', p. 2, <http://hdl.handle.net/10398/7781> [accessed 4 March 2020].
116. Stephen Mezias, et al., 'Much Ado about Nothing? Untangling the Impact of European Premier Film Festivals', p. 3.
117. Seabrook, 'Nobrow Culture'.
118. Paul DiMaggio, 'Cultural Boundaries and Structural Change: The Extension of the High Culture Model to Theatre, Opera, and the Dance, 1900–1940.', in *Cultivating Differences*, ed. by M. Lamont and M. Fournier (Chicago, Ill: University of Chicago Press, 1992), pp. 21–57 (p. 47).
119. Christian Jungen, *Hollywood in Cannes. The History of a Love-Hate Relationship* (Amsterdam: Amsterdam University Press, 2014), p. 30.
120. De Valck, *Film Festivals: From European Geopolitics to Global Cinephilia*, p. 124.
121. Fields quoted in James Quandt, 'The Sandwich Process', pp. 56–57.
122. Jean Cocteau quoted in Cannes Film Festival, <https://www.festival-cannes.com/en/69-editions/history> [accessed 25 May 2020].
123. Michael Guillén, 'Insane Mute: Interview with Chris Fujiwara', *twitch*, 1 September 2010. <https://screenanarchy.com/2010/09/insane-mute-interview-with-chris-fujiwara.html> [accessed 25 May 2020].
124. Mar Diestro-Dópido, 'The Pain in Spain', *Sight & Sound Online*, 19 October 2012, <http://www.bfi.org.uk/news-opinion/sight-sound-magazine/comment/festivals/lff-blog-pain-spain> [accessed 4 March 2020].
125. Falassi cited in Jérôme Segal, 'Film Festivals in the Evolution of a Common Transnational

Identity', in *The 4th Annual Conference on 'Cultural Production in a Global Context: The Worldwide Film Industries'*, Grenoble Ecole de Management, Grenoble, France, 3–5 June 2010 (conference proceedings), p. 2. <http://jerome-segal.de/Publis/Grenoble_Conference_SEGAL_on_film_festivals.pdf> [accessed 4 March 2020]. 'The research for this article was supported by Grant No. 215747 of the 7FP Social Sciences and Humanities Programme of the European Communities for the project 'Art Festivals and the European Public Culture'.

126. Christian Fuchs, 'Transnational space and the "Network Society", in *21st Century Society*, 2, 1 (2007), 49–78 (p. 68).
127. Stefano Odorico, 'Review: Marijke De Valck (2007) Film Festivals: From European Geopolitics to Global Cinephilia', *Film–Philosophy* (12 December 2008), 124–30, <http://www.film-philosophy.com/index.php/f-p/article/view/61/46> [accessed 4 March 2020].
128. Fuchs, 'Transnational space and the "Network Society"', p. 49.
129. Lucy Mazdon, 'The Cannes Film Festival as Transnational Space', *Post Script*, 25, 2 (2006), 19–30 (pp. 22–23).ß
130. Mazdon, 'The Cannes Film Festival as Transnational Space', p. 29. For a detailed introduction to transnational cinema see *Transnational Cinema, The Film Reader*, ed. by Elizabeth Ezra and Terry Rowden (London and New York: Routledge, 2006), p. 2 <http://www.amazon.co.uk/Transnational-Cinema-Film-Reader-Focus/dp/0415371589> [accessed March 2020].
131. Liz Czach, 'Film Festivals, Programming, and the Building of a National Cinema', *The Moving Image*, 4, 1 (2004), 76–88.
132. Elsaesser, 'Film Festival Networks: The New Topographies of Cinema in Europe', p. 99. In his article Elsaesser references Bill Nichols, 'Discovering Form, Inferring Meaning: New Cinemas and the Film Festival Circuit', *Film Quarterly*, 47, 3 (1994), 16–27.
133. De Valck, *Film Festivals: From European Geopolitics to Global Cinephilia*, p. 70.
134. Julian Stringer, 'Global Cities and the International Film Festival Economy', in *Cinema and the City: Film and Urban Societies in a Global Context*, ed. by Mark Shiel and Tony Fitzmaurice (London: Blackwell, 2001), pp. 134–44 (p. 138).
135. Stringer, 'Global Cities and the International Film Festival Economy', p. 135.
136. De Valck, *Film Festivals: From European Geopolitics to Global Cinephilia*, p. 177.
137. SooJeong Ahn, *The Pusan International Film Festival, South Korean Cinema and Globalization*, ed. by Chris Berry and Luke Robinson (Hong Kong: Hong Kong University Press, 2011).
138. *Chinese Film Festivals: Sites of Translation* (New York: Palgrave Macmillan, 2016).
139. Koven, 'Film Festivals as Spaces of Meaning: Researching Festival Audiences as Producers of Meaning'.
140. '1851 London', *ExpoMuseum. The World's Fair Museum Since 1998*, n.d., <http://www.expomuseum.com/1851/> [accessed 4 March 2020].
141. Harbord, *Film Cultures*, p. 43.
142. Eurovision Song Contest, <http://www.eurovisionfamily.tv/blog/read?id=263357> [accessed 4 March 2020]. On the Eurovision Song Contest, see Karen Fricker and Milija Gluhovic (eds), *Performing the 'New' Europe: Identities, Feelings, and Politics in the Eurovision Song Contest* (Houndsmills: Palgrave Macmillan, 2013).
143. Published in European Broadcasting Union, *EBU Technical Review*, 262 (Winter 1994), <http://www.ebu.ch/en/technical/trev/trev_262-editorial.html> [accessed 4 March 2020].
144. De Valck, *Film Festivals: From European Geopolitics to Global Cinephilia*, p. 176.
145. Quandt, 'The Sandwich Process', pp. 76–77.
146. Chris Fujiwara, Review of '*On Film Festivals*, edited by Richard Porton (London: Wallflower Press, 2009)', *FIPRESCI The International Federation of Film critics*, 2010, <http://fipresci.hegenauer.co.uk/undercurrent/issue_0609/fujiwara_festivals.htm> [accessed 25 May 2020].
147. Quandt, 'The Sandwich Process', p. 77.
148. Quintín, 'The Festival Galaxy' in *Dekalog 3: On Film Festivals* (London: Wallflower, 2009), ed. by Richard Porton, pp. 38–52 (p. 30).
149. Pere Portabella, phone interview with Mar Diestro Dópido, 29 June 2011.
150. Tamara Falicov, '"Cine en Construcción"/"Films in Progress": How Spanish and Latin American Film-Makers Negotiate the Construction of a Globalized Art-House Aesthetic', pp.

253–71. See also, 'The "Festival Film": Film Festival Funds as Cultural Intermediaries', in *Film Festivals: History, Theory, Method, Practice*, ed. Marijke de Valck, Brendan Kredell, and Skadi Loist (London, New York: Routledge, 2016), pp. 209–29.
151. Mar Binimelis Adell, *La geopolítica de las coproducciones hispanoamericanas. Un análisis a través de su presencia en los festivales de clase A (1997–2007)* (unpublished doctoral thesis, Universidad Rovira i Virgili, 2011), <https://www.tdx.cat/handle/10803/51762#page=1> [accessed 25 May 2020].
152. Miriam Ross, 'The Film Festival as Producer: Latin American Films and Rotterdam's Hubert Bals Fund', *Screen*, 52, 2, (2011), 261–67.
153. Minerva Campos Rabadán, 'La América Latina de 'Cine en Construcción'. Implicaciones del apoyo económico de los festivales internacionales', *Archivos de la Filmoteca*, 71 (2013). See also her article 'Reconfiguración de flujos en el circuito internacional de festivales de cine: el programa Cine en Construcción', *Secuencias. Revista de Historia del Cine*, 35 (2012), 84–102.
154. For more information see FIAPF, <http://www.fiapf.org/members_governance.asp> [accessed 4 March 2020].
155. Information available at FIAPF, <http://www.fiapf.org/members_governance.asp> [accessed 4 March 2020].
156. Information available at FIAPF, <http://www.fiapf.org/members_governance.asp> [accessed 4 March 2020].
157. Quintín, 'The Festival Galaxy', p. 40.
158. Gaydos, 'Battle Behind the Scenes'.
159. Gaydos, 'Battle Behind the Scenes'.
160. Piers Handling quoted in Gaydos, 'Battle Behind the Scenes'.
161. Celluloid Liberation Front, 'Interview: Rome Film Festival Director Marco Mueller Discusses .is First Year and the Future of Italian Cinema', *Indiewire*, 20 November 2012, <http://www.indiewire.com/article/interview-rome-film-festival-director-marco-mueller-discusses-his-first-year-and-the-future-of-italian-cinema> [accessed 4 March 2020].
162. Charles Masters, 'Fests Play by New Rules', *Backstage*, 24 August 2004, <http://www.backstage.com/news/fests-play-by-new-rules/> [accessed 4 March 2020].
163. Masters, 'Fests Play by New Rules'.
164. John Hopewell, 'Festival organizers rewrite their A-B-C's', *Variety*, 16 May 2004, <https://variety.com/2004/film/news/festival-organizers-rewrite-their-a-b-c-s-1117905025/> [accessed 4 March 2020].
165. Liz Shackleton, 'FIAPF Defends Film Festival Accreditation System', *Screen*, 9 July 2007, <http://www.screendaily.com/fiapf-defends-film-festival-accreditation-system/4033493.article> [accessed 4 March 2020].
166. Shackleton, 'FIAPF Defends Film Festival Accreditation System'.
167. Shackleton, 'FIAPF Defends Film Festival Accreditation System'.
168. Helen De Witt, email exchange with Mar Diestro Dópido, 18 August 2014.
169. For a complete history of FIAPF as well as excerpts that are no longer available on their website, labelled for members only, see Jesper Strandgaard Pedersen and Carmelo Mazza, 'International Film Festivals: For The Benefit of Whom?', *Culture Unbound. Journal of Current Cultural Research*, 3 (2011), 139–65 (pp. 147–48); Dina Iordanova, 'Showdown of the Festivals: Clashing Entrepreneurships and Post-Communist Management of Culture', *Film International*, 4, 23 (2006), pp. 25–38; De Valck, *Film Festivals: From European Geopolitics to Global Cinephilia*, pp. 53–55.

CHAPTER 1

❖

BAFICI, Buenos Aires Festival Internacional de Cine Independiente: The Festival As International Platform

History

- **Date founded**: 1999
- **International/National/Local context**: International festival of independent cinema funded by the Government of the City of Buenos Aires
- **FIAPF (category)**: Not accredited
- **Calendar slot**: Festival's place within the international film festival circuit: April, between Berlin and Cannes (end of summer, beginning of autumn in Argentina)

Infrastructure[1]

- **Are screened films rented or offered?** Both
- **Screening venues 2018**: thirty-six, seven of them cultural centres and open air screenings for free
- **Attendance**: 390,000 attendees

Structure and staffing

- **Permanent programming staff**: six people — the director and five programmers
- **Annual Budget**: $800,000 (approx. 34 million Argentine Pesos) in 2018 from public funds
- **Ticket price**: 50 AR$ (regular ticket); 40 AR$ (students and retired people) — the average price of a cinema ticket in Buenos Aires is around 280 AR$

Directors of BAFICI:

- Andrés Di Tella: 1999–2000
- Eduardo Antín aka Quintín: 2001–2004
- Fernando Martín Peña: 2005–2007
- Sergio Wolf: 2008–2012
- Marcelo Panozzo: 2013–2015
- Javier Porta-Fouz: 2016–

Introduction

At the end of 2008, Argentine academic Gonzalo Aguilar published *Otros Mundos/ Other Worlds*,[2] a book about the New Argentine Cinema that emerged in the 1990s. Aguilar maps out a history of this group of filmmakers by linking together the myriad factors that surrounded their emergence, in the process giving the reader an indispensable reference book on the subject.

It was only in early 2010, as I was writing the review of the English translation of Aguilar's book,[3] when I realized that I too, in a way — albeit with a more modest outsider's approach — aim to achieve something similar. By writing this chapter I am aiming to map the circumstances (historical, political, economical, social) that surrounded the origins of the Buenos Aires Festival Internacional de Cine Independiente (known as BAFICI), in order to begin to engage with it and its role in Argentine film productions. I attempt to do this predominately by way of the people involved in the Festival, both internally: organizers, directors, programmers; and externally: government, audience, filmmakers, as well as exploring the Festival's international position and impact.

It is worth noting also that the name of the Festival suggests a certain ambiguity around the word 'independent', an issue I also discuss in this chapter. It allows for two different interpretations, as its two possible English translations attest. On one hand it can be the Buenos Aires Independent Film Festival; on the other, the Buenos Aires Festival of Independent Film.

As with the New Argentine Cinema, most of the information on BAFICI has been disseminated through many platforms, such as the local and international press, and particularly the Internet. So I will be 'constructing' the history of the Festival from the sources I have accessed. The lack of an 'official' history is also the reason why I have had to largely rely on interviews and oral histories. As such, this chapter draws extensively on information acquired through first person interviews carried out during my own attendance at BAFICI's eleventh edition in 2009. There, I listened to many people and opinions in order to understand the Festival from as many perspectives as possible.

Overall, this chapter grows as much out of research by way of publications and media coverage as out of my desire to try to understand the Festival from the perspective of the people that make it, experience it and ultimately fund it, firmly situating BAFICI within the history of the city and the country where it emerged in 1999.

Establishing a Context for BAFICI: A Wind of Change[4]

The festival of Mar del Plata, located in the coastal city that gives it its name, was originally established in 1954 as an international competitive film festival, and is one of the oldest Latin American film festivals (after Punta del Este, Uruguay, in 1951, followed by Montevideo, which took place the same year as Mar del Plata), as well as the only one in the continent to be awarded A-list category status by FIAPF in 1959 — and held to this day. The festival originated in an attempt to bring attention to the Argentine and Latin American film industries, and so, although the majority of its editions were held in Mar del Plata, in 1964 the festival was celebrated in the city of Buenos Aires, and alternated with the International Film Festival of Rio de Janeiro in its 1967 and 1969 editions — Mar del Plata and Rio film festivals were then the most important cultural events in Latin America.[5] By the time Mar del Plata was founded, the Golden Eras that the film industries of Latin American countries — mainly Mexico and Argentina — had enjoyed in the first half of the century had already fallen foul of US domination of the Latin American box offices and film markets — an ongoing problem even in the twenty-first century. In Argentina alone, as Tamara L. Falikov explains, aside from the internal problems that its film industry was already experiencing across the various sectors — exhibition, distribution and production — 'since the 1950s the United States [...) enjoyed between 60 to 80 percent market share in Argentina', practically going 'unchallenged until recently (from 1997 onwards)'.[6]

Soon after the festival's inception, the coastal city of Mar del Plata would pulsate with the glamour big international stars brought with them, mirroring the other (at that time very few) international film festivals such as Cannes or Venice. This helped Mar del Plata to attract enough attention to position itself in the then emerging international film festival circuit. It was during the decade leading up to the 1968 revolts that the role of international film festivals was reassessed by a generation of new young independent filmmakers. Opposed to the ways in which local governments and ministries of tourism had already successfully exploited the commercial potential of film festivals, these filmmakers (in keeping with the marked shift towards militancy at the time) used international film festivals as launching platforms, making them essential for the visibility of a politically charged Latin American cinema.

Parallel to the greater international visibility of what is recognized as Tercer Cine/Third Cinema,[7] the political and economic instability that occurred in Latin America after the 1968 upheavals, together with the internal struggle generated by the different attempts at democratization in some of these countries, only accentuated the different ways in which Latin American countries would deal with their modes of production, expanding the range of possibilities offered to filmmakers. Argentina's rapidly deteriorating political situation would culminate in a military dictatorship that brought its cultural scene to a halt in 1976, as had already happened in Brazil as early as 1967. Mar del Plata was closed down in 1970 after ten editions.

During subsequent years, the political tensions in Argentina would culminate in a coup d'etat and the Dirty War, which lasted from 1976 to 1983. Under the military dictatorship, film and all other media and culture were subject to the state's full control and censorship. Unsurprisingly, the films dominant at the box office (those that passed the censoring boards) were light entertainment such as comedies and musicals with a definite Argentine flavour; effectively, nationalist propaganda produced for (mainly) national consumption. Nevertheless, there were also subversive comedies that, although at first glance devoid of any criticism, were actually replete with double meanings and cultural references that challenged the regime, such as *Los chiflados dan el golpe* (Enrique Dawi, 1975) or singer and actor Ramón 'Palito' Ortega's films. Of these it was said that 'the more fantastic the films looked, the closer to reality they were'.[8] As for the international titles, many were either cut or censored altogether. However, there was an alternative underground film scene where some of these films were played, particularly in Jewish community centres in the city of Buenos Aires.

It wasn't until 1983 that the Argentine film industry re-emerged, and with democracy came art cinema. From 1983 to 1989 the Argentine political power fell into the hands of the Radical Party, which favoured 'high culture' and promoted homegrown arthouse cinema to be consumed at international film festivals. In the process, the government was attempting to revive the country's 'past glories' via internationally prestigious directors such as Fernando 'Pino' Solanas, Luis Puenzo and Eliseo Subiela. Solanas's *Tangos: El exilio de Gardel/ Tangos: The Exile of Gardel* (1985) collected a total of ten awards in Havana, Argentina, France and Venice; Subiela's *Hombre mirando al sudeste/Man Facing Southeast* (1986) a total of sixteen in Argentina, San Sebastián, São Paolo and Toronto in 1988, and Puenzo's *La historia oficial/The Official Story* (1985) collected twenty-two international awards (from Cannes, Berlin, New York, Toronto, Los Angeles, Spain, Kansas), including an Oscar for best foreign language film.

Yet, despite some international recognition, this period was brought to an end by a political and economic crisis that soon spread throughout Latin America and caused a severe slump in national film markets. By the time conservative Carlos Ménem entered office in 1989, Argentina was already facing an even more severe financial crisis; Ménem's film policies inevitably focused on the blockbuster and alignment with Hollywood commercial/business values.

A particularly barren period ensued, characterized by European co-productions and a fierce fight against the growing power of television and home video consumption. As Argentine journalist and film critic Diego Batlle explains, the result was the almost complete disappearance of Argentine cinema owing to the commercial blockbusters that were inundating the theatres.

> Without either political or private finance, and faced with absolute indifference from the public towards the scarcity of public events and the unattractive films on offer, national production was virtually dead both commercially and artistically.[9]

And with no independent cinema, the visibility of certain commercial projects was consequently far greater. Batlle supports his argument with startling statistics, comparing the few deserted theatres still open at the beginning of the 1990s to the 2190 cinemas in 1959, and the financial state of the Argentine national film market in 1975, in which filmgoers surpassed 3 million, to the unprecedented low in 1994 when '11 new Argentine releases sold barely 323,513 tickets (the most successful, *Convivencia* (1993), by Carlos Galettini, had 138,000 spectators), and overall they were left with a bare 1.8% of sales'.[10] As pressure was exerted on the government by a new generation of filmmakers to create a new film law, countries such as Mexico and Brazil, as well as Argentina, whose once powerful film industries were now severely diminished, developed a series of similar film and audiovisual laws that would control the national and local markets, and which were built mainly on tax incentives. These measures included the creation of taxes for video and TV and the establishment of screening quotas, all engineered to promote and create funds for national cinema.[11] Hence, the Mexican Film Law was created in 1992, Brazil followed a year later, and Argentine and Uruguayan Film Laws were passed in 1994. Mirroring these countries' strategies in response to the positive results they produced, Colombia (2003), Chile (2004) and Ecuador (2006) introduced film laws in the new millennium.

Close scrutiny of the current position of Latin American cinema in the international market reveals that during the last two decades this cinema has managed to achieve prominence on the international film festival circuit as well as commercially, with Mexican and Brazilian filmmakers such as Alejandro González Iñárritu and Fernando Meirelles making the leap from national productions to Hollywood in a relatively short time. Nevertheless, this has not been achieved solely by the increased presence of Latin American films abroad, but above all by a much stronger and more visible range of Latin American international film festivals, for whom the promotion of local talent is a top priority. At the same time, this change in attitude is key to understanding what is one of the most crucial shifts in Latin American film industries in general — and the Argentine film industry in particular — in the last two decades; i.e., the increased involvement of government in film industry financing, as Elena and Díaz López note.[12] In the case of film festivals, most of which are organized and funded through cultural and tourist ministries, intervention in the early stages of film production is far greater.

This more hands-on financial control of cinema by the state has become a cause for great concern, speculation and debate in the case of Argentina. In a Spanish-language study of production within the New Argentine Cinema that was published by BAFICI in 2009, Agustín Campero addresses this question directly, affirming that the influence of the state is now the most important factor shaping many Latin American film markets.[13] To illustrate this, he explains how in 1994, when the new Film Law was passed, the Instituto Nacional de Cinematografía (INC)/National Film Institute changed its name to INCAA (Instituto Nacional de Cine y Artes Audiovisuales/The National Institute of Cinema and Audiovisual Arts) in an attempt to define its own purpose. Under its new name, the Institute, as Falicov also argues, decided that instead of only favouring directors with a proven track record — as it had done until then — it would shift its parameters to cast a 'wider net': that is, to include first and second-time filmmakers in their pool of funding recipients.[14] This initiative clearly follows a distinctly corporate logic, trying to cash in (economically as well as in terms of prestige) on the presence and success that Argentine independent film had enjoyed at international festivals. However, in order to access the Institute's funding, as Campero goes on to explain, non-mainstream films were forced to disguise themselves as 'commercial'[15] with a view to maintain a status quo.

The result of state control of film financing in Argentina was a tendency to homogenization. Even though funding is given to 'new' filmmakers with 'new' ideas, the approved projects often share similar characteristics (they are after all approved by the same people constituting the board), thus contributing to the consolidation of certain film 'clans' formed by the new up-and-coming directors.[16] This posits important questions about the efficacy and equality of any type of national funding itself, a subject that I will not be dealing with in this book. However, as noted in Chapter 2, I will be approaching similarly problematic issues surrounding funding schemes generated in what Tamara L. Falicov denominates the Global North (particularly European film festivals). International funding strategies such as the Hubert Bals and San Sebastián's own Cine en Construcción are aimed at a 'certain' cinema produced in the Global South (one of her case studies is the role that the French Fonds Sud plays in relation to funding African cinema).[17]

Once it was understood by governmental funding bodies for culture that film festivals are an effective way of reaching international audiences (by playing national films outside the country) and hence attracting the attention of foreign distributors, producers and media (as well as being a fast way to acquire international cultural prestige), the position of Latin American film funding bodies clearly shifted from mainly participating at film festivals to funding and organizing (or reviving, as in the case of Mar del Plata after 26 years) their own film festivals. A quick glance at the list of registered film festivals in Latin American countries and Cuba[18] reveals a marked increase in their number, mainly within the first decade of the millennium. The majority of these smaller and newer festivals — regardless of the country — are specialized, or focused on short films, or genre-oriented showcases for horror and/or fantastic cinema, or films aimed at children (thus introducing the festival experience to younger generations and their parents in order to capture new audiences). Nevertheless, Brazil, Mexico and Argentina have managed to regain and maintain their leadership within the continent; their film industries, festival cultures and film producers are established as the most visible and internationalized of the Latin American countries.

The international character of film festivals and their global reach inevitably mean that questions of national identity and national representation are being revisited in relation to these film events. Indeed, many of the current big-name filmmakers' strengths — such as Argentine Juan José Campanella or Mexican Alejandro González Iñárritu — lie precisely in their ability to depict and explore a globalized hybridity, and make strategic business-oriented use of film festivals, which are essentially transnational events. As Marvin D'Lugo notes:

> the tension between those planetary images and the idiosyncrasy of local identity continues to move film authors to seek ways to co-produce new Latin American cultural identities through collaborative practices that have as their ultimate goal not the erasure of the local but a meaningful relocation of it in the global community.[19]

This 'transnational' hybridity is, also an important facet of film festivals (a concept discussed in more detail in Chapter 3 particularly in regards to the LFF), partly a result of the global economy in which they function, and partly due to their own position as alternative means of exhibition and, increasingly, production.

Now more business-focused than its predecessors, the Guadalajara International Film Festival in Mexico, for instance, was established in 1986 as a platform for Latin American films with a particular showcasing for new Mexican cinema. A competitive festival since its origins, its accredited industry numbers rose to five thousand delegates in 2012. It screened over 250 films in its 2012 edition and hosts a FIPRESCI jury; all of which has helped give this event a strong presence in the international festival calendar. Aware of the importance of supporting national and Latin American cinema, the festival founded its Film Market in 2006, which dealt with about two hundred film projects in 2012.[20] It is in part due to their films premiering at this festival that Guillermo del Toro, Alfonso Cuarón and Diego Luna have become international household names during the last twenty years. The international media coverage and subsequent festival touring turned them into recognizable national figures, increasing attention towards the local market.

In Brazil, the new Festival do Rio, inaugurated in 1999, came about as the product of a merger of two other film festivals: the Rio Cine Festival, founded in 1984, and the Mostra Banco Nacional de Cinema, created in 1988. Currently the biggest film festival in Latin America, it hosts BAFTA, CIFEJ and FIAPF awards and is widely considered to be Brazil's foremost platform for 'international business' that 'has opened a door for film *business* in the continent' [my italics].[21] The festival adopts a very different approach to the one pursued by the older International Film Festival of São Paulo (Mostra Internacional de Cinema de São Paulo), which promotes itself as a not-for-profit cultural event. BAFICI would follow a similar pattern to the latter.

BAFICI: The New Face of Independent Cinema

As discussed earlier, as a consequence of the dictatorship, there were no film festivals in Argentina from the 1970s until 1996. That year, following the 1994 reform of the Argentine Constitution, the City of Buenos Aires (politically autonomous from Buenos Aires Province and Argentina since the 1880s) held its first mayoral elections under the new statutes, and had the mayor's title formally changed to 'Chief of Government of the Autonomous City of Buenos Aires'. The winning candidate was from the radical left, Fernando de la Rúa; he would then be followed in quick succession by: Aníbal Ibarra (2000–2006, centre left); Jorge Telerman (2006–2007, a Peronist, publicly dubbed 'the dandy of culture'); Mauricio Macri (2007–2015, staunchly conservative, President of Argentina since 2015); and the current Horacio Rodríguez Larreta (elected in 2015, centre right).

There are now two main international film festivals in the country, Mar del Plata and BAFICI (Buenos Aires Festival Internacional de Cine Independiente), and they are both funded by INCAA and their respective City Hall Culture departments in inverse proportions, i.e.: Mar del Plata receives most of its funding from INCAA, the national film institute, whereas BAFICI is funded mainly by the regional and city governments.

After a hiatus of 26 years that began in 1970, caused by the political instability that led to the coup d'état in 1976 and the start of the Dirty War (1976–1983), nowadays

Mar del Plata, with a budget of around $1.774.000 (70 million Argentine Pesos),[22] currently screens over three hundred films watched by around 130,000 people.[23] In 1996 the festival recovered its FIAPF 'A' category and tried to resurrect its years of glory, not without a fair degree of criticism of the excessive cost and its focus on past Hollywood figures.[24] Nevertheless, as film critic and former director of BAFICI Eduardo Antín [aka Quintín] admitted in the 1999 special edition of the magazine he was editing, *El Amante Cine* (which was dedicated to the newly inaugurated BAFICI, just prior to its first edition), national film critics and cinephiles alike would undertake a pilgrimage each year to Mar del Plata, ignoring its copious commercial programme and focusing their attentions on the (comparatively scarce back then) independent world cinema that was also shown at the Festival. Yet, a quick glance at the history section of the Festival's website gives an immediate impression of Mar del Plata's initial concerns and focus; highlighted there are the celebrities who have visited over the years.[25] Not surprisingly, Mar del Plata was and is largely regarded by the local media as a red-carpet festival that has never had a defined programming stance. The public perception of this festival is that its main agenda has largely been to revive the glam and glitz that the festival enjoyed in the 1960s, by bringing old stars from overseas to be photographed in exchange for high sums of money, something that, as Fernando Martín Peña (former director of BAFICI) points out, 'is completely oblivious to the current economic and political reality of the country.'[26] Peña was invited to direct Mar del Plata in 2008, and nowadays the festival has regained a more balanced position towards its programme, claiming to follow a cinematographic tradition where 'classic cinema coexists with new tendencies, new voices and new technologies',[27] as well as actively promoting Argentine cinema, regaining its status as a must stop in the international circuit for many a film critic pilgrim.

The existence of BAFICI, with its decisively strict cinephile programme (cinephilia is a concept dealt with in this chapter, as well as in the introduction to this book, in particular in relation to film festivals), offered a pronounced contrast with such celebrity-driven tactics. It is precisely BAFICI's cinephile inclinations which seem to have helped it rapidly acquire a privileged position within the international festival circuit, where its virtually 'utopian', anti-commercial stance has led Spanish critic, Violeta Kovacsics, to dub it 'the perfect film festival'[28] — a matter I will deal with in more detail later in this chapter. For now, suffice to say that the buzz generated at both BAFICI and to a lesser extent Mar del Plata is indelibly linked with the new generation of Argentine filmmakers that emerged in the 1990s.

The origins of BAFICI are as convoluted as its directorial trajectory. Unlike San Sebastián and London, where artistic directors are in position for relatively extended durations, BAFICI has had six different directors since its first edition, as follows:

- Filmmaker and writer Andrés Di Tella: 1999–2000
- Film critic, film historian and film archivist Eduardo Antín aka Quintín: 2001–2004
- Film critic, filmmaker and film historian Fernando Martín Peña: 2005–2007

- Filmmaker, screenwriter and critic Sergio Wolf: 2008–2012
- Film critic and film historian Marcelo Panozzo: 2013–2015
- Film critic, programmer and film historian Javier Porta-Fouz: 2015–

As the professions of the directors of the Festival show, cinephilia has clearly been the dominant mode at BAFICI from its outset. As early as 1993, film historian Fernando Martín Peña, the third director of the Festival, set up, in partnership with Sergio Wolf (fourth director of the Festival) and curator Paula Félix-Didier, a film magazine called *Film* (which ceased publication in 1998). This magazine was created two years after the establishment of what was, until that point, the main film magazine in Argentina, *El Amante Cine*, owned and edited by the second director of the Festival, Quintín, together with his wife Flavia de la Fuente (since 2004, the editor has been Javier Porta Fouz, sixth and current director of the Festival).

During the early 1990s, Peña and Wolf noted that, although there were a few young new directors making films in Buenos Aires, they lacked a place in which to show their films. Hence, as an offshoot of their magazine, together, they organized an annual showcase week called Cine Argentino Inédito (Unknown Argentine Cinema, which was similar to what afterwards, under Peña's direction, would be 'Lo nuevo de lo nuevo' [the new of the new] and eventually the Argentine competition in BAFICI) to show films such as *Rapado* (1992) by Martín Rejtman and *Picado Fino/Fine Powder* (1996) by Esteban Sapir — these would later become key films and filmmakers in the newly coined New Argentine Cinema. The films were shown at the Sala Lugones and funded privately by *Film* magazine; they were accompanied by an article by Wolf himself, 'Una generación de huérfanos',[29] which was published in two parts in *Film*, and dedicated to the new group of filmmakers. This event lasted until BAFICI itself started.

In 1995 INCAA concurrently inaugurated a national film contest called 'Historias Breves'. The ten winning shorts were exhibited at commercial cinemas as a collective work that had been subsidized by the Institute. The shorts were made by then unknown but now internationally established directors grouped under the rubric New Argentine Cinema (hereafter referred to as NAC), which included names such as Lucrecia Martel and Pablo Trapero. It is important to note that this was a group of filmmakers who had hardly anything in common aside from being part of the 'Historias' project, and did not in any case constitute a generation. They were rather united by a common history to which they had reacted according to their different temperaments, subjects and experiences — and indeed have continued to do so following vastly different trajectories.

Aside from the emergence of the NAC, theatre also proved to be crucial to the origin of BAFICI. The first Festival Internacional de Buenos Aires or FIBA (Buenos Aires International Festival) was inaugurated by the Ministry of Culture in 1997, two years before BAFICI. Conceived from the beginning as a biennial international festival of contemporary theatre and stage arts, its focus has always been on exhibiting local and national talent internationally, and from its origins FIBA enjoyed success and large audiences, focusing on the Autonomous City of Buenos Aires as one of the world's capitals of theatre. However, as Martín Peña explains, here is where part of the origin of BAFICI also lies, since in that same year he and the team of journalists working on his magazine *Film* helped to shape an initiative by Cecilia Hecht (Managing Director Canal Ciudad Abierta at Gobierno de la Ciudad de Buenos Aires [Buenos Aires City Government]) exploring the possibility of a film festival with similar characteristics to FIBA — one that would focus on the local independent films that were being ignored by the standard channels of distribution. This idea was presented to Darío Lopérfido (the then subsecretary of Cultural Action of Buenos Aires and founder of FIBA), who, when he became Secretary of Culture the following year, decided to go ahead with it, albeit with a different team in charge. Instead, Lopérfido appointed documentary filmmaker Andrés Di Tella as the artistic director of the first Buenos Aires Festival Internacional de Cine Independiente (BAFICI).

In turn, Di Tella himself had already encountered Lopérfido in 1995. After finishing his first documentary feature film *Montoneros: una historia* (1998), Di Tella realized that very few of the international film festivals at that time would accept video, and the only ones that would were those dedicated to video art, a category his own documentary film did not fit. In Buenos Aires, commercial cinemas would not screen it either, and there were no alternative screening rooms to show it. So Lopérfido proposed it be screened at the Centro Cultural Rojas (Rojas Cultural Centre), which belonged to the University of Buenos Aires. *Montoneros* was not only the first film ever made about the guerrilla phenomenon (the 'Montoneros' were a Peronist urban guerrilla group active during the 1960s and '70s in Argentina), but also the first film screened at this centre, with such success that it played regularly there for the next two years. Since that moment, the centre has become the focus of a certain counter-cultural movement against the *Menemismo* (a term widely used to refer to the government of Ménem, which implies conservative, provincial and chauvinist politics) involving music, theatre, the arts, and, from that moment on, film too, proving that an audience already existed in Buenos Aires for an event such as BAFICI.

Organized and run by the city's administration (hence a municipal festival), BAFICI was originally projected to take place in the gap years of the theatre festival. However, the resounding critical and box-office success of its first edition in 1999 would not only secure the Festival an annual spot but marked the consolidation of a new group of filmmakers giving them, as well as the city, a newly found place and identity within the international film market.

One of the most discussed and controversial issues regarding the Festival is the inclusion of the loaded term 'independent' by Lopérfido himself in its title. All of its first four directors relate how the term was questioned and criticized at the beginning by the media. For Di Tella, admittedly,

> It was a word that didn't convince me fully; I didn't find it necessary. Either way, the word independent, at least in Argentina, connoted and came from the independent theatre scene. And that had a very specific meaning, which was the alternative theatre, the off-theatre, or whatever you want to call it. There's something of the spirit of that alternative theatre, that off-theatre, of something made with no money, where the actors take their sandwiches to the dressing

FIG. 1.1. Festival-goers outside Recoleta Venue
Photo © Agustín Maseado

rooms and where instead of money there was a very strong will to do things. This spirit was also in the Argentine cinema that was starting to explode at that moment, and which would later be called New Argentine Cinema.[30]

The early decision to screen films at the Abasto Shopping Centre, which has been used uninterruptedly until and including the 2012 edition, received a lot of criticism.[31] Located in the middle of one of the most emblematic *tangueros* neighbourhoods in Buenos Aires (the statue of Carlos Gardel was erected here in 2000), this huge 1920s art-deco building, whose design was inspired by the Les Halles building in Paris, is on the one hand flanked by small, quiet streets full of the characteristic tango dance halls and shops, and restaurants, and on the other side the hectic and traffic-loaded Avenida Corrientes, which crosses the most bohemian district of Buenos Aires from the Obelisk to the port. The building used to be the Old Abasto Market and ceased to sell its fruits and vegetables in 1984, only to benefit from foreign investment and open its doors as a 120,000 square metre shopping-mall housing designer international brands in 1998. But most importantly, it hosts the Hoyst cinema chain, which were used as the Festival's main screening rooms. It is not uncommon for film festivals around the world — from Budapest to Gijón, Ljubljana and one of BAFICI's own influences, Rotterdam — to use such cinema spaces in shopping malls. In tune with the market spirit that once dominated this place, people gather here once a year for almost two weeks to consume films, exchange opinions and business cards and to make distribution deals over a coffee or lunch in the many restaurants and cafes in the building.

In the celebrated essay that Austrian philosopher and social critic Ivan Illich wrote with Beth Gill, shopping centres are famously referred to as the cathedrals of the present: modern secular temples of consumption,[32] condemned by Fredric Jameson as the clearest postmodern symbol of late capitalism. For Marc Augé, shopping centres are 'empirical non-places'[33] of circulation, consumption and communication, created as a result of the fragmentation and 'decentring' brought by a globalized world. The correlation between shopping centres and film festivals, together with the latter's ephemeral presence in the city, becomes ever more apparent when festivals are celebrated in shopping centres.

Nevertheless, these architectural giants are also undeniably emblematic buildings and their social function and presence have become essential within the landscape of present-day cities. Shopping centres not only give great visibility to film festivals (their mere presence in everyday life functions as a reminder of the cultural residue left by the Festival), but also integrate the participants and the event itself within the greater space of the city, in turn making this event accessible to other possible audiences, instead of ghettoizing it in more alternative locations. The acquisition of this alternative circuit would be, as I will discuss later, one of the main issues brought up in relation to BAFICI. Its new meeting point from 2013 at the Centro Cultural Recoleta attests to that.

Indeed, as Peña notes, the kind of films shown at BAFICI were not only not screened in such places during the rest of the year, but effectively boycotted by the chain. However, as he also admits, aside from being the ultimate symbol of post-

FIG. 1.2. Abasto Shopping Centre
Photo © Agustín Maseado

FIG. 1.3. Programme grid to buy tickets for BAFICI
Photo © Agustín Maseado

modern capitalist space, malls were also a relatively new concept in the 1990s in Buenos Aires — hence a novelty that attracted many people — and the only spaces in the city that could offer the most up-to-date screening conditions. The non-existence of any other technically adequate alternative screening rooms in the city was precisely the reason behind Di Tella's decision to use this venue at the time. It was important, since

> Already, the films we were programming were, let's say, a bit delicate for the audience, because it was an audience that was not used to this kind of film: an Iranian film or an independent film from, I don't know, Kazakhstan. And suddenly, on top of that they had to see them in bad technical conditions: bad projection, bad sound, in totally run-down cinemas, as was the case with the then few screening rooms dedicated to, between inverted commas, 'art cinema'. Deep down, they showed great disregard for the audience, didn't they? It was worth watching these films in good conditions. One of the things that I fought for the most — and which luckily was actually established — is BAFICI's technical rigour.[34]

Di Tella staffed the whole programming team of this first BAFICI edition solely with filmmakers, including Esteban Sapir and Eduardo Millewich, and received the help of a group of young volunteers in the production team, such as Ernau Salupi, now an important producer in Argentina, Sebastián Rochstein, Carolina Constantinoski and Rosa Martínez Rivero (then in charge of the short-films section, and general producer of the Festival in its 2009 edition). In fact, Di Tella's most debatable decision was to use only filmmakers as programmers — in his opinion, this implied a critical freedom that would have probably been lacking had the Festival been programmed by critics. As a filmmaker himself, his main objective was to create a space in which a dialogue could be established between the new Argentine filmmakers and their international equivalents, a focus that perhaps would not have been so essential had the director of the Festival been a film critic instead. To make this happen, Di Tella created the series of co-production forums and filmmaking workshops, which have now developed into what is known as the Buenos Aires Lab, BAL.

Yet critics were going to prove crucial in disseminating the work shown at the Festival by new filmmakers. The new criticism and debate created by the magazines *Film*, *El Amante Cine*, and *Haciendo Cine*, together with newly graduated filmmakers coming out of the booming numbers of university film courses, and the (very few) occasions in which new filmmakers had been able to screen their films, had already created a stir and registered strongly with certain cultural groups in Buenos Aires. All of these factors together created what NAC filmmaker Celina Murga (*Ana y los otros/Ana and the Others* 2003, *Una semana solos/A Week Alone* 2007) refers to as 'the fertile territory in which everything then blossomed'.[35] Hence, to all intents and purposes, the audience had already been created, and this translated into the huge expectancy that the Festival's first edition created and the actual success it enjoyed. As Mariano Martín Kairuz of the cultural newspaper *Página/12* recalls, when BAFICI started, 'there were eight-hour-long queues; half of Buenos Aires was inside the Abasto at a time when the film scene in Argentina was simply terrible.'[36]

Di Tella's main aim was to position BAFICI as far as possible from Mar del Plata and what it was believed to stand for, whilst the Festival's structure, politics and programming focused on basics: trying to get directors to attend the Festival and acquiring films. This was not an easy task at a time when Buenos Aires was not on the international festival circuit; Di Tella vividly recalls running after directors down the corridors of Rotterdam International Film Festival in a bid to persuade them to show their films in the first edition of BAFICI. But the most complicated element was the Festival's organization, since, firstly, none of the people involved had ever attended an international film festival outside the country, as the cost of travelling to Europe or the US was prohibitive; and secondly, because the main fear was making the same mistakes that Mar del Plata was renowned for, such as late changes to the programme, general disorganization and not returning prints to the filmmakers.

The success of BAFICI's first edition in 1999 caught everyone so unawares that a programme for the following year had not even been thought of. Luck was also key in this first year's success, particularly in terms of its media coverage. Although the budget was quite small, and the Festival lacked the international cache and prestige necessary to lure conspicuous personalities identified with the independent film scene, one of the shorts invited was made by Sofia Coppola, who asked if she could bring her father too, causing enough of a stir to get the Festival on the front page of many of the newspapers and magazines — something that was not sought after, but that nonetheless helped turn the Festival into a household name and make it into one of the most important cultural events in the city. This is somehow ironic, for Mar del Plata was highly criticized for its focus on celebrities. Admittedly, the 'use' of big names — independent or otherwise — is something that few festivals can ignore, but it is in the way those festivals relate to the whole notion of celebrity glamour that differentiates them (I deal with this thought-proving issue in relation to one of the self-proclaimed least celebrity-oriented festivals, the Vienna Film Festival, in Chapter 3, focused on the LFF). More pertinently for the national cinema, Pablo Trapero's *Mundo grúa/Crane World* (1999) was screened in this first edition. Significantly, a film self-funded and lacking INCAA's approval (although it was completed with money given by the organization only as a result of BAFICI's intervention) won the best actor and best director awards, and a special OCIC (Organización Católica Internacional del Cine y de lo Audiovisual) Best Film Award. Yet, regardless of its overall success, the commitment of the city's government to a second edition of the Festival receded, and already that second edition was smaller because of the considerable reduction in the ministry's funding. This does not surprise the often outspoken Quintín, who has regularly criticized the local authorities publicly. He observes:

> The second edition had some budget problems which has consistently been an issue with the city because they are lazy and stupid: they are bureaucrats, and when they start a festival, or when they change the director and they fire the previous one, they give money for the first year and you do everything you want, and then they start taking things from you and then you need to be fired in order for the festival to keep its new proportion.[37]

In addition, BAFICI's relationship with INCAA was difficult from the beginning. The success of the Festival and the international recognition of the new Argentine filmmakers had stirred INCAA's interest in the more independent sector of the country's film industry, so the organization increased its involvement: their logo would prominently appear in these films' credits, even though actual funding was generally very low or even non-existent. The national government was headed by Carlos Ménem, whose right-wing Peronism clashed with the radical left politics of De la Rúa, the then city mayor. It is necessary to recall that the city of Buenos Aires has been politically independent from Buenos Aires Province since 1880. And although Buenos Aires is the capital of the Republic of Argentina, Mar del Plata is the capital of Buenos Aires Province. As such, Buenos Aires's local government can be of a different affiliation to the rest of the country. Hence, in a way, BAFICI stood as an emblem of opposition to the 'nationalist' Mar del Plata. However, as Di Tella reminds us, INCAA was investing fifteen or twenty times more money in the festival of Mar del Plata, so it made sense that it supported, if only minimally, the festival of Buenos Aires. INCAA was also the funding body that put up the money necessary to finish Trapero's *Crane World*; from this moment on they would become collaborators with the Festival in the completion and post-production of Argentine films, thereby linking itself to the newly acquired international prestige of the NAC movement. It is important to note that this kind of funding was never given/distributed by INCAA because of any legal requirement to do so. INCAA in fact retained the right to cancel funding if it felt it necessary, leaving the existence of the Festival at their disposal.

BAFICI's dependence on the city's administration soon proved to be problematic. As a municipal festival — and not the 'independent' film festival that its name suggests — everyone who works for it is employed as a civil servant. With no economic autonomy, the Festival is at the mercy of the city government's (frequent) political fluctuations. As soon as the first edition of the Festival finished, Di Tella encountered the first problem when the city's government assumed their economic input ended when the Festival itself ended, and so failed to provide the necessary money to return the prints of the films that had been shown (thus repeating Mar del Plata's mistakes, despite Di Tella's strenuous efforts to avoid doing so). Darío Lopérfido was replaced as secretary by Ricardo Manetti, who — as did Lopérfido — took no notice of Di Tella's phone calls regarding the money for the transportation of the prints. This prompted Di Tella to go to the newspapers and make a public complaint in *La Nación* where the article was run with a picture of former President, Fernando De La Rúa.[38] At this stage, Di Tella was already considering resigning.

It was then that the ministry inaugurated the dynamics that would lead to a rapid succession of festival directors. While Di Tella was on a trip to the Edinburgh Film Festival, his programming team was removed and replaced by another group of programmers, without his prior consultation. In Di Tella's absence, Quintín had been nominated as the Festival's new director (after Peña refused Manetti's offer to co-direct it with the former, owing to a clash of personalities).

Flavia de la Fuente, programmer of the Festival during the 2001–2004 editions (co-editor of *El Amante* with her husband Quintín), was one of the new team of programmers appointed by Jorge Telerman, the newly elected Secretary of Culture in 2001, together with María Valdez, Marcelo Panozzo and Diego Dubcovsky. De la Fuente recalls:

> The production of BAFICI 2001 was chaotic. [...] When we were summoned in September 2000, the director of the Festival was Ricardo Manetti, who was the Director General of Cultural Industries and then Undersecretary of Cultural Industries, a situation which had already provoked conflicts in 1999 and 2000 when Andrés Di Tella was the artistic director of BAFICI. After conducting extensive research in the film world, Telerman approved Quintín as the director of the Festival.[39]

Having made such a last-minute decision, the Ministry (for reasons previously indicated by Quintín) decided to allocate more money for his first year. For most people, including all its former directors, Quintín is the figure that arguably garnered BAFICI its international profile. He would be in charge of the Festival for the next four editions, from 2001 to 2004.

When Quintín was appointed in November as the artistic director for the Festival's third edition in 2001, he took the decision to make this event much bigger:

> I remember that in the previous edition, there were forty films. In those days, before the crisis in Argentina, the international distribution of films [shown at the Festival] was wider than it turned out to be afterwards. Many films in the first and second editions of the Festival opened commercially. There were films whose rights were bought by local distributors and they premiered them at the Festival. So in that way the Festival was showing only forty films that needed to be subtitled, because with the others, in a way we had the commercial prints with subtitles to be released after the Festival. And I changed that, and from forty real films that were not going to have a theatrical release, that number jumped to 150, which allowed us to become more radical in the choices of the programme.[40]

Although this increase was considered by some to be more in tune with 'the spirit of a stamp collector'[41] than that of a Festival programmer, Quintín's programming strategy was undertaken from the perspective of a critic, bringing the most radical and independent films from film festivals around the world, as well as screening key films of the NAC by Lisandro Alonso, Juan Villegas, Albertina Carri, Ulises Rosell, Rodrigo Moreno, Pablo Trapero, Ana Poliak, Raúl Perrone, Rafael Filippelli, Verónica Chen and Ariel Rotter.

Quintín initiated an important shift in programming. A critic himself, he strongly affirms that there is no better programmer than the film critic:

> Because I think critics are reliable and independent. That's one of the biggest mistakes in film festivals. They want films to be evaluated by producers, by people who have interests in the films, or not maybe in that particular film, but in their own film, and they are only trying to push things. And the only independent voice that you can hear in a festival is the voice of the critics. Also, in a way, critics know more about film than the rest of the community. [...] I don't know who else is better than a critic to programme. If not, you end up having the producers and sales agents programming the festival. This should be

> done by an independent voice, a curator. It's like putting in an art museum a
> guy who is selling paintings to run it — that would be the same thing.[42]

This statement does not stand much scrutiny, as Quintín has never been shy about promoting certain directors and attacking others (particularly in the couple's internet blog, La Lectora Provisoria). Likewise, his own personal positions — such as what seems a barely concealed dislike of Lucrecia Martel's films[43] or the self-professed campaigning on behalf of certain filmmakers during his stewardship of BAFICI (his determination and influence gained him the nickname the Black Pope) prove that critics also have their own agendas. Nevertheless, the programming committee of the Festival under Quintín's direction was 'informally' extended (and enriched) by around ten renowned critics from around the world, (mainly male figures including Kent Jones, Jonathan Rosembaum, Adrian Martin, Christoph Huber, Tag Gallager and Olaf Möller), who would act as unpaid advisers on films they saw; a group Quintín refers to as a 'nice mafia'.[44] Some of these critics would in turn be invited to BAFICI to write about the Festival, hence contributing to its rapidly enhanced international profile — a questionable situation in itself, since the same people involved in suggesting certain films would be those writing about them during the Festival.

The economic crisis that had been building in Argentina, and which peaked during BAFICI's 2002 edition, arguably contributed to the Festival's international recognition. The neoliberalist economic policies that the Ménem government had imposed on the country after the dictatorship in order to speed up its opening to the global economy, although initially successful, meant that the presence of foreign investment soon brought about the collapse of the country's economic system, in December 2001. That same year, the government had already invested the same amount in the Festival as it did the previous year: 800,000 Argentine pesos. Although originally the peso was equivalent to the United States dollar — meaning that money would equal $800,000 — by December (when the programme had already been lined up), the value of that figure had fallen to around $150,000. This same money, now much lower in value, had to pay for the already agreed salaries, screening fees, transportation, plane tickets, guests, and so on. It is therefore paradoxical that when asked about this period, the then artistic director Quintín answers with an enthusiastic: 'It was fantastic. That was one of my best memories of the Festival.'[45] Various high-profile programmers, such as the then director of Rotterdam, Simon Field, and Olivier Père from Cannes's Quinzane, launched an international aid campaign for BAFICI. People were sending money, not charging screening fees for their films, paying their own plane tickets and the Festival also managed to get some money from a couple of film foundations in Holland (a country with which the Festival, as discussed later in this chapter, has very strong links). Quintín recounts how nobody had any money as the guests' credit cards were as useless as the locals'; he comments:

> the Festival was held in absolute poverty, but it was a huge success, the only
> thing that was functioning in the city. It was like being in an island of hope
> those days. Everybody who attended [the Festival] was great, and there were
> some riots in the streets so we had a great time; a great time.[46]

Nonetheless, this positive sense of community that adversity brought to the Festival did not transmit to the Argentine films made that year. Although film critic, programmer and fifth director of BAFICI Marcelo Panozzo recognizes there were some 'miracles' (arguably, the greatest miracle were that films such as *Un día de suerte/A Lucky Day* by Sandra Gugliotta, Mariano Llinás's *Balnearios* (2002), and *Tan de repente/Suddenly* (2002) by Diego Lerman were actually made and screened in a Festival that included a retrospective of Raúl Perrone, known as 'the father of minimalist film'),[47] for him 'the origins of the new Argentine cinema, robust, self-confident, unquestionably, were already far behind'.[48]

Quintín's sacking was by far the most controversial of the three first directors' exits from the Festival (Peña's dismissal would follow in 2007).[49] The trigger was an article he wrote in the French film-magazine *Cahiers du Cinéma* in 2003[50] stating that INCAA was killing the domestic production of the more interesting films, accusing the organization of putting obstacles in the way of independent (or partly independent) new directors for funding, and giving state funding to established 'old' directors instead. For this Quintín was considered to be a 'traitor' to the country, since he was publicly attacking the government in the foreign press; some of the responses that Quintín's note elicited also come from members of the Argentine film industry including filmmaker Juan José Campanella.[51] Quintín was fired a total of three times, in 2002, 2003 and 2004; a replacement could not be found on the first two occasions. But the opportunity to end his tenure came in 2004, when the government failed to give any money to the Festival for travel costs and did not answer their calls for six months. At this juncture, Quintín and his team were offered the chance to organize a small festival in Mar del Plata (Marfici) as a sidebar of their main jobs at BAFICI.

> And they paid us very well, and because of that money I could travel abroad and scout films for BAFICI. We didn't even have at that point a courier so we couldn't have somebody send a DVD to watch. So when we did that, they said: you are using the state money to do your own private business, this is against the law. But I didn't have an exclusive contract or anything like it, I didn't even have a contract that explained what my job was, I could be a wall painter... or anybody, somebody who works for the government. And then they fired me because they said I was some kind of crook.[52]

Although Marfici is still running, it has remained a small independent film festival with no specific editorial line.

An article strongly condemning Quintín's firing was published by the Argentine branch of FIPRESCI,[53] accompanied with a statement issued by this same organization,[54] and Jean-Michel Frodon launched a public appeal in the French magazine he then edited, *Cahiers du Cinéma*, which was signed by hundreds of film professionals.[55] This organization comprises most of the important film critics in the country, including Diego Lerer (president of FIPRESCI Argentina and former editor of the film section in the national newspaper *Clarín*) and Quintín.

Fernando Martín Peña, film historian, director of the Buenos Aires Cinematheque and programmer of the MALBA (Latin American Art Museum), would meet with a similar fate to his two predecessors. Beginning his tenure as director in the midst of the international press campaign for reinstatement of Quintín, launched after his dismissal (which also took swipes at BAFICI and questioned Peña's suitability to direct the Festival), Peña in fact soon applied his own personal touch to the Festival. He considered 'old' films equally as important as new ones, and even though the Festival's basic agenda was left untouched — including sidebars such as BAL — the presence of retrospectives was more prominent under his direction, constituting around 40% of the programme.

In many ways, as I go on to explain, Peña addressed himself to two fundamental assets of any film festival: he introduced a remunerated award and provided a meeting place for professionals. One of the main sources of friction between BAFICI and INCAA concerns the economic assistance given to films that are made independently of the national film institute. During the first two editions of the Festival, when a film was selected by BAFICI to be played in its programme, INCAA used to find itself in an illegal position whereby it would have to provide completion funds for films that had not been pre-approved by its classification team.

INCAA produces and/or coproduces around two hundred films a year and offers funding for a large range of films. However, as Murga notes:

> newer and riskier projects look for funding outside the institute. This was the case with the majority of films screened at the Festival's first editions, such as *Mundo Grúa/Crane World*, *La libertad/Freedom*, *Sábado/Saturday*, *Ana y los otros/Ana and the Others*. These films originated completely outside INCAA, and after touring a series of international film festivals, and getting written about in the international press, [and acquiring the coveted international prestige] we managed to get recognition from INCAA, which subsequently awarded a subsidy to these films. This is how new filmmakers are starting to produce their films again.[56]

INCAA's position at that time was therefore not too dissimilar to their position now. As Villegas notes, thanks to the less expensive and more accessible use of new technologies, national production has grown so considerably since those first years (in 1997 there were a total of 28 films made in Argentina),[57] that INCAA has decided to limit access to funds for these kinds of projects: now a film has to be approved by INCAA before filming starts in order to bid for funding.

Reflecting on the influence that the new (protective) Film Law approved in 1994 has on independent filmmaking, Quintín says:

> Today, Argentina's film authorities, along with the industrial establishment, corrected their blunder. You can no longer make films like this [independently from INCAA] and hope for state support. The movie's script must be submitted to a committee before shooting starts, and, if it is rejected, there will be no further chances for support. [...] Instead of being encouraged, this original, inexpensive, and highly efficient production method was repressed. [...] Paradoxically, no one in the world of cinema wants such inexpensive movies, except for new directors and those who clearly choose to be outsiders.[58]

In order to avoid putting INCAA in a situation whereby it would be forced to help a film previously rejected by the organization, Peña and his team introduced (small) monetary awards (both pre- and post-Festival) for blowing the films up to 35mm and/or for post-production. But the most important of these awards, which still exists, is what is now called the Metropolitan Fund (Fondo Metropolitano), paid by the city and administered by BAFICI. This award allows BAFICI to choose three films it wants to blow up, regardless of whether the film is linked to INCAA.

Peña also introduced Intercine, a meeting place for everyone who participates in the Festival (including those whose films had not made it into the Festival) including a large DVD library in which people could watch the films programmed in the Festival, together with other films that had been produced during a given year; guests (producers, distributors or fellow filmmakers) were also given the possibility of watching and buying any of this material. However, after only one edition in charge, the city's government elections brought in a new administration with an opposing political orientation to the national government. The result was that INCAA and the city's ministry cut off all dialogue with the Festival, leaving Peña and his team to piece together the programme based on a minimal budget. Frustrated with the lack of response coming from either government and getting dangerously close to the deadline, Peña, following on Di Tella and Quintín's steps, made his complaint public. In November 2007 he published a letter, addressed to the 'Mysterious Minister', exposing in a sarcastic tone the urgency of the situation to a minister whose identity had yet to be revealed.[59]

Needless to say that Peña's days directing the Festival were now numbered. After a brief, unsatisfactory meeting with Hernán Lombardi, the newly appointed Minister of Culture in the city, held ten days before the new government took power, Peña's relationship with the ministry deteriorated rapidly, and soon, Sergio Wolf (then programmer of the Festival) was being sounded out to direct it. Peña talked with both parties and the decision was taken that the team would stay the same and Wolf would direct (with Peña unofficially co-directing) the 2008 edition.

Under Sergio Wolf's directorship, one of the most important longstanding issues affecting the Festival, its autonomy, has finally been resolved. BAFICI was not created by law, hence it is not institutionally protected against any governmental changes. Wolf, 'together with lawyers Miguel Urainde and Américo Castilla, (both linked to the Festival, and of different political persuasions)',[60] worked on the drafting of a legal document (already approved in 2009) which would preserve the Festival, but also democratize the election of its artistic director. Therefore, instead of the next artistic director being elected by decree or by a government employee, the aim was to develop an election system, as well as to establish limitations and a job description for the position.

Thus, it was proposed (and is now ratified) that six months before the end of each director's term, an advisory board would meet, comprising the former directors of the Festival, who would each in turn summon a filmmaker awarded at the Festival. This group would then meet with the city's Minister of Culture, who in turn would summon three important figures from the Argentine cultural world. These two groups would then propose three candidates for artistic director, one of whom would be nominated by the Minister of Culture. The orderly election of Marzelo Panozzo (film critic and former programmer of the Festival from 2001) as the new

FIG. 1.4. BAFICI directors left to right: Marcelo Panozzo, Sergio Wolf, Javier Porta Fuz, Quintín at a 20th anniversary round table chaired by Diego Papic (far right)
Photo © Agustín Maseado

director for the 2013–2015 editions, bears witness to this. Panozzo had been heavily involved with the Festival throughout its existence, as a programmer for four years under Quintín and for two of the five years that Sergio Wolf was in charge, as well as working on the Festival's daily publication during Peña's direction.[61]

In fact, one of the most surprising things about BAFICI is that regardless of the Festival directors' different programming strategies and backgrounds, and the political, administrative and economic swings of the volatile internal politics of both the city and the national governments, whereby there have been six different directors in the twenty years of the Festival's existence, at the mercy of six mayors and eight Secretaries of Culture, the Festival has always managed to retain its identity. Generally referred to as the 'BAFICI miracle', Di Tella, Quintín, Peña and Wolf all agree that the survival of the Festival, mostly in its first, convoluted years is down to its own strong internal logic and, I would add, to the different but equally uncompromising editorial lines pursued by its directors.

Another possible reason could be, as Wolf mentions, that practically all the people involved in the Festival have been a part of it from the beginning in one way or another, even if their position/s within the Festival have shifted greatly. In 2016, Darío Lopérfido, once more in charge of Buenos Aires's Ministry of Culture (2015–2016), nominated film critic and programmer Javier Porta Fouz as the new director of BAFICI. Porta Fouz, editor in chief of *El Amante* magazine, had already been involved in BAFICI since 2001, and as programmer since 2005, working alongside four of the Festival's directors.[62]

Buenos Aires Lab (BAL): Investing in New Argentine Cinema (NAC)

One of the most important elements of the Festival's future for Wolf was ensuring that Buenos Aires Lab or BAL, the Market section of the Festival, and the collaborations with various international funding bodies, all operated in the most desirable conditions. Many of the initial NAC projects — and afterwards BAFICI's — have to some extent always relied on the support of the Hubert Bals funding incentive.

Supported by the Dutch Ministry of Foreign Affairs, Dutch non-governmental development organizations Hivos-NCDO Culture Foundation, the DOEN Foundation, Dioraphte Foundation and Dutch public broadcasting network NPS, the Hubert Bals Fund is an initiative that Rotterdam, one of the most highly regarded independent festivals in the world, started in 1988 in order to provide financial support for 'remarkable or urgent feature films and feature-length creative documentaries by innovative and talented filmmakers from developing countries close to completion. The HBF provides grants that often turn out to play a crucial role in enabling these filmmakers from countries in the Middle East, Eastern Europe, Africa and Latin America to realize their projects'.[63]

The Hubert Bals Fund is a marked presence at BAFICI;[64] its collaboration with BAL started during the 2003 edition. BAL is an event that aims to support the development and production of independent cinema in Latin America. Through

Fig. 1.5. Buenos Aires Lab (BAL) 2019
Photo © Agustín Maseado

a mix of activities, this event, as its entry on the Festival's website states, mainly focuses on the

> gathering of professionals and the search for financing and it is intended for filmmakers and producers of the region. These activities include the participation of professionals of the worldwide industry (producers, sellers, distributors, TV networks) who have an interest in the Latin American film industry and are aimed at the contact and exchange between both spheres.

BAL is made up of the following three sections:

- Co-production Meetings: between the representatives of the selected Latin American projects and the potential co-producers from the rest of the world. There is a total of four awards, ranging from money, transfer, development and studio time sponsored by Kodak, Cinecolor and the European TV channel ARTE.
- Work in Progress: exhibition of fragments of Argentine films in varying stages of completion. Here there are a total of three awards, covering camera rental, editing, sound or studio postproduction.
- Bridges: the first workshop for producers in Latin America and Europe that will enable both regions to work jointly for five days in Buenos Aires (a section introduced in the 2009 edition of BAFICI).

The appearance of some of BAL's finished projects at the subsequent year's BAFICI turns the role of the Festival from being a platform for new independent films, into the generator of new films itself, securing its own purpose and future continuation.[65]

There are strongly opposing attitudes towards the Festival's close links with such investment and co-production initiatives in its industry section, particularly with regard to their (possible) influence on the shape of the final product. On the one hand Aguilar, discussing the long-term relations that these international funding bodies (such as the Hubert Bals Fund, and Fond Sud Cinèma and even the Sundance Lab) have had with the filmmakers of the new Argentine cinema, claims that

> Whereas earlier filmmakers [in the 1980s] sought artistic co-productions, which often required adaptations or artistic concessions (changes to the screenplay, locations, and casting), these [current] foreign foundations offered the possibility of a financial co-production that did not demand changes to the original project.[66]

On the other hand, Quintín, questioning the interest that the governmental authorities have in these production fund bodies, believes that 'even institutions meant to support Third World projects such as the Font Sud or Hubert Bals, frequently choose what is more established or conventional'.[67] He continues:

> Lost between art and industry, festivals are starting to become useless with regards to either of these two dimensions [artistic and industrial] and to not be clear about what their actual purpose is. In the last few years, they were used as a substitute screening room for the alternative cinema. Their current retreat allows us to suspect something more serious: that the independent cinema, formatted and co-produced in order to bring together art and business, has

managed to establish itself as a product to the detriment of its aesthetic value. Nevertheless, it does not even bring enough profit as a product, which is reflected in the difficulties that festivals are starting to experience.[68]

Quintín's opinion is echoed by Spanish producer Pere Portabella, scholar Falicov and programmer James Quandt, amongst others, as it suggests the existence of what is commonly known as a 'festival film'; i.e., films with certain apparent shared characteristics (as per Wong in the introduction) whose life is, as De Valck notes, confined to the Festival circuit (see introduction).

There is a third perspective that comes into play: the stance of organizations such as Fond Sud or Hubert Bals towards the 'products' themselves. The renewed interest on the part of powerful international film festivals (normally with A-list category, such as Cannes, Mar del Plata, Locarno, Berlin and San Sebastián, or those in another category or not affiliated to FIAPF but comparable in size, such as Toronto and Rotterdam respectively) in 'discovering' new national products in territories yet unexplored, not only paved the way for the string of film waves that have proliferated within the last twenty years: Iranian, Romanian, Mexican, Brazilian and of course, Argentine, but have also been linked to a new form of cultural colonialism that was first examined by film theorist Thomas Elsaesser in his seminal essay 'Film Festival Networks: The New Topographies of Cinema in Europe',[69] and then developed and expanded by Marijke de Valck in her book on film festivals.[70] This occurs partly in response to the increased competition that exists between festivals, which in itself is directly linked to the rapid growth in the number of the festivals over the last two decades.

The state's economic involvement in the film industry and its funding schemes and policies for cinema (and television) are crucial for the possibility of a national cinema and the creation/representation of a national identity. As David Morley and Kevin Robins assert, 'identity [...) is also a question of memory, and memories of 'home' in particular'.[71] Which prompts the question, how intrusive are these organizations? This is a topic I will be dealing with in more detail in Chapter 2, dedicated to San Sebastián. For now, an example: when Lisandro Alonso's first film *La libertad* (2001) was spotted by the programmer of Un Certain Regard in Cannes on a visit to Buenos Aires, he promptly invited the film to that year's edition, but on one condition: that the last scene of the film had to be cut. The film originally ended with the protagonist, a woodcutter — whose everyday movements constitute the subject of Alonso's film — looking directly for the first time at the camera and laughing; a take that — as Page rightly notes in a refreshing analysis of this otherwise critically well-trodden film[72] — asks searching questions about the relationship between the director and his subject, modifying in an instant the (documentary) tone and intention of everything that precedes it. Cannes did not appreciate this sarcasm and Alonso did indeed agree to cut the scene. He went on to become one of the most talked about, although still largely undistributed, filmmakers of the NAC.

National Identity, BAFICI and the New Argentine Cinema

> Nations themselves are narrations. In time, culture comes to be associated, often aggressively, with the nation or the state; this differentiates 'us' from 'them', almost always with some degree of xenophobia. Culture in this sense is a source of identity, and a rather combative one at that.[73]

National identity in the NAC is one of the key issues focused on by Page and Aguilar's respective books. Similarly to Aguilar, Page adopts (not uncritically) a Marxist perspective and also applies postmodern theories to read these films, grounding her discussion in the economic reality of the country from the 1990s onwards — its relations to the global economy and the damage caused by Ménem's neo-liberalist politics that led Argentina into the economic crisis of 2001–2002. In her analysis she argues that the aesthetic and ideological break that the NAC experienced with previous generations is made visible in their own personal detachment from the subject matter of their films (a large number of the NAC films take place in remote parts of Argentina, far from the everyday lived experiences of their directors). This detachment is conveyed through the position of the camera, and, as Aguilar argues, is made without passing any sort of judgment, but rather with an objective indifference.[74]

The realist style of the NAC films has repeatedly led critics to point to the similarities of this group with both the circumstances in which Italian neo-realism flourished, and the influence that this new form of filmmaking had on the highly politicized 1960s and '70s generation of Argentine filmmakers. As theorists Diana Agosta and Patricia Keeton explain, the main contribution of the films made in Latin America and Cuba at the time was the development of a new culture:

> In contrast to the French New Wave, which called for a revolution in film form, without concern for audience accessibility, the Latin American Cinema movement argued that filmmakers must start with where the spectator is in society at this moment, so that artists can make films that involve audiences in a process of redefining truth through their engagement with film images that question reality.[75]

A set of similar technical circumstances has enabled the NAC, and subsequent new Argentine independent filmmakers, to make films outside the system using the new, cheaper and infinitely more accessible digital technologies. However, both Aguilar and Page coincide in pointing out that although the immediacy of digital formats allows for a certain 'realist' aesthetic, these filmmakers' take on reality emerges from a very different political stance both towards Neorealism and their 1970s compatriots. And it is precisely with regards to questions of identity that the gap between the two generations widens. For the 1970s generation, the relationship between public and private had become more intricate and complex, leading to a greater politicization; what Aguilar refers to as 'preaching to the spectator', achieved by the use of a 'realist' or naturalist representational mode combined with the use of Brechtian avant-garde techniques to directly address the spectator. In the NAC the private opens up to the local, and the representation of 'reality' becomes the investigation of realist representational codes[76]; consequently, the rejection of this preaching is not fortuitous, because

> political responses, in the usual sense of the term, are no longer satisfactory, for the very problems that arise no longer respond to traditional norms. The political imperative does not emerge in such a transparent way. Moreover, successive crises (essentially, the failure to restore institutional and economic democracy) meant that new directors preferred to suspend many inherited certainties. (...) "What are we?" stopped being interesting from the moment the community and history that had given this question significance began a process of decomposition or began to be more defined by contemporary global processes than by national ones. (...) In light of the disintegration of the public sphere (whether due to globalization, mass media, or governmental policies), the new filmmakers were not assigned a role in advance. Instead, they used the language of cinema to investigate their own positioning, their own amorphous desires[77].

Therefore, it does not come as a surprise that when asked about the composition of BAFICI's audience, Martín Kairuz and artistic director Wolf both agree that it is predominantly formed precisely by the two aforementioned generations. The Festival brings these two generations together spatially (if not ideologically). This generational encounter becomes the symbol of what the Festival has ultimately created: a common space for a plural community, even if a fragmented one. After all, memory and identity are created through experience and a sense of community.

The establishment and maintenance of this community is precisely what lies behind creating a space to house its identity by showing its films, but also to physically place this community within a demarcated space in Buenos Aires. Key NAC figures, such as filmmakers Celina Murga (*Ana and the Others* 2004, *Una semana solos/A Week Alone*, 2009) and her husband, the filmmaker/critic Juan Villegas (*Saturday*, 1995; *Ocio*, 2010; *Las Vegas*, 2018), or the aforementioned Kairuz — all three BAFICI regulars — refer to it as a festival they feel is theirs; a festival that signifies a place of belonging; 'a place of resistance against the more conservative and commercial cinema.'[78] And yet, as Villegas rightly points out, the big paradox is that at the end of the day, economically BAFICI belongs to the state. Hence one of the most discussed objectives (together with the aforementioned legalization of the Festival) is a proposal to the city's government to build new — or use the already existing — cinemas for public screenings, in order to prolong and spread the spirit of the Festival throughout the year.

In the virtual realm, BAFICI does have a continued presence throughout the year, on the numerous Argentine websites dedicated to film (including those belonging to the main national magazines and newspapers, as well as websites openly opposed to the Festival such as the — now unavailable — <www.ihateyoubafici.com>, Diego Lerer's <www.micropsiacine.com>, and Quintín and Flavia's daily updated blog, active till 2016, *La Lectora Provisoria*, dedicated to literature, theatre, music, sports, the arts and current affairs, but also covering film and film festivals. A short-lived BAFICI Permanente section housed within this blog was inaugurated after the Festival's 2009 edition ended (running for one year, it is no longer available on the website). It took its name from an initiative funded by INCAA within BAFICI, which consists of touring a number of the films (mainly Argentine) screened at a given edition around the Buenos Aires province.

Mirroring this continuation of the Festival, the section in *La Lectora Provisoria* consisted of an ongoing discussion of the films that had been screened at some point in the Festival, always linking them to current news in the film world. The discussions in the blog generally take the form of a dialogue between Flavia and Quintín about BAFICI and its selections, and bloggers are invited to leave their comments. The idea for this section came from a note that Quintín wrote for the website *Otros Cines*[79] (a virtual magazine edited by Diego Batlle), in which he called for a means of expanding BAFICI throughout the year. This is an extract of some of the text included on the website, albeit no longer accessible:

> It is of urgent cultural necessity that the Festival extends beyond those few days in autumn. If there was an instrument capable of measuring throughout the year the enthusiasm of the audience, the quality of the film debates, the feeling that cinephilia is just an illusion with some future (I would almost dare to say with a more adventurous future than the actual cinema), the pointer would mark a very high peak during those [BAFICI] days and would descend abruptly during the rest. Neither practical studies, nor academic dissertations, nor isolated exhibitions have the power to move and stimulate like the endless activities taking place during those days. We need to find a way for BAFICI to continue all year long.[80]

As previously mentioned, in order to promote both the continuation and expansion of the Festival's cinephilic spirit and the bid to reach new and different audiences, INCAA funded the BAFICI Permanente (or Touring BAFICI), which tours the rest of the country, bringing a selection of the Argentine films programmed in the Festival to audiences outside the capital. But in the city, screening some of the Argentine films shown in the Festival still remains a problem. All the four directors of BAFICI that I interviewed agree there is a need for investment in an alternative exhibition circuit with the right technical conditions that would be available for the rest of the year, funded by the city's government. This would be tantamount to a renewal of the spirit of the ebullient cine-clubs which flourished in Buenos Aires in the 1970s, destroyed in the '80s by the lack of protective film laws. The potential revenue derived from this would also benefit the funding body, INCAA.

The widely held opinion and desire that BAFICI should expand beyond the city led the Festival to collaborate more closely with the Universidad de Cine (FUC), one of many private film universities in Buenos Aires, and the one which has been most involved with the NAC movement from its origins. Known simply as FUC, this establishment has not only contributed to the boom of talented filmmakers the country has produced since the 1990s, but also, its position as producer/co-producer is essential in enabling films to be made outside the institute. Founded in 1991 by Manuel Antín (a key filmmaker of the Generación del 60), the main focus for its director was always on production. What is more, Argentine filmmaker Rafael Filippelli explains that with the co-production facilities provided by the FUC:

> there appears, for the first time, a kind of cinema that justifies the word 'independent'. But why? Because a truly independent cinema should be

Fig. 1.6. BAFICI 2019. Left to right: programmer Álvaro Arroba,
Joao Pedro Bénard from the Cinemateca Portuguesa, and
BAFICI's former directors Quintín and Sergio Wolf
Photo © Agustín Maseado

independent of the Film Institute [INCAA]. I think that the University of Film has done a lot to give that word meaning, in as much as it shows that a film can be made outside the Institute, can cost infinitely less than a film funded by a loan or a subsidy from the Institute, and that it can open normally. Some might say that there are only the MALBA, the introduction through BAFICI of the 25 of May Theatre and the Sala Lugones. But aside from those exhibition venues, one could say that these films go to the same or as many festivals as the ones produced by the Institute, and win just as many awards as the others.[81]

Practically all films produced or co-produced by the university find a space in the BAFICI's programme. In 2018 the total number of screening rooms used by the Festival around the city was twenty — albeit according to Batlle the following edition would shorten not only its number of rooms to twelve (not including sidebars, open air screenings and cultural centres), but also total number of films, publications and events.[82] FUC's involvement became more apparent when in 2006 it acquired its own section within the Festival: the Talent Campus Buenos Aires, which is set up in collaboration with the Berlin Festival — Berlinale Talent Campus in Latin America (its other collaborations include Beirut, Durban, Guadalajara, Sarajevo, Tokyo and Rio). The aim of this section is very much in tune with one of Di Tella's original targets when he started the Festival:

> to generate an exchange context for young Latin American filmmakers who will benefit from contact with distinguished figures, and the exchange of ideas and projects by organizing seminars and workshops, held and run by film professionals, scholars and intellectuals from all around the world, such as Chantal Akerman, Florian Koerner, Angela Schanelec, Claire Simon, Heinz Peter Schwerfel, Lisandro Alonso, Colin McCabe, Jean-Michel Frodon, Hugo Santiago, Peter Schumann and Luc Moullet, among others.[83]

This in turn helps to expand the scope and reach of the Festival as it further opens up national talent to the international sphere by making professionals of the latter accessible to current and new generations of filmmakers. It also brings to the fore the position that the Festival adopts on education.

Education in BAFICI puts the emphasis on practical training in filmmaking by way of seminars and meetings organized by Festival sidebars such as the aforementioned BAL or the numerous interviews, events, and Q&As that take place not only as part of the Festival, but also at the events organized by the aforementioned Talent Campus Buenos Aires. Hence, the Festival focuses primarily on the practical side of education, and its target attendees are primarily young filmmakers who are, in one way or another, involved in the film industry already.

This attitude is very different to other similar festivals such as IndieLisboa in Portugal, or indeed some of the festivals which, as Quintín notes, have modelled themselves on BAFICI — amongst which he includes many of those in Latin America, such as FICCO, the Mexico City International Contemporary Film Festival (or Festival Internacional de Cine Contemporáneo), or the Caracas Film and Video Festival in Venezuela — as well as Festivals on which BAFICI has modelled itself, such as Rotterdam. For the organizers of IndieLisboa, also a young Festival of independent film which, founded in 2004, shares many characteristics with the Argentine Festival, one of their priorities is precisely the cinematic education of very young children; in the words of one of the Festival's three directors Rui Perreira, 'this is the future generation that hopefully will be attending, watching and making films in the future'.[84] This happens by way of an extensive array of promotions and workshops involving local schools — an important activity part of the events taking place in both the LFF and San Sebastián. Therefore, it came as a surprise to discover the inclusion of a new section in BAFICI's 2009 edition called BAFICITO (which translates as 'Little BAFICI'); when questioned, Wolf denied this section was part of any educational programme. In fact, the exclusion of any link with education was one of the agreed requirements for including this section in the Festival.

> The experience at festivals that have a strong tradition of a children's section, like Toronto or Berlin, is that this section feels very disconnected from the rest of the Festival. They are organized for schools and in the case of Argentina, all of that implies educational schemes. So you have to choose the films thinking if they need to be approved in order to show them to kids, and then the parents have to authorize the screening and the ministry has to see the films beforehand, and once there they enter into the world of bureaucracy. It implies a kind of limitation of the Festival's artistic profile, and that is the one truly non-negotiable part of the Festival.[85]

BAFICITO was in fact organized primarily so that the festivalgoers who grew up with BAFICI, filmmakers, critics and so on, now with kids of their own, could also attend the Festival. This way the kids also have something to watch while the parents see their films; a position that promotes family relations, but which leaves questions about the visual education of the coming generations untouched.

Paradoxically, just one year since its inception and one year after the interview I held with Wolf, BAFICITO had already acquired a certain degree of importance. In the press conference presenting the programme for the 2010 edition of the Festival that Wolf gave in conjunction with the city's minister of culture, Hernán Lombardi, BAFICITO was regarded as one of the most important sections recently developed at the Festival, as well as one of its most successful in terms of figures. This meant it had expanded and become more focused by comparison with its more experimental version the previous year, and as such, its programming has been gradually tilting towards the promotion of a more family-centred entertainment. In addition, a new award was introduced, whereby the UNICEF Jury chooses the best film with children or adolescents' subject matter.[86] In 2012, in order to expand BAFICI further along the year and with family members in mind, the first edition of BAFICI Animado took place: a four day yearly programme dedicated to animation in film and suitable for both children and adults. Increasingly, the inclusion of children and their families in the festival has acquired more prominence and in 2018 VR film experiences were available for both kids and adults, as reported in the Festival's website, with the emphasis on an event involving local schools and dedicated solely to children. The now larger in number all-inclusive open-air screenings, together with free workshops around the city, have become one of BAFICI's traditions.[87]

FIG. 1.7. Baficito
Photo © Agustín Maseado

BAFICI and Historical Memory

The position that BAFICI takes on educating the country's future generation of filmmakers also draws attention to the way the Festival (and the country) relates to memory and the past.

'El olvido no existe. Forgetting does not exist. The children of the victims take over and tell their testimony 34 years after the 1976 coup'. This was the headline of the issue of the Argentine cultural magazine *Página/12* that was published on 24 March 2010. As an act of remembrance on that same day, there was a call for users of the social network site Facebook to remove the photograph in their profile in order to recall all those 'identities' that were 'erased' during the dictatorship, leaving just the generic (anonymous) Facebook profile. It was a huge success and profiles disappeared all over the website. In that same newspaper, Victoria Ginzberg — the daughter of two 'disappeared' parents — in her article 'Facebook es raro' (or Facebook is Weird) talks not only about how that act made her feel, but also about another act (or maybe we could call it a counter-act) that took place in tandem: whereby people replaced their own profile photo with photos of the *desaparecidos* themselves (relatives, friends, acquaintances), prompting everyone to share and introduce the identities of those people that had been 'erased' during the dictatorship.[88]

For Jewish sociologist Yehuda Elkana, acts of remembrance such as this are controversial, and can be double-edged. In 1988, he published an article titled 'The Need to Forget' in which he stated that

> History and collective memory are an inseparable part of any culture but the past is not and must not be allowed to become the dominant element determining the future of society and the destiny of the people. The very existence of democracy is endangered when the memory of the dead participates actively in the democratic process.[89]

For Edward Said the act of forgetting is a significant cultural fact, and in his powerful essay 'Methods of Forgetting', written in response to Elkana's, he writes:

> Elkana's argument, though intended in a local situation, has universal application. No society should be in the grip of the past, no matter how traumatic, or allow instances of collective history to determine attitudes in the present. Today there is the danger of using an historical trauma remembered too vividly as a screen to obscure or justify what these former victims are doing, which is nothing less than creating victims of their own.[90]

But he then proceeds to explain that forgetting can also become a 'crisis of national significance when one memory is obscured by another[91]'. Hence, for Said, it is imperative that a society not only remembers but also keeps its history alive. For him, retrieving the past may be a moral duty; when Said returned to Palestine he did so not solely for nostalgia and sentimental reasons, or even for political effect; he returned to bear witness.

Said's dual position in recognizing the positive and the negative in both forgetting and remembering, is also shared by Oren Baruch Stier who, writing about the

Holocaust, reflects on forgetfulness of historical trauma and notes:

> The issue of forgetfulness is especially important in the contemporary, technological age, in which historical knowledge appears to be slipping away and everything seems to be focused on the present moment.[92] [...] Forgetting, like remembering, remains an index of the trauma. Recognizing this difference is crucial for an appreciation of the efforts and outcomes of remembering and forgetting as techniques of engagement with and embodiment of the past.[93]

This debate assumes great importance in a country whose recent political past has consisted in 'erasing' a certain ideology through the 'disappearance' of its adherents, and where, on the other hand, public expressions of remembrance undertaken by the Mothers of the Plaza de Mayo in the business district of Buenos Aires are deeply embedded in the country's identity (the killings started in 1973 and the Mothers started demonstrating in 1977, only one year after the military took power, and have not stopped since, visiting the Plaza every Thursday).

Most crucially for this study, this national preoccupation translates into the, by all accounts, vast quantity of films on this very subject that are made each year in Argentina, most of which get sent to BAFICI for selection consideration.[94] Wolf tells me that, comparatively, very few of these films are in fact selected for the Festival, whose interest is in the actual quality of the films and not the film's subject.[95] One of the earliest and most emblematic examples is Albertina Carri's highly divisive *Los Rubios/The Blonds* (2003), which was selected precisely for the controversial take that this filmmaker has on the relation between memory and history. In her film, Carri (the daughter of *desaparecidos*) reconstructs the story of her parents, linking the testimonies of friends and family to her own memories, to question the 'reality' of historical reconstruction based on personal testimony, as well as the entrapments of collective memory which become accepted as history.

Nevertheless, war victims are not the only 'disappeared' in Argentina; for Rowe and Schelling the indigenous people populating the country have been increasingly pushed out of urban centres, as well as slowly erased from the country's official history. It therefore becomes significant that many of the initial group of filmmakers who were part of the NAC in the late 1990s were making films about just such marginalized communities (many have continued to do so). This happened in different ways, such as having the film protagonist retiring to live amongst such communities, as in Trapero's *Nacido y criado/Born and Bred* (2006) or coming back to them for a short time, like Lisandro Alonso's *Liverpool* (2008); as well as filming members of these communities within their own environment, as in Alonso's *La libertad* (2001) and *Los muertos* (2004); or depicting the struggle, rejection and difficulties that these communities face when they migrate to the city, as in Adrián Caetano's *Bolivia* (2001), Martín Rejtman's *Copacabana* (2006) or Alonso's *Fantasma* (2006). Ulises Rosell's documentary of 2012 *El etnógrafo/The Ethnographer*, turns to the twenty years research work of an outsider as it chronicles a British scholar's life and work within the Wichí people. Lucrecia Martel has famously repeatedly surrounded (the term 'imprisoned' would be more accurate here) her protagonists with *desaparecidos*, portraying the practically invisible indigenous people as servants

(*Zama*, 2018), as well as including metaphorical allusions to the fallen during the dictatorship (*La mujer sin cabeza/The Headless Woman*, 2008). Martel's 2020 documentary (her first), entitled *Chocobar*, tells the story of Javier Chocobar, a photographer and land rights activist who was murdered whilst fighting the removal of his Indigenous community from their ancestral land in Argentina.

Inevitably, Argentina's own conflicted position towards remembering and forgetting raises questions about BAFICI's own relation with memory and history, particularly with the preservation of its own history and the formation of its own identity. One of the most interesting characteristics of BAFICI was its total lack of archival material until 2008 — one of the key reasons for my extensive use of interviews in constructing this version of the Festival's 'story' or its oral history. The different teams that have passed through the offices of the Festival have left behind none of the films, the screeners (copies of the films made on DVD), the books published (right from its inception BAFICI followed in the publishing traditions of Guadalajara, Lima, São Paolo or San Sebastián), or even the catalogues that the Festival has produced throughout the years of its existence. Quintín comments:

> There is no kind of archive. That was very badly handled by the authorities. They never gave a budget to someone to take care of the archival material of the Festival. And everything was lost. A mess. We even published a lot of books. That was a thing that we started and it's still ongoing; and the books, nobody knows what happened to them. It's now a proper collection but you cannot have them re-printed anymore because it's a mess; a real mess.[96]

When I asked about press cuttings, Eloísa Solaas, one of the former programmers, confirms that none of those were kept either.[97] As Solaas explains, the situation repeats itself each time the Festival has changed its director. Essentially, there is no department or funding available for archiving the Festival's material, and people have taken everything they worked on when they left.

To some extent this mirrors successive Argentine governments' relation to the maintenance of the nation's cultural heritage, which in the case of film, for example, is illustrated by the publicly denounced negligence with which silent films were treated, resulting in the loss of 90% of the total stock of prints, originally the largest national collection in Latin America. During the dictatorship, the military government created a special force in charge of controlling and censoring all types of scientific, cultural, political and artistic productions. In 1976, this process culminated in the 'Quema de Libros' (burning of books) in which a 'mountain' of books, including novels by Gabriel García Márquez, Pablo Neruda's poems and Osvaldo Bayer's research, were burnt in the name of the Operación Claridad (or Operation Clarity), which consisted in 'hunting' opponents of the regime throughout the cultural realm.[98]

For French philosopher Jacques Derrida:

> There's no political power without control of the archive, if not of memory. Effective democratization can always be measured by this essential criterion: the participation in and the access to the archive, its institution, and its interpretation.[99]

In the light of this, the state's reluctance to provide BAFICI with a space in which to store the material produced or handled by the Festival, a physical space in which to preserve its own memory, becomes even more significant.

This situation has now partly changed, most clearly signalled by a book about the history of BAFICI published to mark the Festival's tenth anniversary and written by people involved with the Festival from its inception; *Cine Argentino 99/08. Bafici 10 Años: análisis, hitos, dilemas, logros, desafíos y (por qué no) varias cosas para celebrar.*[100] For its 20th anniversary a second publication edited by Diego Papic was presented at the Festival's 2018 edition, *Otoños Porteños*, narrating once more, the history of BAFICI from the experience of its protagonists. For Diana Taylor, 'cultural memory is, among other things, a practice, an act of imagination and interconnection',[101] and in this sense, it is important to note the extensive use that BAFICI makes of the Internet, whereby the archive (a physical space) is replaced by the shared, immaterial, 'interconnected' (to use Taylor's term) digital space of the world wide web. This is of course a platform that many festivals use regularly. Yet, for BAFICI, the Internet is not simply a backup, but in many cases, its main source of storage. The information regarding the Festival is not only mainly disseminated on the web, but also 'stored' on it. After Marcelo Panozzo — co-editor of the tenth anniversary book — assumed the director's position in 2013, the archive of the Festival's materials has acquired a new importance. A number of the books published by BAFICI and funded by the City's Government are now available online on the City of Buenos Aires website — from 2013, the Festival's website has become a sub-section within the City of Buenos Aires's own.

Moreover, with film festivals all over the world increasingly digitalizing and uploading all the material they produce (catalogue, programme, media coverage) to the web, this location makes this information instantly accessible to the public. In tune with the Festival's now actual connection with its own past, for its fifteenth edition in 2013 (and coinciding with a change of management) BAFICI included a section celebrating its fifteen years of history, which saw the screening of some of the key Argentine films that defined the Festival (and Argentine cinema in the last decade) such as Martín Reijtman's *Silvia Prieto* (1998), Trapero's *Crane World* (1999), Mariano Llinás *Historias extraordinarias/Extraordinary Stories* (2008) or Santiago Mitre's *El estudiante/The Student* (2011), accompanied by an exhibition.

BAFICI's own position towards accessing (and presenting) the past completely clashes with the Government's disinterest in providing the Festival with archival space for its first decade. A glance at BAFICI's programme over the years reveals a palpable urgency to catch up with all the films (national and international) that, for political or economic reasons, were never screened in the country, so they too might be regarded as archival material. This sense of discovery (or in some cases re-discovery) translates into an impressive retrospective programme comparable to those at the Viennale or San Sebastián festivals, covering the most obscure filmmakers and their most difficult to acquire films, to more recent films (mostly Argentine) that did not manage to get exhibited in the country. For Martín Peña, retrospectives are essential for the proper understanding of the situation of film

Fig. 1.8. BAFICI's 20th Anniversary Party
Photo © Agustín Maseado

today. That is to say, in order to look forward, it is necessary to acknowledge and understand the past, and establish a dialogue between them. With his programming emphasis on understanding the 'cinema of the past', Peña argues:

> There is an independent cinema in the past for me. I think that there has been an independent cinema and that it was as dynamic in the past and it is as unknown to the Argentine public as the cinema of the present is. And that to a certain degree, that has to be represented in the Festival. [...] Because the evolution of cinema is not organic; it's not like a young person who then grows old. One can find something innovative and subversive at any time. And the point is finding it and being able to disseminate it. Independent cinema has always been unprotected, not just now. [...] We offered retrospectives that were also discoveries for the audience of the Festival.[102]

This is still the case in BAFICI, in which year after year the programming of retrospectives are now one of the Festival's most distinctive elements, alongside the newest Argentine films giving the Festival its sense of balance. This balance is for many one of the key motors of its success and its impact.

And while impact and success are notoriously difficult to assess or measure, I would like to turn in the next section to reflect on how these might be considered in relation to BAFICI.

Impact and Success: The Legacy of BAFICI

Practically since its inception, BAFICI has had an aura of utopian space for critics and filmmakers alike. In the 2009 edition critic Tag Gallagher referred to this 'utopian' status of the Festival when introducing one of his several seminars on the Straub-Huillet retrospective, part of that year's programme. As seen, 'perfect' is the word chosen by Spanish critic Kovacsics and the Festival's directors have repeatedly referred to it as a 'miracle' as well as the press and film professionals alike, but is (and how is) the Festival 'successful'?[103] In fact, the real question is if festivals generally are, and will continue to be, successful in the tasks they set themselves?

Here are some of the terms used to measure the success of a film festival:

- Economic, box office
- Cultural value
- International reputation
- Audience attendance and access
- Film premieres
- Press coverage
- Promotion of national cinema/new cinema

As seen, BAFICI has managed to achieve these targets regardless of the problems it has repeatedly encountered within its organization and with regard to funding. It also managed to acquire a resoundingly strong international cache in a relatively short time. In that respect, BAFICI could be compared with Pusan. The annual Asian film festival that takes place in South Korea's city of Pusan, also funded by the local authorities, started at the same time as BAFICI and was linked with a new wave of filmmakers in the country, proving to be fundamental in their promotion. Pusan also acquired a solid presence on the international festival circuit in a relatively short period of time. As for the value of BAFICI, this is a given, not only because it is considered by many as the city's most important cultural event, but also because it is hugely successful in terms of attendance and press coverage[104] and finally, until now, the Festival has not only managed to promote Argentine cinema internationally but also aims to introduce the most challenging international independent cinema to its audience.

The Festival's influence on the creation of other festivals in Latin America is another direct consequence of its success. Quintín names the newly founded Latin American festivals that modelled themselves, to a greater or lesser extent, on the BAFICI formula: FICCO in Mexico City, SANFIC in Santiago de Chile, the Valdivia International Film Festival, Zero Latitude Film Festival in Ecuador, and as we've seen, Quintín's own Independent Film Festival of Mar del Plata, Marfici.

Within Argentina, BAFICI has also proved to be influential. When Mar del Plata became aware of BAFICI's success, its own editorial line started shifting towards BAFICI's, and the A-list festival started including more Argentine independent films than the commercial ones it normally screened. In 2007 Mar del Plata also moved from November to March, its historical date. This decision did not allow enough time to organize the Festival, which is why it was not held that year. This move would also increase the competition between the two festivals for films and press coverage. The following year, 2008, Mar del Plata moved back to November under the direction of Fernando Peña. As the director of Mar del Plata, Peña was accused of taking certain traits from BAFICI and applying them to the coastal festival, such as the section on NAC, very similar to BAFICI's own. Nevertheless, the obvious benefit of having these two festivals, and the increasing overlap of their programmes, is that smaller, more independent (as well as completely independent) films are given a bigger (double) exposure, increasing their chances to secure a distribution deal.

From an internal point of view, when questioned about the success of the Festival, its international cache and its status of utopian space for film and both cinephiles and industry people, the answers of the four artistic directors I got the chance to interview vary. As previously seen, one of the reasons why Sergio Wolf thinks BAFICI has become so successful is down to the people that work in it. People such as Rosa Martínez Rivero, who started as a programmer of short films in the Festival's first edition and is now its producer, or Violeta Baba who began like many others as an 'ángel' (the Festival person allocated to the guests). She became one of BAFICI'S main programmers, co-director of BAL since its inception in 2009, and has been the Latin American delegate for the Venice Film Festival since 2012. These are people who started young and grew up with the Festival, making a career out of their experience; who know it from the inside out and have worked from the bottom up. They know its weaknesses and its strengths, and have a genuinely close and proud relationship with it.

For Quintín, the Festival could no longer be judged to be successful by 2009.

Fig. 1.9. BAFICI 2019 Masterclass given by Julien Temple
Photo © Agustín Maseado

In his opinion, that was the moment for renewal and surprise; to change the perspective of the Festival, as the people involved in it — both outsiders (audience, press, filmmakers) and insiders (programmers, director) — are accustomed to the Festival and they are getting too comfortable with it.

> In our last year 2004 I was thinking that it was time for a change, that something was going on, but I never really had the time to do proper thinking or come up with a new idea. I think that now we need a new kind of festival. I have the feeling that this is as good as it can be, but at the same time we need something better: to rethink how the whole thing works, and which films are shown and where to see them, because people are getting a little bit complacent. I keep on running into people that say that. And this is not Cannes where all the films are new and sold. These films have been at festivals, they were chosen, maybe Thierry Fremaux is very stupid one year and chooses the wrong films, that can happen, but here films come from other festivals, so it's not that they are picking the wrong film. In a way they are consensus films. So something is not working very well. People always try to complain but this year [2009] the complaints were a little too loud.[105]

For some festivals — such as Mar del Plata and many other international festivals — having premieres, accompanied in some cases with red carpet events is key to measuring their success. But for Quintín, as for many others, premieres can also decrease the quality of the overall programme, as there are not enough really good films made in a given year to be premiered at the (ever-increasing number of) film festivals around the world. Nevertheless, BAFICI has also indulged in having its own premieres — predominantly Argentine. A direct consequence of the increasing pressure to include premieres has been that, when Argentine filmmakers have been offered slots in Cannes, San Sebastián or Locarno, in some cases they have chosen them over BAFICI, a decision that directly affects the quality of Argentine films premiering in the international competition; a situation that becomes more noticeable when these films are paired up with better quality international films.

And yet, when I speak to one of BAFICI's newest programmers, the Spanish film critic Álvaro Arroba, he explains that for the last three years, under the direction of Javier Porta-Fouz there has been a greater emphasis on premieres — with a total of 107 international premiers and ninety-nine US and Argentine premieres in the Festival's twentieth anniversary in 2018. Arroba tells me:

> What Porta-Fuz has done, is imprinting the Festival's selection with a bit more ambition, unlike Panozzo [previous director to Porta-Fouz], Wolf, but mainly Panozzo. They all have to be premieres, at least in Argentina and if possible, in Latin America. So we cannot play anything shown six months earlier at Mar del Plata. In that sense, Porta-Fouz treats the films as events, and unlike Mar del Plata, whose films many come from other festivals, our official selection has to be premieres. In fact, last year Mariano Llinás *La flor* [2018, a fourteen hour film divided into three sections] marked a before and after for the Festival, since Llinás kept his film to premiere at BAFICI.[106]

The first part of Llinás film was shown at Mar del Plata previously, but the whole was premiered at BAFICI in 2018, and regardless, went onto compete in the official selection of an A-list international film festival (as Arroba notes), Locarno, winning the Golden Leopard.

In fact, for Wolf the Festival's international visibility has brought a significant change in attitude within the Argentine film community. New filmmakers — who previously sought to show their films first outside the country, in search of sales agents, international press, distributors or producers — now opt to show their films at BAFICI, since the Festival has created a space such that international programmers, critics, et al., trusting the quality of programming, will head to Buenos Aires to see these films. For instance, in 2010, Iván Fund and Santiago Loza's *Los labios/The Lips*, premiered at BAFICI and then competed at Cannes's sidebar, Un certain regard. This in turn brings foreign capital and encourages investment in the Argentine film industry — yet another way of measuring success. This position has also had an impact from a revenue point of view, since attendance is perhaps the most visible point of measure for the success of a festival, and in that respect, audiences have been increasing every year at BAFICI, with 390,000 people attending the Festival in 2018, more than double than its first edition.[107]

But is the international profile of a festival more important than the number of distribution deals made during or as a consequence of the festival? And is BAFICI still successful at promoting national cinema, something that it set itself to do right from the outset?

Towards the end of January 2010, the film trade newspaper *Variety* ran a front page article on the new role that some festivals are acquiring as distributors.[108] This article noted that regardless of the numerous forums that bring together filmmakers with distributors, the number of films shown at film festivals and subsequently picked for distribution is notably less each year. In this article we are told that Sundance, as well as its rival Slamdance, have found ways to not only make sure that their films are exhibited, but also that they carry on being screened during the year, taking full advantage of new technologies as well as their private funds. Hence Sundance's first day offered the possibility of watching eight of its programmed shorts on YouTube; renting a couple of their feature films, plus another eight films would tour North America. But the most important innovation is the use of their own cable channel to broadcast these films during the year. With four hundred entries that make it into the programme and thousands of others that get sent in for consideration, the channel slots would be easily covered throughout the rest of the year. For its part, Slamdance struck a deal with Microsoft to use two of their platforms, Xbox and Zune, to screen Video On Demand (VOD) versions of the films included in their festival programme (VOD allows televisions to stream their content in real time to view, or you can download with a computer, digital video recorder or portable media player for viewing at any time). More recently, the pressure exerted by Netflix's tentacles into film production and distribution has made the streaming platform persona-non-grata at festivals such as Cannes, where its films were banned from competition in 2018, unless they are released on the big screen.[109]

In an interview with a group of Argentine producers included in the book *Aesthetics of Film Production* published by BAFICI in 2009,[110] one of the possibilities for a continuous promotion of Argentine independent film would be introducing a quota for Argentine-produced films to be shown on national television, as well as the possible involvement of the medium itself in co-production. In 2009, the Government passed the New Media Law — Nueva Ley de los Medios — in which this concept was introduced.[111] The outcome of this would be twofold. On the one hand, independent cinema and commercial cinema would be sharing the same medium, and so potentially the gap between their two audiences (as well as their perceived accessibility) would considerably reduce. Thus Argentine films could find a means of distribution within their own country. On the other hand, a project like this raises numerous questions to do with screening and sales rights, as the main concern would be precisely not damaging — by paradoxically exhausting — the possibility of these films having a theatrical release. At the time of sending this book to print, the effects of COVID-19 on cinema distribution/exhibition has thrown into perspective the use of digital platforms, if anything, highlighting once again, festivals' inherent adaptability.

This brings us to the question of distribution and exhibition within Argentina of the kind of cinema promoted by and in BAFICI. The key target of the Festival, and the area in which it has been most successful, would then be in closing the huge gap that exists between commercial and independent distribution in Argentina, building a bridge between these two extremes. For writer and journalist Agustín Campero it is this gap that causes the fragmentation of the audience, and in order to avoid it, he proposes using the facilities in the city's universities. With a total of over fifty universities plus their faculties and satellite buildings, some of these buildings could be fitted with screening rooms (with the capacity for digital projection) at relatively low cost. The main problem with this would be the danger of ghettoizing these films by playing them in an alternative circuit, as this could paradoxically increase the gap between independent and commercial cinema even further. Campero also calls for the creation of a cinematographic policy, to provide funding for production as well as distribution and exhibition[112] (the role of the Universidad del Cine in relation to this is dealt with earlier in this chapter), and agrees with Peña when he notes the difficulty that the government seems to have in long-term planning, and how this is related to the cultural habits of the public, adding that

> Neither schools nor secondary education encourage access to a varied culture, one that would facilitate the possibility of a future vital, intense and rich experience derived from a special relationship with works of any type of art. Added to this, on the film side, there is an exclusion arising from the price of the tickets, the location of the cinemas (highly concentrated geographically) and the fact that the films which are promoted and screened seem very similar to each other.[113]

In 2009, Kairuz noted that one of the consequences of this fragmentation was a drop in cinema attendance figures across the board in Argentina,[114] and a growing sense that film is an expensive entertainment not accessible to everyone, which is being increasingly supplanted by DVD pirate copies (just outside Abasto Plaza street vendors were selling copies during the edition I attended) and the Internet — Julián D'Angiolillo's film screened at BAFICI's 2010 edition, entitled *Hacerme feriante*, deals precisely with this practice. Hence the importance of the state's funding of a national cinema alternative to the straightforward commercial productions to help incentivize the national industry. For Diego Dubcovsky (co-owner with Daniel Burman of the production company BD Cine), film cannot exist in Argentina without the funding coming from INCAA.[115] If INCAA closed, 'it would leave the 50,000 graduates coming out of the film schools every year for the last decade the only option of driving a taxi'.[116] For him, as for many other producers interviewed in the book *Cine argentino: Estéticas de la producción*, eleven years on from the origins of BAFICI and the NAC's boom, this is the most difficult moment for independent Argentine cinema, as there is not enough money coming from INCAA to fund the increasing number of projects, which has affected the involvement of some of the international funds such as Fond Sud, who had to close their doors to Argentine products because the demand is simply too high.[117] This increase in numbers, together with a more protective attitude towards their own national markets, has also significantly reduced the possibilities of (largely commercial) co-productions mainly involving Spain and France.

Paradoxically, the solution may involve looking in and looking back. There is already a distinctive shift in Argentine's newer 'new' generation of filmmakers, as they search for novel ways of collaboration. Coming back full circle to the Festival's own origins, film is now heavily influenced by the national theatre scene in the country. The interaction of film with the city's current theatre scene helps define, influence and generate new ways of film making in Argentina. A cultural cross-over is taking place and today there are a substantial number of filmmakers, screenwriters and actors involved in film making who worked originally in theatre, such as directors Federico León and Santiago Loza, or the cast in Matías Piñeiro's films *Todos mienten/They All Lie* (2009), *Viola* (2012), *La princesa de Francia* (2014) and *Hermia & Helena* (2016), Mitre's *El estudiante* (2011) and *Paulina* (2015), Alejo Moguillanski's *Castro* (2009), and his and Fia-Stina Sandlund's *El escarabajo de oro/ The Golden Beetle* (2014).

In an echo of BAFICI's own origins, cinema is once more linked to the strong local independent theatre scene, an association that generates a pronounced and conscious shift in filmmaking aesthetics. More importantly, three of those films *They All Lie*, *The Golden Beetle* and *Castro* were made by a collective organized outside INCAA and they both shared creative and technical teams and performers. Adopting a position marginal to the state-funded schemes, unsurprisingly they also share as their producer/writer one of the Argentine filmmakers most determined to maintain his independent position from the industry, by refusing to take any funding from INCAA: Mariano Llinás, who proved the viability of this position in 2008, when he picked up the best screenplay award for his *Extraordinary Stories* from the Academy of Motion Picture Arts and Sciences of Argentina, a film (directed, scripted and produced by Llinás) made entirely outside the system. As is his latest feature, *La flor*, fourteen-hours long and filmed over the last ten years, which, as previously mentioned, premiered at BAFICI in 2018, where it won the Best International Film award, before winning the Golden Leopard at Locarno.

Significantly, Llinás did not win the best film at BAFICI ten years earlier in 2008, despite being one the clear favourites. This is unsurprising, since because he works outside the system, Llinás is heavily criticized by a certain sector of the industry (mainly the producers), who consider that, because they do not pay taxes, filmmakers such as he do not contribute economically to the smooth functioning of the system. On the other hand, many maintain it is precisely because this system is corrupt that there is a need to create an alternative. Ironically, Llinas's film lost that year to a film whose subject is precisely the current state of film production in Buenos Aires, *UPA! una película argentina/UPA! An Argentinian Movie* (Tamae Garateguy, Santiago Giralt, Camila Toker, 2007). *UPA!* enjoyed high acclaim from film professionals, for whom — clearly recognizing themselves in this situation — the film captured and denounced with extreme accuracy the way the system has unscrupulously taken control of the production of the new independent cinema in Argentina and turned it into yet another anonymous business based on cronyism. Most importantly, the film was made by the Manifiesto Grupo Acción,[118] yet another collective of filmmakers whose experiences of the horrors of making films with a small budget in Argentina led them to organize themselves in order to fight the system off with new methods of production.

Yet perhaps the most pressing issue in this transition period is the future of cinemas (as repertory cinemas close down all over the world) as well as film festivals themselves: why bother to attend a film festival when the content could be made (or in some cases already is) accessible online. Fourth director of BAFICI, Panozzo's solution was to restructure the Festival's programme into larger sections and to ensure that retrospectives are complete. He explains:

> For instance, the retrospective on Julio Bressane, the Brazilian director, instead of comprising two or three films — as anybody could organize at their home — we are showing all of his seventeen films. It is something that gives you an advantage, something that makes it worth watching them in a physical place. It's a complicated battle and this is a transition year, since from now on BAFICI is going to have to find solutions online by itself. Perhaps in the future it will be a physical and virtual festival simultaneously; this is something that we, the [BAFICI's] producer Paula Niklison and the programmers are talking about all the time. That's the way things are heading but our aim is still to get the biggest number of people to come to the cinema.[119]

With a total of 390,000 people attending the more than four hundred films shown in the 2018 edition,[120] the Festival's success in terms of audience seems incontrovertible. This in turn is reinforced by a greater financial input (40% increase in comparison to the 2017 edition) from the City's Government, reaching $800,000 (approx. 34 million Argentine Pesos at the time of writing) for 2018.[121] Since 2013 the Festival no longer takes place in the Abasto centre, but was relocated to a series of cultural organizations also wholly or partly funded by the government, and in

FIG. 1.10. Outdoor screening of *Let the Right One In* at BAFICI 2012
Photo © Agustín Maseado

2018 its 'meeting point' is Plaza Francia in the scenic neighbourhood of Recoleta, near the National Museum of Fine Arts and the cutting edge shows of Recoleta Cultural Centre. As noted, another noticeable change is that BAFICI no longer has its own independent website. Instead, the Festival's pages are part of the City of Buenos Aires website, appearing under the rubric: Buenos Aires Ciudad-BAFICI-Festivales.[122] Success therefore seems to come at a high price for BAFICI and resurrects an old argument traceable to its origins: the Festival's oft-debated status as 'independent' looks to be its biggest future challenge.

Notes to Chapter 1

All uncredited quotations are from the following unpublished interviews conducted by the author: interview with Sergio Wolf, BAFICI Meeting Point, 29 March 2009 (translated from Spanish by the author); interview with Mariano Martín Kairúz, Abasto Shopping Centre, Buenos Aires, 30 March 2009 (translated from Spanish by the author); interview with Eloísa Solaas, BAFICI offices, 31 March 2009 (translated from Spanish by the author); interview with Celina Murga and Juan Villegas, Abasto Shopping Centre, Buenos Aires, 1 April 2009 (translated from Spanish by the author); interview with Quintín, café opposite the Abasto Shopping Centre, Buenos Aires, 3 April 2009; interview with Andrés Di Tella, by phone, 22 June 2009 (translated from Spanish by the author); interview with Fernando Martín Peña, by phone, 22 June 2009 (translated from Spanish by the author); interview with Álvaro Arroba, by phone, 1 October 2018 (translated from Spanish by the author). All websites were accessed between April 2009 and October 2019.

1. All figures were collected from the Festival's 2018 edition.
2. Gonzalo Aguilar, *Other Worlds*, trans. by Sarah Ann Wells (London: Palgrave Macmillan, 2008)
3. Mar Diestro-Dópido, 'Other Worlds/Crisis and Capitalism in Contemporary Argentine Cinema', *Sight & Sound*, 20, 4 (2010), 93.
4. For an exhaustive account of the origins of Latin American film festivals, see Mar Diestro-Dópido, 'The Film Festival Circuit: Identity Transactions in a Translational Economy', in *A Companion to Latin American Cinema*, ed. by Maria M. Delgado, Stephen M. Hart and Randal Johnson (Oxford: Wiley Blackwell 2017), pp. 99–113.
5. Marijke de Valck, *Film Festivals: From European Geopolitics to Global Cinephilia*, (Amsterdam: Amsterdam University Press, 2007), p. 222. For more information on Mar del Plata, see Mar del Plata Film Festival, <http://www.mardelplatafilmfest.com/28/el-festival/historia/>.
6. Tamara L. Falicov, *The Cinematic Tango. Contemporary Argentine Film* (London and New York: Wallflower Press, 2007), pp. 5–6.
7. A type of cinema that mainly questions the relation of power between colonizer and colonized. For more information see Third Cinema, <http://thirdcinema.blueskylimit.com/thirdcinema.html>.
8. Sol, 'Historia de América. Gobierno argentino. Golpe militar de 1976. Represión. Censura. Prensa. Radio. Prensa. Televisión. Cine y Música. Rodolfo Walsh', in *El rincón del vago*, Salamanca, undated, <http://html.rincondelvago.com/medios-de-comunicacion-en-la-dictadura-argentina.html>.
9. Diego Batlle, 'From Virtual Death to the New Law', in *New Argentine Cinema. Themes, Auteurs and Trends of Innovation*, ed. by Horacio Bernades, Diego Lerer and Sergio Wolf (Buenos Aires: Fipresci Argentina/Ediciones Tatanka, 2002), pp. 17–27 (p. 17).
10. Batlle, 'From Virtual Death to the New Law', p. 17.
11. Joanna Page, *Crisis and Capitalism in Contemporary Argentine Cinema* (Durham and London: Duke University Press, 2009), pp. 2, 201.
12. Elena and Díaz López, *The Cinema of Latin America*, p. 8.
13. Campero, 'Supongamos que existe una política cinematográfica', p. 18.

14. Falicov, *The Cinematic Tango. Contemporary Argentine Film*, p. 2.
15. Campero, 'Supongamos que existe una política cinematográfica', p. 17.
16. Campero, 'Supongamos que existe una política cinematográfica', p. 17.
17. Tamara L. Falicov, 'Migrating from South to North: The Role of Film Festivals in Funding and Shaping Global South Film and Video', in *Locating Migrating Media*, Greg Elmer, Charles H. Davis, Janine Machessault and John McCollough (Lanham, MD: Lexington Books, 2010), pp. 3–22.
18. Data available at Pro Film Festivals, a social network powered by FilmFestivals, <www.fest21.com>.
19. Marvin D'Lugo, 'Cinema: From Mexican Ranchera to Argentinian Exile', in *Rethinking Third Cinema*, ed. by Anthony R. Guteratne and Wimal Dissanayake (Oxford: Routledge, 2003), pp. 101–25 (p. 122).
20. These figures refer to the 2016–18 editions and can be found at the Festival's website, available at <https://moreliafilmfest.com/wp-content/uploads/2019/10/17-ficm-cat-todo.pdf> [accessed 25 May 2020]. The new Festival website does not include a summary of the most current figures.
21. Festival do Rio, <http://www.Festivaldorio.com.br/>.
22. 'Festival de Mar del Plata 2018: Reducen en tres días su duración', *Otros Cines*, 11 September 2018, <https://www.otroscines.com/nota-13761-festival-de-mar-del-plata-2018-reducen-en-tres-dias-su>.
23. See Mar del Plata Film Festival, <http://www.mardelplatafilmfest.com/en/seccion/festival/historia>.
24. Interview with Martín Kairuz.
25. A quick look at the historical background included in the Festival's official website illustrates this: <http://www.mardelplatafilmfest.com/>.
26. Interview with Peña.
27. See Mar del Plata Film Festival, <http://www.mardelplatafilmfest.com/en/seccion/festival/historia>.
28. Kovacsics mentioned this to Sergio Wolf at Cannes. Interview with Wolf.
29. The magazines *El Amante Cine* and *Film* regularly explored the state of film criticism. For a historical introduction to their origins and their relationship to the new Argentine cinema, see Eduardo A. Cartoccio, 'La crítica precursora del Nuevo Cine Argentino: el caso de las revistas *El Amante* y *Film* entre 1992 y 1995', *X Jornadas Nacionales de Investigadores en Comunicación. Una década de encuentros para (re)pensar los intercambios y consolidar la Red*, San Juan, 2006, Instituto Gino Germani — UBA Universidad de Buenos Aires.
30. Interview with Peña.
31. From the 2013 edition and coinciding with the direction of Marcelo Panozzo, this shopping centre has been substituted by the Centro Cultural Recoleta, which inevitably accentuates the cultural value of the Festival as this centre is now its meeting point.
32. Ivan Illich and Beth Gill, 'Temples of Consumption: Shopping Malls as Secular Cathedrals', essay written for Trinity University, <http://www.trinity.edu/mkearl/temples.html>.
33. Marc Augé, *Non- Places. An Introduction to Supermodernity*, trans. by by John Howe (London and New York: Verso, 1995), p. viii.
34. Interview with Di Tell.
35. Interview with Murga and Villegas.
36. Interview with Martín Kairuz.
37. Interview with Quintín.
38. D.B. 'Una polémica independiente. Andrés Di Tella cuestionó la organización del Festival de Cine de Buenos Aires', *La Nación*, 18 June 1999, <http://www.lanacion.com.ar/142604-una-polemica-independiente>.
39. Flavia de la Fuente, 'Odisea del espacio público', in *Cine Argentino 99/08. Bafici 10 Años: análisis, hitos, dilemas, logros, desafíos y (por qué no) varias cosas para celebrar*, Marcelo Panozzo, Leonel Livchits, and Manuel Antín (Buenos Aires: BAFICI & Ministerio de Cultura. Gobierno de la Ciudad de Buenos Aires, 2008), pp. 41–43.
40. Interview with Quintín.

41. Interview with Di Tella.
42. Interview with Quintín.
43. For an example of this see Quintín's article on Lucrecia Martel's *The Headless Woman*, published in *Cinema Scope*. Although the article is putatively about Martel's latest film, it actually focuses more on Lisandro Alonso, Quintín's professed favourite Argentine film director. *Cinema Scope*, 35 (2008), 42.
44. Quintín, 'The Festival Galaxy' in *Dekalog 3: On Film Festivals*, ed. by Richard Porton (London: Wallflower Press, 2009), pp. 38–52 (p. 22).
45. Interview with Quintín.
46. Interview with Quintín.
47. For more information on Raúl Perrone see 'Tribute: Raúl Perrone: The Man from Ituzaingó. Raúl Perrone — The Last of the Independents', a retrospective on the filmmaker organised by the Filmfestival Viennale. Available at the Viennale's website here, <https://www.viennale.at/en/series/tribute-raul-perrone> [accessed 25 May 2020].
48. *Cine Argentino 99/08. Bafici 10 Años: análisis, hitos, dilemas, logros, desafíos y (por qué no) varias cosas para celebrar*, Marcelo Panozzo, Leonel Livchits, and Manuel Antín (Buenos Aires: BAFICI & Ministerio de Cultura. Gobierno de la Ciudad de Buenos Aires, 2008) p. 48.
49. For an article covering the news, see Sebastián Ackerman, 'Festival porteño en crisis', *Página/12*, 18 November 2004, <http://www.pagina12.com.ar/diario/espectaculos/6-43741-2004-11-18.html>.
50. Quintín, 'La nouvelle vague en danger' in 'L'Atlas du cinéma, 2002 en chiffres, vu par les critiques de 40 pays / vu par les critiques de 40 pays', ed. by Charlotte Garson and Charles Tesson, Special Issue of *Cahiers du Cinéma* (April 2003).
51. Juan José Campanella quoted in 'Por una unión en el cine argentino', *Noticine*, 26 June 2003, <http://noticine.com/industria/42-industria/1694-opinion-por-una-union-en-el-cine-argentino.html>.
52. Interview with Quintín.
53. 'The Director of the Buenos Aires International Festival of Independent Cinema Was Fired', FIPRESCI, 18 July 2014, <http://fipresci.hegenauer.co.uk/news/archive/archive_2004/ba_incident.htm>.
54. Statement of FIPRESCI Argentina, FIPRESCI, <http://fipresci.hegenauer.co.uk/news/archive/archive_2004/fipresci_argentina.htm>.
55. 'In Favor of Quintín', FIPRESCI, 18 July 2014 <http://fipresci.hegenauer.co.uk/news/archive/archive_2004/quintin.htm>.
56. Interview with Murga and Villegas.
57. Octavio Getino, *Cine argentino (Entre lo posible y lo deseable)*, <http://www.hamalweb.com.ar/Textos/Getino_CINE_ARGENTINO.pdf>
58. IndieLisboa 2005 catalogue, p. 108.
59. Fernando Martín Peña, 'Es necesario tomar decisiones', *Página/12*, 9 November 2007, <http://www.pagina12.com.ar/diario/suplementos/espectaculos/5-8230-2007-11-09.html>.
60. Interview with Wolf.
61. Daniela Kozak, 'Todo sobre el BAFICI (Entrevista a Marcelo Panozzo)', *la conversación*, 1 June 2013, <http://laconversacion.wordpress.com/2013/06/01/todo-sobre-el-bafici-entrevista-a-marcelo-panozzo/>.
62. Sam Harrison, 'Porteño Corner: Javier Porta Fouz, Director of BAFICI', *Wander Argentina*, 2016, <https://wander-argentina.com/porteno-corner-director-bafici-javier-fouz/>.
63. For more information see Rotterdam Film Festival, <http://www.filmFestivalrotterdam.com/en/about/hubert_bals_fund/>.
64. Due to the decrease in the available budget for 2014, the Hubert Bals Fund has reviewed its policies and regulations. Information regarding these changes — for instance, the Digital Production category is no longer available for applications — see <https://www.filmFestivalrotterdam.com/professionals/hubert_bals_fund/faq/>.
65. Information available at BAFICI, <http://www.bafici.gov.ar/home09/en/balab/index.html>.

66. Aguilar, *Other Worlds*, p. 187.
67. IndieLisboa 2005 Catalogue, p. 108.
68. Quintín, 'La crisis que faltaba', *Perfil*, 23 November 2008, <http://www.perfil.com/columnistas/La-crisis-que-faltaba-20081122-0043.html>.
69. Thomas Elsaesser, 'Film Festival Networks: The New Topographies of Cinema in Europe', in *European Cinema: Face to Face with Hollywood*, ed. by Thomas Elsaesser (Amsterdam: Amsterdam Univ. Press, 2005), pp. 82–107.
70. *Film Festivals: History, Theory, Method, Practice*, ed. by Marijke de Valck, Brendan Kredell, and Skadi Loist (London, New York: Routledge, 2016), pp. 209–29.
71. Markus Reisenleitner, 'Tradition, Cultural Boundaries and the Constructions of Spaces of Identity' in *Spaces of Identity*, vol.1, issue 1, 2001, pp. 7–13 (p. 10). Available at <http://www.yorku.ca/soi/Vol_1/_PDF/Reisenleitner.pdf>.
72. Page, *Crisis and Capitalism in Contemporary Argentine Cinema*, pp. 63–68. For some examples see, Jason Anderson, 'Taste of Armadillo: Lisandro Alonso on La Libertad', in *Cinema Scope*, 9 (December 2001), 36–38; Javier Porta Fouz, 'Un día en la libertad', in *El Amante Cine*, 110 (May 2001); Deborah Young's review in *Variety*, 14 May 2001, p. 24; Michel Ciment's review in *Positif*, 485, 486 (2001), 78–112; Quintín, 'El misterio del leñador solitario', *El Amante Cine*, 111 (June 2001), 2–5.
73. Edward W. Said, *Culture and Imperialism* (London: Vintage, 1993–4), p. xiii.
74. Page, *Crisis and Capitalism in Contemporary Argentine Cinema*, pp. 152–167; Aguilar, *Other Worlds*, pp. 29–31.
75. Diana Agosta and Patricia Keeton, 'One Way or Another: The Havana Film Festival and Contemporary Cuban Film', *Afterimage*, 22, 2 (1994), 7–8. See Diestro-Dópido 2017 for detailed context on this generation of Latin American filmmakers.
76. Aguilar, *Other Worlds*, p. 29.
77. Aguilar, *Other Worlds*, p. 21.
78. Interview with Murga and Villegas.
79. Diego Batlle, 'Lo que queda del BAFICI', *Otros Cines*, April 2009, <http://www.otroscines.com.ar/columnistas_detalle.php?idnota=2670&idsubseccion=11>.
80. La Lectora Provisoria, <http://www.lalectoraprovisoria.com.ar/?p=3445>.
81. Rafael Filippelli quoted in an interview with Sergio Wolf. Sergio Wolf, 'La Universidad Como Productora' in *Cine argentino. Estéticas de la producción*, ed. by Sergio Wolf (Buenos Aires: Ministerio de Cultura, Gobierno de la Ciudad, 2009), pp. 81–90 (p. 83).
82. Diego Batlle, 'BAFICI 2019: Algunas consideraciones tras la presentación de la 21ª edición del festival', *Otros Cines*, 19 March 2019, <https://www.otroscines.com/nota-14393-bafici-2019-algunas-consideraciones-tras-la-presentacio>.
83. For more information see Festival's website at <http://festivalesanteriores.buenosaires.gob.ar/bafici/home10/web/en/talentcampus/index.html> [accessed 25 May 2020].
84. Interview conducted on 4 May 2008 at the IndieLisboa headquarters for Festival report. Mar Diestro-Dópido, 'Viva Lisbon!', *Sight & Sound*, 18, 7 (2008), 8–9.
85. Interview with Wolf.
86. Guido Carelli Lynch, 'El Bafici 2010 viene con un cine más político', in *Ñ Revista de Cultura*, 19 March 2010, <http://www.revistaenie.clarin.com/notas/2010/03/19/_-02163048.htm>.
87. Information available at BAFICI, <http://festivales.buenosaires.gob.ar/2018/bafici/es/noticia&modal=true&target=noticias&title=Más%20de%20390%20mil%20personas%20disfrutaron%20del%20BAFICI>.
88. Victoria Ginzberg, 'Facebook es raro', *Página/12*, 24 March 2010, <http://www.pagina12.com.ar/diario/elpais/subnotas/142578-45907-2010-03-24.html>.
89. Yehuda Elkana, 'The Need to Forget', *Ha'aretz*, 2 March 1988, available at: <http://web.ceu.hu/yehuda_the_need_to_forget.pdf> [accessed 26 May 2020].
90. Edward Said, 'Methods of Forgetting', *Al-Ahram Weekly On-line*, 400 (22–28 October 1998), <http://weekly.ahram.org.eg/1998/400/op2.htm> (no longer available online, although cited on the main website, <http://weekly.ahram.org.eg/2003/658/_edsaid.htm> and reproduced on MasRess, <https://www.masress.com/en/ahramweekly/25005> [accessed 25 May 2020].

91. Said, 'Methods of Forgetting'.
92. Oren Baruch Stier, *Committed to Memory: Cultural Meditations of the Holocaust* (Massachusetts: University of Massachusetts Press, 2009), p. 191.
93. Baruch Stier, *Committed to Memory: Cultural Meditations of the Holocaust*, p. 192.
94. For more information about the *desaparecidos* see the following Human Rights website: <http://www.derechos.org/nizkor/arg/eng.html>.
95. Interview with Wolf.
96. Interview with Quintín.
97. Interview with Solaas.
98. Sergio Ciancaglini, Oscar Raúl Cardoso, María Seoane, Mariana García, Alejandro López Lépori, 'A 20 años del golpe. Los archivos de la represión cultural', in *Clarín Digital*, 24 March 1996.
99. Jacques Derrida, *Archive Fever: A Freudian Impression* (Chicago/London: University of Chicago Press, 1995), p. 4.
100. *Cine Argentino 99/08. Bafici 10 Años: análisis, hitos, dilemas, logros, desafíos y (por qué no) varias cosas para celebrar*, ed. by Marcelo Panozzo, Leonel Livchits, and Manuel Antín (Buenos Aires: BAFICI & Ministerio de Cultura. Gobierno de la Ciudad de Buenos Aires, 2008).
101. Diana Taylor, *The Archive and the Repertoire. Performing Cultural Memory in the Americas* (Durham and London: Duke University Press, 2003), p. 82
102. Interview with Peña.
103. Sergio Wolf, interview with Mar Diestro-Dópido, BAFICI Meeting Point, 29 March 2009 (translated from Spanish by Mar Diestro-Dópido).
104. Interview with Martín Kairuz.
105. Interview with Quintín.
106. Álvaro Arroba, phone interview with Mar Diestro-Dópido, 1 October 2018.
107. Janira Gómez Muñoz, 'El BAFICI festeja sus 20 años con récords y cineastas como John Waters', 16 April 2018, <https://www.france24.com/es/20180415-cultura-bafici-cine-independiente-argentina>.
108. Sharon Swart, 'Film Fests Bringing Pics to the People Directly. Sundance Shares Films though [*sic*] Video on Demand, YouTube, Road Tour', *Variety*, 22 January 2010, <http://variety.com/2010/film/news/film-fests-bringing-pics-to-the-people-directly-1118014192/>.
109. Gwilym Mumford 11 May 2017 Cannes film festival takes on Netflix with new rule, <https://www.theguardian.com/film/2017/may/11/cannes-film-festival-takes-on-netflix-with-new-rule>.
110. Diego Batlle, 'La Era de la Madurez' in *Cine argentino*, ed. by Sergio Wolf, pp. 57–80 (p. 63).
111. For a copy of the different points stated in the original law see official document published online, <http://servicios.infoleg.gob.ar/infolegInternet/anexos/155000-159999/158649/norma.htm> [accessed 25 May 2020].
112. Campero, 'Supongamos que existe una política cinematográfica', p. 22.
113. Campero, 'Supongamos que existe una política cinematográfica', p. 23.
114. Interview with Kairuz. For a detailed breakdown of the state of Argentine audiences during the first decade of 2000, see Tamara L. Falicov, 'Argentine Cinema and the Crisis of Audience' in *The Argentine Film*, ed. by Daniela Ingruber and Ursula Prutsch (Verlag Münster/Berlin/Vienna/Zurich LIT, 2012) pp. 207–18.
115. Round table conducted by Diego Batlle with film producers Diego Dubcovsky, Hernán Musaluppi and Verónica Cura, published as 'La era de la madurez' in *Cine argentino*, ed. by Sergio Wolf, pp. 57–80 (p. 71).
116. Dubcovsky, ibid., p. 61.
117. Sergio Wolf, ed., *Cine argentino: Estéticas de la producción* (Buenos Aires: Ministerio de Cultura, Gobierno de la Ciudad, 2009), pp. 57–80.
118. The published manifesto is available here: 'Manifesto Grupo Acción', *La Nación*, 9 November 2007, <http://www.lanacion.com.ar/960755-manifiesto-grupo-accion>.
119. Natalia Trzenko, 'El Bafici, esa joven tradición cinéfila que cumple 15 ediciones', *La Nación*, 10 April 2013, <http://www.lanacion.com.ar/1571134-el-bafici-esa-joven-tradicion-cinefila-que-cumple-15-ediciones>.

120. BAFICI, <http://festivales.buenosaires.gob.ar/2018/bafici/es/home>.
121. Diego Batlle, 'BAFICI 2018: Anunciaron toda la programación', *Otros Cines*, 13 April 2014, <http://www.otroscines.com/Festivales_detalle.php?idnota=8489&idsubseccion=147>.
122. See BAFICI, <http://Festivales.buenosaires.gob.ar/bafici/es/home>.

CHAPTER 2

❖

Festival de San Sebastián/Donostia Zinemaldia/International Film Festival: A Film Festival of Contrasts

History

- **Date founded:** 1953
- **International/National/Local context:** International Film Festival Competitive
- **FIAPF (category):** A-List
- **Calendar slot: Festival's place within the international film festival circuit:** September, after Venice and Toronto (end of Summer)

Infrastructure[1]

- **Are screened films rented or offered?** Offered
- **Screening Venues:** 25
- **Attendance:** 175,267 attendees
- **Public sector sources of funding:** 44% from the state (funded by the city, local, regional and national Government at 25% each) and 56% from private sponsors.

Structure and staffing

- **Permanent programming staff:** 19 people
- **Annual Budget:** 8,300,000 € (approx.)
- **Ticket price:** 3–7€, similar to an average cinema ticket in San Sebastián

Directors of the San Sebastián Film Festival

- Dionisio Pérez Villar: 1953
- Miguel de Echarri: 1954–1957
- Antonio de Zulueta y Besson: 1958–1963
- Fernández Cuenca: 1964–1966
- Miguel de Echarri: 1967–1977
- Luis Gasca: 1978–1984
- Diego Galán: 1985–1989
- Peio Aldazábal: 1990
- Koldo Anasagasti: 1991
- Rudi Barnet: 1992
- Diego Galán: 1993–2000
- Mikel Olaciregui: 2001–2010
- José Luis Rebordinos: 2011–

Introduction

This chapter focuses on the San Sebastián International Film Festival (known as the Donostia Zinemaldia in the Basque language), which currently holds the much-coveted A-category status that it lost and recovered on several occasions during its volatile 68-year history.[2] The Festival is located in San Sebastián, a small coastal city with a population of 186,370 inhabitants.[3] It is the capital of Gipuzkoa, which belongs to the autonomous community of the Basque Country (Euskal Herria), and is situated twenty kilometres from the border with France in the north of Spain. Notably this municipality was awarded European Capital of Culture status for 2016, shared with Wroclaw in Poland.

A study of the San Sebastián Film Festival inevitably entails analysis of its intrinsically dual identity as both a Basque and Spanish cultural event, which in turn requires a close look at the political tensions between Spain and the Basque Country and their repercussions.

One of the 17 autonomous provinces, or *autonomías*, since the approval of the 1978 Democratic Constitution, with its own co-official regional language, Euskera (Basque) — the language recognized as official throughout Spanish territory is Castilian — the Basque Country still remains a divided territory at its core. On one side there are Basque nationalists; on the whole the Basque Country is a traditionalist region, where folklore and Basque culture are deeply engrained and nourish Basque Nationalism, whose most extreme incarnation is the separatist terrorist group ETA (the acronym stands for Euskadi Ta Askatasuna, 'Basque Homeland and Freedom'). On the other side, there are more progressive elements, since this is also one of the most developed, forward-thinking regions in Spain.[4]

This duality also manifests itself in the relationship that the Basque Country has with the rest of Spain, which in turn is reflected in the Festival's promotion of Basque and Spanish cinema, as well as its relation to different forms of tourism (cultural, geographical and culinary), and the national press and cultural institutions (such as both the Spanish and Basque Cinematheques). This is a Janus-faced position that is also reflected in the balance the Festival attempts to strike between an entertainment event in the form of red carpet galas with the presence of international stars, and the coverage given by specialized press to the actual films themselves as well as the role of the Festival as platform for a more independent cinema.

Concocting the San Sebastián Film Festival; 1953–1955

The San Sebastián Film Festival was born out of what was, in the 1940s and '50s, a common practice in Europe, and, as already outlined in the introduction, one of the principal reasons for organising a Festival of any stripe (whether film, fashion or music): the strategic development of tourism at a favourable time of year in a suitable place. The story of the San Sebastián Film Festival starts around October 1952, the same year a group of representatives from the United States were in Madrid to sign the Hispano-Norteamericano Cinematographic Treaty,[5] which marked the end of autarky in Spain with the introduction of a liberal trade policy. As Spanish film historian Román Gubern notes, the resulting unfettered entry of foreign currency into the country would ignite Spain's so-called 'economic miracle'.[6]

That same year, in a café gathering, a group of ten businessmen from San Sebastián were discussing how their city was famous for being a beautiful place, yet also expensive and boring.[7] Looking to spice things up and elongate the tourist season beyond the 'official' end of the peak holiday, the 15th of September,[8] at first they came up with the notion of an International Week of Song (the Eurovision Song Contest would be first held four years later in 1956 based upon the Sanremo Music Festival, originated in 1951) in collaboration with Biarritz (in the French Basque territory); then a fashion festival; and they even thought of resurrecting the Motor Circuit in the nearby town of Lasarte. It was then only a matter of time before Dionisio Pérez Villar, an entrepreneur well known in the city, suggested a film festival — even if, as he always admitted, he didn't know anything about cinema 'but only wanted to be the organizer, with consultants and collaborators who knew what he didn't'.[9]

The group backed this idea immediately, and tried to gain support from both the Cámara de Comercio, Industria y Navegación/Chamber of Commerce and the Federación Mercantil/Merchants' Federation of Guipúzcoa, but it was not until they presented it to the Centro de espectáculos y turismo/Events and Tourism Centre and the San Sebastián Town Hall that they received any positive response, and most importantly, funding. Both these governmental organs belonged to the Vertical Syndicates (the only workers' unions legal in Franco's Spain from 1940 to 1976), which were very powerful at the time, since they had access to money, venues, staff and a direct line to Madrid, where, under Franco's highly centralized government, all decisions were taken.

The Sindicato Nacional del Espectáculo/Syndicate of Show Business accepted the proposal for a film festival, and in 1953 the city celebrated the First Week of International Cinema of San Sebastián, from 21–27 September in the Theatre Victoria Eugenia. This was the same year that Franco's regime was officially recognized by the United States and the Vatican; both validated Spain internationally, the former 'as a dutiful ally against communism' during the Cold War years, the latter as 'a bastion for the most conservative Catholicism'.[10] The increasing international pressure to open the Spanish economy to global capitalist markets would soon force Franco to surround himself with Opus Dei technocrats, and to create a much more liberal image of Spain as a sort of benign dictatorship. The Festival was an important opportunity to do this, and the government offered its support regarding the programming of Spanish films, a decision that, as the historian of the Festival José Luis Tuduri rightly notes, was clearly made in order to exert its control over what was going to be screened. The Dirección General de Cinematografía/Ministry of Cinematography was supposed to carry out the selection of foreign films for this first edition, but as the opening date loomed and still there was no news from Madrid, Pérez Villar, the Festival director that year, decided to write to the foreign embassies in Spain to ask them to send their best films directly to the Festival;[11] a move that was ultimately endorsed by the

Government. Local folklore, events such as the *tamborada* (or drum playing), dance and music, bullfights, fireworks and fashion shows also strongly featured in the Festival throughout much of its first decade, sometimes at the expense of the films, as will be illustrated further on in this chapter.

Encouraged by these favourable circumstances, Francoist authorities decided to take total control of the Festival's second edition the following year — which was renamed as the first International Film Festival of San Sebastián, since it was officially recognized by FIAPF — and moved it from September to July, placing it right between the Cannes (May) and Venice (September) film festivals. This edition was organized by the National Syndicate of Show Business in collaboration with the Ministry of Cinematography, with film producer Miguel de Echarri (described by José Ángel Herrero Velarde, the Festival's programmer who has been working the longest at San Sebastián, as a 'person addicted to Franco's regime'[12]) appointed as its new director. De Echarri took over the running of the Festival from Dionisio Pérez Villar, the representative of the initial group of businesspeople that founded the event. By this stage, the Spanish authorities had managed to persuade FIAPF to award the Festival the B-category (non-competitive). In fact, de Echarri was a member of the Corporate Body of FIAPF, and together with Ignacio Ferrés Iquino (one of the four vice-presidents of the same body), they would prove to be instrumental in securing that recognition.[13] Not much later, for the 1957 edition, the Festival would finally be awarded the A-category (competitive), placing it on the same level as Cannes, Berlin and Venice.

Three years after San Sebastián's first edition, in 1956, an international film festival was founded in Valladolid (once the capital of Spain and home to one of the oldest universities in the world) and called Week of Religious Cinema and Human Rights, a denomination that it dropped in 1973, when the Festival became the Semana Internacional de Cine (International Cinema Week), widely known as Seminci to this day. As I will explore later on in this chapter, the role of the Catholic Church, in education in general but also in cinema, was an extremely active one in Spain during the Franco years. Nevertheless, the term 'religious' was used loosely here, and, as Herrero Velarde notes, it covered any film that could be considered 'of human interest', an ambiguous phrase that permitted the inclusion of virtually any feature film. Herrero Velarde recalls:

> Valladolid was more serious [compared to San Sebastián], in the sense that it was not interested whatsoever in glamour, but it specialized in art films and auteur cinema. It despised commercial cinema and industrial productions. Seminci's staple filmmaker was Bergman: serious, philosophical, austere. And it obviously wasn't religious. There was never competition between Valladolid and San Sebastián because each of these festivals looked for a very different kind of cinema.[14]

Based on this programming policy, some of the films screened at Valladolid included the likes of Elia Kazan's *On The Waterfront* (1957), Berlanga's *Los jueves, milagro/Miracles of Thursdays* (1958), François Truffaut's *The 400 Blows* (1959), Ingmar Bergman's *The Seventh Seal* (1959), Luis Buñuel's *La vía láctea/The Milky Way* (1969), and most famously, Stanley Kubrick's hugely controversial *A Clockwork Orange*, which premiered at the 1975 edition whilst Franco was still alive. Seminci's risky and innovative programming gained it a strong international reputation, at one point becoming the critical testing ground for European art films through the 1960s and into the '80s, and for some commentators reaching its creative peak under the direction of Fernando Lara, from 1984 to 2004.[15] In the hands of Javier Angulo for the last twelve years, Seminci, in his own words, 'indisputably remains Spain's second most important film festival after San Sebastián, regardless of any other festivals' claims [...], both in seniority and attendance'.[16]

Perhaps the most decisive difference between Valladolid and San Sebastián Festivals is that where the former sought to invite films from the rest of Europe and remains strongly focused on auteur cinema to this day,[17] San Sebastián was from the outset involved in promoting Spain and by extension, Spanish cinema. In the 1950s a new generation of filmmakers — key directors such as the communist Juan Antonio Bardem, the politically unclassifiable Luis García Berlanga,[18] scriptwriter Rafael Azcona and producer Elías Querejeta — and in the 1960s and '70s emerging auteurs such as Carlos Saura, Manuel Summers, Basilio Martín Patino and Víctor Erice, made their films in reaction to the staunch conservatism of Franco-approved national cinema. The latter was typified by the traditionalism of José Luis Sáenz de Heredia's commercial films, which were most representative of the kitsch, religious and folklore-oriented narratives that were the main cinematic output of the regime. These new filmmakers soon awakened serious international interest. Their films were regularly garlanded at the most important international A-list film festivals such as Cannes, Venice and Berlin,[19] as well as San Sebastián. Franco's government recognized the potential of endorsing these films, as well as the Festival's pivotal role as an international platform for extolling the aforementioned 'benign' image of the dictatorship, more in keeping with the government's international economic aspirations.

The inauguration of these two international film festivals, as scholar María del Camino Gutiérrez Lanza points out, not only gave filmmakers access to foreign films, (and in the case of Seminci, its audiences too, since unlike cinephiles in the Basque Country and Cataluña, those from La Meseta — the geographical region that includes the two Castillas, Madrid and Extremadura — could not so easily cross the border into French cinemas in Biarritz), but also sparked international interest in the Spanish film industry.[20] In fact, proximity to the French border enabled many Spanish cinephiles to become acquainted with cinema that was banned for the majority of Spanish spectators. Neorealism, the Nouvelle Vague and the Soviet classics became new reference-points for filmmaking.

By the 1950s Spain had emerged from the all-controlling autarky, an era of economic self-sufficiency instituted during the first two decades of Franco's government. The Press Law that had been passed in 1938, whereby every film had to be submitted to censorship prior to shooting, was still in force. However, the new generation of intellectual groups that had not fought in the war — but who were nevertheless living the consequences of it — were already exerting great cultural opposition to the regime. In 1951, the Christian Democrat Joaquín Ruíz-Giménez was appointed Minister of Education, bringing significant liberalization to Spanish universities. The contradiction between the new generation's aspirations and the reality of the suffocating regime and its curtailment of individual liberties would culminate in the student revolts that took place in Madrid in 1956. This non-conformism was also reflected in literature by the experimental narratives developed by novelists such as Camilo José Cela or Carmen Martín Gayte, who were in turn a significant influence on these new filmmakers. This generation came out of the recently founded (in 1947) Instituto de Investigaciones y Experiencias Cinematográficas or IIEC/Institute for Film Experiment and Research, which became the Escuela Oficial de Cinematografía, EOC/Official Film School in 1960, producing the follow-up generation spearheaded by names such as Saura, Summers and Patino, grouped under the rubric 'the New Spanish Cinema'. I will be exploring the legacy of the EOC later in this chapter.

Writing on the emergence of the new Spanish cinema has generally focused on the Salamanca Conversations,[21] but I am looking at this period of Spanish film history from a different point of view, as I consider the San Sebastián Film Festival to be a pivotal part of the new spirit of liberty that allowed for this more challenging (within boundaries) cinema to be openly promoted internationally. Not only did the Festival itself precede the Salamanca Conversations, but also, in its first ever edition as an official Festival in 1953, San Sebastián had already hosted the First Conference of Spanish Filmmakers, preceding the Conversations by two years. The remit of this conference was to address and discuss the situation of Spanish filmmakers and producers. The issues dealt with were ultimately raised with the National Syndicate of Show Business, and the event welcomed guests such as the French Director General of Cinematography, Jacques Fland, the General Secretary of the Cannes Film Festival, Robert Favre Le Bret, and the president of FIAPF, Charles Delac.[22]

It was under the influence of these Jornadas that two years later the (in)famous Salamanca Conversations took place in Spain. The Ministerio de Información y Turismo/Ministry of Information and Tourism had been created in 1951, with the Dirección General de Cinematografía y Teatro/Department of Cinematography and Theatre set up within it. José María García Escudero became the director of this newly constituted department. A Falangist and devout Catholic who had served as a former deputy colonel of Franco's Air Force, García Escudero had a degree in political science and a doctorate in law, and was a recognized journalist and writer. Despite all that, as film historian and critic Román Gubern rightly notes, García Escudero could 'pass for a liberal'[23] at that time, and it was he who gave permission for the film congress held in Salamanca in 1955[24] to take place. Independent of any cultural institution, the Salamanca Conversations were essentially a democratic act performed within Franco's dictatorship. Once more, the situation of the Spanish film industry was debated; here, Bardem famously described Spanish cinema as:

> Politically inefficient; socially false; intellectually infamous; aesthetically hopeless and industrially stunted.[25]

Perhaps more interesting is the fact that not every participant saw this event as enlightening, as it has generally been portrayed by journalists and academics alike.

Berlanga, one of the participants in the Conversations, adopted a highly critical stance towards this event:

> How many times has the intervention of false prophets scuppered our best possibilities? Already at those so-called wonderful *Salamanca Conversations*, organized and manipulated by the most radical Marxists, it seemed they had found the philosopher's stone to make of Spanish cinema a revolutionary force of resistance. They gave hope to a lot of people, mainly young directors, but the organizers also shamed the directors that had 'sold' themselves to commercial cinema. From the stage, the director of the event pointed the finger accusingly at 'those poor devils' and branded them sell-outs and escapists, accused them of having abandoned the profound social cinema that they advocated [...] Commercial films made millions and millions, not only in Spain but also in France, Italy etc. [...] The accusing organizer got closer to me in triumphalist fashion — I was sitting in the stalls, half scared:
> — And you, Berlanga, the supposed renovator, Bardem's *compañero* under the banner of the New Cinema, aren't you ashamed of making that escapist cinema? [...]
> — It's true, I do make escapist cinema, because what I want is for people to escape from sadness, and to go and see my films.[26]

Cinema was undoubtedly a form of escapism during such controlled and hard times. As film historian Alberto López Echevarrieta points out, the boom in attendance at cinemas — together with the increase in the number of cinemas themselves — coincided with what many regarded as the need for a form of cheap escapism, and/or more often than not, for simply a way of 'having a roof over our heads to protect us from the cold of winter'.[27] In 2006 the Málaga Spanish Film Festival celebrated the 50th Anniversary of the Conversations, organizing a meeting of the survivors. Among the conclusions of this meeting, as Berlanga tells us in his memoirs, guests, organizers and (some) members of the Communist Party alike all agreed with Berlanga's opinion that the Conversations were by and large a big mistake for Spanish Cinema, and that the Communist Party was the 'main instigator of that failed operation'.[28]

In any case, no real solutions emerged from the Conversations. The main difficulty for Spanish filmmakers was to second-guess the censors, as there was no written code they could follow. This was one of the key issues debated in the Conversations, leading to a serious call for the creation of a comprehensible and comprehensively outlined censorship code — which, although it would finally materialize in the Censorship Codes of 1963 and 1975, would in reality remain as vague and imprecise as before.[29]

Amongst the more direct outcomes of the Conversations were: the creation of a law in order to classify films on their merits and their quality (which, as I will later explain, ultimately operated as a censoring tool); the dismissal of Escudero for his involvement in what was considered a communist attack on the regime; and the closure and banning of the film magazine, *Objetivo*.[30]

Strict film censorship as well as ham-fisted dubbing occasionally produced some unintentionally comic and/or outrageous outcomes,[31] most famously the suggested ménage a trois at the conclusion of Buñuel's *Viridiana* (1961). A Ministerial Law was

FIG. 2.1. Orson Welles at the *F for Fake* press conference in 1973
Photo SSIFF/© Archivo Festival

passed in 1939 banning the screening of any film in any other language apart from Spanish[32] — this included regional languages, whose use was also banned outright in public. But more relevantly for the Festival, censorship directly affected the quality of programming during its first years, since Franco's censorship was also liberally applied to what was referred to as the three Ps: *países* (countries), *películas* (films), and *personas* (people).[33] One of the requirements of FIAPF was that films had to be shown in their integrity, in the original version and with no cuts, including those previously censored. In order to understand the impact of censorship, it is important to acknowledge that in this era, programming was done very differently, as former director of the Festival Mikel Olaciregui (2001–2010) notes:

> It is not until 1976 that there is a selection committee as such. Somehow, the Festival was working together with the ministries of foreign affairs of the different countries, be it Russian, Italian, French [...] who'd send a film which they considered would fit the profile of San Sebastián. And this was how it was done during the first 20–25 years of the Festival.[34]

This was indeed a common practice, and even Cannes did not have its own selection committee until 1972.[35] In the case of San Sebastián, this became a problem very early on. Fearing that their films might be rejected outright and therefore miss out on a general release afterwards (free distribution was the normal corollary to a screening at the Festival), the selections presented by the competing countries were almost exclusively, as Tuduri explains, 'white' films, i.e. uncontentious, or in his own words, 'very dull and mediocre' to avoid any problems with the censors.[36] This is also the reason why the first editions of the Festival would rely very little on film, but rather serve as a showcase for the area, with a focus on fashion shows, tourist trips to nearby cities, bullfighting and general entertainment; functioning more like an elite club than a film festival. Nevertheless, and regardless of FIAPF's regulations, on many occasions the version of the film that was watched by the jury (and by Franco, a cinephile who famously turned one of the main drawing-rooms — Salón de Teatro de los Reyes — in his palace in El Pardo, Madrid, into a screening room where he would watch films with invited guests such as Orson Welles[37]) was different to the version shown to the audience; censors would simply cut the film after the jury had viewed it.[38]

Taking Film Seriously: The Tenure of Antonio de Zulueta, the Influence of José María García Escudero and the Promotion of the New(er) Spanish Cinema, 1956–1964

In 1955, FIAPF recognized San Sebastián as a Festival specializing in colour films. Yet the Festival in general was having numerous problems, due to technical deficiencies, the difficulty of access to the city, the application of censorship, the low quality of the films screened, but above all, the manipulation by the government of the Official Document written by the jury at that edition, which turned out to differ considerably from the one read out at the closing ceremony. On these grounds, FIAPF withdrew its recognition of the Festival the following year.

FIG. 2.2. Goran Paskaljević, Raya Martin, José Coronado, Pablo Trapero: members of the Official Jury walking down the red carpet, black for that year's edition, 2010. Photo: Iñaki Pardo/© SSIFF

FIG. 2.3. International Film Students Meeting participants, 2012 Photo: Gorka Estrada/© SSIFF

FESTIVAL DE SAN SEBASTIÁN/DONOSTIA ZINEMALDIA 97

FIG. 2.4. Alfred Hitchcock entering the Victoria Eugenia Theatre
for the World Premiere of *Vertigo*, 1958
Photo SSIFF/© Archivo Festival

Under the General Secretary Ramiro Cibrián Sáiz, San Sebastián still took place in 1956, albeit with no officially recognized prizes, and most damagingly, bereft of any North American films, owing to a decision taken by the Ministry that there would be no tax privileges for the films in competition. This situation was soon rectified for the following edition, which coincided with Franco's almost complete renewal of his Government and the presence of the MPEAA (Motion Picture Export Association of America) in Spain to discuss the conditions for screening North American films in the country. The positive outcome of these negotiations (the North American producers would profit to the tune of millions of dollars in Spain, since exhibition taxes on US films were considerably reduced)[39] translated into US support for the 'official' recognition of the Festival, a status that was recovered in April of that year (1957) with an A-category, only a few months before its July opening. One of the main decisions to be taken before the next edition was a new director of the Festival. Chosen by appointment, the position (unpaid) would be held for the next four years by Antonio de Zulueta y Besson (father of the filmmaker Iván Zulueta), a polyglot with important contacts internationally, and a founder of the Ateneo Cine-Club San Sebastián.

During this time, cine-clubs were very important for film culture in Spain, as many doubled as a political escape-valve: there were many cine-forums organized by the cine-clubs in the San Sebastián area, such as the short-lived Cantábrico, whose screenings often turned into direct political debates. During the first half of the mid-'50s, cine-clubs, salas de arte y ensayo, i.e. art-house cinemas and film societies, or even clandestine screenings and meetings in libraries[40] were like small oases compared to the cautious cinema listings. Two friends and key figures of the new cinema, producer turned filmmaker and notable promoter of Basque cinema Antonio Eceiza and film producer Elías Querejeta, began a collaboration in 1956 with the newly created cine-club San Sebastián, which:

> founded by the Junta Diocesana of Catholic Action, in that same year had already participated in the organization of a Course of Cinematographic Studies, of which it would manage to organize another two editions. In those courses film directors and film critics such as Luis García Berlanga, Juan Antonio Bardem, José María García Escudero, Florentino Soria and Pascual Cebollada participated. Amongst the students were of course Eceiza and Querejeta, but also future filmmakers such as Víctor Erice, Santiago San Miguel, Javier Aguirre and Antonio Mercero.[41]

The importance of the cine-clubs was also reflected in the Festival, and as such, Zulueta created an award in his first year for the 'most appropriate film for cine-clubs' given by Cine-Club San Sebastián; i.e. a prize for the films that were able to make their living outside the commercial circuits as long as the censors looked the other way.[42]

Perhaps unsurprisingly then, it is during Zulueta's tenure that the Festival acquired a distinctly cinephile slant in its programming. Despite the many unsuccessful petitions for the event to be moved to Palma de Mallorca, Barcelona, Torremolinos or Seville in the national press, the following edition made waves, with big film personalities such as King Vidor, Anthony Mann and Kirk Douglas in attendance, and — most importantly of all in terms of the Festival's international image — Alfred Hitchcock. The Master of Suspense chose San Sebastián to promote his latest film, *Vertigo* (1958), and would come back to premiere *North by Northwest* (1959) the following year. A section dedicated to Experimental Cinema was also created, and the retrospectives that have long characterized the Festival were also introduced that year — like the one dedicated to René Clair, organized by the then director of the National Cinematheque Carlos Fernández Cuenca, in collaboration with the Cine-Club San Sebastián.[43] In addition, for the first time in 1957, films from socialist countries were invited to participate (with the exception of the USSR, which would only take part in the Festival for the first time five years later).

However, Zulueta's tenure would soon come to an abrupt end. In 1960, with the help of García Escudero, he organized a Conference of Film Schools for the Festival, which was attended by filmmakers from the IIEC[44] such as José Luis Borau, Miguel Picazo, Basilio Martín Patino, Joaquín Jordá, Bardem, Berlanga, José Luis Sáenz de Heredia, Manuel Summers and García Escudero himself. Film schoolteachers and students were invited from France, Italy, Holland, Mexico and Poland.[45] Although much more monitored and more in tune with the Spanish filmmakers conference organized by the Festival in 1953, this symposium was still seen by the regime as being akin to the Salamanca Conversations of 1955, as the main debate centred once more on the need for a clear definition of the parameters of censorship applied to Spanish films. As a consequence, Zulueta became a scapegoat and was removed from the Festival's directorship.[46] The initiative itself (the meeting of film schools) carried on until 1966 when, as Tuduri notes, an important decline owing to the greater control exerted by the government had seriously undermined its remit. It would take more than thirty years for these school encounters to be finally, and very successfully,[47] re-introduced into the Festival in 2009.

For the next two editions, 1961 and 1962, film and business once more overlapped in the figure of the Festival's new director: the lawyer and manager of the main site of the Festival, the Victoria Eugenia Theatre, Francisco Ferrer Monreal, who was supported ably by a new General Secretary, Pilar Olascoaga, an enterprising and commanding woman who stayed with the Festival until 1991. But what became known publicly as the *Viridiana* scandal — when Buñuel won the Palme d'Or at the Cannes Film Festival in 1961 with his controversial film (the government wanted to destroy the copy but Buñuel's son and Portabella famously smuggled the reels to France on a donkey[48]) — resulted in an increasing distrust and an intensifying of control on the part of the Government with regards to cinema. This led to a decline in the quality of the programming at the Festival, which in turn saw its A-category downgraded once more to a B in 1963.

In the meantime, and owing to the increasing international economic pressure to open up the country and the government's efforts to enter into the European Community — constituted in 1958, it wasn't until 1986 that Spain was finally admitted — Franco appointed a young Manuel Fraga Iribarne as the Minister of Information and Tourism, and re-appointed García Escudero as director of the Department of Cinematography and Theatre in 1962. One of their main targets was to cash in on the international interest and success that several Spanish 'quality' films of the newer New Spanish Cinema — made by those present at the Conference of Film Schools and the Salamanca Conversations, and taught at the IIEC by the likes of Juan Antonio Bardem or Luis García Berlanga, i.e. Borau, Patino, Carlos Saura, Picazo or Summers — were starting to enjoy at major international film festivals. For these filmmakers, as for the previous generation, their presence at these international events was priceless, as it literally allowed heavily censored directors such as Saura to continue making films.[49]

If the role of cinema was as an escape valve for the sheer pressure and suffocation of living under the dictatorship, the role of festivals at the time rapidly shifted from their original associations with tourism and the entertainment industry to a stronger focus on providing a platform for film as culture. As film director and producer (and key player in the regeneration of Spanish independent cinema from the 1960s onwards) Pere Portabella comments:

> At that time festivals undoubtedly had a role to play. Because after WWII in Europe, there was a moment of cultural well-being. This is when Charles [de Gaulle], together with his prime minister, invented [in 1959] the Ministries of Culture. From this moment onwards, there's a respect for what culture is, how it's generated, and so new possibilities open up, like the Nouvelle Vague and many other likeminded people. But already back then festivals were born under the influence of the Hollywood majors, i.e. from the start festivals were thought of as economic platforms. [...] Many filmmakers have started at festivals and made their careers. Of course, for those of us living in a dictatorship, it was the only means of showing our films outside the country, which was fantastic.[50]

Furthermore, the international platform and reach that a film festival like San Sebastián provided was as much a lifeline for the filmmakers as it was for Franco's government: to an extent, it could be said that there was an actual demand on the part of the dictatorship for quality films that could give a different image of Spain. In what is probably one of the most clear-cut examples of the political appropriation of cultural capital on the part of the government (as opposed to the promotion of tourism and the appropriation of folklore, summarized in Franco's favourite (in)famous slogan: 'Spain is different'), this group of filmmakers known for their 'quality' cinema were soon supported by the regime. The government (and the Festival by default) was encouraging a particular type of product aimed at an international audience (such as critics and film professionals at other festivals), an enterprise that makes these films seem an early example of what nowadays is (loosely) called a 'festival film', a slippery, controversial and contested concept that I discuss in more detail in the introduction.

Hence, backed by the government, Escudero promoted and gave financial support to this particular brand of cinema, for which he created the label 'of special interest'. These films were exempt from the full weight of Franco's censorship, at least with regard to their actual making, as they were mainly exported, and many of them remained unseen in Spain. More interestingly, Escudero's new labelling was based on a politics of public subsidies and the assignment of a series of categories which determined where these films could play — hence distributors would not take risks with the films included in the lower categories (i.e. of special interest), which was effectively a form of censorship as they were then not distributed or exhibited in Spain.[51] The fiercest opponents of the regime openly criticized this government-funded New Spanish Cinema generation, accusing them of colluding with the regime and taking its money to produce their films. Producers such as Elías Querejeta, who openly took advantage of this situation, produced the vast majority of this generation's films. Escudero would also make full use of the San Sebastián Film Festival to promote these filmmakers internationally, effectively maximizing their cultural cachet.

It is important to note that not only were the new Spanish films essentially banned from being shown in Spain, but also that although the Festival had already been running for a decade, local audiences were still shut out of the screenings. One of the most significant changes in San Sebastián in 1963 was the new direction that the Festival pioneered with regards to its audience — an initiative that differed from practices in Cannes or Venice. The committee's decision to show competition films to the general public an hour after their official screening at the Victoria Eugenia theatre, at a lower price and at another venue, the Cinema Astoria, as part of a sidebar called Cine de Barrios y Pueblos (Neighbourhood and Town Cinema), was the Festival's first conscious step in acknowledging and attempting to attract local audiences. Nevertheless, programmer Herrero Velarde, one of the attendees, remembers San Sebastián as a resolutely elitist festival:

> During the dictatorship the Festival was only for guests, film critics and people coming from outside the country. The access to screenings was very limited. The Victoria Eugenia was really elitist and you had to dress formally. The spectators didn't even dare to go in; they would look from the outside. I was a season-ticket holder and at first we had to sit in the gods because the stalls were reserved for official authorities, guests and so on. When the dictatorship finished and the Town Hall took care of the Festival, the dress code was changed and the tickets were cheaper, but still people didn't dare to go in, or they just couldn't afford to pay for it.[52]

Effectively, this generated two different audiences: the one attending the screenings at the Victoria Eugenia, comprised of official guests and media, and the one attending the other cinemas (whose numbers would increase over the years), and who were in general militantly anti-establishment.

Spain's gradual opening up to the world was inevitably reflected in the Festival, and the 1964 edition, under the stewardship of Carlos Fernández Cuenca — the then director of the National Cinematheque, a film historian, critic and a regular collaborator on the programming of the Festival — was considered, even by the specialized press, as the coming of age of the Festival. Having been re-upgraded to A-category, that year's programme was regarded as impressive,[53] and included for the first time Soviet classics such as Sergei M. Eisenstein's *Aleksandr Nevski* (1938) as well as complete retrospectives dedicated to French directors Louis Feuillade and Georges Meliès and to Elia Kazan, and striking work made by young European and Spanish filmmakers, such as Miguel Picazo's *La tía Tula/Aunt Tula* (1964).[54] For the first time it was the director, Fernández Cuenca, who made the decisions about who and what to include in the programme of the Festival, instead of waiting for the decisions to be made in Madrid. Significantly, the following year's edition included the first fully Basque film (financed with regional money, in Basque and with a Basque subject) as part of the programme. It was also the first Basque film to be shown in the city since 1936:[55] the short film *Pelotari*, made by Néstor Basterretxea and Fernando Larruquert. Its abstract experimental style and lyricism had already been awarded the Silver Medal at the previous year's IV Competition of International Documentary Film of Bilbao and it was well received by the audience when it was screened at the closing ceremony as a complement to Terence Young's *The Amorous Adventures of Moll Flanders* (1965).[56]

Every Cloud Has its Silver Lining; 1965–1975

But San Sebastián was already facing new challenges. Fernández Cuenca's riskier programming, albeit openly praised, was the cause of instability and his liberal practices with respect to programming were not welcomed in Madrid, affecting the Festival's next editions in 1965 and 1966. The possibility of moving the Festival to Las Palmas also became more concrete when García Escudero received a letter detailing how Las Palmas fully met the necessary requirements. In order to avoid this and keep the Festival in San Sebastián, the latter was given a budget of eight million pesetas (equivalent to almost £47,000 in 1967[57] and around £600,000 today[58]) for the following edition thanks to the support of Fraga and Escudero himself. In addition, a reorganization of the Festival took place, including the appointment of full-time staff and the restructuring of the Press Association in San Sebastián, which would take charge of the Festival's magazine, *Festival*, from that point on. Fernández Cuenca resigned in 1966 and Miguel Echarri came back to the Festival in 1967. Involved with the Festival from its origins, he would remain in charge for the next ten years, a period that the Festival's historian Tuduri revealingly describes as 'the commercial decade of Echarri'[59]; an observation which points to the commercial advantages he allegedly derived as a film producer from this position.

Paradoxically, San Sebastián would benefit directly from the impact that the demonstrations and social unrest of the late 1960s had on the major A-list Festivals. In neighbouring France, the upheavals in 1968 had closed down the Cannes Film Festival that year. The revolts also affected the Venice Film Festival, which along with the Biennale (the annual exhibition of contemporary art to which the Italian festival belongs)

> still had a statute dating back to the fascist era and could not side-step the general political climate. Sixty-eight produced a dramatic fracture with the past. Up until 1980 the Lions were not awarded. [And] as an effect of the dissent, prize-giving was abolished in '68. From 1969 to 1972 the Festival was non-competitive.[60]

The structural and location changes Venice underwent meant that

> from 1974 to 1976, under the direction of Giacomo Gambetti, an attempt was made to fashion a 'different' Festival with 'proposals for new films', tributes,

retrospectives and conventions, with some screenings still in Venice. And finally, the Festival did not take place in 1978.[61]

Effectively, Venice gave up its competition status for the next ten editions. Taking advantage of this crisis, San Sebastián seized the opportunity to move to the same September berth as Venice — where it has remained ever since — ultimately making Venice its most obvious competitor for acquiring films once the latter recovered its competitive status. That same year, 1968, Néstor Basterretxea and Fernando Larruquert's triumphalist *Amar Lur*, an experimental documentary follow-up to *Pelotari*, that also dealt with Basque issues, was shown out of competition.[62] The following year, another Basque film, *Los desafíos/The Challenges*, a debut feature co-directed by Claudio Guerín, José Luis Egea and Víctor Erice, shared the Silver Shell award with Robert Bresson's *Une femme douce/A Gentle Woman* (Bresson famously stormed out of the Festival in anger at this decision). Four years later, in 1973, Erice would win the Golden Shell with *El espíritu de la colmena/The Spirit of the Beehive*, the first Spanish film to take the main prize — and as a Basque director, this was also considered a great triumph for the cinema of the region. 1968 was in fact a significant year in the Basque Country, as ETA (the Basque resistance movement founded by a group of university students in 1952, who, unlike the Basque nationalist Catholic party PNV, called for direct action) claimed its first ever victim,[63] starting a political war that continued until ETA released a ceasefire statement declaring a 'definitive cessation of its armed activity' in October 2011,[64] handed over weapons in 2017,[65] and stated its official dissolution in a letter sent to *El Diario Norte* in April 2018.[66]

The region's political instability in 1968 meant there were three different city mayors in quick succession; at the Festival, spectators were still protesting against the lack of freedom of speech at each screening, and the effects of censorship prompted the film critic Fernando Méndez Leite to call San Sebastián 'a festival fit only for minors'.[67] José Luis Tuduri, the Festival's historian, points out how, in the meantime, Miguel de Echarri was taking advantage of his position as director to bring actors, filmmakers and films that he would then do business with in Spain.[68] Censorship was still all-encompassing, and regardless of the government's support for the new Spanish cinema, some films such as Antonio Drove Fernández-Shaw's graduation film, the daring and controversial documentary short *La caza de brujas/The Witch-Hunt* (1967–1968),[69] 'a study in how to exert power as well as endure it'[70]), were still censored. In fact, four years before Franco's death, the big scandal at the Festival was the non-participation of Spanish cinema. Even though the censors had already passed the film presented, in an unprecedented move the Festival director himself banned Basilio Martín Patino's controversial *Canciones para después de una Guerra/Songs For After the War* because he thought it mocked the Holy Crusade and the success of the Caudillo. The film is a collage of images and songs lifted from Spanish folklore, which adopted a very critical perspective on the Franco regime. Patino's film ended up being banned altogether in Spain by the then Vice-President of the Government, Admiral Carrero Blanco — the most probable successor to Franco, who was killed by ETA in a car bomb two years later. Carrero Blanco, after a private screening of the film at El Pardo, famously declared 'this guy should be shot'.[71]

Yet the truth is that Franco's government was teetering under international pressure and internal tensions, and the country was demanding political change. In 1970 the Burgos Process had seen sixteen alleged members of ETA sentenced between them to seven hundred years in prison, with nine of them receiving the death penalty. The process was condemned internationally, including by the Catholic Church, and owing to the violence of the protests, a state of exception was declared in the Basque Country. So in order to 'lighten' the mood, some films that were currently banned in Spain were allowed to play at that year's Festival edition, such as *M.A.S.H.* (albeit still with some cuts) and Arthur Penn's *Alice's Restaurant*. The Basque filmmaker Gonzalo Suárez screened *Aoom*, a personal favourite of Sam Peckinpah, the story of a man who manages to dissociate his soul from his body in order to escape the imprisonment of the material world.[72] Meanwhile, the gradual opening up of the Spanish economy, and the success of the Carnation Revolution that defeated António de Oliveira Salazar's thirty-six year dictatorship in neighbouring Portugal in 1974, sharpened Spaniards' appetite for freedom. Nevertheless, a year before dying, Franco signed the death penalty for the anarchist Salvador Puig Antich; in response, ETA killed twelve civilians in Madrid.

The growing political pressure also left its mark at the Festival; the presence of films by more politically committed new directors prompted the inauguration in 1974 of the New Talent section, where films by a new breed of filmmakers with a more critical approach were shown — most notably, Pedro Almodóvar's first feature *Pepi, Luci, Bom y otras chicas del montón/Pepi, Luci, Bom* premiered in this section in 1980. That same year, students rose up once more (as they had done in 1956) against the government all around the country, which led in one instance to the controversial and highly publicized closure by the university authorities of the four faculties then constituting the University of Valladolid (Art and Humanities, Medicine, Law and Science).[73] This university was closed from 16–29 January as a result of the longstanding association of its students with the working-class unions and political groups such as the communist party, Maoists, Trotskyites, etc, all of which had been demonstrating regularly from the beginning of the 1974–1975 academic year. And whilst the police continued with a policy of detentions that tended to arise out of conflicts with the public, especially in the Basque Country, armed 'patriotic' groups such as FRAP[74] appeared, who wanted to fight against the regime using the latter's methods. The government enacted a new anti-terrorist law that facilitated the application of the death penalty, put into practice with the sentences handed down to two members of ETA and three of FRAP, which Franco signed two months before he died in November 1975. Once more, there was a flood of petitions for clemency from all around the world, including one from the Pope, but Franco did not give in.[75] As a consequence, several members of the jury expected at that year's Festival edition did not turn up; the Swedish delegation withdrew all their films; the Italian Actors' Union did not let their actors attend the Festival (only Gina Lollobrigida made an appearance). Steven Spielberg showed *Shark*, and some of the Spanish talent attended to show their support for the Festival, such as Pedro Olea and José Luis Borau whose *Furtivos/Poachers* had been banned for months. The Pearl of the Cantabric, an award for a Spanish-language work, was also created that year, and in spite of everything else, the Festival boasted healthy attendance figures.[76] The executions were carried out, although, ironically, Franco died a mere two months later. Famously, on the night of the executions, director/producer Portabella made his film *El Sopar/The Dinner*, a clandestine conversation between four political ex-prisoners held during a dinner.

The Road to Freedom; San Sebastián During the Transition; 1975–1980

The volatile political circumstances that followed Franco's death in November 1975 started off with a General Strike that took place while the Basque Country was virtually closed off in silent mourning for the executions of the political prisoners. Yet, although the following years were very unstable, with terrorist attacks, kidnappings, violent protests and demonstrations happening regularly in Spain, it was clearly the beginning of a new period in Spanish history.[77] The coronation of King Juan Carlos (Franco's successor, as decided by the dictator himself) and the first General Election in 1977 was followed by the approval of a Democratic Constitution in 1978. In 1982 the socialist party PSOE won the first of five consecutive terms. Under the new government, a policy of political autonomy for the Basque Country and Cataluña was implemented in 1980, and divorce and abortion were legalized in 1981 and 1984 respectively.

However, the impact of Franco's death would not be instant. As Berlanga dispiritedly recalls in his memoirs:

> What did we do the day the death of the old dictator was announced? The answer is *nothing*. And that's how it was. The day Franco died and stopped appearing in my dreams as a family member who was excusing himself from the hard time I would give him for his crimes, he also left dry all the thinking brains of the film profession, as well as all the others. If we look at the Spanish production of the time, if we look at the months following his disappearance, we find the same films and projects as before the General's death, or on the other hand, strange and chimerical projects — logical also, because we writers and directors did not know what the hell to do. We were free, but we did not know it yet: we had not yet tasted freedom, we had only intuited it.[78]

Things would take time to change, and Saura's conclusion to his film *Cría Cuervos/Raise Ravens* (1975), released only months after Franco's death, would capture this state of stagnation perfectly. When the three protagonist girls (representing the new generation), set free from the authoritarian figures of the house (the men are all military figures) in which they've been locked in for the summer due to a family bereavement, they happily walk into yet another authoritarian institution: their school, still managed and run by the same people. But as Geraldine Chaplin, Saura's muse and partner at the time, has said about the more political grouping of Spanish filmmakers:

> Back then there was a movement that really believed that we could change the world through film. And Saura was the head of it.[79]

Filmed whilst Franco was lying on his deathbed, Saura's film offered hints of a new beginning, an attempt to break free. Yet the Festival would have to start looking further afield as well, to find newer and younger filmmakers, as the likes of Saura and Berlanga struggled to redefine themselves post-censorship. Regardless of their criticism of the Franco regime, their films represented a Spain that had been, and audiences linked them with both Franco and the dictatorship.

The country's bumpy transition to democracy inevitably had a disruptive effect on the Festival. It was a period of uncertainty and in this climate the central Government virtually washed its hands of the organization of the Festival and left the decision to carry on with that year's edition (regardless of the aforementioned General Strike) to the local authorities. In the end the Festival went ahead, and the official poster directly referred to censorship as it featured three strips of film containing four frames each, all but one crossed out.[80] Even though San Sebastián took place, twenty members of the press left the Festival while it was in process and Elías Querejeta removed *El desencanto/The Disenchantment* (1976) from its programme. Part of the audience threw stones at some participants, such as Mexican actress Dolores del Río, symbol of a Hollywood that had colluded with the regime.

Nevertheless, the 1976 edition was considered by many as the year of the 'big change', as it initiated a new phase in the Festival's history. Miguel de Echarri fell ill (he would die two years later[81]) and Luis Gasca, film editor and comic-book scholar — well-connected in the European industry[82] — stepped in first as General Secretary and then as director; he would remain in charge for the following seven years during which he undertook, in his own words, to 'renew the Festival and change once more the structure; i.e. to evolve'.[83] Mirroring a decentralization from Madrid that was taking place elsewhere in Spain, the government transferred total responsibility for the Festival from Madrid to the City's Council, giving the director and his team complete freedom for its programming — the first ever Selection Committee with a final say on the programming was set up — albeit still receiving funding from the National Government. A new democratic Board of Directors, proposed by De Echarri, was comprised of:

> the Town Hall, Regional Council, Ministry of Information and Tourism, cine clubs, neighbourhood associations, a representative of the film events taking place in the city, and one member of each of the following sectors: production, distribution and exhibition.[84]

Another set of firsts were: the first ever season of Basque Cinema and the First Conversations on Basque Cinema,[85] both organized for the 1977 edition; the first time Buñuel visited the Festival; and the first time a 'special prize' was given, this time to Joan Fontaine, as precursor to what was later called the Premio Donostia (or the Donostia Award, as I will later discuss) in recognition for a lifetime career in film. The first European Festival of Video was also organized in order to expand the scope of the Festival.

And yet, San Sebastián still had a relatively modest international prestige that drove even Spanish filmmakers such as Saura to premiere their films at other, more established and renowned A-list festivals such as Cannes or Berlin, and economic

FIG. 2.5. Pedro Almodóvar with Alaska and Blanca Sánchez entering the Victoria Eugenia Theatre for the screening of *Pepi, Luci, Bom, y otras chicas del montón*. 1980
Photo SSIFF/© Archivo Festival

and political interests were still very much at stake. The most obvious result of this lack of international standing was the poor quality of films offered by the North American studios as well as the Soviet Union. The Festival was more than ever subject to chaotic scenes, such as street revolts and bomb scares during screenings; plus censorship was still a live issue even though Spain was now a democracy (when the Festival played *The Last Temptation of Christ* as late as 1988, its then director, Diego Galán, received complaints for programming the film). All this, plus the attempted coup in 1981[86] in Parliament in Madrid, helped fuel the distrust of foreigners and the international press.

Rethinking the Festival; 1980s and 1990s

The following two decades were most certainly an era of stark contrasts. The Festival was enduring its most difficult period when it lost (for the final time) its A-Category status for the 1980 to 1984 editions, just as Spain itself was enjoying a phase of prolific cultural activity, with Madrid at the centre of a cultural explosion that would become known as *La Movida*. A new generation of artists hungry for change emerged, spearheaded by figures such as Pedro Almodóvar and Iván Zulueta. Almodóvar's first feature, *Pepi, Luci, Bom*, about the adventures in Madrid of three women, respectively emancipated, a masochist and a lesbian, became the most emblematic film of this period, and seemed to perfectly capture the nation's zeitgeist. In contrast, Zulueta's own debut *Arrebato* (1980) testifies to the darker side of drug experimentation and film obsession. This new generation not only shook off the cobwebs in Spanish culture, but also became the focus of interest of a Festival that was as desperately in need of change. Fully embraced and endorsed by San Sebastián, *Pepi, Luci, Bom* premiered in the Festival that year, and Almodóvar went back in 1982 with his controversial second film, *Laberinto de pasiones/Labyrinth of Passion* (1982), which also caused a huge uproar — 'the Almodóvar phenomenon surpassed the screen and became a social phenomenon'.[87] The Festival also supported and endorsed a new generation of actors who became the face of the new cinema such as Antonio Resines, and one of Almódovar's muses, Carmen Maura, who starred in emblematic films such as *¿Qué hace una chica como tú en un sitio como éste?/What is a Girl Like You Doing in a Place Like This?* (Fernando Colomo 1978) and *Ópera Prima* (Fernando Trueba 1980), films which explored their milieu in less confrontational ways than those by Zulueta and Almodóvar. All these figures became regular fixtures at the Festival and have continued to be in the twenty-first century — Trueba won the Best Director Award in 2012 with *El artista y la modelo/The Artist and the Model* (2012) and Carmen Maura received the Donostia Award the following edition. Also, most of them attended the EOC, Escuela Oficial de Cinematografía, or official film school in Madrid — albeit, famously, not in the case of self-taught Almodóvar[88] — and soon were working together on each other's projects, shifting roles from producer to director to actor, as required.

All this was happening in parallel with works by filmmakers from the previous generation known as 'los niños de la Guerra' (the children of the War), such as Pilar

FIG. 2.6. Carmen Maura receiving the Donostia Award from Álex de la Iglesia, 2013
Photo: Iñaki Pardo/© SSIFF

Miró, Víctor Erice, Jaime Chávarri, Pedro Olea, Manuel Gutiérrez Aragón, José Luis Garci and Eloy de la Iglesia (their films regularly played at the Festival) who during the following two decades not only made the most of newfound democratic freedoms to direct films in which they offered revisions of the country's official history but some of them — most notably Miró — also found themselves in positions of professional power.

However, a significant point should be noted here. Spanish cinema of a political stripe can be said to have experienced its golden age during the late 1950s, '60s and early '70s, and what was known as the *comedia madrileña* (Madrid-set comedies) dominated commercial cinema during the '80s. Part of the golden age and running parallel to the *comedias*, Basque filmmakers such as Imanol Uribe, Júlio Médem, Montxo Armendáriz, Juanma Bajo Ullóa and Álex de la Iglesia were themselves laying the foundations of a modern political Basque cinema — thanks in part to being actively promoted by the Festival. Uribe's *La fuga de Segovia/Escape from Segovia* (1981), based on a true story in which some forty members of ETA escaped from a state prison in 1976, screened at the Festival in 1981, which would have been unthinkable only a couple of years previously. By the 1990s, all the Spanish entries for competition at San Sebastián that won the main prize, the Golden Shell, were directed by Basque filmmakers: *Las cartas de Alou/Letters from Alou* (1990) by Montxo Armendáriz; *Alas de mariposa/Butterfly Wings* (1991) by Juanma Bajo Ulloa; *Días contados/Running Out of Time* (1994) and *Bwana* (1996) — a tie with *Trojan Eddie* by Gillies MacKinnon — both by Imanol Uribe.

Yet the principal visual medium during this social and cultural explosion was the National Spanish Television or RTVE (Radio Televisión Española). TV interests increasingly dominated the Ministry of Culture, which was attracted by the medium's accessibility and visibility. In 1983 the socialist government, as part of its policy of providing greater support to the arts, had appointed former director of RTVE and politically controversial woman film-director Pilar Miró as General Director of Cinematography, and thus the figure responsible for cinema in the Ministry of Culture. As a filmmaker, Miró had been prosecuted in a military court because of the re-creation in her 1979 film *El crimen de Cuenca/The Cuenca Crime*, of the torture of three murder suspects at the hands of the Guardia Civil.[89] As a politician, she was responsible for a Film Law that was passed in 1983, known as the Ley Miró, which favoured more specialized auteurist Spanish cinema and was looking firmly at Europe and the kind of 'quality' products that were successful at festivals; exceptionally, the law included a section on 'experimental' cinema. The biggest problem with the Ley Miró was that funding was given prior to shooting and the box office turnover of these films never covered the cost of the films themselves, which ended up indebting the Spanish film industry more and proving its detractors right (particularly distributors and exhibitors of a more commercial type of cinema, generally North American). Albeit hugely controversial and publicly criticized, it was unquestionably the first serious attempt to protect the film industry in Spain (mostly against US box office 'occupation') and to involve television in film production[90]

As director of RTVE, Miró had been instrumental in shaping the content of programmes and restructuring the organization itself; some of the new initiatives included: a revolutionary children's programme that proved to be highly influential on upcoming generations called *La bola de cristal/The Crystal Ball* which was written, directed and hosted by mythical vanguard figures of this 'uprising', such as its presenter, goth-punk Olvido Gara, aka Alaska, one of the protagonists of Pedro Almodóvar's *Pepi, Luci, Bom*, to daily film showings followed by debates such as the still running *¡Qué grande es el cine!/How Great is Cinema!*, directed and presented by more traditional filmmaker José Luis Garci, an Oscar-winner with his 1982 *Volver a Empezar/Begin the Beguine*. Television became the medium that experimented the most. Paradoxically though, the focus of the Ley Miró on a more auteurist cinema ended up seriously affecting one of Spain's most prolific genres at the time: horror. The most malleable genre (full of metaphors, imagined worlds and characters, etc.) for dodging the censors, horror had proliferated during the 1960s and '70s in Spain thanks to the likes of Paul Naschy, Jess Franco and Jorge Grau. But perhaps the most influential of all was the TV series made by Narciso Ibáñez Serrador (known as the godfather of Spanish horror). His cult series *Historias para no dormir/Stories to Keep You Awake* was pivotal in laying the foundations for what is now one of Spain's most successful export film genres. Broadcast weekly uninterruptedly since 1966, the series came to a halt in 1982.

As Olaciregui (who started in television himself) notes in his interview, TVE's most important role regarding film was to provide a whole generation with much of their film education in the form of film programmes, director seasons and debates, planting the seed for cinephilia on which a film festival could capitalize:

> These programmes would show films from anywhere, mainstream and independent. The format was simple but hugely effective: the films were contextualized by introductions and followed by in-depth debates, to which poets, artists, writers, historians, painters, filmmakers and critics contributed. [Although many shows are now relegated to the more experimental TVE2, they still screen almost every night at the time of writing.] The value of all this was immense. For once, works that normally remain underground were plainly visible and accessible. In fact it was the underground that shaped and led popular culture, rather than being sanitized and absorbed by it — as would inevitably happen later.[91]

It should also be noted that TVE became San Sebastián's main sponsor in 2005,[92] joined in 2012 by the energy multinational Gas Natural Fenosa, at which point the Festival was confronting a reduction of public funding of 225,000€.[93]

The political and cultural sea-change of the time coincided with the appointment of a new Festival director who would orchestrate the most far-reaching changes so far — the journalist, historian and highly regarded film critic, Diego Galán. In 1985, Galán, described by the current Festival director José Luis Rebordinos as 'a very imaginative man with an incredible capacity to create; a wonderful seducer who can turn anything boring into something enjoyable'[94] took charge of the Festival, first as consultant and the following year as director. FIAPF's decision to rescind the Festival's A-category status in 1984 had prompted rumours that the

FIG. 2.7. Robert Mitchum with the Donostia Award
for an outstanding contribution to the film world, 1993
Photo SSIFF/© Archivo Festival

FIG. 2.8. Former San Sebastián director Diego Galán with actress Carmen Machi, 2016
Photo: Gari Garaialde/© SSIFF

Festival could close down. (As an interesting side-note, the town's major, Ramón Labayen together with Miró discovered that the actual reason for the removal of the A-category lay, ironically, with Spanish producers representative at the Festival, who for years had not been paying the symbolic annual quotas that Festivals have to pay to FIAPF.[95] In Franco's time the Vertical Syndicates would pay these, but when Franco died, these unions disappeared.[96]) It was a tense political moment, with numerous demonstrations taking place in the Basque Country; many film professionals and would-be guests refused to attend, fearful of the deteriorating situation. But in fact this volatility would be part and parcel of the Festival for many years to come; almost a decade later, in 1993, controversy (both inside and outside the Festival) was still an active ingredient. The actor Robert Mitchum experienced first-hand the idiosyncrasies of the city when he was taken to a restaurant for dinner one night. As his party entered, a full-scale riot kicked off in a nearby area, which was consequently besieged by the police. When they emerged from the restaurant later on, there were children playing in the same street. At such a graphic example of the speed at which changes could take place in the city, Mitchum commented: 'Was I drunk before, or am I now?'.[97]

In addition, local audiences still thought of the Festival as a closed-off, elitist event. This was an issue that, as previously mentioned, had been (unsuccessfully) addressed as early as 1963 when the then director, producer and representative of the International Federation of Film Producers' Association, Miguel de Echarri, had opened up the Festival to the general public (unlike other A-list festivals such as Cannes, which is still almost exclusively for professionals). He achieved this by creating a sidebar called Cine de Barrios y Pueblos (Neighbourhood and Town Cinema), which screened competition films an hour after their official screening, at a lower price and at another venue, in order to lure local audiences. For Galán this issue became pressing; he comments:

> I was going to work on my first day at the Festival and the taxi driver who picked me up from the airport was saying: 'this is rubbish, there are only people from Madrid who come here to eat.' So I made it my aim to convince that taxi driver that the Festival could be for the local people.[98]

In order to do so, and with the complete approval of the General Secretary of the Festival since 1961, Pilar Olascoaga (who has famously declared on more than one occasion that 'the Festival is my pimp and I will do anything to defend it against whoever'[99]), a number of new activities were organized each year in order to bring the Festival closer to the city. These included film seasons that ran throughout the year, the usage of new spaces, such as for instance a programme of sea-related films projected on a huge screen floating on the sea, viewed by the public on the beach; or the use of the city's Antonio Elorza Velodrome from 1985 with a giant screen of 400m^2 and a capacity of almost 3,000 seats. José María Riba, one of the Festival's collaborators, struck a deal with RENFE (the Spanish state's train company) whereby special trains were laid on to ferry children from all the schools in the region to the Velodrome for screenings; that same year their parents would be targeted too, in a section called 'Take your parents to the cinema', a smart way of introducing younger generations to the Festival.

In 1986 — the year Spain was admitted into the European Community — Galán introduced the Donostia Award. This is a career award — given previously only occasionally, under the rubric 'special prize' — granted to a world-renowned film personality, and which exists to this day, luring American and European notables such as Gregory Peck, Bette Davis, Catherine Deneuve, Al Pacino, Max Von Sydow and Julia Roberts to the Festival.[100] In addition, all these events were broadcast by ETB (Basque TV) from 1989 on a channel dedicated almost exclusively to covering the Festival, initially for eight to nine hours daily.[101] All of this had a galvanising effect on the public. The slogan of the Festival became: 'Everyone to the Cinema' and 'Each Spectator Finds His/Her Film'. In Galán's view, San Sebastián was reborn and the people of the city finally embraced the event to an unprecedented degree.

The Old, the New and the Rediscovered; San Sebastián's Commitment to Film Preservation

The Festival's long-established focus on both the past and the future most clearly manifests itself in its on-going collaboration with the Spanish and Basque Cinematheques.[102] Ever since Galán's tenure, three retrospectives are organized each year in collaboration with these cultural organizations — although it is important to note that one of the main reasons Galán made retrospectives so prominent was in order to cover every screen in the city, so that 'no Spielberg was shown during the Festival',[103] i.e. to avoid competition from big mainstream films being shown in the city on general release alongside the Festival. Paradoxically, the San Sebastián's commitment to screening preservation and restoration projects, the equal of its desire to show the new up-and-coming cinema, also seems to reflect the divided nature of the Basque Country, which, as seen in the introduction to this chapter, is at once one of the most modern regions in Spain and at the same time deeply wedded to tradition and its history.[104] The relationship between the Festival and the Cinematheque (then called National and not Spanish, as it is now) dates back to 1954, when the first ever retrospective of Spanish Cinema (1921–1936) was organized for the Festival's second edition, with the Cinematheque producing a catalogue that included the films' credits and critical commentaries.[105] This was the precedent for future annual publication of the Festival catalogues, as well as the book of essays that has accompanied each retrospective since 1986.[106] For comparative purposes, in Chapter 3 I will be looking at the relationship between the London Film Festival and the British Film Institute (the latter, within which the LFF sits, carries out similar functions to Spain's Cinematheque).

The Spanish Cinematheque is an official institution affiliated to the Ministry of Culture in Spain; its objective is to restore, investigate and conserve Spanish film heritage and organize its diffusion. Its film venue, where films are shown daily, is the restored 1920s Cine Doré (famously filmed by Pedro Almodóvar in his 2002 film *Hable con ella/Talk to Her*) located in the central neighbourhood of Lavapiés in Madrid. The Festival's relationship with both the San Sebastián Cinematheque and the Spanish Cinematheque regarding the organization of retrospectives and

collaborations on publications is important. As Olaciregui explains:
> There is always a very large retrospective and then the other ones are more what I would define as ways of perceiving cinema from a more educational perspective. All those retrospectives are always accompanied by the publication of a book of essays, because this is an aspect we work hard at. Because we understand that new generations have to learn about cinema by watching what was made before. I always watched classic cinema on television, but now TV does not broadcast this cinema. And in big cities such as Madrid or London there is a Cinematheque for that; but in San Sebastián there's a screening only once a week or every two weeks, which is nothing compared to the beginning of the '60s and on into the '70s when they organized big seasons of classic cinema, which is where my knowledge also comes from.[107]

In Spain there are a total of fourteen regional cinematheques, organizations whose 'mission is to watch over the cinematographic heritage in different territories'.[108] After the foundation of the Spanish Cinematheque in 1953, the Basque Cinematheque was the first regional cinematheque to be set up, in 1978. The second one was Zaragoza in 1981, and the third was Cataluña in 1982[109]. The Canary Islands, Murcia, Valencia, Andalucía, Galicia and Castilla-León all followed with a total of 16 regional cinemateques. The Spanish Cinematheque also maintains, within its regular activities, frequent interchange with other international cinematheques belonging to the FIAF (Fédération Internationale des Archives du Film), lending prints for programmes, and organising joint seasons and restoration projects. Some members of the FIAF include the BFI and the Film & Video Archive/Imperial War Museum in London, the Scottish Screen Archive in Glasgow, as well as all the Spanish regional cinematheques. The exchanges amongst cinematheques in Spain were introduced by Berlanga in January 1979 during his presidency of the Spanish Cinemateque with the help of the then director of this organization, Florentino Soria — as was the creation of *subfilmotecas* in all the autonomous regions, as well as the introduction of a data-bank of all Spanish cinema which is currently held in Madrid.[110] The Spanish Cinematheque is involved in joint projects with the regional ones, such as programming, restoration and book publishing, as well as with the Academia de las Artes y las Ciencias Cinematográficas de España/Spanish Arts and Sciences Academy, the Asociación Española de Historiadores de Cine/ Spanish Association of Film Historians, and with Spain's most established film festivals, such as San Sebastián, Valladolid, Gijón, Sitges, and Mostra de Valencia as well as universities, museums, and television channels.[111]

Preservation is the Cinematheque's main focus. Hence, in Spain, every cinematographic work with Spanish nationality or co-productions that are beneficiaries of Spanish subsidies or public funding, are legally obliged to submit a print — Entrega Obligatoria (Compulsory Submission) — to the Cinematheque.[112] But as Juan Antonio Pérez Millán, former director of the Spanish Cinematheque (1984–1986) explains, most important, and somehow mirroring the role of film festivals themselves, is the idea of creating a Federation of Cinematheques, which, as he notes, was originally proposed in the 88th issue of the Spanish film magazine *Academia* in Eloísa Villar's article 'Academia/Noticias del cine español' published in March 2003:

'without affecting their independence, it would allow them to coordinate in a stable way the efforts made separately in the fields of recovery, restoration and circulation of cinematographic heritage'.[113] This important obligation is fulfilled through the screenings organized by cinematheques:

> From the years of the political transition, and more specifically, since the general crisis of the historical cine-clubs — who played an important role in the cinematographic culture during the dictatorship — there have been intermittent discussions about the need to organize a 'circuit of cultural exhibition' — along the lines of what has been happening for quite some time in other countries with more of a tradition of associations — that could complement, substitute or serve as the stable alternative [...] to the already existing platforms, which are exclusively commercial, and which are more and more uniform and dependent on the interests of the big distribution companies; [...] contributing within our possibilities [to create] a 'cultural exhibition circuit'.[114]

More relevant for the subject of this book, such a stable alternative circuit would also provide a longer exhibition life for films already screened at festivals. But not everyone agrees with the idea that this is the role of the cinematheques. For Miguel Marías, film critic and former director of the Cinematheque (1986–1988):

> The most serious problem with the Spanish Cinematheque is its legal incapacity to equip itself with the indispensable and ideal human resources in order to carry out efficiently, and with continuity and competency, the large number of complex functions with which it is entrusted, and which it could and should assume, because, amongst other things, nobody else is qualified to guarantee they are carried out [...] if the Cinematheque is mistaken for or reduced to a warehouse — moreover, as often happens, if it's limited (because it looks good) to a kind of cine-club that shows the films that don't open in a given capital. A cinematheque functions with just enough money to pay a group of suckers who do their job because they love it, and often in an irregular and underpaid situation.[115]

As previously noted, Diego Galán accorded greater weight to the publications co-edited by the Festival and the Cinematheque the year Marías took up his position as director of the latter in 1986. Since then a book (often comprised of translated essays as Marías notes[116]) is published annually for each of the retrospectives. For Marías and sections of the film press in Spain — such as the editor of the specialized Spanish film magazine *Caimán Cuadernos de Cine* (former *Cahiers du Cinéma España*), Carlos F. Heredero — some of these retrospectives have not been as rigorous as they should have been — for instance, the one on John Cassavetes in 1992, received a great deal of criticism by the press, and was defined as 'amputated and skeletal.'[117] This concern is reflected in the opinions of film professionals such as Quintín (former director of BAFICI) and Russian film critic and historian Andrei Plakhov[118] for whom retrospectives are the most important element of a festival, and sometimes the main reason for a visit.

Yet more importantly from the point of view of this book is the overlap between the Cinematheque and the Festival (other than the aforementioned possibility of using the former as an exhibition platform akin to a festival) at management level.

Many of the Cinematheque's directors have been involved in one way or another with the Festival down the years, from programming films to actually running the Festival, such as Carlos Fernández Cuenca, former director of the Spanish Cinematheque, in 1964; the former director of the Basque Cinematheque, Peio Aldazabal, in 1990; and Koldo Anasagasti, an independent producer, and director of ETB (Euskal Televista the Basque TV channel), in 1991.

Renewing the Festival; The National and the Local

While the country was readying itself for a burst of intense internationalism in 1992, putting on the Expo in Seville and the Olympic Games in Barcelona, as well as having Madrid as Capital of Culture, the Festival was arguably going through its most chaotic three years, following the resignation of Galán in 1989 (although he would in fact accept an invitation to return in 1993). San Sebastián had three different directors in three years: Aldazábal, Anasagasti and the Belgian cultural host Rudi Barnet in 1992. However, former director of the Festival Olaciregui and long-standing programmer Herrero Velarde with the benefit of hindsight agree that the biggest problem with those three transitional years was not only the general feeling that the level of programming had dropped, but mainly that 'the Festival had lost one of its strongest assets: the just-blooming connection with the general public'.[119] For Olaciregui, in a bizarre echo of the Festival's own beginnings, it was still almost as if there were two parallel festivals.[120] It also proved that employing Barnet, essentially a foreigner unaware of the particular political and cultural idiosyncrasies of the Festival/region/country, and who appeared openly dispassionate and fostered grudges with the national press, was doomed to be a disaster.

Nevertheless, the Festival would soon undergo a dramatic transformation. Galán returned in 1993 (he would stay as director until 2000, and as programming consultant until 2010) and reinstated his programming board, comprising practically the same people that left the Festival in 1989, including Herrero Velarde, José María Arriba, Olaciregui, José María Prado — the director of the Spanish Cinematheque from 1990 till his early retirement in 2016 — plus new face José Luis Rebordinos (who became director in 2011). Under this new 'old' team, the ensuing decade became the Festival's most international period — the glamorous presence of big film stars brought the kind of media attention favoured by local and national governments alike.

Notwithstanding, the newly recovered stability of the Festival was soon undermined by the instability of the relationship between the government and ETA, particularly from 1996 onwards when the right-wing party PP (People's Party) took office after five consecutive terms of the socialist party PSOE in power. In 1998, as part of a truce, president José María Aznar's government relocated over a hundred convicted ETA members to prisons in the Basque region. However, ETA terminated the truce after fourteen months at the end of 1999, which led to a toughening of the government's stance and a withdrawal of the prisoners. Soon, terrorism and the Basque issue were directly implicated in the Festival with the screening in 2003 of perhaps the most polemical film in its history, and arguably in the history of Basque cinema: Julio Medem's *La pelota vasca. La piel contra la piedra/The Basque Ball. Skin Against Stone* (2003). The violent response to Medem's film mirrored reactions to Basque films dealing with Basque identity, politics and culture previously screened at the Festival such as *Ama Lur* (Basterretxea and Larruquert 1968)[121] and Uribe's *El proceso de Burgos/The Burgos Trial* (1979). Medem's documentary confronts Basque independence and identity and ETA head-on and from a myriad of perspectives, through interviews with some of the most important people involved in the conflict. The film famously led to Medem receiving a death threat.[122] Yet the most scandalous public reaction occurred when the then Minister of Culture, Pilar del Castillo (from the governing right-wing party), suggested banning Medem's documentary, declaring that the film 'places the Government and ETA at the same level'.[123] The Festival's response was that it would be banned only if a court decided that it was right to do so.[124] When I asked Olaciregui about the Festival's stance on Basque identity and cinema, he explained:

> I am Basque and Euskera is my mother tongue, and the Festival being Basque is undoubtedly reflected in the idiosyncrasy of the Festival. But we approach a film without any prejudice about its origins, be it Russian, Spanish or Basque; we base our choices on quality. But I wouldn't be honest if I didn't say that obviously, when you see a cinema that is unprotected because it is small, then you look at the films and the projects born there with a special affection. On the other hand, we are not cheating ourselves; film festivals have an amplifying effect that can work for better or for worse. So if you are lucky to screen a film like *Alas de Mariposa/Butterfly Wings* (1991) by Juanma Bajo Ulloa, or the *Basque Ball*, by Médem, which premiered at the Festival, and which, being such a special film with such a political subject, we thought it broke all the expectations (it was huge) — that's when you say: this is what I'm aiming at. But they are also fragile films sometimes, and you have to take care of them. At least you have to make sure that their presence in the Festival is not damaging for them.[125]

In a macabre turn of events, the intervention of José María Aznar's right-wing Government in the war against Iraq was followed by an attack on 11 March 2004 in Madrid by Al Qaida-inspired extremists that killed 191 people and injured almost 2000. Three days later, the Socialist Party PSOE won the General Elections and remained in power until 2011; in 2018 socialist Pedro Sánchez became president after filing a censorship motion against the then PP president, Mariano Rajoy. The intervention against Iraq had previously led to mass public demonstrations in which some Spanish film professionals took part, drawing the ire of the right-wing Spanish press. In fact, for Galán, one of the fundamental problems faced by the Spanish film industry is the damaging relationship between Spanish cinema and the national press, which in his opinion also implicates the audience:

> Spanish cinema comes in many forms, there's not just one Spanish cinema. What there is though is a very strong campaign by the right-wing against subsidies for Spanish cinema. In Spain almost everything is subsidized, but the right-wing press only speaks about the subsidized cinema. Back when the

FIG. 2.9. Kursaal Congress Centre and Auditorium:
(a) The image of Penélope Cruz looks out from the side of one of the
Kursaal's two translucent glass cubes, 2019
Photo: Montse Castillo/© SSIFF
(b) An aerial view of the red carpet in 2016
Photo: Karlos Corbella/© SSIFF

UK and Spain got caught up in that mess over the Iraq war, there were many demonstrations against Spain taking part. And many well-known actors, such as Javier Bardem for instance, made it onto the front pages of the newspapers during the demonstrations. There could be hundreds of thousands of people, but they only showed the actors. And because the government back then was pro-war, they started insulting actors and directors. There was a famous front-page in the right wing daily *La Razón* [i.e. The Reason] where they showed the faces of twelve film directors and wrote next to them how many millions each had been given, as if the money were for them and not to make films. Ever since then it has grown, become larger and left a mark, and there is hostility towards Spanish cinema in general. I think Spain is the only country that detests its own cinema.[126]

Inevitably, the San Sebastián Film Festival also suffers from this attitude. The daily newspapers' stance towards contemporary cinema is defined by film critic and historian Carlos F. Heredero as evincing a 'very serious lack of understanding[127]'; apart from a few exceptions, their views are generally old fashioned, anchored in classic cinema and generally averse to risk-taking films. As a result, San Sebastián finds itself in a difficult position. There is a pronounced incomprehension of the kind of cinema that benefits from screenings at film festivals, which is further accentuated by the Festival's own need to strike a balance between red carpet events and breadth of programming. As film critic Jaime Pena observes, in San Sebastián, until the mid 1990s, support was geared more towards commercial films and the presence of film stars, but since then there has been a more noticeable balance between big films and smaller independent features, mainly because a new group of people became part of the programming team — Roberto Cuetos, Kim Casas and as previously mentioned, Rebordinos — and ultimately part of the management team in 1996. Three years later, the imposing Kursaal Congress Centre and Auditorium was inaugurated, and it has since been the Festival's hub.[128]

In this light, legendary Spanish producer/filmmaker Pere Portabella's comment about how the new technologies have influenced visual culture and the way audiences relate to it is fundamental.

> The market is the market, and culture has always functioned through the support of different states for their cultural industries, more than for the actual sphere of creation, of creative processes. And this is the problem now. For instance, now, the 'what is good for the economy is good for the culture' nostrum means that the money for the industry falls into the hands of producers and those circulating around them. Therefore, there is already a trend in this crisis. For example, I am summoned, together with twenty-four artists and intellectuals, all European and some from North Africa, by Mariano Barroso, the president of the European Commission, to have a long sit down and brain-storm ideas in order to find out what we, the artists, think with regard to the future cultural policy of the European Union. This shows the concern about the new technologies that have absolutely changed the sphere of cultural production. Traditional industries are in crisis: film production companies are failing, distribution companies don't know what to do anymore, and cinemas are playing fashion and sports. So new things can be suggested now — why? Not because traditional industries have changed their opinion, but because new

technologies have socialized the means of production and have democratized information.[129]

One result of this democratization of knowledge and access is the prolific and often radical film criticism emerging from a younger generation on the Internet. These younger critics regularly attend international film festivals such as Cannes, BAFICI, Vienna, Locarno and Rotterdam, and are completely au fait with what is going on in the (rapidly) changing media landscape.[130] These websites that host their writings are committed to an informed, rigorous and engaged film criticism.

Together with these new Internet platforms for film criticism, there has also been a revival of a more specialized film press in print in Spain. The most obvious example is *Caimán Cuadernos de Cine*; Carlos Heredero is the editor of this specialized monthly film magazine published by Caimán Ediciones — until January 2011, the magazine was called *Cahier du Cinéma España*, and was independent from its French namesake, with whom it shared only an agreement over the license of the name. It currently sells around 18,500 copies per month, a figure that has been more or less stable since their first edition in May 2007, and which, as Heredero agrees, shows that there is a readership ready for this kind of publication.

Caimán Cuadernos de Cine also publishes — in collaboration with cultural institutions, such as museums, cinematheques and indeed film festivals like Seminci, Gijón and of course San Sebastián — booklets dedicated to exploring aspects of these organizations' work. This is mutually beneficial as these booklets not only promote the cultural institutions (who cover the costs of producing it) but also help in expanding the distribution of the magazine, in both cases helping to reach new readership/audiences. *Caimán* has been involved in the DVD distribution of more independent and challenging Spanish films such as *Naufragio/Shipwreck* (Pedro Aguilera, 2010), *La vida sublime/The Life Sublime* (Daniel V. Villamediana, 2010), *Diamond Flash* (Carlos Vermut, 2011) as well as international, such as *The Assassin* (Hou Hsiao-hsien, 2015), many of which were screened at San Sebastián. This is the result of the collaboration *Caimán* set up with a small DVD distribution company, Cameo. Both these enterprises agree on a number of films the DVD company is thinking of buying the rights for, which *Caimán* supports by allowing the use of its name on the DVD, and which includes a short article written by one of *Caimán*'s regular collaborators. This puts out into the marketplace films that otherwise would not have made it, and functions as another way of elongating their distribution once they have finished the festival tour and their release (usually small and within independent circuits) in the country.

Nevertheless, for San Sebastián, as Olaciregui illustrates, the balance lies precisely in the space between these two extremes of film coverage. As an A-list, competitive, non-specialist festival, San Sebastián is expected to cater for all audiences — international, national and Basque — a fact which not only is reflected in its programme but also in its press coverage; he notes:

> There are very specialized media with an elevated level of criticism directed at very informed audiences, and then you go from that to the daily, or the fashion magazine. And in a way you have to have a Festival that is able to conjugate

FIG. 2.10. *High Life* press conference with Mia Goth,
Robert Pattinson, Claire Denis, Juliette Binoche, Agata Buzek, 2018
Photo: Pablo Gómez/© SSIFF

and introduce elements that interest all these audiences, all these media, because what is clear is that the success of a festival resides in its continuous exposure in very diverse media. For me it's not enough if *Cahiers du Cinéma* [now *Caimán Cuadernos de Cine*] writes wonderful reviews about us if TVE[131] says that we are only screening films mainly aimed at a minority. We must find a very broad spectrum of films that satisfy very diverse sensibilities and ways of watching film.

Perhaps the most noticeable recent change in relation to press perceptions of the Festival and the government's attitude to Spanish films programmed at San Sebastián revolve around the appointment in 2009 of politician Ignasi Guardans as the then Director of the ICAA[132] by the former PSOE Minister of Culture, Ángeles González Sinde, herself a filmmaker. His controversial intervention in film-funding and its repercussions for the less established and more unconventional Spanish cinema made by a new generation of filmmakers whose films are regularly programmed at San Sebastián, such as Javier Rebollo, Albert Serra, Isaki Lacuesta, Pedro Aguilera, and key independent producers such as Luis Miñarro (also a filmmaker) who is behind many of these new films, crystallizes many of the problems that the Festival confronts of late.

In 2009 the ICAA announced a new law for film subsidies, a law which in the past has existed mainly to provide assistance to independent films. Guardans changed this law so that henceforward, a filmmaker would have to make a film with a minimum budget of two million euros in order to be able to apply for any kind of assistance, and the remaining filmmakers (those with a budget of less than two million euros) would have to enter their projects into a competition for funding. Those films not selected or whose budget is not over two million have no opportunity to apply for any subsidies from the Ministry. The idea is to make fewer films but with bigger budgets. Galán summarizes the law as follows, in a way that tends to reinforce the notion that festivals are absolutely necessary for achieving international projection and distribution:

> It's all a bit chaotic to be honest. The new law didn't change much with respect to the previous one. There have been small changes in the structure, but Guardans was trying to help big-budget Spanish films in particular, thinking that these are the ones that can compete in Europe with other big-budget films. And that is not the reality. Normally, the films that are successful [in the international festival circuit, outside Spain] are paradoxically those with a low budget, which are the ones that go to film festivals, such as for instance José María de Orbe's *Aitá*.[133]

In response to this new film law, a group of more than two hundred filmmakers, *Cineastas Contra la Orden* (Filmmakers Against the Law), appealed to Brussels in November 2009 to have it repealed. In their manifesto, partly quoted in *El País*[134], they claimed that this law did not comply with EU legislation, as it worked against cultural diversity by marginalizing small projects to the advantage of profitable big budget enterprises,[135] measuring films by their cost and not by their public interest or by their content, allegations to which Guardans famously responded: 'Spanish cinema has only *Agoras* [in reference to *Agora/Ágora* (Alejandro Amenábar, 2009), one of the largest in budget and most international films made in Spain in terms of co-production and the presence of international stars] and little nothing films'.[136] Amongst the filmmakers screening 'little nothing films' in competition in San Sebastián the following year in 2010 were Trueba, Lacuesta and Rebollo, a fact that Guardans allegedly took very personally, when he declared after the Festival:

> This decision [to postpone the Law until it was checked by Brussels] is due to the idiocy of some members of Filmmakers Against the Law who haven't got a clue what they are doing and are shooting themselves in the foot.[137]

Guardans was dismissed as director of the ICAA and replaced by Carlos Cuadros in 2011, under whom the law was still passed. In July 2014, Susana de la Sierra, Cuadros's successor, resigned after her proposals to rectify the precarious state of the Spanish film industry — through the increase of tax exception from 18% to 25–30%, amongst other measures — kept on being rejected and/or postponed by the Ministerio de Hacienda/Treasury Department.[138] In 2016, the direction fell on Óscar Graefenhain, and since 2018, Beatriz Navas Valdés, with a background on independent and avant garde cinema, has taken the position as new General Director of ICAA.

For Galán, 'what is really terrible is that this country has to live off subsidies, and that a politician can leave his mark just like that', as the Spanish film industry in particular (and cultural organizations in general) is largely dependent on public funding. Film critic and programmer Jaime Pena agrees with Galán, and points out that some of these reactions stem from the fact that Guardans did not come from the world of film, which was not the case with his predecessor, the film-critic Fernando Lara, who had previously directed Seminci in Valladolid; in addition, neither was he a politician that belonged to the PSOE (the party in power at the time). He was from CiU (Convergència i Unió, which was a Catalan nationalist electoral federation of two political parties) and came from the European Parliament, where he had only been involved with film at a legislative level. The politicization of cultural organizations in Spain is an ongoing problem that results in some of these posts being given as political gifts — behind Guardans appointment lay a desire on the part of PSOE to maintain good relations with CiU.

Perhaps this is key to understanding the situation, since some of the negative reactions towards the promotion and distribution of a more independent Spanish cinema seem to be informed by Guardans' solid relationship with the FAPAE [Spanish Producers' Association]. The new law clearly benefits the FAPAE, who are unhappy with the support that San Sebastián is giving to independent Spanish cinema — although such films prove successful within the international festival circuit, this does not translate into box office revenues (as turned out to be the case with the Ley Miró whose remit, compared to Guardans', stands at the opposite end of the spectrum). I myself attended the 2010 edition of San Sebastián as an accredited film critic, during which *El País* published an article that attacked the Festival's promotion of independent Spanish cinema.[139] It incorporated the opinions of a group of people (mainly FAPAE members) including the likes of Enrique González Macho (then President of the Academy of Cinema), who complained that films such as those by Iciar Bollaín, Álex de la Iglesia and Fernando León de Aranoa — all established filmmakers — were being ignored in favour of other films that did not represent Spanish cinema.[140] To which Olaciregui responded in an interview for the same newspaper (written on his departure):

> I was told by the producers of *Balada triste de trompeta/The Last Circus* (Álex de la Iglesia 2010) that the film was not going to be finished on time and then they premiered it at Venice. With regards to *Y también la lluvia/Even the Rain* (Iciar Bollaín 2010) it was offered when we had already closed the program of Spanish films in the official competition.[141]

During that same edition, Carlos Boyero, the chief film critic of *El País* (who famously has a long history of giving negative reviews to Pedro Almodóvar's films), also publicly criticized the Festival on the basis of the prominence accorded to a certain strain of Spanish independent cinema in the main competition. Boyero's rage was directed particularly at José María de Orbe's *Aitá/Father* (2010),[142] and was in a similar vein to his views on Javier Rebollo's *La mujer sin piano/A Woman Without A Piano*, screened at the Festival the previous year; which he'd described as 'empty stylistics for bores with metaphysical pretensions'.[143] Yet Rebollo's *A Woman Without A Piano* was awarded the Silver Shell for best director that year; when Rebollo collected the award, he roundly declared: 'This award proves that another type of Spanish cinema exists'.[144]

Aside from *Aitá*, the main competition in 2010 included the following Spanish films: *Pa Negre/Black Bread* (Agustí Villaronga 2010) and *Elisa K* (Jordi Cadena, Judith Colell 2010), and what later became a successful box-office hit, *El Gran Vázquez/The Great Vázquez* (Óscar Aibar 2010) (which, although it is not technically a low budget film, could not be classified as a commercial film either), instead of the bigger budget films that Guardans' new Film Law (and, as mentioned, the FAPAE) was seeking to favour. Yet *Black Bread* went on to win nine Goyas (the Spanish equivalent of the Oscars), was announced as Spain's foreign-language Oscar candidate in 2012 and ended up being the seventh highest grossing Spanish film at the box office in the first half of 2011 (eighteenth at the end of the year), amongst a total of 351 Spanish films released that year.[145]

Before he was dismissed, another of Guardans's targets was reducing the number of festivals in Spain, which he planned to attempt by limiting the subsidy available for such ventures. However, on a closer look, it transpires that these state subsidies are relatively insignificant. As noted in the introduction, a quick glance at the situation of film festivals in the world in general — and indeed in Spain in particular — reveals a noticeable increase in their numbers within the last fifteen years. In Spain alone, there are over four hundred film festivals, of which around three hundred are officially recognized and therefore funded in some way or another by the Ministry of Culture. By far the greatest assistance goes to paying, as previously seen, a quarter of the grant aid of San Sebastián's budget — a million and a half euros — and the whole of Huelva's cost, the latter a Festival that specializes in Latin American cinema. The remaining festivals receive minimum help. Pena takes up the theme:

> The big ones like Málaga receive a 50,000€ subsidy in an overall budget of 8 million, so if they lose that it isn't really a problem, but Huelva would disappear; and the rest are subsidized by the Town Hall, the province and/or the regional government. The Ministry gives a lot of money in total, but they are very small figures when broken down. A Festival with a budget of 100,000€ receives something like 5,000€ in funding. Guardans thought that all the festivals in Spain owed their existence to the Ministry. Valladolid (Seminci), with a budget of 2 million, gets 100,000€ from the Ministry, so it could continue without any problem, and they would probably in the process free themselves from demands to screen certain Spanish films, and things like that.[146]

Added to this, the number of festivals held in Spain is greatly reduced if we choose to only consider what might be called 'quality' film festivals. The parameters of what actually constitutes a festival is often stretched when attempts are made to gather these figures, as the majority of these so-called film festivals are in fact an event more comparable to a film week that make up for the lack of films screened during the year. It is therefore safe to speculate that part of the reason for this increase occurs as a direct consequence of the slow disappearance of cinemas in smaller urban locations — as much in Spain as in other European countries such as the UK. In these cases, when there is only one screening place or none at all, locals, generally in collaboration with the cine-clubs and/or cinematheques, organize a festival where they project the films that were never played there.

As such, aside from San Sebastián, the only one with the A-list category in Spain, there are several medium-sized festivals, such as the already mentioned Seminci in Valladolid, a festival comprising the best work screened at other international film festivals (and thus similar to the LFF), and other smaller ones — some of which enjoy considerable international cachet — such as Gijón, Sitges, Las Palmas and Seville — the latter, as Heredero notes, although specializing in European cinema, has an eclectic programme that reputedly lacks a strong sense of direction, but which has been able to occasionally wrest a couple of films here and there from a more established festival such as Valladolid, because it can count on a larger budget. However, the former director of Gijón, José Luis Cienfuegos — who was controversially sacked soon after the right-wing government took power in 2011[147] — was appointed director of Seville and 2012 was his first edition. Cienfuegos's excellent track record at Gijón suggests that Seville — with a similar budget to Seminci — has become already a reference festival. Lastly, there is also Málaga, the self-professed Festival of Spanish Film (Heredero himself was on its board of directors in its first edition), originally conceived as an international platform for showcasing the new Spanish cinema. However, there is a major problem with Málaga (whose budget is currently bigger than that of San Sebastián), which has to do with a strong TV presence. The key sponsor of the festival is the private channel Antena3 under the umbrella of ATRESMEDIA, which means the stars attending it are in most cases from the channel's own TV series, this in turn indicates that the festival promotes a particular kind of TV-financed film. The implication is that Málaga is not internationally recognized for its programming of Spanish cinema, which leaves San Sebastián as the most important international platform for Spanish films.

FIG. 2.11. Welcome drink to Cine en Construcción/
Films in Progress 30 with Festival Director José Luis Rebordinos, 2016
Photo: Karlos Corbella/© SSIFF Archive

Looking In and Looking Out

Not only is San Sebastián the most international platform for Spanish films, the Festival has also, relatively recently, expanded its scope from Spanish in origin to Spanish in language. As such, perhaps one of the biggest challenges of late for the Festival has been the creation in 2001 of Cine en Construcción/Films in Progress, a section that regular programmer José María Riba organized in collaboration with the Toulouse Latin America Film Festival. This initiative endeavours

> to facilitate the completion of rigorously selected Latinamerican films which, though completed, are having difficulty finding their way into the post-production stage, by screening them for a group of professionals, principally from the cross-border domain, who may be able to contribute to their completion.[148]

2001 was also the year of the boom of New Argentine Cinema (for further details, see Chapter 1), and most importantly of the Argentine *corralito* — the name given to the economic measures and restrictions that the Argentine Minister of Economy put into practice as a result of the crisis — a situation that, although it didn't create Cine en Construcción, certainly hastened its establishment within the Festival. As Olaciregui explains:

> We were already thinking of our role as a platform for the industry and about looking for new audiences, and in the midst of the Argentine economic crisis 'el corralito' during our selection process, we were receiving very interesting films from this country. But when you told them to send us a copy in 35mm because it had been selected for the Festival, they'd answer: 'no, I can't get to the post-production of the film, I haven't been able to finish it.' This made us come up with a solution that is now a franchise, one that has been very much replicated by many other festivals, which is Cine en Construcción. We linked up with the Toulouse Film Festival that specializes in Latin-American film, and together we present six films in March and six in September, which are filmed, edited and then presented only to industry people, and which are looking to get financed. This also exemplifies our concern for interesting films not to be left unfinished because they could not find funding.[149]

Cine en Construcción was soon followed by its younger sister, Cine en Movimiento, which pursues the same idea but with Asian countries, and which was introduced four years later in 2005, running till 2012. As Tamara L. Falicov notes, this is a genuinely innovative project, since

> it is the first time that two European film festivals have united to support Latin American [and now Asian] filmmakers in need of postproduction finishing funds. Twice a year, film professionals and Festival staff in Toulouse and San Sebastián screen fictional feature film entries that are works in progress. The winning films obtain post-production completion funding through donations from various film companies, e.g., Exa, Kodak, Molinare, No Problem Sonido, Technicolor-Madrid Film Lab and Titra Film. Out of roughly forty-plus entries each year, the committee selects between four and eight films for funding. Upon their completion, many of the selected films have gone on to screen at one or both of the festivals [Toulouse and San Sebastián].[150]

In similar vein — albeit more in tune with other older funding projects such as Rotterdam's Hubert Bals Fund created in 1988, or Cannes's Fonds Sud Cinema created in 1984 — in 2012 FIAPF also inaugurated the Europe-Latin America Co-Production Forum at the San Sebastián Film Festival covering the whole of Europe and Latin America. However, as Falicov astutely notes, this latter model exemplifies one of the problematic issues around these funding projects. In 2017, the Festival launched one more industry project, this time focusing on European films in non-hegemonic languages called Glocal in Progress. These workshops and funding enterprises generate content for a given festival — hence strengthening the festival's own profile — but in some cases the amount of intervention on the part of the festival can prove to be a drawback. This is the case with Fonds Sud, who claim on their website that they favour producing films with 'a strong cultural identity', but

> a large part of the funding is given for such activities as postproduction work completed in France, hiring French technicians for central crew positions (director of photography, for example) or dubbing the film into French. African filmmakers have alleged that funds such as this will never help nascent film industries develop their infrastructure, to the point where one critic pointed out that ultimately it is the French film industry that is being subsidized (Barlet 2000)[151].

As such, this is directly linked to the theories around the 'neo-colonialism' that Elssaeser and De Valk claim lie at the core of the origins of film festivals in Europe, as discussed in the introduction. Introduced in 2012, San Sebastián's Europe–Latin America Co-Production Forum is therefore also similar to the more invasive Fonds Sud in Cannes, Berlin's World Cinema Fund, the training-oriented Sundance Lab or indeed, BAFICI's own BAL. The main difference with the films presented to Cine en Construcción/Movimiento is that they are no longer the films of independent directors or producers. Rather, they have passed through a series of filters concerning the script, funding etc. This means, as Olaciregui notes, they already have a certain 'reliability' on paper — although as he quickly points out, 'this does not necessarily mean that the results will be of a high standard when the projects are finally filmed.'[152] Nevertheless, San Sebastián's attitude towards these workshops seems to be more cautious than their French or North American counterparts' — for some, both the Sundance Lab and Cinéfondation leave a stamp of sorts on the films they help produce this way, incidentally reinforcing the concept of the 'festival film' (dealt with in the introduction). Regarding San Sebastián's own involvement, Olaciregui explains:

> We have entered this process this year [2010] as observers, because what we have always tried in Cine en Construcción is to create platforms that allow us to observe but also in a way, to keep ourselves out of the equation. It has its positives and its negatives. This is why in Cine en Construcción we don't ask for anything whatsoever in return from the films we select, regardless of whether they are for Toulouse or San Sebastián. We don't even say that it has to be premiered at the Festival. We can offer an invitation but the person is free to go anywhere else. It works the same way if the finished film is not up

to the standards we expected; we have the freedom to withhold an invitation. We help with completing the film, and that's the end of our commitment.[153]

This brings us to the increasingly important position that the industry and production markets such as BAL are currently acquiring in medium-to-large festivals — or indeed in any festival that wishes to make any kind of impact in the current film industry — as the presence of the industry is now intrinsically linked to a market. Both (industry and market) have been present at some point in San Sebastián's previous history. Back in 1988 Diego Galán had already organized an early version of the aforementioned filmmaking workshops called Desayuno con diamantes (Breakfast with Diamonds, the Spanish title for *Breakfast at Tiffany's* [1961]), which he opened to any citizen who wanted to pitch their project to a group of film professionals. And Euroaim Screenings Donostia, an initiative by Rudi Barnet in 1991, was the Festival's first attempt to incorporate some market activity. Most importantly, for Olaciregui the market is the one asset that will enable certain festivals to exist in the near future; the lack of it will mean the disappearance of many of the smaller ones:

> It's never safe to make a diagnosis of this kind of thing, but only those who manage to offer a platform to the industry will survive. Festivals are creating a new economy. There are films that survive because their sales agents are making sure they do by charging the festivals 'renting' fees. Of course San Sebastián is out of this system (apart from the retrospectives, which are comprised of films that already belong to the market) but we don't have to pay fees for any of the rest of the films in the programme. This is how many of these sales' agents, distributors and/or producers make a profit on their films, by screening them in a large number of smaller festivals and charging a fee of about 1,000€ to 3,000€ per festival. If a festival cannot guarantee a platform for the industry, then they are forced to pay a really high percentage in fees for the films that they screen.[154]

Back to the Future

One cannot help but feel that the wheel has come full circle. The future of San Sebastián is increasingly linked to film as business, echoing the Festival's own businessmen founders; and Spanish distributors' tendency to acquire mainly commercial films to screen in Spain operates as a new form of censorship, this time by way of the market rather than dictatorship. Films that do not fit into a neat mainstream category also lack an established screening circuit — this in turn reinforces the position of the San Sebastián Film Festival as an alternative platform within the country, as it has done at key moments in the past. What's more, as Odón Elorza — the Mayor of San Sebastián from 1991 to 2011 — mentions in an article published in *El País*, probably the city's strongest asset in helping it become European Capital of Culture for 2016 was its link to the film and media industries — what he defines as a 'singular and differentiating element',[155] i.e. the fact that the city has an international A-list Festival whose presence is pivotal in attracting cinema and the media industry to San Sebastián. Odón's take on the Festival in this article is revealing, as he chooses to focus not only on big-budget films or on the Festival's importance as a platform for Spanish films — expanded into Spanish language and Basque — but insists more on the internationally regarded auteurs and new filmmakers that populate the festival circuit nowadays. Odón ascribes to them a cultural as opposed to an economic value, revealing a will to acknowledge and support this crucial component of the Festival. It is a position that the new current director, Rebordinos, also stoutly defends — in fact the Golden Shell awarded at his first Festival as director in 2011 went to Isaki Lacuesta's independent, socially minded and formally radical film, *Los pasos dobles/The Double Steps* (2011) and even though the following year this same award went to French director François Ozon's formally inventive *In the House*, it is important to note that the script is based on a confrontational play by one of Spain's key contemporary, and most international, dramatists, Juan Mayorga. The Special Jury Prize that year went to Pablo Berger's silent, black and white reworking of *Blancanieves/Snow White* (2012), an award given the following year to the film's editor, Fernando Franco, for his challengingly bleak yet emotionally rewarding directorial debut, *La herida/Wounded* (2013). In 2014, Carlos Vermut was awarded the Golden Shell for *Magical Girl*, and *Entre dos aguas/Between Two Waters* saw Isaki Lacuesta taking once again the Golden Shell in 2018.

Given that the main objective of the European Capital of Culture project (which began in 1985) is to 'raise [a city's] visibility and profile on an international scale',[156] 2016 undoubtedly situated the Festival once more at the centre of debates around the notion of cultural capital. But in its intrinsically dual identity, the San Sebastián Film Festival has never forgotten that it is also an event, a celebration of the city and a carnival of sorts. So it should not be a surprise that immediately after the city was announced as co-winner, and at a time when the Festival has augmented its scope from promoting Spanish/Basque films to becoming a global platform for Spanish-language cinema through production schemes and a newly established market, the Festival introduced in 2011 a new section called Culinary Zinema — a collaboration with the Berlin International Film Festival and the Basque Culinary Centre — which only shows films that are related in some way to food. This strand highlights one of the city's main features — San Sebastián has more Michelin-starred restaurants per capita than any other city in the world — and by once more turning the local into the global, it gives a clear nod to the Festival's origins, when the city's attractions (bullfighting, sightseeing, drum-playing, gastronomy) were as loudly promoted as the films themselves.

As discussed throughout this chapter, in San Sebastián gastronomy, tourism, identity, politics and culture all go hand in hand, and the Festival mirrors the powerful connections between all these aspects of the city. This multiplicity of perspectives is also echoed in the Festival's content, where, as Geoff Pingree noted back in 2004,[157] 'San Sebastián increasingly had to balance tradition and innovation to survive financially while remaining a showcase for imaginative and challenging work'. In his article, Pingree is referring to the increasing presence of Hollywood films in the Festival's glitzier events, yet, as previously seen, the Festival's commitment to a more challenging strain of cinema (particularly Spanish) has always been a defining trait. What's more, that kind of cinema is definitely increasing its profile during the current regime of Rebordinos.

FIG. 2.12. Festival Director José Luis Rebordinos greeting Viggo Mortensen during the COVID-19 pandemic: SSIFF was one of the very few international film festivals celebrated in 2020
Photo: Montse Castillo/© SSIFF

I would argue, however, that Pingree makes a cunning observation when he describes the Festival as a 'cultural provocateur'. In the latest of Rebordinos's yearly reports on the economic impact of the Festival in the city,[158] the director reveals that the Festival generates in tax already 700,000€ more than the funding it gets from public organizations. But perhaps more importantly, its overall economic impact is 27.3€ million; i.e. almost 20€ million above its annual budget (8.5€ million for 2018). As Rebordinos rightly notes, with hundreds of jobs created by the Festival, these figures prove that at times of crisis, culture generates wealth and jobs. San Sebastián's impact does not simply rest on its promotion of Spanish cinema but rather on its key role within the city's cultural economy.

Notes to Chapter 2

An earlier and briefer draft of this chapter is published as Mar Diestro-Dópido, 'San Sebastián: A Film Festival of Contrasts', in *New Trends in Contemporary Spanish Cinema*, ed. by Fernando Canet and Duncan Wheeler (Bristol: Intellect, 2014), pp. 406–16. All websites were accessed between April 2009 and August 2018. All uncredited quotes are from the following unpublished interviews conducted by the author (all translated from Spanish by the author): interview with José María de Orbe, BFI Southbank press office, 23 October 2010; interview with Diego Galán, Las Vistillas Restaurant, Madrid, 8 April 2011; interview with Carlos F. Heredero, offices of Caimán Cuadernos de Cine, Madrid, 6 April 2011; interview with Mikel Olaciregui, San Sebastián International Film Festival offices, San Sebastián, 4 May 2010; interview with José Luis Rebordinos, San Sebastián International Film Festival offices, San Sebastián, 5 May 2010; interview with Jaime Pena, San Sebastián International Film Festival premises, San Sebastián, 21 September 2010; and interview with José Ángel Herrero Velarde, San Sebastián International Film Festival offices, San Sebastián, 6 May 2010; interview with Miguel Marías, by email, 23 July 2011; interview with Javier Angulo, by phone, 26 February 2020.

1. All figures collected from the Festival's 2018 edition.
2. For more information about FIAPF and the current controversy surrounding the actual value of their categorization see the section dedicated to this organization in the Introduction. More information on the Festival is available at the official website: San Sebastian Festival, <www.sansebastianFestival.com> [accessed 25 May 2020].
3. Information available at the website of the Spanish National Statistics Institute, <http://www.ine.es/en/welcome_en.htm>. Province of Gipuzkoa 2017: 719,282 inhabitants; Donostia 2017: 186,370 inhabitants.
4. For more information about the Basque Country see, Teresa Whitfield, *The Basque Conflict and ETA: The Difficulties of an Ending*. United States Institute of Peace, 1 December 2015. Available at <www.jstor.org/stable/resrep12174> [accessed 25 May 2020].
5. Pablo León Aguinaga, *El cine norteamericano y la España franquista, 1939–1960: relaciones internacionales, comercio y propaganda* (unpublished doctoral thesis, Universidad Complutense de Madrid, 2009), p. 337, <http://eprints.ucm.es/8378/1/T30698.pdf>.
6. Román Gubern, *Función política y ordenamiento jurídico bajo el franquismo (1936–1975)*, (Barcelona: Editorial Península, 1981), p. 49.
7. José Luis Tuduri, *San Sebastián: un festival, una historia. (1953–1966)* (San Sebastián: Euskadiko Filmategia/Filmoteca Vasca, 1989), pp. 15–16.
8. Tuduri, *San Sebastián: un festival, una historia. (1953–1966)*, pp. 15–16.
9. Tuduri, *San Sebastián: un festival, una historia. (1953–1966)*, p. 23.
10. Jesús Angulo, Maialen Beloki, José Luis Rebordinos, and Antonio Santamarina, *Antxon Eceiza: cine, existencialismo y dialéctica* (San Sebastián: Euskadiko Filmategia/Filmoteca Vasca, 2009), p. 23.
11. Tuduri, *San Sebastián: un festival, una historia. (1953–1966)*, p. 19.
12. Interview with Herrero Velarde.

13. Tuduri, *San Sebastián: un festival, una historia. (1953–1966)*, p. 33.
14. Interview with Herrero Velarde.
15. Francisco Cantalapiedra, 'Fernando Lara dice adios a la Seminci tras 20 años como director', *El País*, 29 December 2004, <http://elpais.com/diario/2004/12/29/espectaculos/1104274801_850215.html>; Redacción, 'Nombran a Fernando Lara, revitalizador de la Seminci, director general de cine', *Noticine*, 23 December 2004, <http://noticine.com/industria/3899-nombran-a-fernando-lara-revitalizador-de-la-seminci-director-general-de-cine.html> [accessed 25 May 2020]; Javier Tolentino, 'La Seminci, por atrevida, por valiente', *RTVE.es*, 28 October 2009, <http://blog.rtve.es/septimovicio/2009/10/la-seminci-por-atrevida-por-valiente.html>; For an in-depth study of Seminci in comparison to FICXixón see Núria Triana Toribio, '*FICXixón* and *Seminci*: Two Spanish Film Festivals at the End of the Festivals Era', *Journal of Spanish Cultural Studies*, 12, 2 (2011), 217–36.
16. Interview with Javier Angulo.
17. Victoria M. Niño, 'Javier Angulo: "Me encontré un festival ensimismado y hoy está abierto al mundo"', *El Norte de Castilla*, 13 October, 2019, <https://www.elnortedecastilla.es/culturas/seminci/javier-angulo-encontre-20191013083337-nt.html>.
18. In his memoirs, Berlanga declares his political frustration thus: 'I am a fascist for the communists or the leftwing and I am an indecent red for the right. And I am neither, nor. I'm just an idiot who's still trying to be free in a country where being independent is impossible', Jess Franco, *Bienvenido Mister Cagada. Memorias caóticas de Luis García Berlanga* (Madrid: Aguilar Santillana Ediciones Generales S.L., 2005), p. 210.
19. It is worth noting that, under Franco's censorship, the films were seen outside Spain at the major international film festivals but not within Spain (or at least not in their completed versions), except at film festivals.
20. María del Camino Gutiérrez Lanza, *Traducción y censura de textos cinematográficos en la España de Franco: doblaje y subtitulado ingles-español (1951–1975)* (León: Universidad de León, 2000), pp. 38–40.
21. See, César Santos Fontela, *El cine español en la encrucijada* (Madrid: Ciencia Nueva, 1967), pp. 18–19; Ignacio Rancia, 'Antes de Salamanca, en Salamanca, después de Salamanca', in *El cine español, desde Salamanca: (1955–1995)* (Castilla-León: Junta de Castilla y León, Consejería de Educación y Cultura, 1995), pp. 59–76. For an in-depth historical study of the Conversations see Carlos Aragüez Rubio, 'Intelectuales y cine en el segundo franquismo: de las Conversaciones de Salamanca al nuevo cine español', *Asociación de Historiadores del Presente*, 15 June 2013, <http://historiadelpresente.es/sites/default/files/revistarticulos/5/506intelectualesycineenelsegundofranquismodelasconversacionesdesalamancaalnuevocineespanol.pdf>.
22. Tuduri, *San Sebastián: un festival, una historia. (1953–1966)*, pp. 25–26.
23. Gubern, *Función política y ordenamiento jurídico bajo el franquismo (1936–1975)*, p. 122.
24. Santiago Pozo Arenas, *La industria del cine en España: legislación y aspectos económicos, 1896–1970* (Barcelona: Edicions Universitat de Barcelona, 1984), pp. 121–48 (p. 141).
25. Gubern, *Función política y ordenamiento jurídico bajo el franquismo (1936–1975)*, p. 147.
26. Franco, *Bienvenido Mister Cagada*, pp. 235–36.
27. Alberto López Echevarrieta, *Los cines de Bilbao* (San Sebastián-Donostia: Filmoteka Vasca-Euskadiko Filmotegia, 2000), p. 11.
28. Franco, *Bienvenido Mister Cagada*, pp. 235–37. Despite being banned, the Communist Party was the strongest and most organized party and union against the regime in Spain. For further information on the role of the Communist Party in Spain, including its key role in organizing demonstrations across a range of institutions, including universities, see Dolores Ibárruri, Manuel Azcárate, Luis Balaguer, Antonio Cordón, Irene Falcón and José Sandoval, *Historia del Partido Comunista (Versión abreviada 1960)*, <http://www.papelesdesociedad.info/?Historia-del-Partido-Comunista-de> [accessed 25 May 2020].
29. María Pérez, 'Las películas mutiladas por Franco', *El Mundo*, 13 October 2010, <http://www.elmundo.es/elmundo/2009/10/21/cultura/1256144676.html>. For a thorough study of Franco's censorship in cinema, see Alberto Gil, *La censura cinematográfica en España* (Barcelona: S.A. Ediociones B, 2009).

30. José Ángel Ezcurra, *Crónica de un empeño dificultoso* (Madrid: Jornadas Triunfo en su época, Casa de Velázquez, Ciudad Universitaria, Madrid, February 1994), pp. 7–9, <http://www.triunfodigital.com/TE.pdf>.
31. One of the most widely quoted examples is the changes to which the narrative of *Mogambo* (1953) was subjected. Victor Marswell (Clarke Gable) is cheating on Linday Nordley (Grace Kelly) with Eloise Y. Kelly (Ava Gardner), but in the Spanish dubbed version, Gable and Gardner were made siblings, implying incest (Jo Labanyi, 'Censorship or the Fear of Mass Culture', in *Spanish Cultural Studies An Introduction*, ed. by Helen Graham and Jo Labanyi (Oxford University Press, 1995), pp. 207–14 (p. 210). A similarly problematic outcome was also 'achieved' by the head of the censors who interviewed Luis Buñuel after reading the script for *Viridiana* (for a detailed explanation of the encounter between Buñuel, Portabella and the censor see Mar Diestro-Dópido, 'From Buñuel to Lorca', *Sight & Sound* online edition, October 2011, <https://www.bfi.org.uk/news-opinion/sight-sound-magazine/interviews/pere-portabella-bunuel-lorca> [accessed 25 May 2020]. However, the use of dubbing backfired at the national box office, as Spanish films found themselves in direct competition with foreign films, mainly those from Hollywood. Not only were there no language barriers, but in some instances, the highly qualified and trained professional dubbing actors would improve the acting, and hence the film itself, as one correspondent from *The Times* noted in his report of 1960 (Barcelona Correspondent, 'More Spanish Theatres Lost to the Cinema. World's Most Assiduous Filmgoers', *The Times*, 14 October 1960).
32. Emeterio Díez Puertas, *Historia social del cine en España* (Madrid-Caracas: Editorial Fundamentos, 2003), p. 303.
33. Diego Galán, in *Historia del Zinemaldia (1953–2010)* 2010 [DVD] Spain: ETB/TVE/IBERDROLA (Documentary series about the Festival narrated and directed by Diego Galán).
34. Interview with Mikel Olaciregui.
35. Kieron Corless and Chris Darke, *Cannes: Inside the World's Premier Film Festival* (London: Faber and Faber, 2007), p. 149.
36. Tuduri, *San Sebastián: un festival, una historia. (1953–1966)*, p. 57.
37. Díez Puertas, *Historia social del cine en España*, p. 299.
38. Interview with Olaciregui.
39. Tuduri, *San Sebastián: un Festival, una historia. (1953–1966)*, p. 91.
40. Javier Sada, 'Comienza el ciclo del Cine Club San Sebastián', *Diario Vasco*, 7 October 2009, <http://www.diariovasco.com/20091007/san-sebastian/comienza-ciclo-cine-club-20091007.html>.
41. Angulo et al, *Antxon Eceiza: cine, existencialismo y dialéctica*, pp. 24–25.
42. Angulo et al, *Antxon Eceiza: cine, existencialismo y dialéctica*, pp. 24–25.
43. Tuduri, *San Sebastián: un festival, una historia. (1953–1966)*, p. 117.
44. The Institute of Cinematographic Investigation and Experience had been created in 1947. On 8 November a ministerial law was passed and it became the Official Film School (Escuela Oficial de Cine, EOC).
45. Tuduri, *San Sebastián: un festival, una historia. (1953–1966)*, p. 127.
46. Angulo et al, *Antxon Eceiza: cine, existencialismo y dialéctica*, p. 26.
47. Interview with Olaciregui.
48. Juan Luis Buñuel, 'On Viridiana', in *Luis Buñuel. The Complete Films*, ed. by Bill Krohn and Paul Duncan (Köln, London, Los Angeles, Madrid, Paris, Tokyo: Taschen), pp. 130–31.
49. Carlos Saura in an interview on stage with Professor Maria Delgado on 11 June 2011 at the BFI Southbank NFT1, London. An extract from this interview is included in the DVD of the film, *Cría Cuervos*, 1975 [DVD] UK: BFI.
50. Mar Diestro-Dópido, 'From Buñuel to Lorca'.
51. Román Gubern, 'Notas para una historia de la Censura Cinematográfica en España', in *Un cine para el cadalso: 40 años de censura cinematográfica en España*, ed by Román Gubern and Domènec Font (Barcelona: Euros 1975), pp. 15–44 (p. 17) and J. A. Bardem, 'Una reflexión sobre la censura cinematográfica', in *Arte, política, sociedad. Ensayos*, ed. by J. A. Bardem (Madrid: Ayuso, 1976), p. 18.

52. Interview with Herrero Velarde.
53. Tuduri, *San Sebastián: un festival, una historia. (1953–1966)*, p. 206.
54. Tuduri, *San Sebastián: un festival, una historia. (1953–1966)*, pp. 207–30.
55. Tuduri, *San Sebastián: Un festival, una historia. (1953–1966)*, p. 245.
56. Tuduri, *San Sebastián: Un festival, una historia. (1953–1966)*, p. 246.
57. As per Pacific Exchange Rate Service, <http://fx.sauder.ubc.ca/etc/GBPpages.pdf>.
58. Inflation calculator available at Money Sorter, <http://www.moneysorter.co.uk/calculator_inflation2.html#calculator>.
59. José Luis Tuduri, *San Sebastián: Un festival, una historia. (1967–1977)* (San Sebastián: Euskadiko Filmategia/Filmoteca Vasca, 1992), p. 15.
60. For more information see festival website, La Biennale di Venezia, <http://www.labiennale.org/en/cinema/history/the60s70s.html?back=true>.
61. For more information see festival website, La Biennale di Venezia, <http://www.labiennale.org/en/cinema/history/the60s70s.html?back=true>.
62. Galán, *Historia del Zinemaldia* (1953–2010) DVD.
63. Óscar Gutiérrez, 'El primer día en el que ETA asesinó', *El País*, 4 June 2008, <http://www.elpais.com/articulo/espana/primer/dia/ETA/asesino/elpepuesp/20080604elpepunac_4/Tes>.
64. For the full text in Spanish see 'Texto íntegro del comunicado: Declaración de ETA del fin de la violencia', *El País*, 20 October 2011, <http://politica.elpais.com/politica/2011/10/20/actualidad/1319131779_738058.html>; and for the text in English see, 'Basque ceasefire statement: full text' *Guardian*, 20 October 2011, <http://www.guardian.co.uk/world/2011/oct/20/basque-ceasefire-statement-full-text>.
65. Isla Binnie, 'Basque separatist group ETA says it has 'completely dissolved', *Reuters*, 2 May 2018, <https://www.reuters.com/article/us-spain-eta/basque-group-eta-says-has-completely-dissolved-el-diario-website-idUSKBNI31TP>.
66. E.T.A., 'DOCUMENTO | La carta en la que ETA anuncia su disolución', *El Diario Norte*, 16 April 2018, <https://www.eldiario.es/norte/DOCUMENTO-carta-ETA-anuncia-disolucion_0_767123640.html>.
67. Galán, *Historia del Zinemaldia* (1953–2010) DVD.
68. Tuduri, *San Sebastián: un festival, una historia. (1967–1977)*, p. 22.
69. Note both dates are given in the Cine Doré (Filmoteca) programme, <https://www.culturaydeporte.gob.es/dam/jcr:b228f49d-a615-47d0-abf9-11618bd5e273/programanoviembre.pdf> [accessed 25 May 2020].
70. As described in the Cine Doré (Filmoteca) programme, <https://www.culturaydeporte.gob.es/dam/jcr:b228f49d-a615-47d0-abf9-11618bd5e273/programanoviembre.pdf> [accessed 25 May 2020].
71. Manuel Vázquez Montalbán, *FESTIVAL*, 19 September 1995. Quoted in Miguel A. Arroyo Corral, *Unidad didáctica sobre 'Canciones para después de una Guerra'*, p. 11.
72. Information available at Club Cultura.com El Portal Cultural de la Fnac, <http://www.clubcultura.com/clubcine/clubcineastas/suarez/1peliaoom.htm>.
73. For more information about this, see María del Rosario Díez Abad, 'Crónica de un desafío: el cierre de las facultades de Derecho, Medicina, Ciencias y Filosofía y Letras de la Universidad de Valladolid durante la agonía del franquismo', *Segundas Jornadas II: Imagen y Cultura* (Valladolid: Universidad de Valladolid, n.d.) pp. 289–301, available at Universidad Carlos III de Madrid, eArchivo, <http://e-archivo.uc3m.es/bitstream/10016/9506/1/cronica_diez_ICT_2003.pdf>.
74. The FRAP — Frente Revolucionario Antifascista y Patriota (Revolutionary Front Antifascist and Patriotic) — was set up on 23 January 1971, and two years later called for demonstrations on 1 and 2 May. In Atocha, in central Madrid, this resulted in the biggest demonstration ever organized under the dictatorship. The Francoist press could not conceal these events and listed 145 detained; 1 death; 2 gravely injured and numerous others hurt. Although later there were more demonstrations, this was the first and only time in which the demonstrators could be classified as the victors. A total of 10,000 people took part. <https://issuu.com/elsalmonurbano/docs/grupo-edelvec-frap-27-de-septiembre> [accessed 25 May 2020].
75. Diego Galán, *Pilar Miró: Nadie me enseñó a vivir* (Barcelona: Plaza & Janés Editores, 2006), p. 94.
76. Galán, *Historia del Zinemaldia* (1953–2010) DVD.

77. For further information see RTVE's website dedicated to the TV documentary series based on the history of the Transition including interviews with the key figures of this period. RTVE, <http://www.rtve.es/archivo/la-transicion-serie/>.
78. Franco, *Bienvenido Mister Cagada*, p. 153.
79. Geraldine Chaplin, interviewed by Peter Evans, Cine Lumière, London, 1 October 2011.
80. For all posters of the history of the Festival see the Festival's website. San Sebastian Festival, <http://www.sansebastianfestival.com/es/>.
81. 'Ha muerto Manuel de Echarri organizador del Festival de Cine de San Sebastián', *El País*, 4 July 1978, <http://elpais.com/diario/1978/07/04/cultura/268351202_850215.html>.
82. Echarri was described by Herrero Velarde as a bit disorganized and chaotic; Echarri liked to touch on various topics but did not really go into any of them in much depth. Interview with Herrero Velarde.
83. Galán, *Historia del Zinemaldia* (1953–2010) DVD.
84. Tuduri, *San Sebastián: Un festival, una historia. (1967–1977)*, p. 333.
85. Tuduri, *San Sebastián: Un festival, una historia. (1967–1977)*, p. 351.
86. For an in-depth study of the 23-F see Javier Cercas, *The Anatomy of a Moment*, trans. by Anne McLean (Bloomsbury: London, 2011), originally published in Spanish in 2009.
87. Galán, *Historia del Zinemaldia* (1953–2010) DVD.
88. For an in-depth study of Almodóvar's outsider status regarding the EOC, see Núria Triana-Toribio, *Spanish Film Cultures: The Making and Unmaking of Spanish Cinema* (London: BFI Palgrave, 2016).
89. Galán, *Pilar Miró: nadie me enseñó a vivir*, p. 214.
90. The Ley Miró is covered in historical accounts of Spanish cinema; see for example *A Companion to Spanish Cinema*, ed. by Jo Labanyi and Tatjana Pavlović (Oxford: Wiley-Blackwell, 2013) and *The European Cinema Reader*, ed. by Catherine Fowler (London: Routledge, 2002). For more information and opposing opinions on the law (with the benefit of historical hindsight) see Javier Aguirre, 'Sobre la 'ley Miró'', *El País*, 26 December 1984, <http://elpais.com/diario/1984/12/26/cultura/472863601_850215.html>; Alberto Leal, 'La nueva Ley del Cine', *Mundo Obrero*, 28 February 2007, <http://www.mundoobrero.es/pl.php?id=528&sec=6>; blog posts on Pasadizo.com, <http://www.pasadizo.com/foros/viewtopic.php?t=3483&highlight=pilar+mir%F3>.
91. Mar Diestro-Dópido, 'Women Film Writers Wall of Inspiration', *Sight & Sound Online*, n.d., <https://www.bfi.org.uk/news-opinion/sight-sound-magazine/comment/women-film-critics-inspirations> [accessed 25 May 2020].
92. Redacción, 'TVE patrocina el Festival de San Sebastián hasta 2007', *El País*, 20 July 2005, <http://elpais.com/diario/2005/07/20/radiotv/1121810401_850215.html>.
93. Europa Press, 'El Festival internacional de San Sebastián ve reducida su aportación pública en 225.000 euros este año', *teinteresa.es*, 7 May 2012, <http://www.teinteresa.es/pais-vasco/gipuzcoa/Festival-Internacional-San-Sebastian-aportacion_0_695931324.html>.
94. Interview with Rebordinos.
95. José Luis Barbería, 'El Festival de cine de San Sebastián vive su mayor crisis tras rechazar a Erquicia como director', *El País*, 28 March 1985, <http://elpais.com/diario/1985/03/28/cultura/480812410_850215.html>; and José Luis Barbería, 'El Festival de cine de San Sebastián quiere volver a la altura de Cannes y Berlín', *El País*, 13 May 1985, <http://elpais.com/diario/1985/05/13/cultura/484783206_850215.html>.
96. For more information on the Vertical Syndicates see, Glicerio Sánchez Recio, 'El Sindicato Vertical como instrumento politico y económico del régime franquista', in *Instituciones y sociedad en el franquismo*, special issue of the *Revista de Historia Contemporánea*, 1 (2002), <https://dialnet.unirioja.es/servlet/articulo?codigo=259677> [accessed 25 May 2020].
97. Diego Galán, *Jack Lemmon nunca cenó aquí* (Madrid: Plaza & Janés, 2001), p. 176.
98. Interview with Galán.
99. Maruja Torres, 'Los problemas presupuestarios y de organización hacen reconsiderar a Luis Gasca su continuidad como director del certamen', in *El País*, 22 September 1983, <http://elpais.com/diario/1983/09/22/cultura/433029605_850215.html>.

100. For a full list see the San Sebastián Film Festival official website, <http://www.sansebastianfestival.com/in/indice.php?ap=2>.
101. Interview with Olaciregui.
102. Juan Antonio Pérez Millán, 'De la Filmoteca Nacional al florecimiento de las Autonómicas', in *Filmoteca Española. Cincuenta años de historia (1953–2003)*, ed. by Antonio Santamarina (Madrid: Filmoteca Española/I.C.A.A./Ministerio de Cultura, 2005), pp. 66–82 (p. 73).
103. Interview with Galán.
104. Interview with José María de Orbe.
105. *Anexo 4. Catálogo de Publicaciones*, ed. by Antonio Santamarina (Madrid: Filmoteca Española/I.C.A.A./Ministerio de Cultura, 2005), p. 221.
106. Miguel Marías, 'Las misiones de una Filmoteca y su futuro', in *Filmoteca Española. Cincuenta años de historia (1953–2003)*, ed. by Antonio Santamarina (Madrid: Filmoteca Española/I.C.A.A./Ministerio de Cultura, 2005), pp. 83–100.
107. Interview with Olaciregui.
108. Juan Antonio Pérez Millán, 'De la Filmoteca Nacional al florecimiento de las Autonómicas', p. 74.
109. Pérez Millán, 'De la Filmoteca Nacional al florecimiento de las Autonómicas', pp. 69–70.
110. Franco, *Bienvenido Mister Cagada*, pp. 189–200.
111. Santamarina, *Anexo 4. Catálogo de Publicaciones*, pp. 176–77.
112. Santamarina, *Anexo 4. Catálogo de Publicaciones*, p. 149.
113. Pérez Millán, 'De la Filmoteca Nacional al florecimiento de las Autonómicas', p. 75.
114. Pérez Millán, 'De la Filmoteca Nacional al florecimiento de las Autonómicas', pp. 77–79.
115. Interview with Marías.
116. Interview with Marías.
117. Galán, *Historia del Zinemaldia (1953–2010)* DVD.
118. Andrei Plakhov interview with the author at the London Russian Film Festival offices on 13 December 2011.
119. Interview with Olaciregui.
120. Interview with Olaciregui.
121. Directed by Néstor Basterretxea and Fernando Larruquert, it was the first Basque film (in this case documentary) ever to be screened at the Festival, albeit outside competition, in 1968. The film's experimental form deals with cultural and ideological elements of the Basque country.
122. For more details see, Mar Diestro-Dópido, 'Chaos Theories', *Vertigo*, 3, 8 (2008), <http://www.closeupfilmcentre.com/vertigo_magazine/volume-3-issue-8-winter-2008/chaos-theories/>.
123. José Eduardo Arenas, 'Del Castillo dice que "La pelota vasca" sitúa al Gobierno y a ETA al mismo nivel', *ABC*, 19 September 2003, <http://www.abc.es/hemeroteca/historico-19-09-2003/abc/Espectaculos/del-castillo-dice-que-la-pelota-vasca-situa-al-gobierno-y-a-eta-al-mismo-nivel_208450.html>.
124. Interview with Olaciregui.
125. Interview with Olaciregui.
126. Interview with Galán.
127. Interview with Heredero.
128. Interview with Pena.
129. Diestro-Dópido, 'From Buñuel to Lorca'.
130. Key Spanish websites include: Tren de Sombras, <http://www.trendesombras.com/>; Miradas de cine <https://miradasdecine.es>; Lumière, <http://www.elumiere.net/>; Transit: cine y otros desvíos, <http://cinentransit.com/>; and Letras de cine, <http://letrasdecine.blogspot.com/> [all accessed 25 May 2020].
131. The Spanish state TV channel founded on 28 October 1956.
132. Instituto de la Cinematografía y de las Artes Visuales/Institute of Cinematography and Visual Arts, an autonomous body within the Ministry of Culture, albeit exclusively financed from Government funds, set up in 1986. For more information see the official website: 'Cine y audiovisuales', *Gobierno de España: Ministerio de Cultura y Deporte*, <http://www.mecd.gob.es/cultura-mecd/areas-cultura/cine/inicio.html;jsessionid=BD1E9E7C75A0028E07EA19D1173C1F02>.

133. Interview with Galán.
134. Rocío García, 'Cineastas contra la Orden', *El País*, 17 August 2009, <http://www.elpais.com/articulo/revista/agosto/Cineastas/Orden/elpeputec/20090807elpepirdv_8/Tes>.
135. Rocío García, 'Cineastas contra la Orden', and G. Belinchón, R. García, 'Conmoción en el mundo del cine por la decisión de Bruselas de bloquear las ayudas a rodajes', *El País*, 25 November 2009, <http://www.elpais.com/articulo/cultura/Conmocion/mundo/cine/decision/Bruselas/bloquear/ayudas/rodajes/elpepucul/20091125elpepucul_1/Tes>.
136. Quoted in Rubén Romero, '"El cine español tiene ágoras y peliculitas." Ignasi Guardans tranquiliza a los productores en Sitges', *Público*, 7 October 2009, <http://www.publico.es/culturas/258459/el-cine-espanol-tiene-agoras-y-peliculitas>.
137. G. Belinchón/R. García, 'Conmoción en el mundo del cine por la decisión de Bruselas de bloquear las ayudas a rodajes', *El País*, 25 November 2009, <http://cultura.elpais.com/cultura/2009/11/25/actualidad/1259103601_850215.html>.
138. Rocío García, 'Susana de la Sierra dimite como directora general del ICAA. El Consejo de Ministros nombra a Lorena González como su sustituta en el cargo, *El País*, 17 July 2014, <http://cultura.elpais.com/cultura/2014/07/17/actualidad/1405622273_541843.html>.
139. G. Belinchón/R. García, 'Conmoción en el mundo del cine por la decisión de Bruselas de bloquear las ayudas a rodajes', *El País*, 25 November 2009, <http://cultura.elpais.com/cultura/2009/11/25/actualidad/1259103601_850215.html>.
140. Quoted in R.G/G.B, 'Mikel Olaciregui: "Me voy sin nostalgia"', *El País*, 23 September 2010, <http://cultura.elpais.com/cultura/2010/09/25/actualidad/1285365603_850215.html>.
141. Quoted in R.G./G.B., 'Mikel Olaciregui: "Me voy sin nostalgia"'.
142. In a video blog broadcast on *El País* website on 23 September 2010, Boyero made the following comments on Orbe's *Aitá*: 'I've seen a thing, or a film, whatever you want to call it, that is produced by a certain Luis Miñarro — whose name should prompt you to run away as soon as you see it — called *Aitá*, which is considerable nonsense. It is the prototype of the fake, impostor cinema that enjoys such good press amongst four trendies, and I guess it's justified because it's Basque. This thing called *Aitá* is the most indecent film I've seen at this Festival', <http://cultura.elpais.com/cultura/2010/09/23/videos/1285192803_870215.html>.
143. Carlos Boyero, 'Irreprochable Concha de Oro al Spielberg Chino', *El País*, 27 September 2009, <http://elpais.com/diario/2009/09/27/cultura/1254002403_850215.html>.
144. Agencia Efe, 'Javier Rebollo "Este premio demuestra que hay otro tipo de cine español"', *ABC*, 26 September 2009, <http://www.abc.es/hemeroteca/historico-26-09-2009/abc/Cultura/javier-rebollo-este-premio-demuestra-que-hay-otro-tipo-de-cine-español_103161447234.html>.
145. Provisional data used from 1 January to 30 June 2011. The data is compiled from the information received until now from the companies in charge of exhibition centres, and published on the website of the Ministry of Culture, Education and Sports. Final data available at: <http://www.culturaydeporte.gob.es/dam/jcr:d5478863-2767-4f62-a20f-fed78b0b1724/24-rec-espec-nacionalidad.pdf> [accessed 25 May 2020].
146. Interview with Pena.
147. El País/Agencias, 'El partido de Cascos destituye al director del Festival de Cine de Gijón', *El País*, 11 January 2012, <http://cultura.elpais.com/cultura/2012/01/11/actualidad/1326236404_850215.html>; José Luis Cienfuegos's Open Letter (echoing those of Di Tella, p. 99 and Peña, p. 108 regarding BAFICI), 12 January 2012, <http://www.filmin.es/blog/carta-abierta-de-jose-luis-cienfuegos>.
148. For more information see San Sebastián Festival, <http://www.sansebastianfestival.com/in/pagina.php?ap=4&id=2025>.
149. Interview with Olaciregui.
150. Tamara L. Falicov, 'Migrating from South to North: The Role of Film Festivals in Funding and Shaping Global South Film and Video', in *Locating Migrating Media*, ed. by Greg Elmer, Charles H. Davis, Janine Marchessault and John McCullough (Lanham, MD: Lexington Books, 2010), pp. 3–22 (p. 15).
151. Falicov, 'Migrating from South to North: The Role of Film Festivals in Funding and Shaping Global South Film and Video', p. 4.

152. Interview with Olaciregui.
153. Interview with Olaciregui.
154. Interview with Olaciregui.
155. Quoted in Odón Elorza, 'San Sebastián, de cine', *El País*, 18 September 2010, <http://www.elpais.com/articulo/pais/vasco/San/Sebastian/cine/elpepiesppvs/20100918elpvas_9/Tes>.
156. For more information see European Commission Culture website, <http://ec.europa.eu/programmes/creative-europe/index_en.htm>.
157. Geoff Pingree, 'How Easily a Feisty Film Festival Goes Glittery', *The New York Times*, 25 September 2004, <http://www.nytimes.com/2004/09/25/movies/25seba.html?_r=0>.
158. R. A., 'El impacto económico del Zinemaldia multiplica por siete la inversión pública', *El diario vasco*, 1 May 2018, <https://www.diariovasco.com/culturas/zinemaldia/impacto-economico-zinemaldia-20180501002951-ntvo.html>. For yearly breakdowns of the figures in the Statistics Reports published by the Festival, see the annual accounts published on the Transparency Portal of the Festival's website.

CHAPTER 3

❖

The BFI London Film Festival: A Public Festival of Festivals

History

- **Date founded:** 1957
- **International/National/Local context:** International Public Film Festival
- **FIAPF (category):** Recognized by FIAPF in 1958 as non-competitive. Opted out in 2010 for the 2011 edition
- **Calendar slot: Festival's place within the international film festival circuit:** October after Toronto, Vancouver, Venice and before Rome and Vienna

Infrastructure

- **Are screened films rented or offered:** Mostly invited and supported by inviting talent, hospitality, press campaign, etc.
- **Screening Venues:** 14 venues across London
- **Attendance:** 205,630 attendees[1]
- **Projection facilities and formats (aspect ratios):** All plus digital
- **Access: sign interpreted screenings and audio described screenings:** Where films have these available, usually only major release titles
- **Public/Private sector sources of funding:** DCMS Lottery money, City and Regional funding plus private sponsors. Request for percentage information was declined.[2]

Structure and staffing

- **Permanent staff:** Nine people: four of them work across the Exhibition Department on Southbank
- **Annual Budget for the festival:** Request for budget information declined (see footnote 2).
- **Ticket price:** Standard ticket price from £10.00 to £30.00 for Headline Galas; £5 tickets for 16–25 year olds. Prices are similar to the average price of a ticket in central London and slightly more expensive than tickets for the BFI Southbank.

Directors of the BFI London Film Festival

- Derek Prouse: acknowledged Programmer of the LFF's first ever edition in 1957
- David Robinson: acknowledged organizer of the 1958 edition

- James Quinn: Director of the BFI from 1955
- Between 1957 and 1963, brochures are not signed by a festival director and the programme is attributed to 'those of us who have organized' the festival
- Richard Roud: 1963–1969 Programme Director
- Ken Wlaschin: 1970–1983 Programme Director
- Derek Malcolm: 1984–1986 Director
- Sheila Whitaker 1987–1996 Director; Head of Programming at the BFI National Film Theatre (1984–1986)
- Adrian Wootton: 1997–2004 Director; Head of BFI Southbank (1993) with overall responsibility for all the BFI's public exhibition activities
- Sandra Hebron: 2003–2011 Artistic Director. Wootton and Hebron crossed for one year when Wootton was director and Hebron was Artistic Director.[3]
- Clare Stewart: 2011–2017 Head of Exhibition whose responsibilities include the role of Director of the London Film Festival, BFI
- Tricia Tuttle: 2018– Tuttle led the LFF in 2018 as interim Artistic Director and took her permanent post as Artistic Director from December 2018. The role also incorporates Flare: London's LGBTQ+ Film Festival

Introduction

There are no written accounts covering the 64-year history of the BFI London Film Festival (LFF), which is a surprise, given its size and importance. The nearest equivalent to a history of the Festival was published in 1981 to mark its first twenty-five years; a 116-page document entitled *Water Under the Bridge*, comprising two essays and a reply to one of the essays; all three amount to nineteen pages. The rest comprises a filmography including all the films screened at the LFF from 1957 to 1981. The first essay, 'Whose Festival?', written by the pamphlet editor, British film and television producer Martyn Auty, focuses predominantly on the LFF's identity and its impact on the national film scene. Auty's essay is followed by a two-page response to his comments on the LFF, written by the then director of the Festival, Ken Wlaschin and entitled 'Film Culture vs Film Makers'. The second essay, written by Wendy Dalton, entitled 'London Film Festival Economics', centres on the Festival's finances and its relationship with the British Film Institute (BFI). Yet the pamphlet's historical content is minimal. A full analysis of this document follows in the next section of this chapter, particularly its critical stance vis-à-vis the Festival's programming strategy and identity.

In 2006, to mark the fiftieth edition of the LFF, the then artistic director, Sandra Hebron, and her team commissioned a collection of three pamphlets to mark this historic milestone, edited by film programmer and writer Gareth Evans. These were not intended to be a historical celebration in any conventional sense. Instead of adopting an inward-facing view of the Festival itself, the pamphlets look outwards at the contemporary situation regarding film festivals and their audiences, and at the effects the Festival had had on filmmakers whose work it had screened. The three pamphlets focused on:

— the role of festivals internationally, entitled, 'International Visions';
— filmmakers whose work had been 'discovered' at festivals, but who had then sunk into obscurity, entitled 'Lost and Found'. This was accompanied by an NFT season featuring some of these filmmakers' work;
— audience members' experiences of attending the Festival over the years (including filmmakers as part of that cohort), entitled 'Two Weeks in Autumn'.[4]

It would not be until 2012 that the BFI as a whole had its own history recorded, in a volume published by Manchester University Press (and not, as one might have expected, by BFI/Palgrave Macmillan). The book, edited by Geoffrey Nowell-Smith and Christophe Dupin, is entitled *The British Film Institute, the Government and Film Culture, 1933–2000*. Owing to difficulties accessing archival material and historical documents — stored in no order in boxes at the BFI's archive at Berkhamsted — this AHRC-funded project took a team of three researchers from 2004 to 2008 to catalogue and digitize the archives — the book was finally completed in 2011. Nowell-Smith and Dupin's book is therefore unique, since its content — the result of extensive research — has never before been gathered and published in one volume. Nowell-Smith and Dupin's book has thus proved crucial in providing valuable context for an understanding of the history of the LFF, even if the space dedicated to it is relatively small. Finally, the only volume published on the BFI's film magazine *Sight & Sound*, to celebrate its fiftieth anniversary in 1982, summarizes the magazine's history very briefly in its seven-page introduction, and then offers a selection of articles published throughout those fifty years.[5] Unlike other film festivals' websites (BAFICI and San Sebastián, amongst many others), the LFF's does not have a section containing a summary of its history within its website, nor sections updated throughout the year where archival material — such as films, awards, events — is stored and can be consulted. Instead, the website has a 'Festival' website within the BFI's 'What's On?' section with content from the latest edition. The only two features found under the BFI umbrella website is a brief history of the Festival which was written in 2018, to mark its sixty years.[6] This is also the case with the BFI's other film festival, BFI Flare: London LGBTIQ+ Film Festival.

It is interesting to note that the LFF, Flare, *Sight & Sound* and the BFI's stance with regard to their own histories is in direct contrast to the central activity of the BFI itself, which is dedicated to the collection and preservation of Britain's cinematic heritage. For Professor Ian Christie, '[The BFI has] no history, a sense of history. It's as if it has no memory, like it has always happened at the present time. It is an institution without a memory really. But that's what the BFI, London, Britain, has sort of wanted'.[7]

In the context of this book, such an absence of a documented history reveals a marked contrast with BAFICI and the San Sebastián Film Festival. In Argentina and Spain, their relatively recent violent pasts have underlined the tensions between differing accounts of history, but it has also meant that the necessity to record those histories in order to be able to revisit and analyse them afterwards has never been questioned. This is reflected in the festivals' own preservation of historical accounts. BAFICI's 21-year history is documented by way of substantial amounts of literature, both on the films screened at the festival and reflections on the festival itself, a history of which was published to mark its tenth anniversary and ten years later, the book *Otoños porteños: Historias del Bafici en sus primeros 20 años* accompanied the festival's 20th anniversary; BAFICI also provided the impetus and subject for César Aira's 2011 novel *Festival*, available (together with most of the publications produced by the festival) online.[8] San Sebastián not only has a comprehensive two-volume account that covers 24 years of its 68-year history, but also numerous co-operative ventures with the Spanish Cinematheque, and there has even been a TV series covering the complete history of the Festival up until 2010.[9]

At the end of her essay in *Water Under the Bridge*, Wendy Dalton wonders where the LFF will be situated in another 25 years. In fact, although special events and celebrations took place during the Festival's fiftieth anniversary in 2006,[10] aside from the three pamphlets mentioned above there was no commemorative written document reflecting on the historical trajectory of the Festival, either funded by the organization itself or published externally. Why this lack of interest in the history and politics of the LFF? Professor Ian Christie's statement below offers some clues and hints:

> I think it's true to say the LFF has never been seen as having a strong character that you could write about. I don't mean that necessarily in a completely negative way, although it sounds negative. Ken Wlaschin, who was LFF artistic director for a long time, said once that his job was like being a traffic policeman — bringing things in, in an orderly fashion, and getting them shown. He [...] was saying it perhaps a little defensively, but I think he expressed it absolutely accurately. [...] But that's just the international menu being brought to London for those lucky enough to be able to get in to see them. Why would you write about that, because there isn't a strong editorial line, and in fact a strong editorial line wasn't wanted. If a festival director [...] said, I'm not going to show that, [...] I'm going to show this, the questions from all sides would be: Why? Who told you it's your job to choose? So it'd be very hard to write about.[11]

And yet, as former artistic director of the Festival Sandra Hebron argues, an editorial stance is implied and articulated, by virtue of selecting certain films and rejecting many others.[12] I would also add that there is an implied hierarchy in the organization of the programme, i.e. the section where a film is placed, the order in which the sections are placed in the brochure, and the allocation of galas amongst others. Nevertheless, Christie's particular criticism, generally focused on the Festival's origins, is one that has recurred over the years, and is echoed later in this chapter by Matthew Flanagan, Tony Rayns, and Nowell-Smith. Yet, for Gilbert Adair writing in 1981, the breadth and variety of the Festival can be a positive thing:

> A critic, briefed to 'cover' an event as indiscriminately eclectic as the LFF has become, can't be blamed for endeavouring to impose a modicum of cohesion on his material, at however great a risk of violence to the overall 'incoherence' (a word I do not necessarily use in a pejorative sense).[13]

The positive 'incoherence' to which Adair refers somehow compels the attendee to adopt a more active role at the festival, as it gives the festivalgoer a certain freedom

FIG. 3.1. Third London Film Festival, 1959
© BFI Archive

to discover and create their own festival — an idea I too alighted upon in my own coverage of the 2012 edition.[14]

I do not propose to provide a detailed historical account of the LFF, but rather to explore key issues that have recurred throughout the Festival's history in order to try to answer Wendy Dalton's aforementioned question. I will therefore look at how the Festival developed and changed in the years after she wrote her piece in 1981, by exploring its origins, its relationship with British cinema, the tensions between the Festival's approach to education and its focus on industry, and its relationship with the BFI and the UK Film Council (UKFC). My study of the LFF is based primarily on the (limited) literature produced by the Festival, which principally consists of annual programme introductions written by the LFF directors themselves, and brochures that have accompanied the Festival at certain junctures such as the twenty-fifth and fiftieth anniversaries, all stored and accessible at the BFI Reuben Library; as well as extensive interviews with former LFF Artistic Director Sandra Hebron (2003–2011[15]), historian and former Head of Education at the BFI Geoffrey Nowell-Smith,[16] film scholar and former BFI staff member, Professor Ian Christie[17] and on and off LFF programmer from 1977 to 2013, Tony Rayns.[18]

The rationale for choosing these four interviewees was as follows. Hebron, as well as being a co-supervisor of the PhD this book is based on, is a recent longstanding director of the Festival. Rayns is both longstanding and arguably the LFF's most influential programmer, covering a vast geographical territory. Nowell-Smith held several elevated positions at the BFI and has written the only book ever published on the BFI's history. Ian Christie, as well as holding high offices in the BFI at various junctures, is a London-based film historian of international repute. Together, these four interviewees represent varied authoritative perspectives on the Festival, both insider and outsider (although the latter still BFI-associated).

Once Upon a Time. The LFF's Origins

As indicated by its official title, the London Film Festival (it was rechristened BFI London Film Festival in 2007 as part of a BFI-wide rebranding designed to raise awareness of all events and activities under its umbrella) sits within a broader group of organizations/departments in the British Film Institute (BFI), a governmental organization founded in 1933 and granted a Royal Charter on 18 July 1983.[19] The BFI's inception took place at a time when film — as the former controller of the NFT Leslie Hardcastle recalls — was 'not taken seriously; you could count film books and journals on one hand and outdated silent films were being thrown away in their hundreds.'[20] For Hardcastle, the arrival of the BFI was like 'coming over the Appalachians in a covered wagon', as, he explains.

> In those days [...] what we were doing was unheard of. Twelve years after the War, we suddenly had something called a 'Film Festival', showing films from Poland, Japan, France, and all in the face of a fundamentally hostile film industry. We were very proud of ourselves.[21]

It is therefore unsurprising that the BFI's educational remit did not sit comfortably at first in the midst of a highly censored film scene in the UK. In 1912, The British

Board of Film Censors (BBFC) had been established by the film industry itself owing to distributors' fear of censorship by local authorities. The BBFC's remit stated that 'No film will be passed that is not clean and wholesome and absolutely above suspicion'. Films are given either 'U' (for universal exhibition) or 'A' (more suitable for adults) certificates. Although the BBFC has no legal powers to censor films, its advice is largely still followed by local authorities, which have the power to withdraw cinema licenses. The BBFC was at the peak of its powers in 1933, a year in which the board objected to a record 504 films out of the 1,713 submissions.[22] As Geoffrey Nowell-Smith explains, the BFI was far from welcomed by the film trade at the time:

> The BFI was founded mainly by people who believed in film as an instrument for education, and the film trade was very worried about this organization. So when it was set up with Government approval, it was restricted in what it could do. It was not supposed to involve itself in any matters affecting the trade; because I think that was mainly what the trade was concerned about — that they were a load of busybodies who worked in education who might want to interfere in censorship. That was a heavily censored period already, but they thought it might be even more censorious if there was a government body that could interfere.[23]

Regardless, the BFI gradually became bigger and commenced its central activity, the establishment of an archive, in 1935, which necessitated, as Nowell-Smith notes, 'quite a lot of cooperation from the trade'[24] for the collection of the films. It also took over the film magazine *Sight and Sound*[25] — originally published by the British Institute of Adult Education — starting with its 1934 Spring edition. The BFI's National Film Library (later renamed National Film and Television Archive and currently known as the BFI National Film Archive) was set up a year later, in 1935, and was originally run by Ernest Lindgren, its first curator and an instrumental figure (together with his French contemporary and arch-foe[26] Henri Langlois, co-founder of the Cinémathèque Française) in the establishment of an international network of archivists and cinephiles.

Yet the BFI did not start screening films until 1952, when former Chairman of Granada TV Denis Forman — appointed Director of the BFI in 1948 (1948–1955) — managed to secure one of the exhibition buildings of the Festival of Britain celebrations in 1951 for the BFI. Inaugurated by King George VI, the Festival of Britain was organized to mark the centenary of the Great Exhibition of 1851, and was intended to demonstrate Britain's contribution to civilization, past, present, and future, in the arts, science and technology, and industrial design.[27]

Once this first edition of the Festival had ended, the then Labour government planned to demolish the South Bank (one of the areas in which the Festival of Britain had taken place), including a temporary cinema building known as the Telekinema,[28] where all the latest technical experiments in the moving image took place. A four hundred-seat state-of-the-art cinema, it had the necessary technology to screen both films (including 3D films[29]) and large-screen projected television.[30] But this cinema was used by so many people during the exhibition that the London County Council (LCC) supported the building of a permanent structure. With extra help from the Government and the film trade, Forman turned this building into a prototype of the National Film Theatre, otherwise known as the NFT — which, as Hardcastle explains, was built under the arches of Waterloo Bridge because it was cheaper, since 'the builders could work there even during bad winter weather'.[31]

In 1957 the present NFT building (rechristened BFI Southbank in 2007[32]) was completed and inaugurated by Princess Margaret, also marking the beginning of the London Film Festival itself, which opened the next day, 16 October, showing fifteen features from thirteen different countries over the course of eleven days. Among these titles were Federico Fellini's *Nights of Cabiria* (1957), René Clair's *Porte des Lilas* (1957), Leopoldo Torre Nilsson's *La casa del ángel/The House of the Angel* (1956), Akira Kurosawa's *Throne of Blood* (1956) and Satyajit Ray's *The Unvanquished* (1956).

Wendy Dalton explains the early financing of the LFF:

> The costs were underwritten by the *Sunday Times*[33] and a total of fifteen films were screened — none of them British, which caused much outraged press comment at the time [...]. Ticket prices ranged from three to seven shillings [equivalent of £3–7 today].[34] In the second year, the London County Council took over sponsorship of the Festival and subsequently the emphasis shifted to a budgetary break-even requirement i.e. ticket sales plus LCC/GLC Grant had to cover the operating costs of the Festival.[35]

Arguably the most important and influential aspect of the renovation of world cinema exhibition in London brought to pass by the BFI was its workforce. As Nowell-Smith explains, Forman surrounded himself with a group of young people, amongst them Penelope Houston, who in 1947 was editor of the influential film magazine *Sequence*, founded by Gavin Lambert, Lindsay Anderson and Karel Reisz in 1947 (and published up until 1952) at Oxford University. Lambert would become editor of *Sight & Sound* from 1949 to 1956 (Houston then took over the position, remaining editor until 1990), and Karel Reisz became programmer of the NFT. *Sight & Sound*, which had been reduced to half its size after the War, became more widely read as a result of the expansion of BFI membership, one category of which included a subscription to the magazine. Nowell-Smith recalls:

> The increase [in memberships] reached a high point of 34,000 people with the NFT-type membership and 15,000 with the *Sight & Sound*-type membership. This was already achieved by Denis Forman in 1949–50, and it represented a complete renovation of the BFI. The only thing that didn't change [its structure] yet continued to grow is the archive, which was overseen by the same curator who arrived in 1934 and stayed there until 1971–1972, Ernest Lindgren. So, really, Lindgren and Forman are the creators of the BFI, greatly helped by [Lambert] the editor of *Sight & Sound*.[36]

The appetite for a more specialized kind of cinema in London had therefore been stoked, not only for archival material, but also for those films that generally could only be seen at festivals by professionals. Showing these latter films would constitute an avowed aim of the LFF, as explained by Austro-Hungarian émigré filmmaker G. M. Hoellering, a former colleague of Brecht[37] and the Managing Director of the Academy of Cinema, in his welcoming note in the Festival's first ever brochure:

It has long been a matter of regret that the audience at the great internation [sic] film festivals is largely restricted to members of the press and the film trade. Inevitably, the ordinary, intelligent cinema-goer, who has been taking an increasing interest in what goes on at these festivals, feels out of things [...]. It is therefore an excellent thing for London that the London Film Festival is now giving a normal [sic] audience the chance of attending a festival of the cream of festival films [...].

We at the Academy have always tried to bring to London films from all over the world, as soon as they become available, and we feel that the London Film Festival will be a stimulus from which both we and our audience will benefit.

We hope, finally, that the organizers of this Festival will not overlook those fresh, experimental works of the international free cinema which are of such signal importance for the development of the art of film, and which even at the great international festivals don't always receive the attention they deserve.[38]

It is worth noting that, from the outset, in the brochure published for the Festival's first edition in 1957, aside from the more obvious information accompanying the films — such as the name of their director, the year of production (not all were made in the same year), their country of origin (WWII had shaken national identities and boundaries less than a decade previously) — each film was accompanied not only by their respective prizes but also the precise international film festival that had awarded them. This was the basis for the Festival describing itself as a 'Festival of Festivals', which of course constituted an exercise in self-promotion.

Later in this chapter I will examine in greater detail the phrase 'Festival of Festivals' — which was applied to the LFF right from its inception — and the debate it generated when the Festival was still formulating its own identity in its early days. But by giving equal importance to the film, the director and the festival where it was awarded, the LFF was already selling itself not only as the platform for difficult-to-see films from around the world, but also as an event where the films had accrued cultural capital as opposed to being straightforwardly commercial. The Festival's aim was to screen to 'English audiences the Grand Prize winner from every major film festival held during the past 12 months, including Cannes, Berlin, Moscow, San Sebastián, Locarno, Tehran, San Remo and Lisbon'.[39]

In that sense, the films themselves trailed the glamour of the festivals where they had been awarded, as well as the exoticism of the (often remote) countries where they were made, an exoticism that could also be ideological (for example, films from 'behind the Iron Curtain', such as USSR and Poland). Also implicit in the Festival of Festivals appellation is a cosy pact between programmers and audiences, where the latter is congratulated on the 'excellence' of its taste. It is important to remember that NFT members constituted the majority of the LFF's audience, as they had (and still have) priority for buying tickets for a rather limited (then three hundred-seat) NFT1 auditorium where the films at the Festival were screened. This somewhat 'elitist' approach to cinema would be heavily contested during the 1960s and '70s, underlining the LFF's most defining trait: the constant dialectic between the Festival's cultural status and its value as a commercial event, as I will discuss later.

After those early days during the first decade when the programme was kept relatively small, the Festival started to grow rapidly, becoming more varied in

FIG. 3.2. LFF Team 1994, with Sheila Whitaker at the wheel of a London black cab
© BFI Archive

the process in terms of countries of origin, and with more sections, more genres and more invited guests. But most importantly, a new screening room, NFT2, was inaugurated in 1970, which helped increase the number of invited films from twenty-eight in 1970 to forty-five in 1971. This also increased the cost of the Festival, as Wendy Dalton explained in 1981:

> Originally budgeted to cost some £16,000 that year [1970], and to earn the same amount, in fact it cost £23,000 and earned £22,000: a shortfall of £1,000. From that year on [1971], the NFT commenced supporting the London Film Festival from its DES Grant and the break-even requirement ceased.[40]

By 1989, under Sheila Whitaker, screenings were held in the mornings, afternoons, evenings and some late nights — albeit always careful to respect the strict limitations imposed by FIAPF[41] on the number of screenings per film — but despite that the LFF still had no full-time staff. (FIAPF recognized the Festival as an official event in its second year, although the Festival opted out of membership from the 2011 edition onwards, maintaining that the accreditation did not represent value for money; it should be noted that there don't appear to have been any negative consequences in the wake of this decision.[42]) Films came free of rental charge and by 1972 (two years after the extra screen, NFT2, was inaugurated) the number of films had rocketed from the original fifteen to fifty — a special mention of this year as 'the largest since its inception' is made in the Festival's brochure by its director Ken Wlaschin. The LFF almost doubled its size during the following decade to a total of ninety features for its twenty-fifth anniversary in 1981, and has been showing an average of two to three hundred films at each edition during the last decade.

The LFF and British Cinema

One of the main focuses of Chapters 1 and 2 of this book was the differing historical contexts in which BAFICI and San Sebastián developed. This has been attempted not only through historical accounts, but also with respect to questions of national identity and in particular the festivals' active relationships with their national/regional cinema. In the case of BAFICI, it was the emergence of the New Argentine Cinema that somehow defined the festival and, in a way, helped it to establish itself as an international event. At its outset the festival benefited greatly from the attention and awards that the new generation of Argentine filmmakers was garnering at other film festivals all over the world. In the case of San Sebastián, similarly the emergence of a new (and, given the strict censorship under Franco's dictatorship, highly unlikely) cinema of political engagement, led the government to endorse it, since it too could benefit from the international attention it received, using it to promote an image of Spain as a benign dictatorship. The location of this festival in the Basque Country triggered questions concerning national and regional matters, as well as the festival's promotion of the cinema produced in Spain and the Basque Country.

In the case of the LFF, at first glance the Festival's relationship with British cinema does not seem one of its defining traits. After all, the films programmed have been defined, right from the Festival's origins, by a stance of looking outwards rather than inwards, i.e. it was always about bringing films from outside the UK to British audiences. A small detour is required here to note how the LFF 'audience' is principally referred to as English rather than British or London-based in programme catalogues up until 1976, particularly under the direction of Ken Wlaschin — who incidentally, was American, as was Richard Roud — as exemplified by his previously mentioned quote from 1975.[43] What's more, as I have already noted, NFT programmer Derek Prouse's first ever selection for the Festival did not include a single British film among the fifteen selected, for which it was highly criticized, as Dalton recalls in her essay[44] — one of the drawbacks of building a programme on the 'awarded' films of other festivals if none of them are British.

Yet, as discussed in the introduction to this chapter, the origins of the LFF are intrinsically linked to the Festival of Britain, described by Roy Strong as 'a great reawakening of the arts after years of privation'.[45] This Festival was in part an attempt to enhance the UK's powers of recovery after WWII, a bid to restore the country's status in the international realm, even if the reality was one of an economy on its knees after the wartime struggle. The war was the main catalyst of decolonization; as a result, Britain lost its colonies in Africa, and acceded to the Indian independence movement.[46] Britain's withdrawal from India took place in 1947. At home, the shattered British economy had become overshadowed after WWII by the United States and the Soviet Union, a fact that did not stop the incoming Labour government from embarking on an extensive and expensive programme of social reform.

After the war, British cinema followed a similar trajectory to the rest of the country's economy. The high standing of studio-related figures of the 1950s such as Michael Powell, David Lean and Carol Reed gradually gave way to a new, more diverse situation (including the closing down of both Ealing and London Films studios), that incorporated the likes of the Bond franchise and the Beatle's films, the *Carry On* series, as well as a younger generation of filmmakers such as Nicolas Roeg and Donald Cammell who famously collaborated on *Performance* (1970). The majority of these films were attached to and celebrated a certain version of Britishness that peaked in psychedelic Swinging London, and which attracted international directors such as Roman Polanski and Michelangelo Antonioni to make films in the UK.

Although during the 1950s and '60s there were British films included in the Festival programme, it is not until 1974 that the then Festival director, Ken Wlaschin (1970–1976) makes a direct mention of the flowering of new British films of less commercial and more independent provenance. For the first time in the director's introductory blurb to the Festival's brochure, there is a special mention of two new British filmmakers (space normally dedicated exclusively to renowned international figures such as Robert Bresson, Jacques Tati, Orson Welles, Rainer Werner Fassbinder, Alain Resnais, Jacques Rivette, etc.), highlighted among the total of fifty films and seventy shorts screened at that edition — even if both these directors are practically unknown nowadays:

> The LFF is particularly pleased to be able to present two new British directors as well. Michael Joyce made his delightful *Nice Try* totally independently with an almost unbelievable budget of only £3000, while Peter K. Smith's powerful *A Private Enterprise* was financed by the British film [sic] Institute's Production Board.[47]

It is important to note that in his introduction Wlaschin also includes a mention of the British Film Institute's Production Board. Created on a shoe-string budget in 1952 as the Experimental Film Fund, it was renamed and revamped in 1964 as the BFI Production Board, and, more importantly, its budget was further boosted at the beginning of the 1970s, as Michael Brooke, film-critic and co-creator of BFI Screenonline explains:

> In 1971–1972 the Production Board received a substantial increase in its funding, thanks to a large increase in the BFI's government grant, and income from the Eady levy (which ploughed a percentage of ticket sales back into the industry). Some of this money was specifically intended for the BFI to fund low-budget feature-length films on a regular basis.[48]

During its life the Production Board was responsible for funding the work of now established British filmmakers such as the late Bill Douglas, Terence Davies, Peter Greenaway and Sally Potter. As an aside, following the election of Tony Blair as Labour Prime Minister in 1997, the BFI Production Board was abolished in 2000 and its function absorbed into the newly-created UK Film Council — itself abolished in 2011 after Tory re-election and re-merged with the BFI as discussed further on in this chapter.

Turning attention back to the 1970s, this resurgence of younger (predominantly left-leaning) and more independent British talent backed by the BFI would figure greatly in the Festival's programme the following year, 1975. Not only did two British films open the Festival — Kevin Brownlow and Andrew Mollo's *Winstanley* (1975), and David Gladwell's *Requiem for a Village* (1975) — but in the same year, Wlaschin dedicated two thirds of his programme introduction to the new British cinema, as well as the role that BFI production played in its flourishing:

> For the first time ever the LFF is able to offer during its opening week seven complete programmes of independent new British films. [...] Some of them could be considered heirs of the short-lived Free Cinema, the British documentary movement of the 1950s which produced such outstanding directors as Lindsay Anderson and Karel Reisz.
> [...]
> Perhaps it is worth re-stressing the fact that the BFI itself produced four of these films under the guidance of Production Board head Barrie Gavin (and his predecessor Mamoun Hassan) with only minimal funds. If the British film industry is to grow strong again, perhaps the revival will come through such (ultimately) governmental funding.[49]

Wlaschin continues the theme in his 1977 programme introduction, this time with a greater sense of urgency and a plea for more funding directed toward the national industry. At the same time, Wlaschin's insistence on the approachability of these films should be noted: i.e. they're not only for 'buffs':

> The British Independent Cinema may be alive and well and growing but it certainly hasn't been over-watered. All of these films have tiny budgets and most of the features were made for only a few thousand pounds. Infinitesimal amounts by industry standards. Given a little more financial moisture, these directors could create a new wave, British style. It's only money that's needed: witness the startling recent revivals of the Australian and German cinemas after government help was given. Also one should point out that the films featured in these programmes are in no way intended only for cinema buffs and the experimentally minded.[50]

Particularly relevant here is the outspoken, non-conformist character of the programme notes in the Festival catalogue, soon to be replaced by a blander, more ingratiating and PR-driven mode of address as the Festival moved beyond the politicized 1970s era. The tone of the Director's catalogue introductions become more emollient and inclusive, as for instance during Sheila Whitaker's tenure (1987–1996), tending to focus exclusively on promoting the contents of the Festival, and that's generally how they have remained ever since.

The escalating economic and social unrest in the UK culminated in the Winter of Discontent only a year later in 1978. The effect on the Festival was a reduction from twenty-one days (long by any standard[51]) to sixteen the following year, with Wlaschin complaining in that year's brochure about the level of economic support given by the Government to the Festival. By 1979, British cinema had become New British Cinema with capitals, attempting to put it on a par with previous Australian, German and French new waves.

For Christie the relation between the BFI and a certain sector of British cinema has always been far from straightforward:

> The BFI has always had a very edgy and very complex relationship with British cinema. It's been anti-mainstream British cinema for most of its career, and very much influenced by the rise of the new independent film culture, some of which of course came from Britain. Bill Douglas was pretty much a creation of the BFI through its backing for his films. And Bill Douglas picked up if you will from where Humphrey Jennings left off. The BFI was always on the side of the Humphrey Jennings strand, and the Free Cinema strand and then the Bill Douglas strand. And then, I think it began to get complicated. Essentially at the end of the 1970s, because there were other elements appearing in British film culture that didn't really belong to the BFI, there was a kind of confusing situation. The BFI had quite a conflicted relationship with the rise of gay cinema, it didn't back *Nighthawks* [1978], it didn't back Jarman, at least not until I came onto the production board with the mission to reconnect with Jarman; which we did, with *Caravaggio* [1986]. But before that people like Derek [Jarman] were pretty much pushed aside and ignored by the BFI.[52]

The LFF, on the other hand, was welcoming British cinema back with open arms in 1982, the year after its own twenty-fifth anniversary. Wlaschin described the national scene as a renaissance, partly aided by the newly established Channel 4 and its investment in local and regional talent through the creation of the franchised workshops (which lasted until 1990[53]). The presence of Channel 4 also meant a dramatic expansion in the kind of films that could be seen on UK TV in the 1980s, which included international cinema as well as British. The 1982 LFF edition included a total of eight Channel 4 productions — the year before the British Film Institute had celebrated its fiftieth anniversary, part of which had included activities at the LFF.

But not everyone was supportive of the LFF's endorsement of national cinema. In response to the British film feast at the Festival in 1982, film critic Richard Combs (editor of the *Monthly Film Bulletin* for seventeen years), writing for *Sight & Sound*, adopts a more critical stance:

> [T]he 26th festival came on strong with a hype of its own, about the rebirth of the British cinema. No less than four opening galas were held, 'spotlighting four separate strands of independent production', and baptising the 'New British Cinema' as confidently as its German and Australian cousins of recent years. There is a distasteful opportunism about this proclamation — not confined to the festival, there has also been a glut of flag-waving ballyhoo in the press of late — based simply on the fact that more films than usual were made in Britain in the past year. Given the diversity of aims, methods and achievements in those gala films, the all-embracing rubric seems anomalous; and given that two of the four, *The Draughtsman's Contract* and *Hero*, were made with the backing of Channel 4, whose impact on the kind of films being made in this country is as yet debatable, it is also dangerously premature.[54]

Thirty years and twenty-nine Festival editions later, there are echoes of Combs' take on the subject in director Sandra Hebron's own attitude to the LFF promoting British talent (in relation to the then recent re-incorporation of the UKFC back into the BFI):

> In my view we are an international festival but we have responsibility to showcase films from the UK — if those films are good. We've never been a festival, and we've been criticized sometimes for never being a festival, that has privileged British films over the international films. We select British films into the festival because they are good, not because they are British. But I think what you are really alluding to is the idea that the BFI now funds films, and is there an expectation that the festival will play those films? Well, if you recall, since 2009 the festival was directly funded by the Film Council, which was funding films at the time too. So the question is not a new one. And I actually remember someone from the Film Council who worked in the production bit saying about the LFF in 2009 — 'Well, now we are funding them, so they'll have to show our films'. My response was: you know what? We don't have to show your films; that's not a condition of funding. And we will show the films you funded only if they are any good.[55]

In 1997, Angus Finney did a feasibility study on the possibility of having an A-list competitive London Film Festival/Market, which would have been called the LIFFAM — London International Film Festival and Market — to be held in October (instead of November until that year). Commissioned by the British Film Institute and the Producer's Alliance for Cinema and Television, this study took place at the time Sandra Hebron was Festival Programmer under the direction of Adrian Wootton. The objective was:

> To review what developments might be made to the scope and function of the existing London Film Festival and informal film sales market in the light of representations made by industry bodies and other parties.[56]

Based on over seventy interviews with industry professionals, amongst the results, some of the highlights include an 'overwhelming support for a fully-fledged "A" grade competitive festival in London'.[57] However, the latter raised a question put by more than two-thirds of the interviewees: 'Where are these films for competition going to come from? Are there going to be enough "A" grade films for a London festival competition in November, let alone October?'[58]

But perhaps more interestingly here is the reaction of these interviewees regarding an all-British competition separate from an international competition. This proposal was 'scorned by Polygram and other distributors and sellers'[59] who were reportedly in fact 'extremely upset that none of them had been formally consulted'[60] (underlining in original).

> There was an overall rejection of a British-only competition strand in any new (or existing) London film festival. Quality will be lacking; and the UK is a notoriously poor place to launch British films. If London is to up the stakes, it needs to do it on a fully international level, rather than leading with its potentially most vulnerable foot first.[61]

The argument against a 'British only' strand was made on the grounds that the 'UK press and public have a peculiar love-hate attitude to British pictures, and that sellers in particular would do better seeing them screen in Spain, Italy and Canada than en masse in the UK'.[62] In an interview given more than twenty years later, the newly appointed Artistic Director's, Tricia Tuttle, recalls one of her first impressions when she moved to London from her original US in the late 1990s to work as a volunteer at the LFF was being 'struck by the fact that British people who worked in the industry were so negative about British cinema.'[63]

Nevertheless, in 2008 promoting the British film industry was heavily emphasized in the former UKFC's Festival Strategy and the application guidelines that UK film festivals — including the LFF — had to meet in order to receive funding. The first objective for a festival outlined in the document is as follows:

> **Objective 1**: To help ensure that, taken together, UK film festivals deliver significant economic, company, and global value for the UK film industry.[64]

A few pages later, in a section where festival values are described, the final of these values, following on from market development, company, cultural, educational and social, is global value, which is defined as follows:

> Some UK festivals have an impact on the international stage. Global value is concerned with positively representing UK culture around the world, and building partnerships with other countries. This can be achieved by international activity outside of the UK. It may range from basic coverage and awareness, to active participation and contribution.[65]

British cinema would carry on being highlighted throughout the Festival's history in the form of a section dedicated exclusively to it, as part of what became a predominantly Anglo-Saxon programme under the direction of Sheila Whitaker and, to a larger extent, under her successor, Adrian Wootton, who remains an LFF programme advisor for Italian cinema.

Previous to both, Derek Malcolm, following in Wlaschin's footsteps, carried on with the expansion of the Festival from the NFT venues to Leicester Square, the traditional location for international premieres. It was in this more accessible and media-oriented space that both Whitaker and Wootton would place English-language films, guaranteeing greater visibility for the Festival and generating more press coverage. British cinema, like French, was appointed its own separate section in the programme, (the remaining contemporary feature films were divided into European and World). In 2009, the already existing UK Film Talent Award (started in 2004) was renamed Best British Newcomer, the same year that the inaugural Star of London award — designed by sculptor Almuth Tebbenhoff[66] — was introduced. Both these awards would be given out at the Festival's first dedicated awards ceremony, which followed on the heels of the LFF being granted UKFC funding. Although not a competitive Festival at this point, the introduction of the Best Film Award helped in 'raising the international profile of the LFF' — mainly through press coverage — a buzz phrase ever since the Festival received its extra funding. Historically the LFF has given a series of awards for particular areas, like the Sutherland award [1958], a long-standing BFI award for imaginative, original filmmaking in contemporary cinema, and the documentary award [the Grierson Award, 2005]. Yet, as Hebron clarifies, 'we gave awards but we don't have a competition'; she explains:

> When the Festival was fifty years old we did a big consultation exercise with the industry and with our audiences about what they thought of the Festival and if there were things that they would change. And there was a massive chorus of people within the industry wanting a best film award — which to be quite honest, was not something that I'd ever been personally, desperately, interested in, and nor did I necessarily think that is what we needed. But there was very much a kind of request from the industry that we should do that. So I guess they spoke, and we listened.[67]

This in itself is indicative of the much greater importance that the industry has acquired on the festival circuit generally, not only at the LFF. The glamour and excitement that awards bring, and the 'international profile' it creates, as well as the media coverage, make even more apparent the LFF's ongoing dialectic, a balancing act between notions of cultural value and entertainment, arguably most evident during Sandra Hebron's tenure. By the 2011 edition, Hebron's last, the press notes heralded 'a packed industry programme' whose highlights included 'the Film London Production Finance Market, plus new initiatives to champion British filmmakers'.[68]

The award for Best British Newcomer is still running, although the LFF's programme underwent its most drastic structural change for quite some years in 2012. There has only ever been one other attempt to significantly alter its programme structure, which took place in 1979 under Wlaschin and lasted only one year. In that case, the brochure did not display separate sections, as there were no categories in the programme — referred to by Wlaschin as 'artificial 'ghettoes'' —

FIG. 3.3. Leicester Square booking office for the London Film Festival, 1991
© BFI Archive

so films were ordered alphabetically by country. The ghettoes came back by popular demand the following year. This rigid disposing of the geographical divisions that have dominated the Festival's programme for decades (European, British, French, World cinema) was once more challenged in 2012, when the Festival was overseen for the first time by Clare Stewart (the former director of the Sydney Film Festival) under the newly created role of Head of Exhibition, BFI in 2011 — a job which also incorporates the running of BFI Southbank. Stewart took over in 2012, after Sandra Hebron's resignation, which was also the third and last year of funding from the UKFC. In 2013 Stewart's role became BFI Head of Festivals, no longer programming the Southbank, and her tenure ended with the 2017's edition to embark on a yearlong sabbatical. The 2018 edition was taken over by then Deputy Tricia Tuttle, designated the Festival's Artistic Director from January 2019.

In a way this reorganization of one of the top tiers of power at the BFI, an exercise that became more commonplace after the repeated cuts to the arts introduced by the Conservative government after their election in 2010 (in coalition with the Liberal Democratic party), constitutes a step backwards in history, and arguably a restitution of the BFI's preferred mode, since it is has only been for part of the tenure of Sheila Whitaker (from 1987–1996[69]), Derek Malcolm's short period as director (1984–1986) and Sandra Hebron's tenure that the Festival has had its own separate artistic director as opposed to director or festival programmer. Prior to Whitaker's tenure, the Head of Programming at the NFT had always been the Director of the LFF. Under Clare Stewart's management, the Festival's division into strands based on nationalities was abolished — including the British one — just as Wlaschin had done in 1979 and it has remained the same under Tricia Tuttle's own directorship from 2018. This time, however, the intention was radically different. In this instance, the use of experiential pathways (love, debate, dare, laugh, thrill, journey, sonic, and from 2017, create, featuring films that 'celebrate artistic practice in all its channels and forms the electricity of the creative process, reflecting London's position as one of the world's leading creative cities') signals not only a reframing of the Festival as an event, but perhaps more significantly, as an individual experience, as opposed to something more cultural, informative, and above all, collective. The publicity campaign that accompanied the Festival in 2012 — a trailer called 'Feel It' — to some extent echoes the individualism that is increasingly reflected in our consumption of film (iPads, plasma televisions...). The trailer portrays a woman sitting on her own in an empty cinema as she experiences a wide range of emotions.[70] The logic of this within the trajectory of the Festival itself is discussed in the following sections.

The 'Festival of Festivals' Debate

Perhaps the most important and defining debate about the LFF's identity, a recurring one throughout its now sixty-four years of existence, centres on its long-held and oft-proclaimed status as a 'Festival of Festivals'.

The celebration of the first twenty-five years of the Festival in 1981 brought with it not only special events such as seminars, special screenings in collaboration with the BFI and two extra publications (including a glossy A4 version of the programme with some articles and stills from the films screened), but also, and more notably, a vigorous debate about the very identity of the Festival itself, perhaps most clearly outlined in Martyn Auty's contribution to the dossier on the first twenty-five years of the LFF entitled *Water Under the Bridge*. Published by the BFI, this dossier, far from being just a marketing tool, is highly critical of the LFF. The purpose of the dossier, as Auty explains it, was

> to present a retrospective survey, but also to take a polemical look at the Festival, paying particular attention to criticisms of its weaknesses, to anticipate new directions for the Festival, and to broach the question of the Festival's contribution to the national film culture (a notion that embraces film production, patterns of distribution and exhibition, composition of audiences, variations in the critical consensus and more general awareness).[71]

As is generally the case in the present-day LFF coverage is largely based on analysis of the films' perceived worth, rather than there being any attempt to analyse individual films in relation to their context within the Festival or the larger world, or to engage in any critical analysis of the Festival as a curatorial exercise, that would focus on the coherence or otherwise of the programme overall (except for rare exceptions — such as Matthew Flanagan's two features published in the online film journal *senses of cinema*, focusing mainly on the Experimenta section of the Festival in 2013[72] as well as his frustrations with the 2009's edition[73]).

The LFF's late position within the Festival calendar (initially November-December, and from Hebron's tenure, October, placing the Festival more squarely on the pre-awards season circuit after Cannes, Venice and Toronto) has always enabled it to select films shown and/or awarded at other international festivals in order to bring them to British audiences. Some of these films would have probably not been picked up by a distributor to be shown in the UK. In other words, either the LFF helped them find distribution and/or the Festival was the only place that they would be seen in the UK.

Derek Prouse, the person who first voiced the idea of having a Festival of Festivals in London — at the time NFT programmer — recalls the origins of the LFF (italics kept as per original):

> Strange... truth *will* out, even after twenty-five years. I imagine that nobody but Dilys Powell and myself remembers that the London Film Festival owes its birth largely to her husband, Leonard Russell, who was at the time the Literary Editor of *The Sunday Times*.
>
> I was then programme planner at the NFT and also Dilys's understudy at *The Sunday Times*. As I recall, we were all dining at their house when I raised the suggestion of a London Film Festival, a Festival of Festivals...
>
> Months went by; words from Dilys would tell me that Leonard was fighting to get the owner of *The Sunday Times*, Viscount Kemsley, to support the idea.
>
> In the end, he did. I was already covering other festivals for the newspaper, which made it easier to make contact with filmmakers. The grant from the newspaper allowed me to invite such guests as Visconti, Mastroianni, Kurosawa, René Clair to visit the Festival with their films.[74]

Limiting the size of the programme to the best of other festivals initially kept the number of films to between twenty and thirty for the first thirteen years. However, the gradual expansion of the Festival, particularly since 1970, when NFT2 opened its doors, has foregrounded the issues of selection criteria and quality. In his report, Auty reflects on the notion of quality, this slippery, difficult to measure category, describing it as some mythical standard of excellence. Yet, as he suggests:

> this quality is never defined, let alone interrogated, by its advocates, who simply assume that it may be readily recognized, understood and tacitly transmitted within the consensus of 'taste'. The extent to which these anachronistic positions (based squarely on concepts of individualism) survive and continue to be nurtured by our social institutions is a persistent problem for the film culture and for those concerned with the mediation of popular culture in its widest context.[75]

Practically every LFF brochure starts with (or at the very least contains within its blurb) the phrase 'bigger and better' and in many ways, the question of quality was clearly defined by the prize-winning status of the films offered at the Festival — which I would argue is a somehow tangible ascription of value.

However, the issue of 'quality' would soon be undercut by one of 'quantity', since the LFF was unable to get all of the awarded films it wanted from the festival circuit — some distributors would choose to bypass the Festival in order to premiere their films to the general audience, leaving a large number of slots that had to be filled. This explains why the Critics' Choice award came into being in 1980 under Wlaschin; British critics were invited to select films that they had watched in the various international festivals they had attended in order to fill in those slots. Of course, this was only a professional individual's choice, as opposed to the collective decision of a jury or a selection panel, however compromised. Bringing the prize-winning films from around the world also added an extra dimension to the Festival programme. Since readers of the more specialist film magazines would know in advance the films that had been awarded, it became a sort of guessing game which of these films the Festival organizers had managed to acquire for the programme, further highlighting the festival's innate character as an event.

It is precisely the 'eventful' quality of the Festival that most clearly demarcates the LFF from the BFI for Dalton, who correctly points out that similar, less commercial films to those shown in the Festival — if not even more avant-garde and experimental and indeed just as 'exotic' — are screened at the NFT throughout the year. And yet, these films do not attract as much attention and sense of occasion as the 'festival film' does. Being presented and screened in a festival gives a film a certain quality (even if many of them are already in general distribution by the end of the festival) by being part of the celebration of a collective event. Hebron comments on this:

> When I first came to the Festival I certainly had an anxiety about the relationship between the Festival and the BFI. Partly because the Festival had and still has a much stronger identity than the BFI. And one of the things we've done is work quite hard on people understanding that the LFF is part of the BFI. It's certainly one of the things that Anthony Minghella wanted when he

became Chair of the BFI — for the Festival and the BFI to be more closely aligned.[76]

Yet the question still remains, where do audiences go when the Festival is over? Do they return to the same venue for more of these experiences, or do they settle back into their regular film-going routines? The answer to these questions in the earlier days of the Festival was more straightforward, as the majority of the audience, as Nowell-Smith notes, was composed of NFT members in the first place. But the expansion of the Festival in later years (in number of films as much as venues) would make the influence of the Festival two-fold, as the venues themselves can constitute a discovery on the part of the viewer — particularly the NFT, located in London's Southbank. Yet, the opposite may also be true. When Hebron and her team approached VUE in Leicester Square, a chain that specializes in big blockbusters, there was a fear that this move might alienate part of the audience. Perhaps it is important to note that in 2013 another film-chain giant Cineworld's interest in expanding its target audience somehow mirrored VUE when the former acquired the UK's leading repertory-style art-house chain, Picturehouse.[77] In 2013, Cineworld Shaftesbury Avenue was the dedicated venue for Press and Industry screenings during the Festival together with the NFT. VUE and Cineworld's collaboration with the LFF illustrate one of the ways that the influence of the Festival can/may extend beyond its limited number of days. Although the Festival comes to an end, the screening facilities remain in place, acting as reminders throughout the year of the Festival itself. Regarding VUE, Hebron explains:

> VUE were very keen for us to go there because they wanted to slightly change their programming policy all year round. So they wanted to screen some of the films that we had screened in the Festival, and obviously we are still talking about films that have distributors, but they wanted to get that audience into their cinemas so they could run a slightly more adventurous programme for the rest of the year. So they obviously felt that there was some potential for that as well.[78]

Odeon West End, the main home of the LFF for years (demolished in 2015), was definitely lost in 2014 when Stewart and her team introduced a new venue for the Festival, eight hundred-seat pop up cinema, the Embankment Garden, to make up for the loss of seats. In 2018 the iconic Odeon Leicester Square, epicentre of big premieres and red carpet photo-calls was also rendered out of action due to extensive renovation work, which proved to be Tuttle's most difficult challenge. She explains:

> Last year, Leicester Square provided 35,000 in admissions, and to try to ensure that we can continue to serve audiences is really, really important. That was incredibly difficult and we ended up meeting that challenge by twinning Cineworld in Leicester Square and Embankment Garden Cinema in order to give us that sort of capacity.[79]

This not only spreads the influence of a festival beyond its limited period, but, perhaps more importantly, in the case of the LFF it further reinforces what has become (or perhaps always was) the Festival's defining trait: its (delicate) position

THE BFI LONDON FILM FESTIVAL   163

FIG. 3.4. Red carpet ready for the LFF 2019 Opening Gala, premiering
The Personal History of David Copperfield at the Odeon Leicester Square
© BFI London Film Festival Archive

negotiating between high and low-culture, popular and specialized, cinema as art and as entertainment, which by and large are not mutually exclusive. *The New Yorker*'s John Seabrook refers to 'the space between the familiar categories of high and low culture' as *nobrow*:

> In Nobrow, paintings by van Gogh and Monet are the headliners at the Bellagio Hotel while the Cirque du Soleil borrows freely from performance art in creating the Las Vegas spectacle inside. In Nobrow, artists show at K mart, museums are filled with TV screens, and the soundtrack of *Titanic* is not only a best-selling classical album but one that supports the dying classical enterprises of old-style highbrow musicians.[80]

In his report, Auty is determined that a festival should rise above the dichotomy of cinema as culture and industry, and offer something new. In his opinion, this is what the Edinburgh International Film Festival had always been able to do, reinforcing his view with a quote from Colin McArthur on the EIFF, which for both Auty and McArthur was a paragon, the 'perfect' festival:

> One thing is certain: film festivals can 'excel' or distinguish themselves by breaking out of the twin jaws of 'culture' and 'commerce' and establishing new perspectives on cinema. Edinburgh is the living proof of this argument. Writing about that festival in *Tribune* (September 1977), Colin McArthur noted: 'Its form challenges the dominant model of the cultural festival as a consumers' delight — a laying out of the exotic delicacies, the sampling of which is obligatory for the local bourgeoisie and tourists... with concomitant appeals to instant judgement and 'taste'. The form of the Edinburgh Film Festival suppresses the invitation to consume and foregrounds the invitation to produce, to engage in a pleasurable <u>work</u> process'.[81] (Underlining in original)

In the LFF's twenty-fifth anniversary brochure former director Wlaschin also points to the fact that, unlike Cannes and Venice, the Festival does not have a beach and has never been tourist-oriented, at least in the traditional sense, referring to it as 'unique' because:

> It gives no prizes, has no full-time staff [neither of which is the case today], gets most of its operating revenue from its audiences and has always been organized for cultural rather than trade or touristic reasons.
> It is not the oldest festival (Venice started in 1932), nor the biggest (Cannes has over 600 films), nor even the longest (Los Angeles lasted 22 days in 1981). It has no starlets, no beaches, no yachts and it's orientated towards neither glamour, film theory, politics nor sales.[82]

Yet the very act of 'discovering' new film cultures around the world and showing them like hunters' prey constitutes a form of tourism in itself. In his essay, Auty compares this to the colonization of 'exotic' cultures during Victorian times. This critique of the way festivals operate in regards to the 'discovery' and 'colonising' of other national cinemas precedes by over a decade the ideas of Bill Nichols',[83] considered the first attempt to disentangle the notion of the festival circuit, to be followed by Julian Stringer,[84] Thomas Elsaesser,[85] and Marijke de Valck's seminal study of the festival circuit (all discussed in the introduction),[86] as well as Azadeh Farahmand's[87] own reading of the circuit in relation to Iranian cinema. Auty reflects that:

> The fundamental question that needs posing here is what it means to 'discover' a film-maker or a national cinema. The process is both ethnocentric — an Icelandic cinema, for example, may 'not exist' for British film-goers until it has been accorded a season — and colonialist insofar as the 'unknown' film-maker is brought back from some movie safari and put on show. In this respect film festivals bear an ideological resemblance to the great Victorian exhibitions where exoticism was assimilated into the fabric of imperialist cultures.[88]

One such exhibition was the Great Exhibition that took place in Alexandra Palace, London, in 1851, whose one hundredth anniversary was commemorated by the Festival of Britain — the latter, as I noted in the introduction, was in many ways a model for the LFF itself.

Wlachin's response to Martyn Auty's comments on the LFF was also published in the celebratory dossier:

> Martyn Auty and a certain coterie of critics within the BFI associated with the Edinburgh Film Festival believe that the London Film Festival should not be like itself but like Edinburgh. [...] During the 1970s Edinburgh has grown in importance as a forum for film theorists while London has grown in importance as a festival for films. The LFF is interested in cinema, the EFF is interested in cinema culture. [...] The Auty viewpoint therefore is that film-makers are less important than the people who write about them. The LFF has been structured to promote film-makers while the EFF has been structured to promote film critics. [...] London, one could therefore argue, is of more value to the film-maker than Edinburgh. [...] To sum up: the LFF is not primarily organized for critics, theorists, distributors nor consumers but for the film-makers themselves, the real creative force of the cinema. That is its raison d'être.[89] (Underlining in original)

Wlaschin's focus on the films and the filmmakers as the defining elements of the programme clearly mirrors the coverage that the LFF has traditionally received from the national and international press. A boost in numbers of press attendees took place in 2013, whereby a total of 11,072 press and industry delegates who attended 143 screenings, the latter up from approximately eighty-five in recent years, as noted in the Festival's press release.[90] Figures have carried on rising and in 2018 there were a total of 17,173 admissions in press and industry, and 2368 at education and industry events, with a total of 3,600 press guests.[91] However, focusing on the films at the expense of a curatorial context leaves a programme of 229 features films and 159 shorts in its 2018 edition looking 'arbitrary', according to critic Tony Rayns, an opinion he had already voiced back in 1975, and which, when I interviewed him in 2013, three months after his resignation as a programme adviser, he still held. Rayns wrote in 1975:

> The range is broad enough to be sure of pleasing all of the people some of the time, but the uniformly gushing tone of the programme booklet blurbs and the absence of any defined selection criteria make it pretty hard to sort out the worth-while from the dreck. At its most useful, the LFF serves to bring to London a lot of movies that might not otherwise be seen here. At its most

spurious, it dignifies lousy movies by making them appear more interesting than they could ever be in any context.[92]

What Rayns identifies as the Festival's usefulness is echoed by Argentine critic, programmer, and acting president of FIPRESCI Argentina Diego Lerer, who during his attendance at the LFF's 2012 edition, when I asked him what he thought of the Festival, he replied that he kept on coming back as for him, it was useful because he could watch all the films he had missed at other festivals such as Cannes, and which had not played at Venice.[93] He then expressed this opinion in his own blogging about the Festival:

> Many films together and not much time to be able to write about them. This is a quick summary of my experience at London. Unlike other big festivals (Cannes, Venice, Berlin, Toronto... etc) London does not have the urgency of the day to day — most of the films have already been shown somewhere else — and the continuous walking from screen to screen throughout the city does not leave enough time to sit down and write about the films. (...) [T]his festival is functioning as a 're-take' of what I didn't see during the year.[94]

In 2013 Rayns also draws attention to the large number of films that played at the LFF (with figures not dissimilar to 2018: 235 features and 134 short films), and defines the Festival as a 'big impossible machine'. In his experience, Rayns finds that over the years there has been, what he refers to as a 'glaringly obvious and rather embarrassing' disproportion between the attention given to the big films as opposed to the smaller films, and concludes that, 'in that light I think that you sense that change in the personality of the Festival'. That the Festival was there for different reasons. 'It became much less in the service of the films that it was promoting, it was more about itself.'[95]

Although the key words in Rayns's 1975 critique are 'broad' and 'pleasing', for Hebron, on the other hand, the breadth of the Festival is actually its greatest strength, as it indicates inclusivity as opposed to elitist specialization. This position mirrors Wlaschin's own, expressed when he stated in 1981 that under his direction 'a first film from Iceland can rub shoulders with a Hollywood horror film in the LFF and the same audience can appreciate both', a change he refers to as a 'development'.[96] Rayns, working at that time as a programmer for the Festival, recalls how Wlaschin, 'made it national policy to broaden the Festival.' The LFF expanded dramatically under Ken Wlaschin and opened up to all kind of things that, in Rayns's words, 'would have been unimaginable under Richard Roud, including popular genre film'.[97]

Pursuing Wlaschin's policy further of opening up the Festival, it was the then *Guardian* film critic and historian, Derek Malcolm, in his three years as director, who most definitively embraced the LFF's expansion; nevertheless, his is the lone voice of discrepancy as regards the 'Festival of Festivals' label. Malcolm opened his short tenure (1984–1986) with a written rant against, first of all, the sense of exclusivity emanating from the Festival, which he termed a 'bonanza for the National Film Theatre members'; to counter this, he spread the Festival into eight different venues to 'persuade Londoners that this really is their Festival' — an attitude which recalls that of Diego Galán at San Sebastián. Malcolm goes on to dispense with what he refers to as 'another canard', alluding directly to the institution of a programming agenda that LFF critics such as Rayns feel has been sorely lacking:

> that the LFF is the 'Festival of Festivals', which relies only on films shown at other festivals round the world. That is no longer true. Of course, most of our movies come from Berlin, Cannes, Venice, etc. But a larger number than ever are our own choices, which other festivals may well pick up. We do have original thoughts of our own! I would like, in short, to think of the twenty-eighth LFF chiefly as a celebration of cinema in all its forms, from the frankly commercial to the overtly experimental. I think that's a just summation of the programme, and the only proviso has been that each film is good of its kind. We can no longer afford, and not just for financial reasons, to think of 'festival films' and 'others'. The cinema, which in my view is by no means dead yet, is too broad a church for that old-fashioned conception.[98]

For Hebron, being inclusive and inviting should also be one of the strongest points of the Festival.[99] And so it's Stewart who, when interviewed by film critic Charles Gant, explains how her own remit when she started was precisely to reach out to the audiences whilst keeping the 'very strong programme identity' that she inherited. She recalls:

> But I also perceived there was, from an external point of view, a perception that the festival was a bit of a closed shop; that it was for BFI members and for the industry.[100]

Ergo, as she explains to Gant, her analysis developed into 'a two-pronged mission: to expand the audience by making the programme and festival look and feel more accessible'. This is an angle also shared by Tuttle, who turns the screw a bit tighter and focuses on the most important thing that any festival relies on for its own future: the younger generation. After her debut in 2018 as interim director, she remarks that one of the things she found very exciting was that, in the last few years, she had seen across the BFI what she describes as 'a real interest in attracting younger audiences and that corresponding to new programming voices coming into the BFI.' Tuttle pointedly further remarks:

> Also, no one has quite grappled yet with the SVoD and VoD market and the changes that has brought about. Business models are shifting and changing. Festivals, in a way, are playing a role that arthouse cinemas used to play 25/30 years ago in introducing audiences to the broadest range of global cinema. It's a really important part of what we do and that's one of the reasons why diversity, in every sense, is so important to us. Audiences can't get that on a year-round basis in the regular cinema culture.[101]

The Eternal Dichotomy: Culture vs. Entertainment

The most important asset of the LFF has always been its capacity to retain a balance between the cultural value of cinema and film as an entertainment industry, with all the attendant glamour. This dichotomy is perhaps best captured by Michael Brooks in his brief history of the BFI Production Fund. In it, he identifies one of new Labour's buzzwords, their use of the term 'cultural industries', which for him suggests that 'a commercial element was paramount'.[102] This is a concept of culture as business that Adorno had already identified in 1944, when he wryly stated in his seminal essay on the Culture Industry that:

> Movies and radio no longer pretend to be art. The truth that they are just business is made into an ideology in order to justify the rubbish they deliberately produce. They call themselves industries; and when their directors' incomes are published, any doubt about the social utility of the finished products is removed.[103]

During her tenure, Hebron re-introduced a focus on smaller, more experimental and/or independent films, and brought back the more avant-garde-orientated BFI-programming of its early years, placed throughout the programme and focused in the Festival's Experimenta section. This can be viewed as an attempt to reinstate and reclaim a certain cultural value for the Festival in the wake of the Whitaker and Wootton (particularly the latter) years, when the LFF was oriented more clearly towards box office and the presence of film stars on the red carpet in order to capture press attention and extend its audience.

This debate over the 'balance' between the Festival's cultural capital and its value as an industry, red-carpet event, as previously illustrated, had already been played out in the wake of the Festival's twenty-fifth anniversary dossier. But perhaps more significantly, it was echoed and reignited in 2008, the year the LFF did not succeed in its application for extra funding from the UKFC (it did, however, receive it the following year, in 2009), in turn resurrecting the old debate over the relative merits of Edinburgh and London.

This time the trigger for the debate was a small article published in *Time Out* by the editor of the film section, Dave Calhoun. That same year, 2008, populist television executive Greg Dyke was appointed the new Chairman of the BFI by the UKFC (responsible for allocating a portion of the BFI's funds since it was created in 2000). As Calhoun points out, this was a shock to many in the British film industry, as Dyke did not come from the world of cinema. In one of the first interviews he gave, to *The Times*, Dyke declared that the LFF needed to be 'bigger and glitzier'. In particular:

> For what it is, the festival is successful. But I think the idea of making it bigger and glitzier is quite attractive. You want the festival to be for buffs and the general public. A glitzier festival is a good idea. It does something for London.[104]

As an aside, and echoing Wlaschin and Malcolm themselves down the years, Dyke also highlights what Elsaesser identifies as one of film festivals' many defining traits, city branding,[105] when he emphasizes what the Festival can do for London (instead of for England, or for the UK).

More relevantly here though, in his article titled 'Greg Dyke and The Future of the British Film Institute', Calhoun responded thus:

> Why is this so worrying? Mainly because it raises questions about where Dyke is getting his ideas from and, crucially, what he perceives to be the role of the BFI. Firstly, a radical change for the LFF would go against the better advice of those who know the event the best: the people that run it, who, in private, have

spent much of the past year listening patiently to the ideas of bodies outside of the BFI, like the UKFC, Film London and the London Development Agency who would all like to see it change (all are funders of the event). Secondly, on what evidence is Dyke, days into the new job, making these suggestions? Is he a regular at the festival and familiar with its programme? Thirdly, and most worrying for signs of the direction of his tenureship, his comments seem similar to noises emanating from the UKFC, noises which I'm aware that the current custodians of the LFF at the BFI oppose: that the London Film Festival should become bigger, more populist, and more glamorous, and perhaps move its date from October, not for cultural reasons but so that the festival can act as a flag-waver for the British film industry purely in trade terms, and so that distributors can gain more mileage from its programme. [...] Such proposals suggest that programming [...] hasn't come into the equation at all.[106]

He goes on to explain that although these ideas are valid for the industry, they take little account of the public's feelings. Mention is also made of turning the LFF into a competitive festival — 'the only reason for this would be to raise the Festival's profile within the industry and to shine a light on the city'. Calhoun closed his article by opening the debate to the public, and invited readers to give their opinion online about Dyke's declarations. Most notably though, Festival director Sandra Hebron herself personally entered into the debate and commented on the public responses in an article published six weeks later in the same magazine. Hebron's answer acknowledged both cultural and industry concerns.[107]

Below is a summary of Hebron's comments on the readers' replies. Before that, it should be pointed out that the dialogue that *Time Out* inaugurated on this occasion can be viewed as a revisiting of contested issues pertaining to the LFF throughout most of its existence. The most interesting aspect this time round was — thanks to the Internet — the public's expression of opinions, thus fulfilling one of the Festival's (and the BFI's) remits: that the LFF is an audience/public festival. Here, the audience is given a voice, possibly for the first time in the Festival's existence; and more importantly, this voice is answered by the Festival's artistic director — incidentally, this is also a first in the history of the LFF. Those answers, summarized below, supply perhaps the most accurate definition of the LFF's identity.

After first reminding *Time Out* readers that the LFF was founded as a 'public "Festival of Festivals" to enable audiences in London to see films that had premiered at other international events', Hebron also mentions the important role that the industry had played in the Festival, especially in the previous five years. One of the concerns raised not only by readers, but also repeatedly by the film professionals I have talked to, is the Festival's breadth of scope, reflected in the steadily increasing number of films invited every year. It could be argued that this is simply a reflection of the ever-increasing number of films being made. Hebron clarifies that only 10% of the films sent for consideration to the LFF are selected for the actual programme, and the key section of her article reads as follows:

> The postings about the programme display a tension which also surfaces in the discussion of the logistics of the festival. Some readers want the festival to be intimate, exclusive, cinephile. Others favour a more inclusive and democratic approach. We try to strike a balance between the two, so that our core of

FIG. 3.5. LFF 1997 Helena Bonham Carter posing on the red carpet
© BFI Archive

knowledgeable filmgoers can attend with serious purpose, but where space is still maintained to introduce new audiences to unfamiliar work. A festival should be somewhere that allows audiences to take chances, and that includes people who like to watch films in the Odeon West End.[108]

The balance that Hebron refers to not only reflects the multiple nature of cinema from its inception — Edison's money-oriented initiatives, the Lumière brothers recording of 'reality', the pure entertainment of Méliès's camera magic tricks — but also the notion of diversity that lies at the core of the BFI's mission statement. Nevertheless, for Ian Christie, it also constitutes the most difficult task for the Festival, what he refers to as 'a hopeless situation':

> I feel very sorry for the LFF because there are so many expectations wished upon it, because [independent cinema] is not being shown anywhere else and they are in an experimental film section. What sort of sense does it make having a sort of avant-garde section in what is a mainstream film festival? It's only the BFI and the LFF trying to cater for the LUX crowd, because when the LUX cinema collapsed it would have been an outpost for showing that kind of work. The LFF rather knowingly in that sense took on that responsibility too, so it seems that now it's a dog's dinner; it's trying to do everything for everybody.[109]

When I put these comments to Hebron, she pointed out that a London-based audience member could and still can see independent cinema in venues throughout London during the year; that is not entirely accurate to describe the LFF as a mainstream festival; that independent cinema was and still is screened extensively in sections other than Experimenta. And finally, that the LUX was still in existence for several years after the Experimenta section started.

In 2008 Edinburgh was awarded £1.88 million[110] of UKFC funding for a proposal based on its becoming, under the stewardship of the then director Hannah McGill, 'the world's leading festival of discovery'. This would entail a reduction of its red-carpet events, and switching from its traditional slot in August to June, thus separating itself from the main Edinburgh International Festival, which it had been part of since its inception in 1947. For the LFF, in order to get the £1.8 million that it would eventually be granted the following year, to be spent over the course of three years,[111] Hebron and her team were asked to rethink their strategy. Their original proposal was considered only a modest expansion of the LFF, when in fact, as *Variety* reporter Adam Dawtrey noted, the UKFC had, echoing Dyke, a 'bigger and glitzier' future in mind:

> The UKFC wants London to become one of the world's foremost red carpet festivals, with major premieres and a big dollop of razzle-dazzle, though not necessarily a competition. [...] 'They made a bid, but it was a Band-Aid on the existing operation', confirms UKFC chairman Stewart Till. 'So we said, 'Let's go on with the 2008 festival as it stands, let's not stick a Band-Aid on it, and let's work together on a strategy of creating a London Film Festival in 2009 and beyond that is the festival everybody in the British film industry wants'.[112]

Reiterating Dyke's point of view about the LFF, film producer Stewart Till (CBE, chairman and chief executive of United International Pictures) is quoted in the article declaring:

London, for its budget, is fantastic [...]. But the UK is the Western world's second most important industry, and the Film Council feels very strongly that it needs to work with the BFI to create a much bigger festival. We need to double the current budget to £7–£8 million [...], and the Film Council can contribute part of that alongside other sponsors.[113]

As Dawtrey notices, that would put London in the same league as A-list festivals such as Berlin or Venice, and the newly founded Rome, at that time also a 'best of' festival that held its first edition in November 2006. Nevertheless, the same year the LFF's application was rejected, Hebron and her team secured the premiere of one of the most high-profile films ever, and certainly the most high-profile British film, *Quantum of Solace*, the latest James Bond — in an edition which trumpeted its 'unprecedented number of premieres'.[114]

Unsurprisingly, although the Festival's calendar position didn't shift, a number of important changes did take place during the next three editions, the last of Hebron's tenure. There was a total of six changes attached to the funding in order to raise the profile of the Festival. In an interview conducted on 5 February 2010 with Hebron, also attended by the then Head of Projects and Development Anne-Marie Flynn (Managing Director of BFI Festivals from 2018), I was provided with a summary of these changes. Firstly, the number of World and European premieres would have to increase. More European journalists should be invited to the Festival. And press conferences should be held for most of the gala screenings. The latter had never been done at the LFF, in spite of the Festival's scope, because the budget had not allowed for it. The other points were as follows. To take the Festival city-wide for one night with a big popular screening. To develop the online press coverage of the Festival in order to entice more people to engage with its programme. And finally, a general desire to increase the overall production values of the Festival, to professionalize particular areas of the Festival. That would mean an increase of investment in opening and closing nights as well as the gala screenings, and an increase in the number of filmmakers invited as well as the overall amount of money allocated for their attendance at the Festival, to ensure the right amount of buzz is created around those events.

The majority of these changes mirror in many ways the enhanced role that the industry now has throughout the whole festival circuit. It should also be noted that these changes — premieres, online coverage, industry meetings and seminars — were already taking place to a greater or lesser degree at the Festival before it was granted the funding. Others, such as the number and quality of guests, have always been the bread and butter of any festival, even more so of a populist one like the LFF. In 1975 Ken Wlaschin was already stressing the presence of directors at the Festival in the introductory blurb of the catalogue; and as previously mentioned, when recalling the origins of the LFF, the original programmer Derek Prouse highlights as the highest achievement the presence of international auteurs at the Festival, as previously mentioned in this chapter. Commenting on the 1959 LFF, the critic of the *Daily Mail* announced that he was 'not sure what useful purpose is served by any film festival'[115] and points out that 'This is a festival with little money for conscious glamour — in any case, South Bank in October is hardly the best

Fig. 3.6. NFT 1987 Riverside entrance
© BFI Archive

Fig. 3.7. Terry Gilliam samples LFF's lively atmosphere, 1998
© BFI Archive

place for festival film-flam'[116]. Yet he goes on to describe the packed houses and lively atmosphere, as well as the extensive press coverage, concluding that:

> the London Film Festival is now firmly established as a centrepiece of the National Film Theatre year. Nevertheless, some leading critics still show a strange reluctance to recognize this annual treat for what it is: a stimulating variation on the weekly round and an opportunity to assess what the real cinema is capable of achieving.[117]

Back into the present, however, perhaps the most pronounced shift that occurred in recent years is the source of the Festival's funding. One outcome of the then Coalition government's cuts in culture funding was the abolition of many of Labour's famous *quangos* (a quasi-autonomous non-governmental organization), one being the UKFC, which was merged under the umbrella of the BFI. From 1 April 2011 the BFI has become the lead body for film in the UK, which includes

> a role as a lottery distributor, with responsibility for funding film development and production; training; distribution and exhibition; supporting film UK-wide; film certification, the Cultural Test and co-production; strategic development; industry research and statistics; and the MEDIA Desk UK. The role of the British Film Commission in encouraging inward investment work transfers to Film London.[118]

This also meant that at the point where the three-year funding granted by the UK Film Council (UKFC) to the LFF ended, the Festival would then receive part of its funding from the BFI — an organization, it should be noted, that is more culture-focused than the industry-driven UKFC. Yet, this transition required a significant degree of negotiation with the Department for Culture, Media and Sport (DCMS),[119] including a suggestion that the Festival should be directly funded by the DCMS as a cleaner political solution. This shift moves the BFI away from its traditional cultural focus to one more industry oriented, as the appointment of Clare Stewart in 2011 as Head of Exhibition, BFI, shows. Her position 'brings all of the BFI's film exhibition activity together and is responsible for the cultural and commercial performance of BFI Southbank, BFI Festivals including the BFI London Film Festival, and BFI IMAX'.[120] In 2014 the DCMS made a further adjustment whereby the UKFC itself was abolished and absorbed by the BFI, bringing the role of the industry within the BFI, and by extension the LFF, a little bit closer. In fact, the LFF's embrace of the industry, including a Film London-led collaboration on a production finance market,[121] is proving to be the means by which the real 'rise in international profile' is taking place. As San Sebastián's former director, Mikel Olaciregui, argues, the one and only reason a festival will survive nowadays in the midst of the festival boom is by having the industry attached to it.[122]

With a total of 229 feature films in the Festival's 2019 programme, it is now hard to envisage a curatorial line for the LFF — even just covering it as a critic is a daunting task, as I note myself in my report of the 2012 edition.[123] This was an issue already raised by film critic/academic Matthew Flanagan in his coverage of the Festival in 2013:

> There is no such thing as a 'London film', in the vein of what might be a 'Sundance' (take your pick) or 'Viennale' film (a new Straub or Rousseau, perhaps), and nor does there need to be. Measures of scale are rarely significant as indicators of quality or vitality either — what the small may gain in character or individuality, the large can compensate with resources and scope. However, it is worrying that London seems so timid with regard to taking a stance, articulating an outlook, supporting or even attempting to nurture a particular type, or idea, of modern cinema.[124]

Programmer Tony Rayns opens up this issue further and locates the problem beyond the LFF itself, echoing Christie's view on the national press:

> In this country I don't think anybody, certainly nobody in the press, is very interested in issues of what a film festival's orientation should be, or how it should be run. They are very happy to take it as the BFI wants it, which is, as you know, a glamorous event. So the *Evening Standard* is happy to become a sponsor because they will get red carpet photos of Scarlet Johansson or whoever on their front page day after day, which suits them just fine. They think this is what the public wants and they are involved in getting that. *The Sun* for example gives extensive coverage of the West End part of the Festival and takes no notice at all of the rest of it. It goes completely unnoticed. If it's at the NFT or at the ICA, the Ritzy or somewhere else, they couldn't care less.[125]

I would argue that a strong curatorial line is something that London will probably never have, since its location would seem to dictate otherwise: London is one of the most globalized, multiculturally diverse and transnational capital city in the world. And it is precisely the 'multiplicity in programming voices' that the LFF's new director, Tuttle sees as the key tool to attract new audiences.[126] The Festival not only has to compete with the many and varied events that already take place in the capital, but also has to cater to the sheer variety of cultures, backgrounds, ethnicities, etc. that constitute the city. In that respect it is quite surprising that it was not until 2010 that some of the Festival's new bigger budget was allocated to 'dressing up' the city, i.e. using banners and posters all over the city to publicize it, in line with using a portion of the UKFC funding for marketing.

Viewed from the perspective of its host city, the many comparisons that have been made between London and Edinburgh seem superficial; the LFF clearly has more in common with a Festival like Toronto, even if London and Edinburgh do compete for certain smaller, European art-house films. The key is making the most of what a city like London can give to the Festival — not only economic benefits, which is where much of its energy seems to be focused in its new phase, but also cultural ones too. Take for instance the invited studio films and attendant guests. Glamour can take many forms; three festivals completely different to the LFF, BAFICI, Vienna, and Locarno, widely perceived as specialized, curated festivals, by and large use the same tools as London to market themselves, albeit within the parameters of their own interests and the particular identity of the Festival. All three screen hundreds of films, and share — particularly so in the case of BAFICI — a clearly marked interest in the industry, the market and the training of new filmmakers. The aura of glamour at programme-driven festivals such as Vienna has prompted Austrian academic Barbara Wurm to describe what she identifies as the paradoxically egalitarian and exclusive nature of these festivals as 'leftist glamour' in her coverage of Vienna's 2010 edition (its forty-seventh).

> A general assumption is in the air — and it has been hanging there for a while now — that the Viennale is governed by leftist glamour. [...] To be egalitarian and exclusive at the same time seems like an ideal image in a way. No one can refrain from appearances, as we all know, and nobody will be asking for that. We are so far beyond blue-collar retro-look requirements, that nowadays it is probably rather non-stylishness that may arouse ideological suspiciousness (besides, an intentional anti-fashion-attitude is part of a very specific Viennese way of life anyway, I guess). Nevertheless it is — again — stylishness we are talking about, when it comes to the Viennale.[127]

In the final analysis, it is really down to the context in which the films — big or small, commercial or independent — are framed. When George Clooney comes to the LFF to promote a commercial but nevertheless political film like *The Ides of March* screened as one of the Festival's galas in 2011, it is indicative of one of Hebron's publicly professed changes: not to take any old Hollywood film just because it is offered, but rather to go for those with a certain amount of relevance and substance, and then to use the glamour and star wattage they bring to shed some light on the more obscure sections of the Festival, even, if she admits that when you are running 'a more generalist festival [...] the balance is a delicate one'.[128]

Hebron's reasoning is echoed by Simon Field, who at the time of directing Rotterdam (1997–2004), applied what in the Netherlands they refer to as the 'sandwich process', i.e.:

> how you use bigger films to get audiences to support your festival and its smaller — but equally important — films. They become not an alibi so much as a support system. You need the profile in the press, which comes with the big films and the films that are being sold to local distributors. They become a rationale that drives the festival, at all sorts of levels: they are the films the audiences often want to see, they represent the interests of the studios and the independents; they are, sadly, what the press wants to cover. The danger is that the balance begins to shift.[129]

The problem, of course, is how to maintain that delicate balance, when — using Toronto as an example — as Fields explains:

> all films are described as fabulous, and when some parts of the festival disappear beneath an overcrowded programme. The noise of the 'upper' part of the festival drowns out other areas. When you get the feeling that rhetoric, and the marketeers have taken over, you begin to be concerned that the marginal films aren't at the centre of anyone's interest.[130]

Also referring to Toronto, film critic and editor of *Dekalog 3: On Film Festivals*,[131] Richard Porton echoes this problem in commenting that 'all that many people see is that the glitz and the sort of celebrity infatuation tend to overshadow the real films of substance'.[132] Whereas in Locarno, this delicate balance is perhaps achieved, in Porton's opinion, by inviting 'movie stars past their prime, so they aren't just on junkets', and who therefore bring their experience in film as a pedagogical tool. This echoes Diego Galán's own original logic behind San Sebastián's Donostia Award given to celebrate a film personality's career. As he reasons, in this way the function of the celebrities invited (pursued by a certain section of the audience and press, and sponsors alike) is not simply as 'flower-pots' for the press.[133]

If, for Hebron, Fields, Galán — and to some extent Porton — glamour can be used as one of the alluring tools to invite viewers to explore other — less accessible — sections of the Festival, then providing a context to these sections becomes essential. As James Quandt indicates in his conversation with Simon Fields, Toronto's effort to make this happen (topping the LFF by screening approximately a hundred films more) is the publication of a festival daily, where, in Quandt's words, the festival makes sure that 'at least ninety per cent of it is directed towards the films that don't otherwise get much coverage, the smaller films. They have made a concerted effort to compensate for the media's attention on stars and Hollywood'. Fields responds thus:

> Which is absolutely correct. We tried to do the same thing with the Daily in Rotterdam because a similar problem occurs there. Veteran visionary directors of the independent cinema like Werner Schroeter and Tonino De Bernardi are now marginal directors even at a festival like Rotterdam. You have to ensure they get that coverage, but as a festival gets bigger it becomes harder and harder to create that attention — which filmmakers does one choose to feature in the Daily among so many deserving cases?[134]

One of the oft-praised aspects of the Edinburgh Film Festival is, as Nowell-Smith points out, its publishing of informative essays and articles and books to accompany the programme — particularly when the Festival focused on the promotion of documentary films, and specially under Chris Fujiwara's tenure as director, 2010–2014 — largely written by film critics instead of the Festival's programmers, and of great importance in introducing the films and providing a context for the viewer. Equally, one of the most surprising findings about the LFF is that, despite its relation to the BFI, it does not offer anything like this. The blurbs accompanying the films in the LFF catalogue don't provide much context aside from a short synopsis, and read more like promotional tools than film criticism. And although both the BFI's own website and *Sight & Sound* have for some years been publishing film-critics' recommendations leading up to the LFF, the bulk of the content published online with regard to the Festival does take place during or after the Festival, and not before. Both BAFICI and San Sebastián (the latter through its link with the Spanish equivalent to the BFI) have offered since their inception a large number of publications dedicated to a given retrospective, or director or group of works screened at the festival, and their websites further expand the context and literature on the films they are showing — they both also include access to contextual historical material on the festival itself.

I would argue that it is precisely this contextualization of the work shown at the Festival that can have greater impact in drawing new audiences to other, lesser-known parts of a given festival, but it is something that no LFF director has either pursued or managed to realize throughout its history. Nowell-Smith believes this is because it would mean a lot of extra work, as well as the collaboration of other departments of the BFI, such as Palgrave Macmillan, its publishing arm since 2008.

> There's not much you can do because of the lack of infrastructure of people who have been keeping up with what's happening in different countries. And the universities don't really help here, I don't think. [...] I think that although the number of films in the Festival is enormous, the back-up knowledge is not being assembled. And there was always criticism of the Festival when it was a bit smaller, that you are dumped a lot of films but there's nothing written on them. If you go to Berlin, when you arrive you get a thick book which has probably taken a year to put together, and although they haven't had too long to work on the films they've selected within the last two months, even so, a huge amount of work goes into them, in terms of background, supporting material.

When I put this question to Hebron she explained that, during her tenure, this kind of catalogue was costed several times, but found to be both resource heavy and a very difficult proposition to raise money for as the money raised tends to be strictly spent on what it was raised for: 'both sponsors and public funders are equally strict on this, and the BFI as an organisation was never able to underwrite the production of this kind of catalogue'.[135]

Notwithstanding, Hebron highlights an important point, perhaps the most relevant ingredient in any festival, i.e. the role of sponsors and funders with regards to the shape and content of the festivals they pay for. It goes beyond my remit to tackle this issue here, since although I had access to much of the LFF I did not attend any meetings with sponsors, funding bodies, etc., or indeed budgets, considered as sensitive information and never made public. In this regard, mention of scholar Rhyne Ragan's study on the relationship between stakeholders and film festivals becomes relevant, as it raises issues to do with who the festival is addressing: a specialized audience like BAFICI, film professionals like Cannes, or a more general audience.

Funding, the Future and Contextualizing the LFF's Programme

A hint of a change in this regard is currently occurring at the BFI. The monumental Gothic season that took place at BFI Southbank from September 2013 to January 2014 was accompanied by a total of eight Gothic-related BFI Film Classics covering some of the films screened at the season, as well as a companion volume dealing with different aspects of the Gothic, from sexuality to foreign politics, feminist theory and science. This initiative was previously introduced, albeit on a smaller scale, during 2012's Alfred Hitchcock retrospective, which was accompanied by a compendium covering different aspects of the filmmaker's life and career. The Gothic season has been followed by further blockbuster programmes dedicated to Sci-Fi (2014), Love (2015), Black Star (2016) and Thrillers (2017), accompanied by their own compendia. In the case of the LFF, an informed, accessible (and readily available during the festival) introduction to and contextualization of the films programmed would almost certainly boost the sense of discovery that took root at the LFF's inception; and could potentially lure the casual viewer back to sample more films during the same edition.

Although demonstrably an effective way of generating increased box office revenues and capturing new audiences,[136] the 'blockbuster' approach is debatable in terms of selection of material. In fact, it is interesting that Rayns extends the blockbuster influence to the way the BFI is programmed in general, when he criticizes the retrospectives currently being screened at the Southbank:

> The NFT for example used to be one of the great treasures in the world for retrospectives of directors, or national cinemas, or whatever. And people went to enormous lengths to track down prints to make sure that these things were complete. That every last short was shown, nothing was missing. It was a retrospective as complete as it was humanly possible to make it. Now, under Clare Stewart, they are greatest hits retrospectives. They just show the main stuff, the films that people have maybe heard of, none of the rarities, or as few rarities as they can get away with.[137]

It is important to note that, unlike San Sebastián and BAFICI, the LFF does not include retrospectives as part of its programme, although until 2012 there was a section dedicated to screening recently restored films from archives all around the world. Under Clare Stewart's direction, these films are now dispersed and threaded into the relevant experiential pathways (under 'Treasures'), albeit retaining a designated Gala. The absence of retrospectives is arguably a further illustration of the Festival's problematic relationship with memory, whether its own, or in this case, film history. It could be argued that there's no need to include retrospectives, because they are shown at the NFT throughout the rest of the year. By way of comparison, however, the other two festivals I deal with in this book, as well as others including Vienna, Toronto, Edinburgh and Berlin, are strongly linked to their respective national cinematheques, local film museums or film societies, and still collaborate with them to organize specialised retrospective programmes for the festival. I would argue that such retrospectives not only represent, as previously mentioned, strong attractions in themselves for many a festivalgoer, but also provide a sense of the medium's past to help contextualize the contemporary films on offer.

The LFF's shift to a more commercial stance — from an initial focus on arthouse film towards inclusion of Hollywood studio fare — was already discussed by Auty in 1981, who compared it to a similar transition undertaken by the BFI's film magazine *Sight & Sound*, attributing both to responses to external pressure:

> *Sight and Sound*'s support for the LFF is not simply a product of the fact that both activities emanate from departments within the same body — i.e. the BFI (after all some BFI departments are openly critical of the LFF), it is also due to a shared ideology that began as cultural elitism and dwindled into aimless pluralism in the face of concerted attacks from progressive wings of the film culture.[138]

Flanagan echoes this view to an extent in his report on the LFF's 2009 edition.[139] But more importantly, he contributes to the debate about the relationship that the Festival has developed with 'business' — a topic that is acquiring such relevance in the festival world that, as Flanagan notes, it prompted Mark Peranson, programmer and editor of the film magazine *Cinema Scope*, to write an article on this very subject, in which he divides film festivals into two increasingly differentiated categories: those which prioritize the audience and those which focus on business.[140]

Peranson's preference is for a happy co-existence of both models, although he bitterly laments the rise of the sales agent, one of the direct consequences of festivals' closer ties with the industry. In the case of the LFF, this co-existence seems to be taking place within the Festival itself. At the 2009 edition, Flanagan identified the more pronounced presence of the industry as placing the Festival in a kind of middle of the road position, responding too much — as Auty had already pointed out in 1981 — to external forces, which caused the Festival to become diluted:

> At first glance it [the LFF] appears to belong to the latter [audience], but displays far too many conservative hallmarks of the former [business] to even come close to an audience-based ideal in its current state. The festival is of course propped up by corporate sponsorship, hosts a number of prominent premieres (this year: *Fantastic Mr. Fox* and *Nowhere Boy*) and enjoys a visible Hollywood studio presence, but at the same time it refrains from functioning as a notable market or competition event, invests little in new work, and solicits the bulk of its programming from elsewhere. London is pitched as a survey, an overview, a service for the city, and advertises itself as such — the ubiquitous trailer shows a number of residents dazzled by the bright lights of 'the best in world cinema' that the programmers dump before their eyes, seemingly rapt and satiated. Perhaps the festival does succeed in providing what its habitual audience desires of it, but if that is the case then we should be asking much more.[141]

The official press releases summarizing the Festival's audience figures and attendees seems to demonstrate quite clearly this dichotomy between an interest in reaching both existing and new audiences and the increasingly important role of the industry (and international press) at the LFF. Even if the bulk of the release trumpets the talent that attended the Festival, one of its main attractions is the fact that stars of the stature of Tom Hanks, Amy Adams, Tom Ford and Leonardo DiCaprio can share the same space as lesser known directors, etc.

Both the Festival's reliance on the presence and accessibility of international guests — as well as a then limited yet already present will to accommodate the industry side within the Festival — has been a trait throughout its existence. This is particularly true in relation to the increasing effectiveness as inviting these guests produced a greater interest in the Festival, as well as the role that the Festival itself started acquiring as middleman between the films and the industry. An early hint can be traced back to 1966. At the LFF's tenth anniversary success was measured by Roud — in his introduction to that edition's brochure — by the number of filmmakers such as Fellini, Antonioni and Truffaut whose films the Festival were able to screen, and by the fact that the gap 'which used to exist between production and eventual UK distribution of the best of the year's work in films [...] in many cases no longer exists'. In that same year, an industry-related change was introduced, which Roud refers to as an 'important innovation'. He notes:

Fig. 3.8. Still from the
BFI London Film Festival 2009 publicity campaign
© BFI London Film Festival Archive

> All the films shown at the National Film Theatre this year will be screened twice and, with one or two possible exceptions, only twice. This will not entirely solve the problem of forty-thousand members trying to get into a five-hundred-seat house but it should help. This new system is fairer not only to the members but also to the eventual distributors and exhibitors of the festival films.[142]

In addition to the existing press and industry screenings, from 2013 the LFF also organized private passes, with 17,173 in press and industry admissions, and 2368 at education and industry events in 2018.[143]

As discussed earlier, the presence of the industry at film festivals is not unique to the LFF. When I asked Porton if he thinks this has increased since he edited the *Dekalog*, he offered the following assessment.

> Every festival now has to have an industrial component, has to have a talent campus, and now they have critics' academies, it's the latest thing. Which is fine, I guess it's good to nurture young critics but it is just part of the package I suppose. It's almost as if they are working in sync with each other and they all have to take on these new adjuncts. I guess a few of them now have the equivalent of the Hubert Bals. It's become a corporate model. The most extreme is the Tribeca Festival, which is not even clearly a film festival; they've gone into distribution and online activities. They are sponsoring sporting events. It's almost a Disneyfication of a film festival. Although that's an extreme case, but it could be a model for the future.[144]

Porton's complaint about the 'sameness' (as Adorno would put it[145]) that is dominating the festival form is one of the main preoccupations of Mark Cousins in his Film Festival Manifesto, where he states that film festivals 'are undergoing formal torpor. Too many of them use the same techniques — a main competition, sidebars, awards, late-night genre cinema, VIP areas, photo-calls, etc'[146] and calls for festivals to be *'authored'* (his italics).

But it is Porton's 'Disneyfication' that becomes particularly relevant here, as it draws attention not only to the changing nature of festivals, their innate adaptability, but to the spread of their activities (gastronomy in San Sebastián, sports in Tribeca). In that respect there's a strong connection to the eventful and 'discovery' aspect of festivals, and, unavoidably (in the majority of cases), their dependence on box office attendance. As a 'Festival of Festivals', the LFF depends on attracting an audience, as does an organisation like the BFI — particularly on attracting a young audience. The annual statistics published by the BFI in 2017 for the previous year show that young people aged 15–24 made up the largest proportion of the UK cinema audience, at 29%. The attendance for UK films was popular across all demographic groups, with a particularly strong appeal for those aged forty-five and over, and older audiences also showed a strong preference for UK independent films.[147] The importance of the audience for any public event is not a new debate, but it has certainly become the buzzword in the digitally-oriented film world that we inhabit, since audiences' viewing habits have changed as much as cinema has changed in the three key areas of production, distribution and exhibition.

The question of audiences has been a significant factor in recent funding decisions. From 2013 to 2017 the BFI allocated Lottery funding of £1 million per year to the newly established Film Festival Fund to support regional festivals 'which provide audiences across the UK with a greater film choice, as well as increasing audiences for specialized and independent British film'. Its second priority is 'to enhance film festivals in the UK that have an international reach and profile' — which applies to the LFF. But perhaps more significant is the fact that this fund belongs to the also newly established Audience Fund, a £22 million investment strategy over four years, from 2013–2017 to 'boost audience choice across the UK' and which comprises four elements: the UK Audience Network for Film, the Programming Development Fund, the Community Venues Fund, and the aforementioned Film Festival Fund, all under the umbrella Film Forever. The fund is divided into two strands and both emphasize audience development above any other activity. The BFI website includes a detailed document on new ways of reaching audiences for distribution.[148] Film Forever has now been replaced by the Film Audience Network, which is at the heart of the BFI's latest strategy BFI2022.[149] Christie himself participated in two large research projects — *Stories We Tell Ourselves* (2009)[150] and *Opening Our Eyes* (2011)[151] — on audiences in Britain and has just published a book entitled simply *Audiences*.[152]

In 2012, the opening and closing galas of the Festival were simultaneously screened in fifty cinemas across the country with the red carpet action shown via satellite link in order to — as specified in the press release — 'put the UK audience at the heart of the festival-going experience'. Since then, a larger number of galas and special screenings are shown across the UK every year adding a total 36,120 admissions UK wide in 2018. In addition, in 2014, the BFI launched a new VOD service, the BFI Player, which has since then been giving 'UK audiences access to all the stars and behind-the-scenes action during the Festival'.[153] The emphasis now appears to be on engaging audiences through superficial, picture-led, celebrity-driven website coverage, at the expense of more analytical, in-depth written material available at the various screening sites (*Sight & Sound*'s and the BFI's online coverage of the Festival) — i.e. programme notes at screenings (such as the BFI provides throughout the year), or more commonly and usefully, a daily newspaper containing interviews and reviews, as is the case at many festivals nowadays, from San Sebastián and BAFICI to Locarno.

The importance of such written work, readily available to the festivalgoer, is identified by film scholars Jesper Strandgaard Pedersen and Carmelo Mazza in their extensive study of value in film festivals. They regard it as a tool to ascribe value to the festival and its contents, whereby 'official publications concerning the festival (e.g. festival programmes, flyers, festival newspapers, etc.) directly issued by the festival organization [are published] in order to capture its profile and self-presentation to the public'.[154] Rayns also believes that such written apparatus enhances the way an audience engages with a festival, drawing principally on his own experiences at Asian film festivals such as Pusan, where extensive written programmes and essays, as well as publications organized by the festivals, are an important part of the cultural offer.

184   The BFI London Film Festival

Fig. 3.9. BFI Flare Gala of *A Fantastic Woman* as part of the LFF 2017.
Q&A with talent and myself
Photo © Tiina Heinonen

But Rayns also acknowledges that times have changed, and that, regarding new (and I would add, particularly, younger) audiences, the Festival 'could be potentially quite useful'. He explains:

> It's complicated to talk about this because times have changed so much. Cinema itself is not meaningful or important to people in the same way that it was twenty years ago. There is an audience, it's mostly now an older audience, there are relatively few young people but the few young people are aberrations, they are the exceptions not the mainstream. Don't care very much about film as a medium. And they are not very interested in film history, not very interested in film culture, they are not what you would call film buffs or what were called film buffs in an earlier age. So since there is no young audience coming up of the kind that sustained the Festival for so many years. Since there is no young audience coming up with the same needs and the same taste. It's impossible to say that the Festival needs to go back to the way it was, it's not going to happen. And it would make no sense anyway. But I definitely think the Festival could change in a way that would make it more user friendly, more in touch with the needs of the filmmakers who come, make it more of an experience for them. And more for the audience as well, so you wouldn't just pay through the nose to go and see a film and if you are lucky the filmmaker is there to answer some questions after the film.[155]

Contrary to Rayns's somewhat pessimistic view on the subject of cinephilia in present times, Laurent Jullier and Jean-Marc Leveratto, in their chapter exploring the notion as it pertains to the digital age,[156] argue that it is precisely now, with the 'democratizing' assistance of the Internet, that anybody can be a cinephile. Whereas before, according to their analysis, cinephilia was restricted to those who could actually access film festivals and film societies, etc. in order to see the lesser known films and cinemas, nowadays much content is available online. As they see it, cinephilia was something strongly related to the French Nouvelle Vague, whereas contemporary cinephilia knows no boundaries, and is more an individualized experience as it does not require joining a group of people at a given film theatre.[157] The LFF has been taken this to its advantage for over ten years, inviting bloggers and film lovers alike to the Festival in order to benefit from the buzz their online activity generates.[158]

The buzz, the audience, the celebration, the events. Mark Cousins concludes his Film Festival Manifesto alluding to 'the whole issue of festivity itself', for it to be

> restored to the centre of the world of film festivals. [...] film festivals should realise that, especially in the age of online, it's the offline communality of film festivals, the fact that we are all getting together to do the same thing, that is part of the source of their joy.

In the light of these comments, I would therefore argue that London, given the etymology of the word 'festival', holds close to a definition of 'festive', a notion that Strandgaard and Mazza apply to the much younger Festa del Cinema di Roma, established in 2006 and conceived as a 'popular event', and which instead of using the word 'festival' uses the actual origin of this word in its name (as discussed in the introduction). In Latin 'festa' means a celebration, a holiday, a party, and most significantly in relation to the discussion of the LFF in this chapter, a feast; or what Russian literary theorist Mikhail Bakhtin calls 'a primary human cultural form'.[159]

> FCR is thought of as a 'Festa' (Feast) rather than a 'Festival' in order to underline it as an event for the public at large rather than a competition for a prestigious award. As the Latin says 'in nomen omen' (the destiny is in the name), and the label 'festival' defines an event for the film industry and a celebration of stars. Festa sounds like a popular word, drawing on the participation of people and, in the mind of the founders, spreading throughout the entire city involving its inhabitants. A Festa is thought of as an event for the audience just as much as for the industry.[160]

When I recall my own personal experience of attending the Festival in the days before I had any links with either the LFF or the BFI, when I was simply a film lover living in London, my principal memory is one of sheer excitement. A particular pleasure, before the Festival had even started, was scouring the pages of the catalogue to try to make some sense of the hundreds of films, events, special screenings, etc. luring me from its pages. But above all else there was excitement at the prospect of a feast (as much as money allowed). The LFF does have hugely self-celebratory (if you like) red-carpet public events that take over several locations in London, including Leicester Square — as all film premieres in the capital do. But lesser known and more cult filmmakers can and do share the same space — in press releases, programmes and other materials issued by the Festival, as well as being participants in Q&As, debates, interviews, etc. In my years as a regular member of the audience, I personally discovered many of the filmmakers that have become fixtures of my own cinephilic landscape, from Lucrecia Martel to Eugène Green, and was able to explore and gain knowledge of their work and craft. London is undoubtedly a celebratory event that still manages to excite more and more people, a fact reflected clearly in the steady increase in attendance figures every year. For all that the Festival organizers seem keen to open London up to the international scene by inviting more international press, as well as broaden its scope nationally, the truth is that the LFF broadly remains a 'Festival of Festivals' for its city.

The BFI London Film Festival 187

Notes to Chapter 3

All uncredited quotes are from the following unpublished interviews conducted by the author: interview with Sandra Hebron, her office at the BFI Southbank. on 5 February 2010 (together with Anne-Marie Flynn); 28 September 2011; 16 November 2011; via email, 22 August 2014; interview with Ian Christie, his office in Birkbeck University of London, 12 December 2012; interview with Geoffrey Nowell Smith, *Sight & Sound* offices, 14 November 2011; interview with Tony Rayns, Boquería Restaurant London, 8 July 2013; interview with Richard Porton, BFI, 15 August 2014; interview with Diego Lerer, Southbank, 24 October 2011 (translated from Spanish by the author); interview with Helen De Witt, via email, 18 August 2014.

1. Figures published on the BFI LFF's website, <https://www.bfi.org.uk/news-opinion/news-bfi/announcements/lff-62-draws-close> [accessed 10 March 2020].
2. An official request for detail of the financial modeling of the LFF was refused on the basis that the data is protected by a commercial sensitivity exemption, which permits the BFI to withhold certain financial information when responding to Freedom of Information or other requests.
3. As opposed to a festival director, the Artistic Director job title was given to make clear that the role involves overall programming responsibility; not all Festival Directors have this.
4. *50/06. Lost and Found: Two Weeks in Autumn. International Visions*, ed. by Gareth Evans (BFI: The Times BFI 50th London Film Festival, 2006).
5. *Sight and Sound: A Fiftieth Anniversary Selection*, ed. by David Wilson (London: Faber & Faber and BFI Publishing, 1982).
6. 'A brief history of the BFI London Film Festival', BFI, 23 August 2018, <https://www.bfi.org.uk/news-opinion/news-bfi/features/brief-history-bfi-london-film-festival> [accessed 10 March 2020].
7. Interview with Christie.
8. Buenos Aires Ciudad. Buenos Aires Cine website, <http://www.opcionlibros.gov.ar/libros/cine.php?libro=cineargentinoesteticas> [accessed 25 May 2020].
9. Diego Galán, in *Historia del Zinemaldia (1953–2010)* 2010 [DVD] Spain: ETB/TVE/IBERDROLA (Documentary series about the festival narrated and directed by Diego Galán).
10. Geoffrey Macnab, 'London Film Festival Plans 50th Anniversary Events', *Screen Daily*, 23 May 2006, [accessed 10 March 2020].
11. Interview with Christie.
12. Interview with Hebron, via email.
13. Gilbert Adair, 'London 25. Tom Milne and Gilbert Adair write about some of the films in the 1981 London Film Festival', *Sight & Sound*, 51, 1, (Winter 1981–1982), 16–19 (p.16).
14. Mar Diestro-Dópido, 'The Pain in Spain: Three Spanish Films at London 2012', *Sight & Sound*, 20 November 2012, <https://www.bfi.org.uk/news-opinion/sight-sound-magazine/comment/festivals/lff-blog-pain-spain> [accessed 10 March 2020].
15. It is worth reiterating here that Sandra Hebron was one of the two main supervisors of the PhD project this book is based on.
16. Geoffrey Nowell-Smith joined the BFI as Head of Education in 1978 and moved sideways to become Head of Publishing in 1980. Then from 1989 until 1992 he was Senior Research Fellow. Before his employment he was a member of the BFI Production Board from 1976 to 1978. He was also indirectly employed by the BFI when he was Editor of *Screen* between 1977 and 1978.
17. Ian Christie was Regional Programme Adviser from 1976–1980; then Head of Exhibition, and later Head of Exhibition and Distribution, until 1993. He then became Head of Special Projects, developing the Centenary of Cinema projects, from 1993–1995, when he was 'loaned' to Oxford University to head up the development of Film Studies. He has been Professor of Film and Media History at Birkbeck since 1999.
18. Tony Rayns has worked as programmer for East Asian Cinema intermittently since 1977. He briefly resigned from this post when Derek Malcolm was appointed as director in 1984 and, although invited back by Sheila Whitaker, he did not return to the LFF until the latter left after the 1996 edition. Rayns was in fact invited back as programmer by Adrian Wootton the

following year and resigned in 2013 following a public falling-out with the then LFF director Clare Stewart.
19. British Film Institute: Royal Charter, 19 April 2000, <http://www.bfi.org.uk/sites/bfi.org.uk/files/downloads/bfi-royal-charter-2000-04.pdf> [accessed 10 March 2020].
20. Leslie Hardcastle, 'In the beginning... A view of how the National Film Theatre and the London Film Festival came into being, from Leslie Hardcastle, Controller of the NFT', in LFF 25th Anniversary LFF brochure, unpaginated.
21. Leslie Hardcastle, 'In the beginning...'
22. British Board of Film Classification, <http://www.bbfc.co.uk/about-bbfc>.
23. Interview with Nowell-Smith.
24. Interview with Nowell-Smith.
25. *Sight and Sound* dropped the conjunction 'and' in 2002 and substituted it with '&' from that date on. I will use the current version henceforth for consistency.
26. For more information on the opposing views regarding archiving film between Henri Langlois and Ernest Lindgren, see Penelope Houston *Keepers of the Frame: The Film Archives* (London: British Film Institute, 1994).
27. '1951: King George opens Festival of Britain', *BBC online*, On This Day 1950–2005, n.d., <http://news.bbc.co.uk/onthisday/hi/dates/stories/may/3/newsid_2481000/2481099.stm> [accessed 10 March 2020].
28. For more information about the role of film at the Festival of Britain, see Sarah Easen, 'Film and the Festival of Britain' in Ian MacKillop and Neil Sinyard (eds.), *British Cinema on the 1950s: A Celebration*, (Manchester University Press, 2003), pp. 51–63. Available at, <https://www.manchesteropenhive.com/view/9781526137272/9781526137272.00011.xml> [accessed 25 May 2020].
29. See 'Articles', British Universities Film & Video Council, n.d., <http://bufvc.ac.uk/publications/articles > [accessed 10 March 2020].
30. Ben Johnson, 'The Festival of Britain 1951', Historic UK: The History and Heritage Accommodation Guide, n.d., <http://www.historic-uk.com/HistoryUK/HistoryofBritain/The-Festival-of-Britain-1951/> [accessed 10 March 2020].
31. Leslie Hardcastle, 'In the beginning...'.
32. Geoffrey Macnab, 'The NFT is no more, long live the BFI Southbank', *Guardian*, 6 March 2007, <http://www.theguardian.com/film/filmblog/2007/mar/06/thenftisnomorelongliveb> [accessed 10 March 2020].
33. As noted later in this chapter, film critic Dilys Powell of the *Sunday Times* was one of the main initiators of the LFF, which explains why the *Sunday Times* was involved in the financing.
34. 'Currency converter: 1270–2017', National Archives, <http://apps.nationalarchives.gov.uk/currency/results.asp#mid> [accessed 10 March 2020].
35. Wendy Dalton, 'London Film Festival: Economics', in *Water Under the Bridge: 25 Years of the London Film Festival*, ed. by Martin Auty and Gillian Hartnoll (London: British Film Institute, 1981), p. 15.
36. Interview with Nowell-Smith.
37. Daniel Snowman, *The Hitler Emigrés: The Cultural Impact on Britain of Refugees from Nazism* (Pimlico: Chatto & Windus, 2002).
38. G. M. Hoellering, LFF brochure, 1957, p. 2.
39. Wlaschin, LFF brochure, 1975, n.p.
40. Wendy Dalton, 'London Film Festival: Economics', in *Water Under the Bridge: 25 Years of the London Film Festival*, ed. By Martin Auty and Gillian Hartnoll (London: British Film Institute, 1981), pp. 15–19 (p. 16).
41. A brief explanation of the role of FIAPF is included in the introduction of this book, along with an explanation of the controversy and actual value of their accreditation system.
42. Interview with Helen De Witt.
43. Wlaschin, LFF brochure, 1975, n.p.
44. Wendy Dalton, 'London Film Festival: Economics', p. 16.
45. Roy Strong described the 1951 South Bank Exhibition in his preface to that festival's twenty-

five-year retrospective in Mary Banham and Bevis Hillier, *A Tonic to the Nation: The Festival of Britain 1951* (London: Thames & Hudson, 1976), p. 2.
46. For a detailed breakdown of the events following WWII in the UK, including a comprehensive bibliography, see John Darwin, 'History: Britain, the Commonwealth and the End of Empire', BBC Online, 3 March 2011 <http://www.bbc.co.uk/history/british/modern/endofempire_overview_01.shtml> [accessed 10 March 2020].
47. Ken Wlaschin, LFF brochure, 1973, p. 3.
48. Michael Brooke, *The BFI Production Board: The Features,* BFI Screen Online, n.d., <http://www.screenonline.org.uk/film/id/1348538/> [accessed 10 March 2020].
49. Ken Wlaschin, LFF brochure, 1975, n.p.
50. Ken Wlaschin, LFF brochure, 1977, p. 45.
51. For comparative purposes, international film festivals generally do not run for longer than a fortnight, as is the case with Venice and Edinburgh. Cannes runs for twelve days, the same as BAFICI, followed by Toronto at eleven days, and San Sebastián at nine.
52. Interview with Christie.
53. For more information about the workshops see Margaret Dickinson, Anne Cottringer and Julian Petley, 'Workshops: A Dossier', *Vertigo,* 1, 1 (Spring 1993), <http://www.closeupfilmcentre.com/vertigo_magazine/volume-1-issue-1-spring-1993/workshops-a-dossier/> [accessed 10 March 2020].
54. Richard Combs, 'Richard Combs, Gilbert Adair and Nick Roddick write about some of the films that were shown in the 26th London Film Festival. LFF', in *Sight and Sound,* 52, 1 (Winter 1982/83), 14–17 (p. 14).
55. Inerview with Hebron, 28 September 2011.
56. Angus Finney, *The London Film Festival/Market: A Feasibility Study',* (Commissioned by the British Film Institute and the Producer's Alliance for Cinema and Television, 14–24 February, 1997), pp. 1–17, (p. 1).
57. Finney, *The London Film Festival/Market,* p. 1.
58. Finney, *The London Film Festival/Market,* p. 5.
59. Finney, *The London Film Festival/Market,* p. 5.
60. Finney, *The London Film Festival/Market,* p. 5.
61. Finney, *The London Film Festival/Market,* p. 1.
62. Finney, *The London Film Festival/Market,* p. 5.
63. Greg Wetherall, 'The BFI and London Film Festival today — Interview with Artistic Director Tricia Tuttle', *The Hot Corn,* 9 October 2018, <https://hotcorn.com/en/movies/news/bfi-london-film-festival-today-interview-artistic-director-tricia-tuttle/> [accessed 10 March 2020].
64. UK-Wide Film Festival Strategy.
65. UK-Wide Film Festival Strategy.
66. Peter Knegt, 'London Fest Sets 191 Features; Adds New Awards', *Indiewire,* 9 September 2009, <http://www.indiewire.com/article/london_fest_sets_191_features_adds_new_awards> [accessed 10 March 2020]. Jason Best, '53rd BFI London Film Festival. The Star of London Awards', *Whatsontv,* 6 October 2009, <https://www.whatsontv.co.uk/news/53rd-bfi-london-film-festival-the-star-of-london-awards-325682/> [accessed 10 March 2020]; LFF press release, BFI, <https://www.youtube.com/watch?v=u_JDQsVgsIM> [accessed 25 May 2020].
67. Interview with Hebron, 28 September 2011.
68. '55th BFI London Film Festival Unveils Packed Industry Programme', BFI, <http://www.bfi.org.uk/sites/bfi.org.uk/files/downloads/bfi-press-release-55th-bfi-london-film-festival-unveils-packed-industry-programme-2011-10-06.pdf> [accessed 10 March 2020].
69. Whitaker was Head of Programming of the NFT (now BFI Southbank) and director of the LFF from 1984–1986. She eventually took over the LFF full-time from 1987 to 1996.
70. The trailer is available to watch online on the BFI website: <http://www.bfi.org.uk/news/video-2012-festival-trailer> [accessed 10 March 2020].
71. Auty, *Water Under the Bridge,* pp. 1–2.
72. Matthew Flanagan, '"There is nothing moving in cinema": The Experimenta Weekend

at the 56th BFI London Film Festival', *senses of cinema*, Festival Reports, 66 (March 2013), <http://sensesofcinema.com/2013/festival-reports/there-is-nothing-moving-in-cinema-the-experimenta-weekend-at-the-56th-bfi-london-film-festival/> [accessed 10 March 2020].
73. Matthew Flanagan, 'Circles of Confusion: The 53rd London Film Festival', *senses of cinema*, 53, (December 2009), <http://sensesofcinema.com/2009/festival-reports/circles-of-confusion-the-53rd-london-film-festival/> [accessed 10 March 2020].
74. Derek Prouse, 'From Derek Prouse, who programmed the first London Film Festival', 25th Anniversary LFF brochure, 1981, n.p.
75. Auty, *Water Under the Bridge*, pp. 4–5.
76. Interview with Hebron, 28 September 2011.
77. Julia Kollewe, 'Cineworld buys Picturehouse: Arthouse cinema deal will make chain's co-founder Lyn Goleby a multi-millionaire', *Guardian*, 6 December 2012, <http://www.theguardian.com/business/2012/dec/06/cineworld-buys-picturehouse> [accessed 10 March 2020].
78. Interview with Hebron, 28 September 2011.
79. Wetherall, 'The BFI and London Film Festival today — Interview with Artistic Director Tricia Tuttle'
80. John Seabrook, 'Nobrow Culture', *The New Yorker*, 20 September 1999, <http://www.johnseabrook.com/nobrow-culture/> [accessed 25 May 2020].
81. Colin McArthur in Auty, *Water Under the Bridge*, p. 5.
82. Ken Wlaschin LFF brochure, 1981, n.p.
83. Bill Nichols, 'Global Image Consumption in the Age of Late Capitalism', *East-West Film Journal*, 8, 1 (1994), 68–85.
84. Julian Stringer, 'Raiding the Archive: Film Festivals and the Revival of Classic Hollywood', in *Memory and Popular Film*, ed. by Paul Grainge (Manchester: Manchester University Press, 2003), pp. 81–96.
85. Thomas Elsaesser, *European Cinema: Face to Face with Hollywood* (Amsterdam: Amsterdam University Press, 2005), pp. 82–107.
86. Marijke De Valck, *Film Festivals: From European Geopolitics to Global Cinephilia* (Amsterdam: Amsterdam University Press, 2007).
87. Azadeh Farahmand, 'Disentangling the International Festival Circuit: Genre and Iranian Cinema', in *Global Art Cinema: New Theories and Histories*, ed. by Rosalind Galt, and Karl Schoonover (eds), (New York: Oxford University Press, 2010), pp. 263–83.
88. Auty, *Water Under the Bridge*, p. 6.
89. Ken Wlaschin, 'Film Culture vs Film Makers', in Auty, *Water Under the Bridge*, pp. 13–14.
90. '57th BFI London Film Festival Boasts "Strongest Programme In Years"', BFI, <http://www.bfi.org.uk/sites/bfi.org.uk/files/downloads/bfi-press-release-london-film-festival-draws-to-a-close-2013–10–20.pdf> [accessed 10 March 2020].
91. 'A hugely popular 62nd BFI London Film Festival Draws To A Close', BFI, <https://www.bfi.org.uk/sites/bfi.org.uk/files/downloads/bfi-press-release-a-hugely-popular-62nd-bfi-london-film-festival-draws-to-a-close-2018–10–22.pdf> [accessed 10 March 2020].
92. Tony Rayns, quoted on the programming policy of the LFF's 1975 edition, in 'Luck and Judgement', *Time Out*, November, 1975, p. 10, in LFF dossier available in the BFI Archive.
93. Interview with Lerer.
94. Diego Lerer, 'Diario de Londres 2: Bruno Dumont, Jeff Nichols, Sean Durkin', *Micropsia*, 23 October 2011, <https://www.micropsiacine.com/2011/10/diario-de-londres-2-bruno-dumont-jeff-nichols-sean-durkin/> [accessed 25 May 2020].
95. Interview with Rayns.
96. Ken Wlaschin, LFF brochure, 1981.
97. Interview with Rayns.
98. Derek Malcolm LFF brochure, 1984, n.p.
99. Interview with Hebron, 28 September 2011.
100. Charles Gant, 'How Clare Stewart transformed the BFI London Film Festival', *Screendaily*, 4 October 2017, <https://www.screendaily.com/features/how-clare-stewart-transformed-the-bfi-london-film-festival/5122932.article> [accessed 10 March 2020].

101. Wetherall, 'The BFI and London Film Festival today — Interview with Artistic Director Tricia Tuttle'.
102. Michael Brooke, 'The BFI Production Board: The Features', *BFI screenonline*, n.d., <http://www.screenonline.org.uk/film/id/1348538/> [accessed 10 March 2020].
103. Theodor W. Adorno and Max Horkheimer, 'The Culture Industry: Enlightenment as Mass Deception', in *Dialectic of Enlightenment* (Great Britain: Verso Classics, 1979–1997 [1944]), pp. 120–67 (p. 121).
104. Tim Teeman, 'Greg Dyke: our man in the stalls at the BFI', *The Times Online*, March 6 2008, article copied and pasted online by Pam Cook in her blog *bfiwatch* on the same day, <http://bfiwatch.blogspot.co.uk/2008/03/greg-dyke-bbc-and-bfi.html> [accessed 10 March 2020].
105. Elsaesser, 'Film Festival Network', p. 84.
106. Dave Calhoun, 'Greg Dyke and The Future of the British Film Institute', *Time Out*, 12 March 2008, <http://www.timeout.com/london/film/greg-dyke-and-the-future-of-the-british-film-institute> [accessed 10 March 2020].
107. Sandra Hebron, 'Points taken', *Time Out*, 8–14 May 2008, p. 82.
108. Hebron, 'Points Taken'.
109. Interview with Christie.
110. Adam Dawtrey, 'UKFC Lifts Edinburgh Festival Budget', *Variety*, 17 March 2008, <http://variety.com/2008/film/news/ukfc-lifts-edinburgh-festival-budget-1117982526/> [accessed 10 March 2020].
111. Ali Jaafar, 'London Fest Gets $2.7 million', *Variety*, 10 May 2009, <https://variety.com/2009/biz/news/london-fest-gets-2-7-million-1118003443/> [accessed 10 March 2020].
112. Adam Dawtrey, 'Brit fest scene is a tale of two cities', *Variety*, 24–30 March 2008, p. 7.
113. Stewart Till, quoted in Adam Dawtrey, 'Brit fest scene is a tale of two cities'.
114. 'Festival screening for new Bond film. The new Bond film Quantum of Solace is to get its first public screening at this year's London Film Festival, organisers have announced...', BBC, 10 September 2008, <http://news.bbc.co.uk/1/hi/entertainment/7608105.stm> [accessed 25 May 2020].
115. Prouse, quoted in Auty, *Water Under the Bridge*, p. 9.
116. Prouse, quoted in Auty, *Water Under the Bridge*, p. 10.
117. Prouse, quoted in Auty, *Water Under the Bridge*, p. 10.
118. BFI Film Fund official information available at <https://www.bfi.org.uk/supporting-uk-film/film-fund> [accessed 25 May 2020].
119. For more information see Adam Dawtrey, 'How is the BFI suddenly able to take over from the UK Film Council?', *Guardian Film Blog*, 29 November 2010, <http://www.theguardian.com/film/filmblog/2010/nov/29/uk-film-council-bfi-ed-vaizey> [accessed 10 March 2020].
120. 'Clare Stewart Appointed Head of Exhibition, BFI', 8 July 2011, <http://www.bfi.org.uk/sites/bfi.org.uk/files/downloads/bfi-press-release-clare-stewart-appointed-head-of-exhibition-bfi-2011-07-08.pdf> [accessed 10 March 2020].
121. For more information about this industry event see Film London official website, <http://filmlondon.org.uk/pfm> [accessed 10 March 2020].
122. Olaciregui, Mikel, interview with Mar Diestro-Dópido, San Sebastián International Film Festival offices, San Sebastián, 4 May 2010.
123. Mar Diestro-Dópido, 'The Pain in Spain', *Sight & Sound Online*, 19 October 2012, <http://www.bfi.org.uk/news-opinion/sight-sound-magazine/comment/festivals/lff-blog-pain-spain> [accessed 10 March 2020].
124. Matthew Flanagan, '"There is nothing moving in cinema": The Experimenta Weekend at the 56th BFI London Film Festival'.
125. Interview with Rayns.
126. Wetherall, 'The BFI and London Film Festival today — Interview with Artistic Director Tricia Tuttle'.
127. Barbara Wurn, 'Leftist Glamour? or, Home Runs and Explorations: The 47th Viennale: Vienna International Film Festival', *senses of cinema*, Festival Reports, 54 (April 2010), <http://sensesofcinema.com/2010/festival-reports/vienna-international-film-festival/> [accessed 10 March 2020].

128. Interview with Hebron, 28 September 2011.
129. Simon Fields quoted in James Quandt, 'The Sandwich Process: Simon Field Talks about Polemics and Poetry at Film Festivals' in *Dekalog 3: On Film Festivals*, ed.by Richard Porton (London: Wallflower Press, 2009), pp. 53–80 (pp. 56–57).
130. Fields quoted in Quandt, 'The Sandwich Process', p. 57.
131. *Dekalog 3: On Film Festivals*, ed. by Richard Porton (London: Wallflower Press, 2010).
132. Interview with Porton.
133. Interview with Diego Galán, Las Vistillas Restaurant, Madrid, 8 April 2011.
134. Fields quoted in Quandt, 'The Sandwich Process', p. 57.
135. Interview with Hebron, via email.
136. Figures requested but not provided.
137. Interview with Rayns.
138. Auty, *Water Under the Bridge*, p. 8.
139. Flanagan, 'Circles of Confusion'.
140. Mark Peranson, 'First You Get the Power, Then You Get the Money: Two Models of Film Festivals', *Cineaste*, 33, 3 (Summer 2008), 37–43. Reprinted in *Dekalog 3: On Film Festivals*, ed. by Richard Porton (London: Wallflower Press, 2010), pp. 116–31.
141. Flanagan, 'Circles of Confusion'.
142. Roud, LFF brochure 1966, p. 2.
143. 'A hugely popular 62nd BFI London Film Festival Draws To A Close', BFI, <https://www.bfi.org.uk/sites/bfi.org.uk/files/downloads/bfi-press-release-a-hugely-popular-62nd-bfi-london-film-festival-draws-to-a-close-2018-10-22.pdf> [accessed 10 March 2020].
144. Interview with Porton.
145. Theodor W. Adorno and Max Horkheimer, 'The Culture Industry: Enlightenment as Mass Deception', in *Dialectic of Enlightenment* (Great Britain: Verso Classics, 1979–1997 [1944]), p. 120–67 (p. 121).
146. Mark Cousins, Film Festival Manifesto, *Film Festival Academy*, 2012, <https://www.filmfest.net.au/2015/09/23/the-film-fest-manifesto/> [accessed 25 May 2020].
147. For a summary of the statistics published in the BFI Yearbooks from 2002 see, <https://www.bfi.org.uk/education-research/film-industry-statistics-research/statistical-yearbook> [accessed 25 May 2020]. The whole of the BFI Statistical Yearbook 2014 is available at www.bfi.org.uk/statisticalyearbook2017/
148. 'Film Forever', BFI, July 2013, <https://www.bfi.org.uk/sites/bfi.org.uk/files/downloads/bfi-film-festival-fund-overview-2013-07.pdf> [accessed 11 March 2020].
149. 'BFI2022: Supporting the future of UK film', BFI, <https://www.bfi.org.uk/2022/> [accessed 11 March 2020].
150. UK Film Council, *Stories We Tell Ourselves: The Cultural Impact of UK Film 1946–2006* (Great Britain: Narval Media/Birkbeck College/Media Consulting Group, 2009).
151. UK Film Council/British Film Institute, *Opening Our Eyes: How Film Contributes to the Culture of the UK* (Great Britain: Northern Alliance with Ipsos MediaCT, 2011).
152. *Audiences*, ed. by Ian Christie (Amsterdam: Amsterdam University Press, 2012).
153. '57TH BFI London Film Festival Boasts "Strongest Programme in Years"', BFI, <http://www.bfi.org.uk/sites/bfi.org.uk/files/downloads/bfi-press-release-london-film-festival-draws-to-a-close-2013-10-20.pdf> [accessed 11 March 2020].
154. Jesper Strandgaard Pedersen and Carmelo Mazza, 'International Film Festivals: For The Benefit of Whom?', *Culture Unbound. Journal of Current Cultural Research*, 3, 2011 (pp. 139–165) p. 144
155. Interview with Rayns.
156. Laurent Jullier and Jean-Marc Leveratto, 'Cinephilia in the Digital Age' in *Audiences*, ed. by Ian Christie, pp. 143–54.
157. Jullier and Leveratto refer to a Cinephilia Dossier published by the U.S. academic journal *Framework* in 2004, and guest-edited by Jonathan Buchsbaum and Elena Gorfinkel. 'What's Being Fought by Today's Cinephilia(s)? dossier, ed. by Jonathan Buchsbaum and Elena Gorfinkel *Framework. The Journal of Cinema and Media*, 50 (Fall 2009).
158. For details of Lerer's coverage of the LFF, for example, see p. 247.

159. Mikhail M Bakhtin, *Rabelais and His World*, trans. by Hélène Iswolsky (Bloomington: Indiana University Press, 1968/1984), p. 11.
160. Jesper Strandgaard Pedersen and Carmelo Mazza, 'International Film Festivals', p. 153.

CONCLUSION

❖

The End of Festivals?

By way of conclusion I propose to continue more or less from where I left off in Chapter 3, in order first to note the challenges that festivals in general are facing at present, then to look at the particular ways in which these challenges are being dealt with by each of my three case studies. Finally, I summarize the contribution I hope to have made to the emerging field of film festival studies with this study.

As outlined in Chapter 3, audience, technology and industry are not just the current preoccupations for cultural organizations such as the BFI, but a serious concern for film festivals all over the world. This concern became a micro-zeitgeist of sorts, expressed in related activities that seemed to peak in 2009, perhaps triggered by the economic crisis that had engulfed the Western world in 2008. Part of the aftermath of the crisis in countries such as the UK and Spain were severe cuts to cultural organizations, creating an atmosphere of anxious self-interrogation. Practically every film festival I attended between 2008 to 2011 had organized panels bringing together important festival world guests to discuss what became a general topic at the time: the future of film festivals. It was certainly so at the three case studies in this book, as well as other festivals such as Venice in 2011.

One such panel took place in Toronto in 2009. The event was covered by *Indiewire*'s Peter Knegt, who in his article summarizes some of the key issues raised by its four panellists: host Sean Farnel, (Director of Programming at Hot Docs), Cameron Bailey (Co-Director of the Toronto International Film Festival), Geoff Gilmore (Chief Creative Officer, Tribeca Enterprises), Janet Pierson (Producer of SXSW Film Conference and Festival), and Sky Sitney (Artistic Director, SILVERDOCS — now AFI Docs).[1] The key problematic aspects of film festivals identified by the panel were: the way festivals are incorporating markets for producers and buyers, forcing the festival to turn away from its original role as exhibitor and get more involved in business transactions and production; the disappearance of arthouse spaces and film critics, and how this has put pressure on film festivals to act as a substitute;[2] audiences' changing film habits; the place of programming for the filmmaking community (as opposed to programming for audiences); and working with distributors.

The German film magazine *Schnitt* echoed this preoccupation with the changing shape of festivals and their future and dedicated its February 2009 issue to the same question: the future of film festivals. The magazine invited festival directors from all over the world to contribute, and for the first time in its history it was published in both English and German, to 'accommodate a discussion of international relevance'.[3] In it, Marco Müller (current artistic director of Pingyao, formerly of Turin, Pesaro, Rotterdam, Locarno, Venice, Rome and Macau) proposed taking on board the entertainment side of film to aim for a broad and inclusive programme,[4] a not dissimilar argument to Hebron's, whose contribution focuses on the digital 'kindergarten' that festivals are still mired in.[5] Jean-Pierre Rehm (director of FIDMarseille) asserts that the task of a festival is, by definition, to trust in the future,[6] whilst Hans Hurch (then director of the Viennale) focuses on the role of the film festival as 'a social sphere of collective cultural experience', and argues that 'a future festival cannot be legitimized as a marketplace, nor as a media event, nor as a cinematic musealization nor as politico-cultural surplus, but by its work in order to create a public for the filmic'.[7] For Lars Henrik Gass (director of the International Short Film Festival Oberhausen) the transformations that festivals are undergoing signal only one possible future: 'to change from being a marketplace to becoming a brand and taking responsibility to refinance their products. The only sure thing is that screening films will no longer be enough'.[8]

Oliver Père (former director of Cannes's Directors Fortnight and Locarno, now Head of ARTE France), states that cinema, since its creation, 'has been a window to the world, to the people, to the soul of the artist and his models. A film festival must be a window to that window'.[9] Père not only references Bazin's conception of cinema as a 'window on the world', but more importantly here, with its focus on the festival's function as exhibitor, Père brings attention to the question: does a festival remain so if it gets involved in distribution and nowadays in production too? Or does it become something else? Film critic and programmer Neil Young takes this to an extreme when he alleges that, in his opinion, Cannes is not a film festival per se, because of its strong ties with the film industry. In this light, for Young, Cannes becomes

> an industry event in the context of which audiences either do not figure or figure only as extras that serve as background for glitzy events.[10]

In a 2014 interview, Carlo Chatrian, then director of the Locarno Film Festival, declared (referring to Toronto) that, 'A Locarno, nous sommes en dehors de la logique de supermarché' (or 'In Locarno we are outside of the logic of the supermarket').[11] Young and Chatrian's opinions are somehow echoed in filmmaker and producer Pere Portabella's take on the subject; he does not see the role of the industry as a new thing, but rather it has been a major player in festivals since their inception:

> Festivals were born under the influence of the [Hollywood] Majors, i.e. from the start they were thought of as large platforms in the most financial sense of the word. This has become decadent now –– because of film's own decadence –– and for years film festivals have been purely a market for films, which follow certain classicist canons, with good casting and strong media-friendly figures. [...] There can be certain fissures, flashbacks and those kind of things, but [n]owadays, festivals are worse than a market, it's the swan song.[12]

Yet for Marco Müller the key to the success and survival of film festivals lies precisely in the dialogue between festivals and the industry:

> A festival shouldn't be a surrogate of all that doesn't work in the distribution circuit; it shouldn't represent a sort of alternative universe to the marketplace. A festival makes sense in relation to what starts happening in the wider film world the day after the festival ends. There needs to be a dialogue, an exchange between the festival and the market so that films screened here don't die after the event but are launched into a longer trajectory. I'm interested in the waves that a festival ignites and the motion its films are set in. Films should be recognized outside the festival they're being shown and within the international arena.[13]

To paraphrase Gass's conclusion regarding the future of film festivals, 'The only sure thing is that screening films will no longer be enough'.[14] And this, more often than not, not only applies to spreading festivals' many functions, but also to further involving their audiences.

Fast forward to 2016, and *Screen Daily* magazine published an article online in which a group of smaller, non-commercial film festival professionals are asked the question 'What's the purpose of film festivals in the 21st Century?'.[15] Democracy is a word shared by all participants in relation to global digitalization, and so is giving the public and the filmmakers the chance to establish a dialogue, enhancing the festival-goers' experience, as well as their key role as an alternative exhibition platform for non-commercial films. But so is recovering the form in which film is supposed to be shown; as Selena Valyyavkina, programmer of the Message2Man International Film Festival in Russia comments: 'In the century of "clip thinking" a film festival is very often the only place where you can actually watch and enjoy film, without fast forwarding it, without pausing it'. For Neil Fox, Projects Manager of the Edinburgh International Film Festival, 'Film Festivals are places of discovery and ritual'; and contrary to the believe by many a film professional, the growing number of film festivals is seen by Ana Cerar, Programme Coordinator of Kino Otok — Isola Cinema in Slovenia, a festival I myself attended in 2012, 'The number of film festivals around the globe is becoming a strength, not weakness: a progressive model of cooperation between festivals helps distribute filmmakers' work in an alternative, friendly way.

Eventbrite, an event management and ticketing website based in the US, offers its services to allow its users to 'browse, create and promote local events'. Their latest report claims to draw on 'recent research, to give you the latest festival innovations, emerging technologies, and marketing tips'.[16] Under the title 'The Future of Festivals: 8 Trends You Need to Know', anybody can access the report which focuses on the use of new technology such as Instagram to increase word of mouth, ticketing services, etc., and the hunger for personalized unique experiences. And yet, its most important bit of information comes right at the report's introduction with the following statistic,

> Over 75% of millennials and 59% of Baby Boomers say they value experiences over possessions.

Followed by the eternal question summarizing decades of festival professionals' headaches:

> How can you tap into your attendees' desires, and build strong connections that bring them back year after year?

The answer is as malleable and current as the festivals themselves — always in constant flux, forever foreseeing that same question.

Responding to a slight change of angle, and moving from the festival itself to its key players, i.e. the films, in 2011 on the San Sebastián website you could win a pair of tickets to attend the closing ceremony by entering your answer to the question: 'Tell us what you think of the future of film', presumably in the hope that the answers would shed some light on people's current film-watching habits. The issue of accessibility, as well as the festivals' need to keep abreast of technological changes, led BAFICI, San Sebastián and London within a short period of more or less two years (2010–2012) to massively upgrade and improve their websites (in the case of the LFF, it was part of the BFI's own website redesign). These festivals' websites now present a much more user-friendly environment, with written blogs, tweeting, video-blogging from the festival, press conferences, footage of opening galas, etc., and its own Festival TV in the case of San Sebastián. The festivals marketing climate in which I began my research in 2008 is very different to the environment that festivals now operate in (the colossal impact of COVID-19 included).

Indeed, the current director of San Sebastián, José Luis Rebordinos, has an all year-round blog where he and his team of programmers write regularly about their activities (attendance at other festivals, or particular films/screenings) and any film-related news, such as budgets or governmental changes. BAFICI offers access to every activity being carried out by the Festival and maintains an archive of every event that's taken place at the Festival, including catalogues, awards, industry meetings, guest lists, and published books. In the case of the LFF, the BFI website, where the Festival's site is housed, offers video on demand of some of the films screened at the Festival, as well as the rest of the BFI's own content, from the digital version of *Sight & Sound* and access to its archive, to educational material and library access. In addition, all three festivals have a strong presence on Internet social networks such as Facebook, Twitter, Flickr, etc.

In many ways, festivals could be said to constitute the temple in which Guy Debord's notion of the 'spectacle' is consecrated. But Debord also conceives this spectacle not simply as the reduction of human experiences to a collection of images, but rather as a '*social relationship* between people that is mediated by images'[17] (my italics). Baudrillard takes this notion and turns it on its head when speaking about the way the digital is dominating our means of communication in his book *The Ecstasy of Communication*, and bemoans that

> Obscenity begins precisely when there is no more spectacle, no more scene, when all becomes transparence and immediate visibility, when everything is exposed to the harsh and inexorable light of information and communication. We are no longer a part of the drama of alienation; we live in the ecstasy of communication.[18]

In this light, I would argue that Baudrillard's notion is doubly relevant when applied to festivals. On the one hand festivals are source and space where the spectacle is held. But on the other hand, they are readily capable of adapting to new ways of socializing brought about by the digital realm, and can establish a dialogue with, or participate in, the Baudrillardian 'ecstasy of communication'; more so, when one relates Baudrillard's digital 'ecstasy' to Bakhtin's notion of the cultural 'feast'.[19] It is within the capacity of festivals to establish a space where tensions such as these are played out, setting up a productive dialectic that I would argue is important for festivals' long-term survival. Or in other words, what Hursch refers to in his *Schnitt* contribution as 'a social sphere of collective cultural experience'.

Further making use of the visual, one of the most entertaining and revealing marketing devices of any festival is its promotional trailer. Indeed, my three case studies illustrate that these trailers also perfectly exemplify the variety of stances that film festivals adopt with regard to their audiences.

In the case of San Sebastián the festival's emphasis on its links to film history and its own history create an image that is modern but situated within a certain classicism and tradition -- mirroring the idiosyncrasies of the Basque Country. This classicism is expressed by the festival's preference for prioritizing their marketing posters over their trailers (which are simply an image of the logo). This poster-led marketing has featured throughout its existence; in some cases posters were used to denounce the political situation in Spain, such as the one designed for the 1976 edition (the first one after Franco's death). Their design has come to be recognized as the expression of the Festival's identity and personality. All posters can be accessed on the official website.

But it was under Diego Galán -- who, as discussed in Chapter 2, actively opened up the Festival to the audience -- that the posters evinced a particularly pronounced celebration of cinema under the auspices of the design company Artimaña (who have worked with the festival since 1995). The poster for the forty-sixth edition in 1998 best exemplifies this, as the actual process of designing the poster became an attraction in itself. The idea was to recreate the synchronized swimming used in Hollywood musicals by Busby Berkeley. The aim was to get a specialized swimming team of Madrid to evoke the shape of the famous *concha* symbol of the festival for the poster (a shell, it gives its name to San Sebastián's main award, which in turn refers to the main beach that fronts the city).[20]

Nowadays, the focus has slightly shifted in order to encourage audiences to participate further, and the actual design of the poster is chosen through open competition. From 2012, and coinciding with the Festival's sixtieth anniversary, San Sebastián has held an online poster contest where everyone is invited to produce a design for that year's edition. With all the posters available online, the audience is invited to vote for the one they think is best producing a selection of a total of ten, and a final decision by a jury. The results are all published online; the preference seems to be for figurative imagery alluding to cinema iconography based on a cutting-edge idea of design. Hence, San Sebastián uses film history to embrace a communal film imaginary that connects with its contemporary audiences.

In the case of the LFF the more creative marketing goes into the Festival's trailer, comprising a mini film that is played before every film. But there's a big difference in the majority of LFF trailers compared to San Sebastián, as the protagonist is not just the audience but also the city. Two different examples, from the 2003[21]

Fig. C.1. Still from the BFI London Film Festival 2011 publicity campaign
© BFI London Film Festival Archive

and 2009[22] editions (also available on YouTube), suffice to reveal the LFF trailers' common traits: humour, the city, and the audience.

In the 2003 trailer, filmmaking itself takes over the city. A random man who aspires to be a filmmaker pretends to be shooting takes involving bystanders: a child, a worker, a pigeon, framing them with his hands and asking them to play for the camera. The common element is the city, used as the identifiable background. In 2009 the LFF's trailer foregrounded the audience, as did the campaign in 2012.[23] But whereas the latter, as discussed in Chapter 3, focused on an individual woman sitting in an empty cinema, the trailer in 2009 takes the camera out of the cinema and brings film to the city's varied citizens. One by one they are all lured by a flickering light, sometimes on their own, sometimes in company. In 2011,[24] the city is once more present. Yet, here a red carpet is the protagonist, shown being rolled out throughout the city's streets, ending up in what looks like an older version of the NFT.

The different voice-overs at the end of these trailers are also revealing. In 2003, it announces 'The Times BFI London Film Festival; bringing film to the *public*'. In 2009, we have 'the world's best new films, here in *London*'. And similarly, in 2011, the festival is said to be 'bringing the world's best new films to *London*' (all my italics). They are all imbued with a sense of film's alluring power, decidedly all-inclusive and strongly located within the city. It is significant to note that two years after the appointment of Clare Stewart as artistic director in 2011, and the boosting of premieres that followed, the Festival's promotional trailers are no longer short films focusing on the audience, but an amalgam of the films populating that year's programme where that year's festival's most important figures -- total number of features, premieres, venues, etc. -- are projected onto the images (all publicity campaigns are available on YouTube).

Like the LFF, BAFICI also uses trailers that are played before every film shown. However, their focus has been entirely different to both London and San Sebastián. Picking up on a tradition followed by festivals such as the Viennale, in 2010 the festival commissioned some of the so-called New Argentine Cinema filmmakers to direct a one-minute trailer for the Festival. The most symbolic of them, Lisandro Alonso's *Owl*,[25] consists of a fixed camera holding a close up on an owl for a minute. Humour tends to be their main ingredient, although usually in a more slapstick vein than Alonso's understated effort.

In *Bigotes/Moustaches*,[26] *El cuadro más triste del mundo/The Saddest Picture in the World*,[27] *Payasos/Clowns*,[28] *Portal*[29] (all made in 2007) and *Playa/Beach* (2009),[30] a small group of about four people experience something together -- a moustache, a painting, a song, a time-space travelling experience, the beach, respectively. But when they share their experience afterwards, each time one of them fails to engage. From 2011 the trailers adopt a slightly different perspective and encourage audiences to watch something other than commercial films, for example in *Cazadores/Hunters*[31] (2011). The concluding quote reflects this: 'The more independent films you watch, the less you stereotype. And vice versa.'

So whereas London and San Sebastián's efforts are definitely inclusive in their address to their potential audiences (in the case of London, at least until 2013), BAFICI's mode of address emerges from the festival's creation of what I would assess as an exclusive, yet fully accessible, space. BAFICI's slogan at the end of its videos up until 2011 is self-explanatory: 'If it's not for you, it's not for you.'

Not only that, but to some extent, the clue is in the name, and each festival's title reveals their attitude not only to audiences but also to the industry and indeed film itself. BAFICI has 'independent' in its name, San Sebastián 'international'. The LFF has neither independent nor international in its title, but has at different points in its history (and especially so in recent years) included the name of its parent organization, as well as its main sponsor, uniquely within the festival circuit; it was for example known for many years as *The Times* BFI London Film Festival.

And yet, there is a powerful overarching element that connects all three festivals: their absolute determination to include their audiences, to take their audiences with them every step of the way. So to return to that thorny question of the future of film festivals, in many ways the capitalist dictum of supply and demand could be applied. I would nevertheless argue that it is only by going 'back to the future'[32] (as with Müller's contribution to *Schnitt*), that the future of festivals can be located; by regarding them as an essential part of the cultural landscape in which film is received, a form of ritual that precedes their current incarnation, and which is innate to human interaction. This is in many ways what this book has been centrally concerned with: how each of these festivals 'speaks to' and within the context in which it has been created and which has evolved throughout its history. Once again I'm compelled to return to Bakhtin's notion of the feast as a cultural form, which implies that there will always be a hunger, an atavistic desire for a communal, ephemeral live experience. Finding new ways (as well as the tried and tested) to respond to what Cousins refers to as a 'need'[33] in his Manifesto is what, in my opinion, constitutes the key to the survival of film festivals.

The thrust of this book has taken me on a similar journey. From the origins, to the present, and back to the future of these three case studies, my focus has largely been on the 'communities' that have shaped these festivals, transforming them into what they are in the present, which may be something very different to what they were even twelve years ago when I embarked on the research I conducted for this book. For one of the difficulties of studying these events resides precisely in their 'live' condition; their intrinsically ephemeral quality. Unlike films — a huge part of film festivals' content — festivals cannot be reproduced but have to be experienced. And they are unique in themselves, but more importantly, for each individual.

This is where I believe this book contributes to the emerging academic field of film festival studies; through the attempt to reproduce, by way of my own and others' multiple experiences, the intricacies that shape film festivals. By focusing on the history of each of my three case studies, I have tried to concentrate on crucial details and not generalities. I have done this by exploring one of the most overlooked aspects of these events — the point of view of the 'communities' that constitute the festival cosmos: organizers, funders, filmmakers, producers, critics, directors, programmers, guests, educational bodies, and more.

The myriad personal testimonies of those directly involved in film festivals gathered together in this book have allowed me to create a space in which an overarching dialogue between the varying ecologies of my three case studies plays out. Threaded throughout is a nuanced understanding of how these festivals operate at different levels of exchange — political, social, economic, cultural — as well as the relationships that these three case studies establish for themselves within the multiple layers of the festival circuit, through their roles as exhibitors, distributors, producers, and above all, events.

As indicated by the quotation that opens this book, all histories are constructions and therefore partial, their narratives dependent on access — to people, texts, other research material. The main difficulty with the cross-over approach to these festivals was precisely the inaccessibility of certain people and research items. Nonetheless, I maintain that the synergies that have emerged within this study through the conjunction of oral testimony and extensive academic research are its most valuable contribution, having enabled me to construct unique and insightful histories of each of the three festivals. This book is only but one version of them.

Notes to the Conclusion

1. Peter Knegt, 'On the Future of Fests: Thoughts From the Top', *Indiewire*, 12 May 2009, <http://www.indiewire.com/article/on_the_future_of_film_festivals_thoughts_from_leading_figures> [accessed 11 March 2020].
2. See *Sight & Sound*'s Nick James's editorial on the 'disappearance' of film critics from the UK printed press in the last five years. Nick James, 'Goodbye Mr French: Fleet Street Cuts Back Its Film Critics', *Sight & Sound*, 23, 11 (November 2013), 5. See also, Nick James, 'Rip It Up: Revitalizing Film Criticism', *Film Quarterly*, 62, 3 (Spring 2009), <http://www.filmquarterly.org/2009/03/spring-2009-volume-62-no-3/> [accessed 10 March 2020].
3. Unsigned, 'The Future of Film Festivals', *Schnitt*, 54 (February 2009), 7.
4. Marco Müller, 'Back to the Future', *Schnitt*, 54 (February 2009), 13–15 (p. 13).
5. Sandra Hebron, 'In the Digital Kindergarten', *Schnitt*, 54 (February 2009) 17–19 (p. 17).
6. Jean-Pierre Rehm, 'Film Museums of the Now', *Schnitt*, 54 (February 2009), 27–31 (p. 27).
7. Hans Hurch, 'The Film Festival as a Space of Experience', *Schnitt*, 54 (February 2009), 31–33 (p. 31).
8. Lars Henrik Gass, 'Trade Market Becomes Trade Mark', *Schnitt*, 54 (February 2009), 43–45 (p. 43).
9. Olivier Père, 'A Showcase for the Cinema', *Schnitt*, 54 (February 2009), 19–21 (p. 19).
10. Neil Young speaking at Tromsø IFF, Norway, January 2010, cited in Dina Iordanova, 'Notes on Film Festivals vs. Industry Events', *DinaView*, 30 September 2010, <http://www.dinaview.com/?p=1490> [page no longer live].
11. Julien Gester, 'Carlo Chatrian: A Locarno Nous Sommes en Dehors de la Logique de Supermarché', *Libération*, 6 August 2014, <http://next.liberation.fr/cinema/2014/08/06/a-locarno-nous-sommes-en-dehors-de-la-logique-de-supermarche_1076520> [accessed 11 March 2020].
12. Interview with Pere Portabella, by phone , 29 June 2011.
13. Celluloid Liberation Front, 'Interview: Rome Film Festival Director Marco Mueller Discusses his First Year and the Future of Italian Cinema', *Indiewire*, 20 November 2012, <http://www.indiewire.com/article/interview-rome-film-festival-director-marco-mueller-discusses-his-first-year-and-the-future-of-italian-cinema> [accessed 11 March 2020].
14. Lars Henrik Gass, 'Trade Market Becomes Trade Mark', p. 45.
15. 'What's the purpose of film festivals in the 21st Century?', *Screendaily*, 19 August 2016, <https://www.screendaily.com/comment/whats-the-purpose-of-film-festivals-in-the-21st-century/5108598.article> [accessed 11 March 2020].

16. 'The Future of Festivals: 8 Trends You Need to Know', *EventBrite*, n.d., <https://www.eventbrite.co.uk/blog/academy/the-future-of-festivals/> [accessed 11 March 2020].
17. Guy Debord, 'The Society of the Spectacle', trans. by Black & Red in 1977, point 4. Originally written in 1967. Reproduced at *Marxists.com*, <https://www.marxists.org/reference/archive/debord/society.htm> [accessed 11 March 2020].
18. Jean Baudrillard, 'The Ecstasy of Communication', trans. John Johnston in *The Anti-Aesthetic: Essays on Postmodern Culture*, ed. by Hal Foster (Port Townsend, Washington: Bay Press, 1987), pp. 126–34 (p. 130).
19. Mikhail Bakhtin, *Rabelais and his World*, trans. by Hélène Iswolsky (Bloomington: Indiana University Press, 1968, revised edition 1984), p. 11.
20. The actual recreation was televized and the video can still be seen on YouTube. '1998 making off cartel 46° festival de cine de san sebastián', YouTube, 7 July 2010, <https://www.youtube.com/watch?v=mvXzREbu360> [accessed 11 March 2020].
21. 'The Times/BFI London Film Festival — Director (2003, UK)', YouTube, <https://www.youtube.com/watch?v=diLuz2pilcE> [accessed 25 May 2020]
22. 'BFI 53rd London Film Festival (2009, UK)'. Available at <https://www.youtube.com/watch?v=u_JDQsVgsIM> [accessed 25 May 2020].
23. 'Feel It', <https://www.youtube.com/watch?v=gk49fkpt5rY> [accessed 25 May 2020].
24. 'The 55th BFI London Film Festival Trailer', YouTube, 13 October 2011, <https://www.youtube.com/watch?v=5n9JacMaKHE>.
25. 'BAFICI [11°] Corto institucional: "Lechuza" por Lisandro Alonso', YouTube, 18 November 2010 <https://www.youtube.com/watch?v=tp2rqMBPUxM> [accessed 11 March 2020].
26. 'Bigotes', Youtube, 8 April 2008, <https://www.youtube.com/watch?v=hCF5zr5Zhks> [accessed 11 March 2020].
27. 'El cuadro más triste del mundo', YouTube, 9 June 2007 <https://www.youtube.com/watch?v=3dfiFCwJBXY> [accessed 11 March 2020].
28. 'Payasos', YouTube, 8 April 2008, <https://www.youtube.com/watch?v=bJ4vOAjb9MU> [accessed 11 March 2020].
29. 'Portal — Bafici — Festival cine independiente Buenos Aires', YouTube, 31 March 2007, <https://www.youtube.com/watch?v=tUv3igBmTJ8> [accessed 11 March 2020].
30. 'BAFICI PLAYA', YouTube, 1 April 2009 <https://www.youtube.com/watch?v=ExyJARnEulo> [accessed 11 March 2020].
31. 'bafici cazadores', YouTube, 7 April 2011, <https://www.youtube.com/watch?v=UKL_yThHIa8> [accessed 11 March 2020].
32. Marco Müller, 'Back to the Future', pp. 13–15.
33. Mark Cousins, Film Festival Manifesto, *Film Festival Academy*, 2012, <http://www.filmfestivalacademy.net/publications/film-festival-form-a-manifesto> [accessed 11 march 2020].

BIBLIOGRAPHY

❖

ACKERMAN, SEBASTIÁN, 'Festival porteño en crisis', *Página/12*, 18 November 2004,<http://www.pagina12.com.ar/diario/espectaculos/6-43741-2004-11-18.html> [accessed 12 March 2020]

ADAIR, GILBERT, 'London 25. Tom Milne and Gilbert Adair Write about Some of the Films in the 1981 London Film Festival', *Sight & Sound*, 51, 1 (Winter 1981–82), 16–19

ADORNO, THEODOR W., and MAX HORKHEIMER, *Dialectic of Enlightenment*, ed. by Gunzelin Schmid Noerr, trans. by Edmund Jephcott (Stanford: Stanford University Press, 2002), pp. 94–136

ADORNO, THEODOR W., *The Culture Industry: Selected Essays on Mass Culture* (London: Routledge, 2001)

AGENCIA EFE, 'El Festival de San Sebastián genera 27 millones en impacto económico', *El Mundo*, 12 July 2013, <http://www.elmundo.es/elmundo/2013/07/12/paisvasco/1373628016.html> [accessed 11 March 2020]

—— 'Javier Rebollo "Este premio demuestra que hay otro tipo de cine español"', *ABC*, 26 September 2009, <http://www.abc.es/hemeroteca/historico-26-09-2009/abc/Cultura/javier-rebollo-este-premio-demuestra-que-hay-otro-tipo-de-cine-español_103161447234.html> [accessed 11 March 2020]

AGOSTA, DIANA and PATRICIA KEETON, 'One Way or Another: The Havana Film Festival and Contemporary Cuban Film', *Afterimage*, 22, 2 (1994), 7–8

AGUILAR, GONZALO, *Other Worlds*, trans. by Sarah Ann Wells (London: Palgrave Macmillan, 2008)

AGUIRRE, JAVIER, 'Sobre la 'ley Miró', *El País*, 26 December 1984, <http://elpais.com/diario/1984/12/26/cultura/472863601_850215.html> [accessed 11 March 2020]

AHN, SOOJEONG, *The Pusan International Film Festival, South Korean Cinema and Globalization* (Hong Kong: Hong Kong University Press, 2011)

AIRA, CÉSAR, *Festival* (Buenos Aires: Ministerio de Cultura, Gobierno de la Ciudad, 2011), <http://www.opcionlibros.gov.ar/libros/cine.php> [accessed 11 March 2020]

ANDERSON, JASON, 'Taste of Armadillo: Lisandro Alonso on *La Libertad*', *Cinema Scope*, 9 (December 2001), 36–38

Angulo, Javier, interview with Mar Diestro-Dópido, by phone, 26 February 2020

ANGULO, JESÚS, MAIALEN BELOKI, JOSÉ LUIS REBORDINOS, and ANTONIO SANTAMARINA, *Antxon Eceiza: cine, existencialismo y dialéctica* (San Sebastián: Euskadiko Filmategia/Filmoteca Vasca, 2009)

ARAGÜEZ RUBIO, CARLOS, 'Intelectuales y cine en el segundo franquismo: de las Conversaciones de Salamanca al nuevo cine español', *Asociación de Historiadores del Presente*, 15 June 2013, <http://historiadelpresente.es/sites/default/files/revista/articulos/5/506intelectualesycineenelsegundofranquismodelasconversacionesdesalamancaalnuevocineespanol.pdf> [accessed 11 March 2020]

ARENAS, JOSÉ EDUARDO, 'Del Castillo dice que "La pelota vasca" sitúa al Gobierno y a ETA al mismo nivel', *ABC*, 19 September 2003, <http://www.abc.es/hemeroteca/historico-19-09-2003/abc/Espectaculos/del-castillo-dice-que-la-pelota-vasca-situa-al-gobierno-y-a-eta-al-mismo-nivel_208450.html> [accessed 11 March 2020]

ARROBA, ÁLVARO, INTERVIEW WITH MAR DIESTRO-DÓPIDO, BY PHONE, 1 OCTOBER 2018 (translated from Spanish by Mar Diestro-Dópido)
ARROYO CORRAL, MIGUEL A., *Unidad didáctica sobre 'Canciones para después de una Guerra'*, p. 11, <http://platea.pntic.mec.es/curso20/68_elcine-profundizacion/2010/4_canciones_p_despues_d_u_guerra_miguel_angel_arroyo.pdf> [accessed 11 March 2020]
AUGÉ, MARC, *Non-Places: An Introduction to Supermodernity*, trans. by John Howe (London and New York: Verso, 1995)
AUSTIN, GUY, *Contemporary French Cinema: An Introduction* (Manchester: Manchester University Press, 1996), pp. 1–17
AUTY, MARTIN and GILLIAN HARTNOLL, eds, *Water Under the Bridge: 25 Years of the London Film Festival* (London: British Film Institute, 1981)
B., D, 'Una polémica independiente. Andrés Di Tella cuestionó la organización del Festival de Cine de Buenos Aires', *La Nación*, 18 June 1999, <http://www.lanacion.com.ar/142604-una-polemica-independiente> [accessed 11 March 2020]
BALLARD, J. G., *Super-Cannes: A Novel* (New York: Picador, 2000)
BAKHTIN, MIKHAIL, *Rabelais and His World*, trans. by Hélène Iswolsky (Bloomington: Indiana University Press, 1968, revised edition 1984)
BARBERÍA, JOSÉ LUIS, 'El Festival de cine de San Sebastián vive su mayor crisis tras rechazar a Erquicia como director', *El País*, 28 March 1985, <http://elpais.com/diario/1985/03/28/cultura/480812410_850215.html> [accessed 11 March 2020]
——'El Festival de cine de San Sebastián quiere volver a la altura de Cannes y Berlín', *El País*, 13 May 1985, <http://elpais.com/diario/1985/05/13/cultura/484783206_850215.html> [accessed 11 March 2020]
BARCELONA CORRESPONDENT, 'More Spanish Theatres Lost to the Cinema. World's Most Assiduous Filmgoers', *The Times*, 14 October 1960
BARDEM, J. A., *Arte, política, sociedad. Ensayos* (Madrid: Ayuso, 1976)
BARUCH STIER, OREN, *Committed to Memory: Cultural Mediations of the Holocaust* (Massachusetts: University of Massachusetts Press, 2009)
The Basque Conflict, <http://www.elkarri.org/en/pdf/BasqueConflict.pdf> [accessed 10 March 2020], and as content in Elkarri. Social movement for dialogue and agreement website, <http://www.elkarri.org/en/textos/quienes1.php> [accessed 10 March 2020]
BATLLE, DIEGO, 'BAFICI 2014 Balance positivo (y los desafíos que persisten)', *Otros Cines*, 13 April 2014, <http://www.otroscines.com/Festivales_detalle.php?idnota=8489&idsubseccion=147> [accessed 11 March]
——'BAFICI 2019: Algunas consideraciones tras la presentación de la 21ª edición del festival', *Otros Cines*, 19 March 2019, <https://www.otroscines.com/nota-14393-bafici-2019-algunas-consideraciones-tras-la-presentacio> [accessed 11 March 2020]
——'From Virtual Death to the New Law', in *New Argentine Cinema. Themes, Auteurs and Trends of Innovation*, ed. by Horacio Bernades, Diego Lerer and Sergio Wolf (Buenos Aires: Fipresci Argentina/Ediciones Tatanka, 2002), pp. 17–27
——'La era de la madurez', in *Cine argentino. Estéticas de la producción*, ed. by Sergio Wolf (Buenos Aires: Ministerio de Cultura, Gobierno de la Ciudad, 2009) pp. 57–80, <http://www.opcionlibros.gov.ar/libros/cine.php?libro=cineargentinoesteticas> [accessed 11 March]
——'Lo que queda del BAFICI', *Otros Cines*, April 2009, <http://www.otroscines.com.ar/columnistas_detalle.php?idnota=2670&idsubseccion=11> [accessed 11 March]
BAUDRILLARD, JEAN, 'The Ecstasy of Communication', trans. by John Johnston, in *The Anti-Aesthetic: Essays on Postmodern Culture*, ed. by Hal Foster (Port Townsend, Washington: Bay Press, 1987), pp. 126–34
BAZIN, ANDRÉ, 'The Festival Viewed as a Religious Order', *Cahiers du Cinema*, June 1955,

trans. by Emilie Bickerton and reproduced in *Dekalog 3: On Film Festivals*, ed. by Richard Porton (London: Wallflower Press, 2009), pp. 13–19

BELINCHÓN, G. and R. GARCÍA, 'Conmoción en el mundo del cine por la decisión de Bruselas de bloquear las ayudas a rodajes', *El País*, 25 November 2009, <http://www.elpais.com/articulo/cultura/Conmocion/mundo/cine/decision/Bruselas/bloquear/ayudas/rodajes/elpepucul/20091125elpepucul_1/Tes> [accessed 11 March]

BERGER, JOHN, *Ways of Seeing* (London: British Broadcasting Corporation and Penguin Books, 1988)

BERRY, CHRIS and LUKE ROBINSON, eds, *Chinese Film Festivals: Sites of Translation* (New York: Palgrave Macmillan, 2016)

BEST, JASON, '53rd BFI London Film Festival. The Star of London Awards', *Whatsontv*, 6 October 2009, <http://blogs.whatsontv.co.uk/movietalk/2009/10/06/53rd-bfi-london-film-festival-the-star-of-london-awards/> [accessed 11 March]

BINIMELIS ADELL, MAR, *La geopolítica de las coproducciones hispanoamericanas. Un análisis a través de su presencia en los festivales de clase A (1997–2007)* (unpublished doctoral thesis, Universidad Rovira i Virgili, 2011), <https://www.tdx.cat/handle/10803/51762#page=1> [accessed 25 May 2020].

BINNIE, ISLA, 'Basque separatist group ETA says it has "completely dissolved"', *Reuters*, 2 May 2018, <https://www.reuters.com/article/us-spain-eta/basque-group-eta-says-has-completely-dissolved-el-diario-website-idUSKBN1I31TP> [accessed 11 March]

BOURDIEU, PIERRE, 'The Forms of Capital', trans. by Richard Nice, in *Handbook of Theory and Research for the Sociology of Education*, ed. by J. Richardson (New York: Greenwood, 1986), pp. 241–58. Article reproduced at Marxists.org, <https://www.marxists.org/reference/subject/philosophy/works/fr/bourdieu-forms-capital.htm> [accessed 11 March]

—— *Distinction: A Social Critique of the Judgement of Taste*, trans. by Richard Nice (Oxon: Routledge, 2010)

BOYERO, CARLOS, 'Irreprochable Concha de Oro al Spielberg Chino', *El País*, 27 September 2009, <http://elpais.com/diario/2009/09/27/cultura/1254002403_850215.html> [accessed 11 March]

BROOKE, MICHAEL, 'The BFI Production Board: The Features', *BFI screenonline*, n.d., <http://www.screenonline.org.uk/film/id/1348538/> [accessed 11 March]

BUCHSBAUM, JONATHAN and ELENA GORFINKEL, eds, 'What's Being Fought By Today's Cinephilia(s)?', *Framework: The Journal of Cinema and Media*, 50 (Fall 2009)

BUÑUEL, JUAN LUIS, 'On Viridiana', in *Luis Buñuel. The Complete Films*, ed. by Bill Krohn and Paul Duncan (Köln, London, Los Angeles, Madrid, Paris, Tokyo: Taschen), pp. 130–31

BURTON, JULIENNE, 'The Old and the New: Latin American Cinema at the (last?) Pesaro Festival', *Jump Cut*, 9 (1975), 33–35, <http://www.ejumpcut.org/archive/onlinessays/JC09folder/PesaroReport.html> [accessed 11 March]

CALHOUN, DAVE, 'Greg Dyke and The Future of the British Film Institute', *Time Out*, 12 March 2008, <http://www.timeout.com/london/film/greg-dyke-and-the-future-of-the-british-film-institute> [accessed 11 March]

CAMPANELLA, JUAN JOSÉ, 'Por una unión en el cine argentino', *Noticine*, 26 June 2003, <http://noticine.com/industria/42-industria/1694-opinion-por-una-union-en-el-cine-argentino.html> [accessed 11 March]

CAMPERO, AGUSTÍN, 'Supongamos que existe una política cinematográfica', in *Cine argentino. Estéticas de la producción*, ed. by Sergio Wolf (Buenos Aires: Ministerio de Cultura, Gobierno de la Ciudad, 2009), pp. 17–23, <http://www.opcionlibros.gov.ar/libros/cine.php?libro=cineargentinoesteticas> [accessed 11 March]

CAMPOS RABADÁN, MINERVA, 'La América Latina de "Cine en Construcción". Implicaciones del apoyo económico de los festivales internacionales', *Archivos de la Filmoteca*, 71 (2013)

―― 'Reconfiguración de flujos en el circuito internacional de festivales de cine: el programa Cine en Construcción', *Secuencias. Revista de Historia del Cine*, 35 (2012), 84–102
CANTALAPIEDRA, FRANCISCO, 'Fernando Lara dice adios a la Seminci tras 20 años como director', *El País*, 29 December 2004, <http://elpais.com/diario/2004/12/29/espectaculos/1104274801_850215.html> [accessed 11 March]
CARELLI LYNCH, GUIDO, 'El Bafici 2010 viene con un cine más político', in *Ñ Revista de Cultura*, 19 March 2010, <http://www.revistaenie.clarin.com/notas/2010/03/19/_-02163048.htm> [accessed 11 March]
CARTOCCIO, EDUARDO A., 'La crítica precursora del Nuevo Cine Argentino: el caso de las revistas El Amante y Film entre 1992 y 1995', in *X Jornadas Nacionales de Investigadores en Comunicación. Una década de encuentros para (re)pensar los intercambios y consolidar la Red* (San Juan: Instituto Gino Germani — UBA Universidad de Buenos Aires, 2006), <http://www.redcomunicacion.org/memorias/pdf/2006cacartoccio.pdf> [accessed 11 March]
CELLULOID LIBERATION FRONT, 'Interview: Rome Film Festival Director Marco Mueller Discusses His First Year and the Future of Italian Cinema', *Indiewire*, 20 November 2012, <http://www.indiewire.com/article/interview-rome-film-festival-director-marco-mueller-discusses-his-first-year-and-the-future-of-italian-cinema> [accessed 11 March]
CERCAS, JAVIER, *The Anatomy of a Moment*, trans. by Anne McLean (Bloomsbury: London, 2011)
CIANCAGLINI, SERGIO, OSCAR RAÚL CARDOSO, MARÍA SEOANE, MARIANA GARCÍA, and ALEJANDRO LÓPEZ LÉPORI, 'A 20 años del golpe. Los archivos de la represión cultural', *Clarín Digital*, 24 March 1996, <http://edant.clarin.com/diario/96/03/24/claridad.html> [accessed 11 March]
CIMENT, MICHEL, 'La Libertad', *Positif*, 485, 486 (July/August 2001), 78–112
COMBS, RICHARD, 'Richard Combs, Gilbert Adair and Nick Roddick Write about Some of the Films that were Shown in the 26th London Film Festival. LFF', *Sight and Sound*, 52, 1 (Winter 1982/83), 14–17
CORLESS, KIERON and CHRIS DARKE, *Cannes: Inside the World's Premier Film Festival* (London: Faber and Faber, 2007)
COUSINS, MARK, FILM FESTIVAL MANIFESTO, *Film Festival Academy*, 2012, <http://www.filmfestivalacademy.net/publications/film-festival-form-a-manifesto> [accessed 11 March 2020]
CHRISTIE, IAN, ed., *Audiences* (Amsterdam: Amsterdam University Press, 2012)
―― interview with Mar Diestro-Dópido, Christie's office in Birkbeck University of London, 12 December 2012
CZACH, LIZ, 'Film Festivals, Programming, and the Building of a National Cinema', *The Moving Image*, 4, 1 (2004), 76–88
DALTON, WENDY, 'London Film Festival: Economics', in *Water Under the Bridge: 25 Years of the London Film Festival*, ed. by Martin Auty and Gillian Hartnoll (London: British Film Institute, 1981), p. 15
DAWTREY, ADAM, 'UKFC Lifts Edinburgh Festival Budget', *Variety*, 17 March 2008, <http://variety.com/2008/film/news/ukfc-lifts-edinburgh-festival-budget-1117982526/> [accessed 11 March 2020]
―― 'Brit Fest Scene is a Tale of Two Cities', *Variety*, 24–30 March 2008, p. 7
―― 'How is the BFI Suddenly able to take over from the UK Film Council?', *Guardian Film Blog*, 29 November 2010, <http://www.theguardian.com/film/filmblog/2010/nov/29/uk-film-council-bfi-ed-vaizey> [accessed 11 March 2020]
DAYAN, DANIEL, 'Looking for Sundance: The Social Construction of a Film Festival', in *The Film Festivals Reader*, ed. by Dina Iordanova (St Andrews: St Andrews Film Studies, 2013), pp. 45–58

DEBORD, GUY, 'The Society of the Spectacle', trans. by Black & Red (1967), reproduced by Marxists.com, <https://www.marxists.org/reference/archive/debord/society.htm> [accessed 11 March 2020]

DE LA FUENTE, FLAVIA, 'Odisea del espacio público', in *Cine Argentino 99/08. Bafici 10 Años: análisis, hitos, dilemas, logros, desafíos y (por qué no) varias cosas para celebrar*, ed. by Marcelo Panozzo, Leonel Livchits, and Manuel Antín (Buenos Aires: BAFICI & Ministerio de Cultura. Gobierno de la Ciudad de Buenos Aires, 2008), pp. 41–43

DERRIDA, JACQUES, *Archive Fever: A Freudian Impression* (Chicago/London: University of Chicago Press, 1995)

de Orbe, José María, interview with Mar Diestro-Dópido, BFI Southbank press office, 23 October 2010

DE VALCK, MARIJKE, BRENDAN KREDELL, and SKADI LOIST, eds, *Film Festivals: History, Theory, Method, Practice* (London, New York: Routledge, 2016)

DE VALCK, MARIJKE, *Film Festivals: From European Geopolitics to Global Cinephilia* (Amsterdam: Amsterdam University Press, 2007)

DE WITT, HELEN, interview with Mar Diestro-Dópido, via email, 18 August 2014

DEVESA FERNÁNDEZ, MARÍA, *El impacto económico de los festivales culturales: el caso de la Semana Internacional de Cine de Valladolid* (Madrid: Fundación Autor, 2006)

DI CHIARA, FRANCESCO and VALENTINA RE, 'Film Festival/Film History: The Impact of Film Festivals on Cinema Historiography. Il cinema ritrovato and beyond', *Cinémas: revue d'études cinématographies/Cinémas: Journal of Film Studies*, 21, 2–3 (2001), 131–51, <http://www.erudit.org/revue/cine/2011/v21/n2-3/1005587ar.html> [accessed 11 March 2020]

DICKINSON, MARGARET, ANNE COTTRINGER and JULIAN PETLEY, 'Workshops: A Dossier', *Vertigo*, 1, 1 (Spring 1993), <http://www.closeupfilmcentre.com/vertigo_magazine/volume-1-issue-1-spring-1993/workshops-a-dossier/> [accessed 11 March 2020]

DIESTRO-DÓPIDO, MAR, 'The Film Festival Circuit: Identity Transactions in a Translational Economy' in *A Companion to Latin American Cinema*, ed. by Maria M. Delgado, Stephen M. Hart and Randal Johnson (Oxford: Wiley Blackwell, 2017), p. 99–113

——'Women Film Writers Wall of Inspiration', *Sight & Sound Online*, n.d., <http://old.bfi.org.uk/sightandsound/newsandviews/comment/women-film-writers-wall-of-inspiration.php> [accessed 11 March 2020]

——'Viva Lisbon!', *Sight & Sound*, 18, 7 (July 2008), 8–9

——'Chaos Theories', *Vertigo*, 3, 8 (Winter 2008), <http://www.closeupfilmcentre.com/vertigo_magazine/volume-3-issue-8-winter-2008/chaos-theories/> [accessed 11 March 2020]

——'Other Worlds/Crisis and Capitalism in Contemporary Argentine Cinema', *Sight & Sound*, 20, 4 (April 2010), 93

——'From Buñuel to Lorca', *Sight & Sound Online*, October 2011, http://www.bfi.org.uk/news-opinion/sight-sound-magazine/interviews/pere-portabella-bu-uel-lorca> [accessed 11 March 2020]

——'Cindy Hing-Yuk Wong: Film Festivals: Culture, People, and Power on the Global Screen', *Journal of Cultural Economics*, 36, 4, 2012, 353–56

——'The Pain in Spain', *Sight & Sound Online*, 19 October 2012, <http://www.bfi.org.uk/news-opinion/sight-sound-magazine/comment/festivals/lff-blog-pain-spain> [accessed 11 March 2020]

——'San Sebastián: A Film Festival of Contrasts', in *New Trends in Contemporary Spanish Cinema*, ed. by Fernando Canet and Duncan Wheeler (Bristol: Intellect, 2014), pp. 406–16

——'The Film Festival Circuit: Identity Transactions in a Translational Economy', in *A Companion to Latin American Cinema*, ed. by Maria M. Delgado, Stephen M. Hart and Randal Johnson (Oxford: Wiley Blackwell, 2017), pp. 99–113

Díez Abad, María del Rosario, 'Crónica de un desafío: el cierre de las facultades de Derecho, Medicina, Ciencias y Filosofía y Letras de la Universidad de Valladolid durante la agonía del franquismo', *Segundas Jornadas II: Imagen y Cultura* (Valladolid: Universidad de Valladolid, n.d.) pp. 289–301. Available at Universidad Carlos III de Madrid, eArchivo, <http://e-archivo.uc3m.es/bitstream/10016/9506/1/cronica_diez_ICT_2003.pdf> [accessed 11 March 2020]

Díez Puertas, Emeterio, *Historia social del cine en España* (Madrid-Caracas: Editorial Fundamentos, 2003)

DiMaggio, Paul, 'Cultural Boundaries and Structural Change: The Extension of the High Culture Model to Theatre, Opera, and the Dance, 1900–1940', in *Cultivating Differences*, M. Lamont and M. Fournier (Chicago, Ill: University of Chicago Press, 1992), pp. 21–57

'The Director of the Buenos Aires International Festival of Independent Cinema Was Fired', FIPRESCI, 18 July 2014, <http://fipresci.hegenauer.co.uk/news/archive/archive_2004/ba_incident.htm> [accessed 10 March 2020].

Di Tella, Andrés, interview with Mar Diestro-Dópido, by phone, 22 June 2009 (translated from Spanish by Mar Diestro-Dópido)

D'Lugo, Marvin, 'Cinema: From Mexican Ranchera to Argentinian Exile', in *Rethinking Third Cinema*, ed. by Anthony R. Guteratne and Wimal Dissanayake (Oxford: Routledge, 2003), pp. 101–25

Elena, Alberto and Marina Díaz López, *The Cinema of Latin America* (London and New York: Wallflower Press, 2003)

Elkana, Yehuda, 'The Need to Forget', *Ha'aretz*, 2 March 1988, available at: <http://web.ceu.hu/yehuda_the_need_to_forget.pdf> [accessed 26 May 2020].

Elorza, Odón, 'San Sebastián, de cine', *El País*, 18 September 2010, <http://www.elpais.com/articulo/pais/vasco/San/Sebastian/cine/elpepiesppvs/20100918elpvas_9/Tes> [accessed 11 March 2020]

Elsaesser, Thomas, *European Cinema: Face to Face with Hollywood* (Amsterdam: Amsterdam University Press, 2005)

—— 'Film Festival Networks: The New Topographies of Cinema in Europe', in *European Cinema: Face to Face with Hollywood*, ed. by Thomas Elsaesser (Amsterdam: Amsterdam Univ. Press, 2005), pp. 82–107

El País/Agencias, 'El partido de Cascos destituye al director del Festival de Cine de Gijón', *El País*, 11 January 2012, <http://cultura.elpais.com/cultura/2012/01/11/actualidad/1326236404_850215.html> [accessed 11 March 2020]

E.T.A., 'DOCUMENTO | La carta en la que ETA anuncia su disolución', *El Diario Norte*, 16 April 2018, <https://www.eldiario.es/norte/DOCUMENTO-carta-ETA-anuncia-disolucion_0_767123640.html> [accessed 11 March 2020]

Europa Press, 'El Festival internacional de San Sebastián ve reducida su aportación pública en 225.000 euros este año', *teinteresa.es*, 7 May 2012, <http://www.teinteresa.es/pais-vasco/gipuzcoa/Festival-Internacional-San-Sebastian-aportacion_0_695931324.html> [accessed 11 March 2020]

European Broadcasting Union, *EBU Technical Review*, 262 (Winter 1994), <http://www.ebu.ch/en/technical/trev/trev_262-editorial.html> [accessed 4 March 2020].

European Film Market Berlin. <https://www.efm-berlinale.de/en/HomePage.php> [accessed 3 March 2020].

Evans, Gareth, ed., *50/06. Lost and Found. Two Weeks in Autumn. International Visions* (BFI: The Times BFI 50th London Film Festival, 2006)

'Exploring the festival model. The British Arts Festivals Association's Capacity to Endure conference last year focussed on how festivals should be valued as an integral and sustainable part of society. Published online by Arts Professional', *ArtsProfessional*, 7

February 2013, <https://www.artsprofessional.co.uk/magazine/262/feature/exploring-festival-model> [accessed 11 March 2020]

EZRA, ELIZABETH and TERRY ROWDEN, eds, *Transnational Cinema, The Film Reader* (London and New York: Routledge, 2006).

FALASSI, ALESSANDRO, *Time Out of Time: Essays on the Festival* (Albuquerque: University of New Mexico Press, 1987) pp. 1–10

FALICOV, TAMARA L., *The Cinematic Tango: Contemporary Argentine Film* (London and New York: Wallflower Press, 2007)

—— 'Migrating from South to North: The Role of Film Festivals in Funding and Shaping Global South Film and Video', in *Locating Migrating Media*, ed. by Greg Elmer, Charles H. Davis, Janine Marchessault and John McCullough (Lanham, MD: Lexington Books, 2010), pp. 3–22

—— 'Argentine Cinema and the Crisis of Audience' in *The Argentine Film*, ed. by Daniela Ingruber and Ursula Prutsch (Verlag Münster/Berlin/Vienna/Zurich LIT, 2012), pp. 207–18

—— '"Cine en Construcción"/"Films in Progress": How Spanish and Latin American Film-Makers Negotiate the Construction of a Globalized Art-House Aesthetic', *Transnational Cinemas*, 4, 2 (2013), 253–71

—— 'The "Festival Film": Film Festival Funds as Cultural Intermediaries', in *Film Festivals: History, Theory, Method, Practice*, ed. by Marijke de Valck, Brendan Kredell, and Skadi Loist (London, New York: Routledge, 2016), pp. 209–29

FARAHMAND, AZADEH, 'Disentangling the International Festival Circuit: Genre and Iranian Cinema', in *Global Art Cinema: New Theories and Histories*, ed. by Rosalind Galt and Karl Schoonover (New York: Oxford University Press, 2010), pp. 263–83

'Festival de Mar del Plata 2018: Reducen en tres días su duración', *Otros Cines*, 11 September 2018, <https://www.otroscines.com/nota-13761-festival-de-mar-del-plata-2018-reducen-en-tres-dias-su> [accessed 10 March 2020]

'Festival screening for new Bond film. The new Bond film Quantum of Solace is to get its first public screening at this year's London Film Festival, organisers have announced...', BBC, 10 September 2008, <http://www.bbc.co.uk/london/content/articles/2008/09/10/film_festival_08_launch_feature.shtml>.

FINNEY, ANGUS, 'Circles of Confusion: The 53rd London Film Festival', *senses of cinema*, 53 (December 2009), <http://sensesofcinema.com/2009/festival-reports/circles-of-confusion-the-53rd-london-film-festival/> [accessed 11 March 2020]

—— *The London Film Festival/Market: A Feasibility Study* (British Film Institute and the Producer's Alliance for Cinema and Television, 14–24 February 1997)

—— '"There is nothing moving in cinema": The Experimenta Weekend at the 56th BFI London Film Festival', *senses of cinema*, 66 (2013), <http://sensesofcinema.com/2013/festival-reports/there-is-nothing-moving-in-cinema-the-experimenta-weekend-at-the-56th-bfi-london-film-festival/> [accessed 11 March 2020]

FOWLER, CATHERINE, ed., *The European Cinema Reader* (London: Routledge, 2002)

FRANCO, JESS, *Bienvenido Mister Cagada. Memorias caóticas de Luis García Berlanga* (Madrid: Aguilar Santillana Ediciones Generales S.L., 2005)

FRICKER, KAREN and MILIJA GLUHOVIC, eds, *Performing the 'New' Europe: Identities, Feelings, and Politics in the Eurovision Song Contest* (Houndsmills: Palgrave Macmillan, 2013)

FUCHS, CHRISTIAN, 'Transnational Space and the "Network Society"', 21st *Century Society*, 2, 1 (February 2007), 49–78

FUJIWARA, CHRIS, REVIEW: 'On Film Festivals, edited by Richard Porton (London: Wallflower Press, 2009)', *FIPRESCI The International Federation of Film critics*, 2010, <http://www.fipresci.org/undercurrent/issue_0609/fujiwara_festivals.htm> [accessed 11 March 2020]

'The Future of Festivals: 8 Trends You Need to Know', *EventBrite*, n.d., <https://www.eventbrite.co.uk/blog/academy/the-future-of-festivals/> [accessed 11 March 2020].

'The Future of Film Festivals', *Schnitt*, 54 (February 2009), 7

G., R. and G. B, 'Mikel Olaciregui: "Me voy sin nostalgia"', *El País*, 23 September 2010, <http://cultura.elpais.com/cultura/2010/09/25/actualidad/1285365603_850215.html> [accessed 11 March 2020]

GALÁN, DIEGO, interview with Mar Diestro-Dópido, Las Vistillas Restaurant, Madrid, 8 April 2011

——*Jack Lemmon nunca cenó aquí* (Madrid: Plaza & Janés, 2001)

——*Pilar Miró: nadie me enseñó a vivir* (Barcelona: Plaza & Janés Editores, 2006)

CHARLES GANT, 'How Clare Stewart transformed the BFI London Film Festival', *Screendaily*, 4 October 2017, <https://www.screendaily.com/features/how-clare-stewart-transformed-the-bfi-london-film-festival/5122932.article> [accessed 11 March 2020]

GAYDOS, STEVEN, 'Battle Behind the Scenes' *Variety*, 24 August 2003, <https://variety.com/2003/scene/markets-festivals/battle-behind-the-scenes-1117891416/> [accessed 11 March 2020]

GARCÍA, ROCÍO, 'Cineastas contra la Orden', *El País*, 17 August 2009, <http://www.elpais.com/articulo/revista/agosto/Cineastas/Orden/elpeputec/20090807elpepirdv_8/Tes> [accessed 11 March 2020].

——'Susana de la Sierra dimite como directora general del ICAA. El Consejo de Ministros nombra a Lorena González como su sustituta en el cargo, *El País*, 17 July 2014, <http://cultura.elpais.com/cultura/2014/07/17/actualidad/1405622273_541843.html> [accessed 11 March 2020]

GASS, LARS HENRIK, 'Trade Market Becomes Trade Mark', *Schnitt*, 54 (February 2009), 43–45

GELARDI, ANDREA, 'Bologna and its Cineteca: Building Trans-cending Networks', *Excursions*, 8, 1 (June 2018), 1–28

GESTER, JULIEN, 'Carlo Chatrian: A Locarno Nous Sommes en Dehors de la Logique de Supermarché', *Libération*, 6 August 2014, <http://next.liberation.fr/cinema/2014/08/06/a-locarno-nous-sommes-en-dehors-de-la-logique-de-supermarche_1076520> [accessed 11 March 2020]

GETINO, OCTAVIO, *Cine argentino (Entre lo posible y lo deseable)*, <http://www.hamalweb.com.ar/Textos/Getino_CINE_ARGENTINO.pdf> [accessed 11 March 2020]

GIL, ALBERTO, *La censura cinematográfica en España* (Barcelona: S.A. Ediciones B, 2009)

GILES, DAVID, *Illusions of Immortality: A Psychology of Fame and Celebrity* (New York: St. Martin's, 2000)

GINZBERG, VICTORIA, 'Facebook es raro', *Página/12*, 24 March 2010, <http://www.pagina12.com.ar/diario/elpais/subnotas/142578-45907-2010-03-24.html> [accessed 11 March 2020]

GÓMEZ MUÑOZ, JANIRA, 'El BAFICI festeja sus 20 años con récords y cineastas como John Waters', *france24*, 16 April 2018, <https://www.france24.com/es/20180415-cultura-bafici-cine-independiente-argentina> [accessed 11 March 2020]

GUBERN, ROMÁN, 'Notas para una historia de la Censura Cinematográfica en España' in *Un cine para el cadalso: 40 años de censura cinematográfica en España*, ed. by Román Gubern and Domènec Font (Barcelona: Euros 1975), pp. 15–44

——*Función política y ordenamiento jurídico bajo el franquismo (1936–1975)* (Barcelona: Editorial Península, 1981)

GUILLÉN, MICHAEL, 'Film Festival Yearbook 2: Film Festivals and Imagined Communities', *The Evening Class*, 24 February 2010, <http://theeveningclass.blogspot.co.uk/2010_02_01_archive.html> [accessed 11 March 2020]

——'Insane Mute: Interview with Chris Fujiwara', *twitch*, 1 September 2010, <https://

screenanarchy.com/2010/09/insane-mute-interview-with-chris-fujiwara.html> [accessed 25 May 2020]

GUNNING, TOM, '"Now You See It, Now You Don't": The Temporality of the Cinema of Attractions', in *The Silent Cinema Reader*, ed. by Lee Grieveson and Peter Krämer (New York: Routledge, 2004), pp. 41–50

—— 'The Cinema of Attractions Early Film, its Spectator and the Avant-Garde', in *Early Cinema. Space. Frame. Time*, ed. by Thomas Elsaesser (London: British Film Institute, 2006), pp. 56–62

GUTIÉRREZ, ÓSCAR, 'El primer día en el que ETA asesinó', *El País*, 4 June 2008, <http://www.elpais.com/articulo/espana/primer/dia/ETA/asesino/elpepuesp/20080604elpepunac_4/Tes> [accessed 11 March 2020]

GUTIÉRREZ LANZA, MARÍA DEL CAMINO, *Traducción y censura de textos cinematográficos en la España de Franco: doblaje y subtitulado ingles-español (1951–1975)* (León: Universidad de León, 2000)

HARBORD, JANET, *Film Cultures* (London: Sage Publications, 2002)

—— 'Film Festivals-Time-Event', in *Film Festival Yearbook 1: The Festival Circuit*, ed. by Dina Iordanova and Ragan Rhyne (St. Andrews: St. Andrews Film Studies, 2009) pp. 40–46

'Ha muerto Manuel de Echarri organizador del Festival de Cine de San Sebastián', *El País*, 4 July 1978, <http://elpais.com/diario/1978/07/04/cultura/268351202_850215.html> [accessed 10 March 2020]

HARDCASTLE, LESLIE, 'In the beginning... A view of how the National Film Theatre and the London Film Festival came into being, from Leslie Hardcastle, Controller of the NFT', in LFF 25th Anniversary LFF brochure, n.p.

HEBRON, SANDRA, interview with Mar Diestro-Dópido, her office at the BFI Southbank, 5 February 2010 (together with Anne-Marie Flynn)

—— interview with Mar Diestro-Dópido, her office at the BFI Southbank, 28 September 2011

—— interview with Mar Diestro-Dópido, her office at the BFI Southbank, 16 November 2011

—— interview with Mar Diestro-Dópido, via email, 22 August 2014

—— 'In the Digital Kindergarten', *Schnitt*, 54 (February 2009), 17–19

—— 'Points Taken', *Time Out*, 8–14 May 2008, p. 82

HEREDERO, CARLOS F., interview with Mar Diestro-Dópido, offices of Caimán Cuadernos de Cine, Madrid, 6 April 2011

HERRERO VELARDE, JOSÉ ÁNGEL, interview with Mar Diestro-Dópido, San Sebastián International Film Festival offices, San Sebastián, 6 May 2010

HARRISON, SAM, 'Porteño Corner: Javier Porta Fouz, Director of BAFICI', *Wander Argentina*, 2016, <https://wander-argentina.com/porteno-corner-director-bafici-javier-fouz/> [accessed 11 March 2020]

HOELLERING, G. M., LFF brochure, 1957, p. 2

Hong Kong International Film & TV Market, <http://www.hktdc.com/fair/hkfilmart-en/Hong-Kong-International-Film---TV-Market--FILMART-.html> [accessed 3 March 2020].

HOPEWELL, JOHN, 'Festival organizers rewrite their A-B-C's', *Variety*, 16 May 2004, <https://variety.com/2004/film/news/festival-organizers-rewrite-their-a-b-c-s-1117905025/> [accessed 11 March 2020]

HOUSTON, PENELOPE, *Keepers of the Frame: The Film Archives* (London: British Film Institute, 1994)

HURCH, HANS, 'The Film Festival as a Space of Experience', *Schnitt*, 54 (February 2009), 31–33

Ibárruri, Dolores, Manuel Azcárate, Luis Balaguer, Antonio Cordón, Irene Falcón and José Sandoval, *Historia del Partido Comunista (Versión abreviada 1960)*, <http://www.pce.es/descarga/historia_pce_version1960_reducida.pdf> [accessed 11 March 2020]

IndieLisboa, catalogue, 2005

Illich, Ivan and Beth Gill, 'Temples of Consumption: Shopping Malls as Secular Cathedrals', Trinity University, <http://www.trinity.edu/mkearl/temples.html> [accessed 11 March 2020]

'In Favor of Quintín', FIPRESCI, <http://www.fipresci.org/news/archive/archive_2004/quintin.htm> [accessed 10 March 2020]

Iordanova, Dina, 'Showdown of the Festivals: Clashing Entrepreneurships and Post-Communist Management of Culture', *Film International*, 4, 23 (2006), 25–38

——ed., 'Film Festivals Dossier', Special Issue of *Film International*, 6, 4 (2008), 4–81

——'Notes on Film Festivals vs. Industry Events', *DinaView*, 30 September 2010, <http://www.dinaview.com/?p=1490> [site no longer active].

Iordanova, Dina and Ragan Rhyne, eds, 'The Film Festival Circuit', *Film Festival Yearbook 1: The Festival Circuit* (St. Andrews: St. Andrews Film Studies, 2009)

Iordanova, Dina and Stefanie Van de Peer, eds, *Film Festival Yearbook 6: Film Festivals and the Middle East* (St Andrews: St Andrews Film Studies, 2014)

Jaafar, Ali, 'London Fest Gets $2.7 million', *Variety*, 10 May 2009, <https://variety.com/2009/biz/news/london-fest-gets-2-7-million-1118003443/> [accessed 11 March 2020]

James, Nick, 'Rip It Up: Revitalizing Film Criticism', *Film Quarterly*, 62, 3, Spring 2009, <http://www.filmquarterly.org/2009/03/spring-2009-volume-62-no-3/> [accessed 12 March 2020]

——'Goodbye Mr French: Fleet Street Cuts Back Its Film Critics', *Sight & Sound*, 23, 11 (November 2013), 5

Johnson, Ben, 'The Festival of Britain 1951', in *Historic UK: The History and Heritage Accommodation Guide*, n.d., <http://www.historic-uk.com/HistoryUK/HistoryofBritain/The-Festival-of-Britain-1951/> [accessed 11 March 2020]

Jonathan Rosenbaum, <http://www.jonathanrosenbaum.com/?cat=5> [accessed 4 March 2020].

Jullier, Laurent and Jean-Marc Leveratto, 'Cinephilia in the Digital Age' in *Audiences*, ed. by Ian Christie (Amsterdam: Amsterdam University Press, 2012), pp. 143–54

Jungen, Christian, *Hollywood in Cannes: The History of a Love-Hate Relationship* (Amsterdam: Amsterdam University Press, 2014)

Knegt, Peter, 'On the Future of Fests: Thoughts From the Top', *Indiewire*, 12 May 2009, <http://www.indiewire.com/article/on_the_future_of_film_festivals_thoughts_from_leading_figures>[accessed 11 March 2020]

——'London Fest Sets 191 Features; Adds New Awards', *Indiewire*, 9 September 2009, <http://www.indiewire.com/article/london_fest_sets_191_features_adds_new_award> [accessed 11 March 2020]

Koehler, Robert, 'Cinephilia and Film Festivals' in *Dekalog 3: On Film Festivals*, ed. by Richard Porton (London: Wallflower, 2009), pp. 81–97

——'What the Palm Springs Film Festival Tells Us About the State of Cinema', *filmjourney.com*, 22 January 2019, <https://filmjourney.org/?p=3630> [accessed 11 March 2020]

Kollewe, Julia, 'Cineworld buys Picturehouse: Arthouse Cinema deal will make Chain's co-founder Lyn Goleby a Multi-millionaire', *Guardian*, 6 December 2012, <http://www.theguardian.com/business/2012/dec/06/cineworld-buys-picturehouse> [accessed 11 March 2020]

Koven, Mikel, 'Film Festivals as Spaces of Meaning: Researching Festival Audiences as Producers of Meaning', *From the Mind of Mikel: A University of Worcester Film Studies Blog*, 6 September 2013, <http://fromthemindofmikel.wordpress.com/2013/09/06/film-festivals-as-spaces-of-meaning-researching-festival-audiences-as-producers-of-meaning/> [accessed 11 March 2020]

Kozak, Daniela, 'Todo sobre el BAFICI (Entrevista a Marcelo Panozzo)', *la conversación*, 1 June 2013, <http://laconversacion.wordpress.com/2013/06/01/todo-sobre-el-bafici-entrevista-a-marcelo-panozzo/> [accessed 11 March 2020]

Labanyi, Jo, 'Censorship or the Fear of Mass Culture', in *Spanish Cultural Studies: An Introduction*, ed. by Helen Graham and Jo Labanyi (Oxford University Press, 1995), pp. 207–14

Labanyi, Jo and Tatjana Pavlović, eds, *A Companion to Spanish Cinema* (Oxford: Wiley-Blackwell, 2013)

Leal, Alberto, 'La nueva Ley del Cine', *Mundo Obrero*, 28 February 2007, <http://www.mundooobrero.es/pl.php?id=528&sec=6> [accessed 11 March 2020]

León Aguinaga, Pablo, *El cine norteamericano y la España franquista, 1939–1960: relaciones internacionales, comercio y propaganda* (unpublished doctoral thesis, Universidad Complutense de Madrid, 2009), <http://eprints.ucm.es/8378/1/T30698.pdf> [accessed 11 March 2020]

Lerer, Diego, 'Diario de Londres 2: Bruno Dumont, Jeff Nichols, Sean Durkin', *Micropsia*, 23 October 2011, <http://micropsia.otroscines.com/2011/10/diario-de-londres-2-bruno-dumont-jeff-nichols-sean-durkin/> [accessed 11 March 2020]

—— interview with Mar Diestro-Dópido, Southbank, 24 October 2011 (translated from Spanish by Mar Diestro-Dópido)

López Echevarrieta, Alberto, *Los cines de Bilbao* (San Sebastián-Donostia: Filmoteka Vasca-Euskadiko Filmotegia, 2000)

Lumière, <http://www.elumiere.net/> [accessed 4 March 2020]

MacKillop, Ian and Neil Sinyard, eds, *Exhibition. From British Cinema in the 1950s: An Art of Peacetime* (Manchester University Press, 2002)

Macnab, Geoffrey, 'London Film Festival Plans 50th Anniversary Events', *Screen Daily*, 23 May 2006, <http://www.screendaily.com/london-film-festival-plans-50th-anniversary-events/4027387.article> [accessed 11 March 2020]

—— 'The NFT is no more, long live the BFI Southbank', *Guardian*, 6 March 2007, <http://www.theguardian.com/film/filmblog/2007/mar/06/thenftisnomorelongliveb> [accessed 11 March 2020]

Malcolm, Derek, LFF brochure, 1984

Marché du Film, <http://www.marchedufilm.com/en> [accessed 3 March 2020].

Marías, Miguel, interview with Mar Diestro-Dópido, by email, 23 July 2011

—— 'Las misiones de una Filmoteca y su futuro', in *Filmoteca Española. Cincuenta años de historia (1953–2003)*, ed. by Antonio Santamarina (Madrid: Filmoteca Española/I.C.A.A./Ministerio de Cultura, 2005), pp. 83–100

Marlow-Mann, Alex, ed., *Film Festival Yearbook 5: Archival Film Festivals* (St Andrews: St Andrews Film Studies, 2013)

Martin, Adrian, 'Cinephilia as War Machine', *Framework: The Journal of Cinema and Media*, 50, 1 and 2 (Spring and Fall 2009), 221–25

Martín Kairúz, Mariano, interview with Mar Diestro-Dópido, Abasto Shopping Centre, Buenos Aires, 30 March 2009 (translated from Spanish by Mar Diestro-Dópido)

Martín Peña, Fernando, 'Es necesario tomar decisiones', *Página/12*, 9 November 2007, <http://www.pagina12.com.ar/diario/suplementos/espectaculos/5-8230-2007-11-09.html> [accessed 11 March 2020]

―――interview with Mar Diestro-Dópido, by phone, 22 June 2009 (translated from Spanish by Mar Diestro-Dópido)
MASTERS, CHARLES, 'Fests Play by New Rules', *Backstage*, 24 August 2004, <http://www.backstage.com/news/fests-play-by-new-rules/> [accessed 11 March 2020]
MAZDON, LUCY, 'The Cannes Film Festival as Transnational Space', *Post Script*, 25, 2 (2006), 19–30
MEZIAS, STEPHEN, JESPER STRANDGAARD PEDERSEN, SILVIYA SVEJENOVA and CARMELO MAZZA, 'Much Ado about Nothing? Untangling the Impact of European Premier Film Festivals', *Creative Encounters*, Working Papers 14 (Copenhagen Business School: Institut for Interkulturel Kommunikation og Ledelse, 2008), 1–31
MOERAN, BRIAN and JESPER STRANDGAARD PEDERSON (eds), *Negotiating Values in the Creative Industries: Fairs, Festivals and Competitive Events* (Cambridge: Cambridge University Press, 2011)
MÜLLER, MARCO, 'Back to the Future', *Schnitt*, 54 (February 2009), 13–15
MULVEY, LAURA, *Visual and Other Pleasures* (Hampshire: Palgrave, 1989)
MURGA, CELINA and JUAN VILLEGAS, interview with Mar Diestro-Dópido, Abasto Shopping Centre, Buenos Aires, 1 April 2009 (translated from Spanish by Mar Diestro-Dópido
NAYMAN, ADAM, 'Reviewed Works: *Dekalog 3: On Film Festivals* by Richard Porton; *Film Festival Yearbook 1: The Festival Circuit* by Dina Iordanova, Ragan Rhyne; *Film Festival Yearbook 2: Film Festivals and Imagined Communities* by Dina Iordanova, Ruby Cheung', *Cinéaste*, 35, 3 (Summer 2010), 62–63.
NICHOLS, BILL, 'Discovering Form, Inferring Meaning: New Cinemas and the Film Festival Circuit', *Film Quarterly*, 47, 3 (1994), 16–27
―――'Global Image Consumption in the Age of Late Capitalism', *East-West Film Journal*, 8, 1 (1994), 68–85
NIÑO, VICTORIA M., 'Javier Angulo: "Me encontré un festival ensimismado y hoy está abierto al mundo"', *El Norte de Castilla*, 13 October, 2019, <2019https://www.elnortedecastilla.es/culturas/seminci/javier-angulo-encontre-20191013083337-nt.html> [accessed 11 March 2020]
NOWELL SMITH, GEOFFREY, interview with Mar Diestro-Dópido, *Sight & Sound* offices, 14 November 2011
ODORICO, STEFANO, 'Review: Marijke De Valck (2007) Film Festivals: From European Geopolitics to Global Cinephilia', *Film-Philosophy*, 12 December 2008, pp. 124–30, <http://www.film-philosophy.com/index.php/f-p/article/view/61/46> [accessed 11 March 2020]
OLACIREGUI, MIKEL, interview with Mar Diestro-Dópido, San Sebastián International Film Festival offices, San Sebastián, 4 May 2010
OSTROWSKA, DOROTA, 'Film Festival Workshop, St Andrew's University, Scotland, 4 April 2009. Conference Report', *Screen*, 51, 1 (2010), 79–81
PAGE, JOANNA, *Crisis and Capitalism in Contemporary Argentine Cinema* (Durham and London: Duke University Press, 2009)
PANOZZO, MARCELO, LEONEL LIVCHITS, and MANUEL ANTÍN, eds, *Cine Argentino 99/08. Bafici 10 Años: análisis, hitos, dilemas, logros, desafíos y (por qué no) varias cosas para celebrar* (Buenos Aires: BAFICI & Ministerio de Cultura. Gobierno de la Ciudad de Buenos Aires, 2008)
PENA, JAIME, interview with Mar Diestro-Dópido, San Sebastián International Film Festival premises, San Sebastián, 21 September 2010
PERANSON, MARK, 'First You Get the Power, Then You Get the Money: Two Models of Film Festivals', *Cineaste*, 33, 3 (Summer 2008), 37–43. Reprinted in *Dekalog 3: On Film Festivals*, ed. by Richard Porton (London: Wallflower Press, 2010), pp. 116–31
PÈRE, OLIVIER, 'A Showcase for the Cinema', *Schnitt*, 54 (February 2009), 19–21

Pérez, María, 'Las películas mutiladas por Franco', *El Mundo*, 13 October 2010, <http://www.elmundo.es/elmundo/2009/10/21/cultura/1256144676.html> [accessed 11 March 2020]

Pérez Millán, Juan Antonio, 'De la Filmoteca Nacional al florecimiento de las Autonómicas' in *Filmoteca Española. Cincuenta años de historia (1953–2003)*, ed. by Antonio Santamarina (Madrid: Filmoteca Española/I.C.A.A./Ministerio de Cultura, 2005), pp. 66–82

Pingree, Geoff, 'How Easily a Feisty Film Festival Goes Glittery', *The New York Times*, 25 September 2004, <http://www.nytimes.com/2004/09/25/movies/25seba.html?_r=0> [accessed 11 March 2020]

Porta Fouz, Javier, 'Un día en la libertad', *El Amante Cine*, 110 (May 2001)

Porton, Richard, ed., *Dekalog 3: On Film Festivals* (London: Wallflower Press, 2009)

—— interview with Mar Diestro-Dópido, BFI, 15 August 2014

—— 'The Festival Whirl. The Utopian Possibilities — and Dystopian Realities — of the Modern Film Festival', *Museum of the Moving Image*, 8 September 2009, <http://www.movingimagesource.us/articles/the-festival-whirl-20090908> [accessed 11 March 2020]

Pozo Arenas, Santiago, *La industria del cine en España: legislación y aspectos económicos, 1896–1970* (Barcelona: Edicions Universitat de Barcelona, 1984)

Prouse, Derek, 'From Derek Prouse, who programmed the first London Film Festival', 25th Anniversary LFF brochure, 1981, n.p.

Quandt, James, 'The Sandwich Process: Simon Field Talks about Polemics and Poetry at Film Festivals' in *Dekalog 3: On Film Festivals*, ed. by Richard Porton (London: Wallflower Press, 2009), pp. 53–80

Quintín, 'El misterio del leñador solitario', *El Amante Cine*, 111 (June 2001), 2–5

—— interview with Mar Diestro-Dópido, café opposite the Abasto Shopping Centre, Buenos Aires, 3 April 2009

—— 'La crisis que faltaba', *Perfil*, 23 November 2008, <http://www.perfil.com/columnistas/La-crisis-que-faltaba-20081122-0043.html> [accessed 10 March 2020]

—— 'La nouvelle vague en danger', in, 'L'Atlas du cinéma, 2002 en chiffres, vu par les critiques de 40 pays / vu par les critiques de 40 pays', ed. by Charlotte Garson and Charles Tesson, Special Issue of *Cahiers du Cinéma* (April 2003)

—— 'The Headless Woman', *Cinema Scope*, 35 (Summer 2008), 42

—— 'The Festival Galaxy', in *Dekalog 3: On Film Festivals*, ed. by Richard Porton (London: Wallflower, 2009), pp. 38–52

Rabinovitz, Lauren, *Points of Resistance: Women, Power & Politics in the New York Avant-garde Cinema, 1943–71* (Urbana and Chicago: University of Illinois Press, 2003)

Rancia, Ignacio, 'Antes de Salamanca, en Salamanca, después de Salamanca', in *El cine español, desde Salamanca: (1955–1995)* (Castilla-León: Junta de Castilla y León, Consejería de Educación y Cultura, 1995), pp. 59–76

Rayns, Tony, interview with Mar Diestro-Dópido, Boquería Restaurant London, 8 July 2013

—— 'Luck and Judgement', *Time Out*, November 1975, p. 10, in LFF dossier available in the BFI Archive

Rebordinos, José Luis, interview with Mar Diestro-Dópido, San Sebastián International Film Festival offices, San Sebastián, 5 May 2010

Redacción, 'Nombran a Fernando Lara, revitalizador de la Seminci, director general de cine', *Noticine*, 23 December 2004, <http://h2031287.stratoserver.net/industria/42-industria/3899-nombran-a-fernando-lara-revitalizador-de-la-seminci-director-general-de-cine.html> [accessed 10 March 2020]

—— 'TVE patrocina el Festival de San Sebastián hasta 2007', *El País*, 20 July 2005, <'http://elpais.com/diario/2005/07/20/radiotv/1121810401_850215.html> [accessed 10 March 2020]

REHM, JEAN-PIERRE, 'Film Museums of the Now', *Schnitt*, 54 (February 2009), 27–31
REISENLEITNER, MARKUS, 'Tradition, Cultural Boundaries and the Constructions of Spaces of Identity', *Spaces of Identity*, 1, 1 (2001), 7–13, <http://www.yorku.ca/soi/Vol_1/_PDF/Reisenleitner.pdf> [accessed 10 March 2020]
RHYNE, RAGAN, *Pink Dollars Gay and Lesbian Film Festivals and the Economy of Visibility* (unpublished doctoral thesis, New York University, 2007)
—— 'Film Festival Circuits and Stakeholders', in *Film Festival Yearbook 1: The Festival Circuit*, ed. by Dina Iordanova with Ragan Rhyne (St. Andrews: St. Andrews Film Studies, 2009), pp. 9–39
ROMERO, RUBÉN, '"El cine español tiene ágoras y peliculitas." Ignasi Guardans tranquiliza a los productores en Sitges', *Público*, 7 October 2009, <http://www.publico.es/culturas/258459/el-cine-espanol-tiene-agoras-y-peliculitas> [accessed 10 March 2020]
ROSENBAUM, JONATHAN, 'Reply to Cinephilia Survey', *Jonathan Rosenbaum*, 21 June 2009, <http://www.jonathanrosenbaum.net/2009/06/reply-to-cinephilia-survey/> [accessed 10 March 2020]
ROSS, MIRIAM, 'The Film Festival as Producer: Latin American Films and Rotterdam's Hubert Bals Fund', *Screen*, 52, 2 (Summer 2011), 261–67
ROSSER, MICHAEL, 'BFI Launches US Distribution Fund', *Screen International*, 13 January 2014, <http://www.screendaily.com/news/bfi-launches-us-distribution-fund/5065271.article> [accessed 10 March 2020]
Rotterdam Cinemart, <http://www.filmfestivalrotterdam.com/en/cinemart/> [accessed 3 March 2020]
Roud, Richard, LFF brochure 1966, p. 2
ROWE, WILLIAM and VIVIAN SCHELLING, *Memory and Modernity: Popular Culture in Latin American Cinema* (London and New York: Verso, 1991)
SAID, EDWARD W., *Culture and Imperialism* (London: Vintage, 1993–1994)
—— 'Methods of Forgetting', *Al-Ahram Weekly Online*, 400 (22–28 October 1998), <http://weekly.ahram.org.eg/1998/400/op2.htm> [no longer available online, although cited in the main website, <http://weekly.ahram.org.eg/2003/658/_edsaid.htm>]. Reproduced at Ziomania, <http://ziomania.com/edward-said/57.htm> [accessed 10 March 2020.
SADA, JAVIER 'Comienza el ciclo del Cine Club San Sebastián', *Diario Vasco*, 7 October 2009, <http://www.diariovasco.com/20091007/san-sebastian/comienza-ciclo-cine-club-20091007.html> [accessed 10 March 2020]
SÁNCHEZ RECIO, GLICERIO, 'El Sindicato Vertical como instrumento político y económico del régime franquista', in *Instituciones y sociedad en el franquismo*, Special Issue of *Revista de Historia Contemporánea*, 1 (2002) <http://publicaciones.ua.es/filespubli/pdf/15793311RD12141118.pdf>
SANTAMARINA, ANTONIO, ed., *Anexo 4. Catálogo de Publicaciones* (Madrid: Filmoteca Española/I.C.A.A./Ministerio de Cultura, 2005)
SANTOS FONTELA, CÉSAR, *El cine español en la encrucijada* (Madrid: Ciencia Nueva, 1967)
SAURA, CARLOS, interview with Maria Delgado, 11 June 2011, BFI Southbank NFT1, London. An extract from this interview is included in the DVD of the film, *Cría Cuervos*, 1975 [DVD] UK: BFI
SEABROOK, JOHN, 'Nobrow Culture', *The New Yorker*, 20 September 1999, <http://www.booknoise.net/johnseabrook/stories/culture/nobrow/> [accessed 10 March 2020]
SEGAL, JÉRÔME, 'Film Festivals in the Evolution of a Common Transnational Identity', in *The 4th Annual Conference on 'Cultural Production in a Global Context: The Worldwide Film Industries'*, Grenoble Ecole de Management, Grenoble, France, 3–5 June 2010, <http://jerome-segal.de/Publis/Grenoble_Conference_SEGAL_on_film_festivals.pdf> [accessed 10 March 2020]

senses of cinema, <http://sensesofcinema.com/> [accessed 4 March 2020]
SHACKLETON, LIZ, 'FIAPF Defends Film Festival Accreditation System', *Screen*, 9 July 2007, <http://www.screendaily.com/fiapf-defends-film-festival-accreditation-system/4033493.article> [accessed 10 March 2020]
SNOWMAN, DANIEL, *The Hitler Emigrés: The Cultural Impact on Britain of Refugees from Nazism* (Pimlico: Chatto & Windus, 2002)
SONTAG, SUSAN, 'The Decay of Cinema', *New York Times Magazine*, 25 February 1996
SOLAAS, ELOÍSA, INTERVIEW WITH MAR DIESTRO-DÓPIDO, BAFICI OFFICES, 31 MARCH 2009 (translated from Spanish by Mar Diestro-Dópido)
SOL, 'Historia de América. Gobierno argentino. Golpe militar de 1976. Represión. Censura. Prensa. Radio. Prensa. Televisión. Cine y Música. Rodolfo Walsh', in *El rincón del vago*, Salamanca, n.d., <http://html.rincondelvago.com/medios-de-comunicacion-en-la-dictadura-argentina.html> [accessed 10 March 2020]
STAM, ROBERT, 'Third World Film and Theory', in *Film Theory: An Introduction* (Department of Cinema Studies, New York University: Blackwell Publishers, 2000), pp. 92–102
STATEMENT OF FIPRESCI ARGENTINA, FIPRESCI, <HTTP://WWW.FIPRESCI.ORG/NEWS/ARCHIVE/ARCHIVE_2004/fipresci_argentina.htm> [accessed 12 March 2020]
STRANDGAARD PEDERSEN, JESPER and CARMELO MAZZA, 'International Film Festivals: For the Benefit of Whom?', *Culture Unbound: Journal of Current Cultural Research*, 3 (2011) 139–65
STRINGER, JULIAN, 'Global Cities and the International Film Festival Economy', in *Cinema and the City: Film and Urban Societies in a Global Context*, ed. by Mark Shiel and Tony Fitzmaurice (London: Blackwell, 2001), pp. 134–44
—— 'Raiding the Archive: Film Festivals and the Revival of Classic Hollywood', in *Memory and Popular Film*, ed. by Paul Grainge (Manchester: Manchester University Press, 2003), pp. 81–96
—— *Regarding Film Festivals*, Dissertation (Indiana University, Department of Comparative Literature, 2003)
—— 'Regarding Film Festivals: Introduction', in *The Film Festivals Reader*, ed. by Dina Iordanova (St Andrews: St Andrews Film Studies, 2013), pp. 59–68
STRONG, ROY, 'Preface', in *A Tonic to the Nation: The Festival of Britain 1951*, ed. by Mary Banham and Bevis Hillier (London: Thames & Hudson, 1976), p. 2
SWART, SHARON, 'Film Fests Bringing Pics to the People Directly. Sundance Shares Films though [*sic*] Video on Demand, YouTube, Road Tour', *Variety*, 22 January 2010, <http://variety.com/2010/film/news/film-fests-bringing-pics-to-the-people-directly-1118014192/> [accessed 10 March 2020]
TAYLOR, DIANA, *The Archive and the Repertoire. Performing Cultural Memory in the Americas* (Durham and London: Duke University Press, 2003)
TEEMAN, TIM, 'Greg Dyke: our man in the stalls at the BFI', *The Times Online*, 6 March 2008, article copied and pasted online by Pam Cook in her blog bfiwatch on the same day, <http://bfiwatch.blogspot.co.uk/2008/03/greg-dyke-bbc-and-bfi.html> [accessed 10 March 2020]
THE MANAGEMENT, ed., *Twenty Years of Cinema in Venice [1932–1952]. The Venice Biennial: International Exhibition of Cinematographic Art* (Rome: Edizioni Dell'ateneo, 1952)
TOLENTINO, JAVIER, 'La Seminci, por atrevida, por valiente', *RTVE.es*, 28 October 2009, <http://blog.rtve.es/septimovicio/2009/10/la-seminci-por-atrevida-por-valiente.html> [accessed 10 March 2020]
TORONTO INTERNATIONAL FILM FESTIVAL, <http://www.tiff.net/> [accessed 3 March 2020].
TORRES, MARUJA, 'Los problemas presupuestarios y de organización hacen reconsiderar a Luis Gasca su continuidad como director del certamen' in *El País*, 22 September

1983, <http://elpais.com/diario/1983/09/22/cultura/433029605_850215.html> [accessed 10 March 2020]

Triana Toribio, Núria, 'FICXixón and Seminci: Two Spanish Film Festivals at the End of the Festival Era', *Journal of Spanish Cultural Studies*, 12, 2 (2011), 217–36

—— *Spanish Film Cultures: The Making and Unmaking of Spanish Cinema* (London: BFI Palgrave, 2016)

Trzenko, Natalia, 'El Bafici, esa joven tradición cinéfila que cumple 15 ediciones', *La Nación*, 10 April 2013, <http://www.lanacion.com.ar/1571134-el-bafici-esa-joven-tradicion-cinefila-que-cumple-15-ediciones> [accessed 10 March 2020]

Tuduri, José Luis, *San Sebastián: un festival, una historia (1953–1966)* (San Sebastián: Euskadiko Filmategia/Filmoteca Vasca, 1989)

—— *San Sebastián: un festival, una historia. (1967–1977)* (San Sebastián: Euskadiko Filmategia/Filmoteca Vasca, 1992)

Turan, Kenneth, *Sundance to Sarajevo: Film Festivals and the World They Made* (Berkeley: University of California Press, 2002)

UK Film Council, *Stories We Tell Ourselves: The Cultural Impact of UK Film 1946–2006* (Great Britain: Narval Media/Birkbeck College/Media Consulting Group, 2009)

UK Film Council/British Film Institute, *Opening Our Eyes: How Film Contributes to the Culture of the UK* (Great Britain: Northern Alliance with Ipsos MediaCT, 2011)

Vallejo, Aida, and Maria-Paz Peirano, eds, *Film Festivals and Anthropology* (Cambridge: Cambridge Scholars Publishing, 2017)

van Gennep, Arnold, *The Rites of Passage* (London: Routledge, 2004)

'What's the purpose of film festivals in the 21st Century?', *Screendaily*, 19 August 2016, https://www.screendaily.com/comment/whats-the-purpose-of-film-festivals-in-the-21st-century/5108598.article> [accessed 10 March 2020]

Whitfield, Teresa, *The Basque Conflict and ETA: The Difficulties of an Ending.* United States Institute of Peace, 1 December 2015. Available at <www.jstor.org/stable/resrep12174> [accessed 25 May 2020].

Wetherall, Greg, 'The BFI and London Film Festival today — Interview with Artistic Director Tricia Tuttle', *The Hot Corn*, 9 October 2018, <https://hotcorn.com/en/movies/news/bfi-london-film-festival-today-interview-artistic-director-tricia-tuttle/> [accessed 10 March 2020]

Willemen, Paul, 'Through the Glass Darkly: Cinephilia Reconsidered', *Looks and Frictions* (London: British Film Institute, 1994)

Wilson, David, ed., *Sight and Sound: A Fiftieth Anniversary Selection* (London: Faber & Faber and BFI Publishing, 1982)

Wise, Damon, 'Cannes 1968: The Year Jean-Luc Godard and François Truffaut Led Protests That Shut Down the Festival', *Deadline*, 18 May 2018, <https://deadline.com/2018/05/cannes-film-festival-1968-protests-anniversary-commentary-news-1202380606/> [accessed 10 March 2020]

Wlaschin, Ken, LFF brochure, 1973

—— LFF brochure, 1975

—— LFF brochure, 1977

—— LFF brochure, 1981

—— 'Film Culture vs Film Makers', in Martin Auty and Gillian Hartnoll, eds, *Water Under the Bridge: 25 Years of the London Film Festival* (London: British Film Institute, 1981), pp. 13–14

Wolf, Sergio, ed., *Cine argentino: Estéticas de la producción* (Buenos Aires: Ministerio de Cultura, Gobierno de la Ciudad, 2009), pp. 57–80.

—— interview with Mar Diestro-Dópido, BAFICI Meeting Point, 29 March 2009 (translated from Spanish by Mar Diestro-Dópido)

—— 'La Universidad como productora', in *Cine argentino. Estéticas de la producción*, ed. by Sergio Wolf (Buenos Aires: Ministerio de Cultura, Gobierno de la Ciudad, 2009), pp. 81–90

WONG, CINDY HING-YUK, *Film Festivals: Culture, People, and Power on the Global Screen* (New Brunswick, NJ: Rutgers University Press, 2011)

YOUNG, DEBORAH, Review of *La Libertad*, *Variety*, 14 May 2001, p. 24

YOUNG, NEIL, 'You, The Jury: The XXV FIDMarseille', *Sight & Sound*, 24, 9 (September 2014), 20

WURN, BARBARA, 'Leftist Glamour? or, Home Runs and Explorations: The 47th Viennale: Vienna International Film Festival', *senses of cinema*, 54 (April 2010), <http://sensesofcinema.com/2010/festival-reports/vienna-international-film-festival/> [accessed 12 March 2020]

ZALLO, RAMÓN and MIKEL AYUSO, *The Basque Country: Insight into its Culture, History, Society and Institutions* (Donostia/San Sebastián: Eusko Jaurlaritzaren Argitalpen Zerbitzu Nagusia, 2009) <http://www.kultura.ejgv.euskadi.net/r46-714/es/contenidos/informacion/ezagutu_eh/es_eza_eh/adjuntos/eza_en.pdf> [accessed 12 March 2020]

ZIELINSKI, GER, 'Dossier: Film Festival Pedagogy: Using the Film Festival in or as a Film Course', *Scope: An Online Journal of Film and Television Studies*, 26 (February 2014), <www.nottingham.ac.uk/scope/documents/2014/february/zielinksi.pdf> [accessed 12 March 2020]

'1851 London', *ExpoMuseum. The World's Fair Museum Since 1998*, n.d., <http://www.expomuseum.com/1851/> [accessed 4 March 2020]

'1951: King George opens Festival of Britain', *BBC online*, On This Day 1950–2005, n.d., <http://news.bbc.co.uk/onthisday/hi/dates/stories/may/3/newsid_2481000/2481099.stm> [accessed 10 March 2020].

INDEX

❖

2004 Madrid train bombings 118–20

Abasto Shopping Centre 44–47
'act of display' 19
Adair, Gilbert 144–46
Agora/Ágora (Alejandro Amenábar) 123
Aguilar, Gonzalo 34, 58, 5
Aguilera, Pedro:
   Naufragio/Shipwreck 121
Aibar, Óscar:
   El Gran Vázquez/The Great Vázquez 125
Aldazábal, Peio 117
Almodóvar, Pedro 104, 108, 111, 114
   Hable con ella/Talk to Her 114
   Laberinto de pasiones/Labyrinth of Passion 108
   Pepi, Luci, Bom y otras chicas del montón/Pepi, Luci, Bom 104, 108, 111
Alonso, Lisandro 68
   Fantasma 68
   La libertad/Freedom 53, 59
   Liverpool 68
   Los muertos/The Dead 68
   Owl 200
   El Amante Cine magazine 4, 40, 41, 47
Anasagasti, Koldo 117
Angulo, Javier 91
Antín, Eduardo, *see* Quintín
Antín, Manuel 62
Antonio Elorza Velodrome 113
Argentina:
   1998–2002 Argentine great depression 51, 60, 128
   politics in 35–37, 39, 42, 49, 51
Armendáriz, Montxo:
   Las cartas de Alou/Letters from Alou 110
Arroba, Álvaro 75–76
audience 7–8, 61, 101, 113–14, 121–23, 149, 152, 162–64, 182–85
Augé, Marc 44
Auty, Martyn 142, 160–61, 164–65, 180

Bajo Ulloa, Juanma:
   Alas de mariposa/Butterfly Wings 110, 118
Bakhtin, Mikhail 7, 11, 187
Bardem, Javier 120
Bardem, Juan Antonio 91, 92–93
Barnet, Rudi 117, 130
Basque conflict 5, 88, 103–05, 110, 117–18
   see also Euskadi Ta Askatasuna (ETA)

Basterretxea, Néstor:
   Amar Lur 103, 138 n. 121
   Pelotari 102
Batlle, Diego 36, 64
Baudrillard, Jean 197–98
Bazin, André 10, 18–20, 195
Berger, Pablo:
   Blancanieves/Snow White 130
Bergman, Ingmar:
   The Seventh Seal 90
Berlanga, Luis García 93, 105–06, 115, 134 n. 18
   Los jueves, milagro/Miracles of Thursdays 90
Berlin International Film Festival 2, 17, 64, 179
BFI London Film Festival (LFF) 3–8, 18, 141–87, 197, 198–200, 201
   audience 7–8, 149, 152, 162–64, 182–85
   criticism of 172–74
   expansion of 166
   fiftieth anniversary of 142–43, 157
   funding 169–71, 179, 185
   London, relationship with:
      marketing 198–200
      programming 7, 149–53, 165–67, 176
      retrospectives 180
BFI Production Board 153
BFI Southbank (building) 148
Birkbeck, University of London 2
La bola de cristal/The Crystal Ball (TV show) 111
Bollaín, Iciar:
   Y también la lluvia/Even the Rain 124
Bourdieu, Pierre 11, 14
Boyero, Carlos 125, 139 n. 142
Bresson, Robert:
   Une femme douce/A Gentle Woman 103
British Art Festivals Association (BAFA) 9
British film industry 7, 156
British Film Institute (BFI) 3, 5–7, 18, 143, 146–48, 154, 159, 161, 174, 179–80
   see also BFI London Film Festival (LFF)
Brownlow, Kevin:
   Winstanley 153
Buenos Aires Festival Internacional de Cine Independiente/Buenos Aires Independent Film Festival (BAFICI) 3–8, 16, 25, 33–34, 39–58, 61–81, 143–44, 151, 197, 200–01
   1998–2002 Argentine great depression 51
   audience 7–8, 61
   education programme (BAFICITO) 64–65

funding 49–51, 56–58
influence 72–73
Intercine 54
La Lectora Provisoria blog 61–62
marketing 198–200
programming 47, 50, 75–76
touring 62
Buenos Aires Lab (BAL) 56–58
bullfighting 95, 131
Buñuel, Luis 106
La vía láctea/The Milky Way 90
Viridiana 93, 99, 135 n. 31

Caetano, Adrián:
Bolivia 68
Cahiers du cinéma: España magazine 52
see also Caimán Cuadernos de Cine magazine
Caimán Cuadernos de Cine magazine 121–23
see also *Cahiers du cinéma* magazine
Calhoun, Dave, 168–69
Campanella, Juan José 38, 52
Campero, Agustín 37, 77
Cannes Film Festival 13, 18–20
capitalism 20
carnival 11
Carri, Albertina:
Los Rubios/The Blonds 68
Catholic Church 90, 104
celebrity 48
censorship:
in Argentina 35, 36–38, 69
in Spain 91–95, 101, 103, 108
in United Kingdom 146–47
Channel 4 (UK) 154–55
Chatrian, Carlo 8, 195
Christie, Ian 143, 144, 146, 154, 171, 185, 188 n. 17
cine-clubs 13, 98
Cine Doré 114
Cine en Construcción (Films in Progress) 4, 23, 38, 128–29
Cine en Movimiento 128–29
Cinéfondation 129
cinema of attractions 19
Cinema Scope magazine 17, 182
CineMart Rotterdam 7
cinephilia 6, 15–18, 40–41, 186
Cineworld 162
Clair, René:
Porte des Lilas 148
Clarín newspaper 52
Cocteau, Jean 20
Colomo, Fernando:
¿Qué hace una chica como tú en un sitio como éste?/What is a Girl Like You Doing in a Place Like This? 108
colonialism:
cultural colonialism 21, 59
neo-colonialism 129

Combs, Richard 155
Communist Party of Spain 93, 134 n. 28
community 61
consumption 7, 10–11, 13, 44, 159
Cousins, Mark 183, 186, 201
Film Festival Manifesto 183, 186, 201
COVID-19 77, 197
criticism, see film criticism
cultural capital 14, 167–68
cultural imperialism 21
cultural memory 67–72

Debord, Guy 8, 197
de Orbe, José María:
Aitá/Father 125
De Valck, Marijke 2, 10, 12–14, 19, 20–22, 59
De Witt, Helen 25
Los desafíos/The Challenges (Claudio Guerín, José Luis Egea and Víctor Erice) 103
Derrida, Jacques 69
Devesa Fernández, María 15
Di Chiara, Francesco 15
Di Tella, Andrés 42–44, 47–50, 64
dictatorship 5, 35, 39, 67, 69, 89, 90–92, 100–04, 136 n. 74, 151
Diestro-Dópido, Mar 2, 11, 20, 34, 146, 174
Donostia Award 114
Douglas, Bill 154
Drove Fernández-Shaw, Antonio:
La caza de brujas/The Witch-Hunt 103
dubbing 135 n. 31
Dupin, Christophe 143
Dyke, Greg 168–69

Eceiza, Antonio 98
Echarri, Miguel 90, 102, 103, 106
Edinburgh Film Festival 164–65, 178
elitism 101, 113, 149
Elkana, Yehuda 67
Elsaesser, Thomas 1, 13–14, 21, 59, 168
Erice, Víctor:
El espíritu de la colmena/The Spirit of the Beehive 103
Escuela Oficial de Cinematografía (official film school in Madrid) 92, 108
European Capital of Culture project 131
European Network for Cinema and Media Studies (NECS) 2
Eurovision Song Contest 22
Euskadi Ta Askatasuna (ETA) 88, 103–04, 110, 117–18
see also Basque conflict
experience 196
experimentation 92, 99, 102, 103, 110, 149, 153–54, 160, 161, 168, 171
Expos 21
Falassi, Alessandro 9–12, 20
Falicov, Tamara L. 4, 22, 37, 38, 128–29

Fascism 12
Fédération Internationale de la Presse Cinématographique/International Federation of Film Critics (FIPRESCI) 17
Fédération Internationale des Associations de Producteurs de Films/International Federation of Film Producers Associations (FIAPF) 6, 23–25, 95, 129
Federico Fellini:
  Nights of Cabiria 148
Fernández Cuenca, Carlos 101–02
Festival do Rio 39
'festival film' 4, 22–23, 59, 100, 129, 161, 167
Festival of Britain 152
festivals, history of 8–18
FICXixón 15
FIDMarseille 10–11
Field, Simon 11, 19–20, 177–78
film criticism 17, 47, 121
Film Festival Research Network (FFRN) 2
Film Festival Yearbook 2
Film magazine 41, 42
film subsidies 123–24
Filmoteca Española/Spanish Cinemateque 114–17
financial crisis of 2007–08 194
Flanagan, Matthew 174–76, 180–82
Fonds Sud 38, 129
Franco, Fernando:
  La herida/Wounded 130
Franco, Francisco 25, 89–92, 93–95, 99–100, 103–06
Franco, Jesús (Jess) 111
Frémaux, Thierry 75
Fuente, Flavia de la 49–50, 61–62
Fujiwara, Chris 15–16, 22, 178
Fund, Iván:
  Los labios/The Lips 76
funding 37–39, 49–50, 56–59, 78, 100–01, 123, 125–26, 169–71, 185

Galán, Diego 5, 8, 111–14, 116, 118–20, 123, 124, 130, 178, 198
García Escudero, José María 92, 99–102
Gasca, Luis 106
geopolitics 4, 19–22, 164
Gilmore, Geoffrey 24–25
Gladwell, David:
  Requiem for a Village 153
glamour 18–20, 157, 168, 174, 177–78, 182–83
globalisation 4, 20, 22
Glocal in Progress 129
Guadalajara International Film Festival 39
Guardans, Ignasi 123–26
Gubern, Román 89, 92
Guerín, José Luis 103
Gugliotta, Sandra:
  Un día de suerte/A Lucky Day 52

Gunning, Tom 19

Harbord, Janet 11–12, 22
Hardcastle, Leslie 146, 148
Hebron, Sandra 144, 146, 155, 157, 161–62, 168, 169–72, 177, 179
Heredero, Carlos F. 116, 120, 121, 126
Herrero Velarde, José Ángel 90, 101, 117
Hispano-Norteamericano Cinematographic Treaty 88–89
Historias Breves 41
Hitchcock, Alfred 99
Hollywood 18–19, 153–54
Hong Kong International Film Festival (HKIFF) 2
Houston, Penelope 148
Hsiao-hsien, Hou:
  The Assassin 121
Huber, Christoph 16, 51
Hubert Bals Fund (HBF) 22, 56–59, 129
Hurch, Hans 9, 195

Ibáñez Serrador, Narciso:
  Historias para no dormir/Stories to Keep You Awake 111
de la Iglesia, Álex:
  Balada triste de trompeta/The Last Circus 124
Instituto de la Cinematografía y de las Artes Audiovisuales/Institute of Cinematography and Visual Arts (ICAA) 123–24
IndieLisboa film festival 64–65
Instituto Nacional de Cine y Artes Audiovisuales/The National Institute of Cinema and Audiovisual Arts (INCAA) 37, 39, 41, 48–49, 52–54, 62–64, 78
International Film Festival Circuit 4, 35, 37
International Film Festival of Rio de Janeiro 35
International Film Festival of São Paulo 39
Iordanova, Dina 2–3, 14

Jameson, Frederick 44
Jullier, Laurent 16

Kazan, Elia:
  On The Waterfront 90
Knegt, Peter 194
Koehler, Robert 16–17
Kubrick, Stanley:
  A Clockwork Orange 90–91
Kurosawa, Akira:
  Throne of Blood 148
Kursaal Auditorium 120

Lacuesta, Isaki:
  Entre dos aguas/Between Two Waters 130
  Los pasos dobles/The Double Steps 130
Lara, Fernando 91, 124

Larruquert, Fernando:
    Amar Lur 103, 138 n. 121
    Pelotari 102
Lerer, Diego 52, 61, 166
Lerman, Diego:
    Tan de repente/Suddenly 52
Leveratto, Jean-Marc 16, 186
Ley Miró/Ley del Cine 110–11, 124
Llinás, Mariano 78–79
    Balnearios 52
    Historias extraordinarias/Extraordinary Stories 78–79
    La Flor/The Flower 75–76
Locarno International Film Festival 177–78, 195
London Film Festival, *see* BFI London Film Festival (LFF)
Lopérfido, Darío 42, 56
Loza, Santiago:
    Los labios/The Lips 76

Málaga Film Festival 126
Malcolm, Derek 157, 166–67
Mar del Plata International Film Festival 34–35, 39–40, 48, 49
Marché du Film 7
Marfici film festival 52
Marías, Miguel 116
market 20–23
marketing 15
Martel, Lucrecia 51, 68–69
    Chocobar 69
    La mujer sin cabeza/The Headless Woman 68–69
    Zama 68–69
Martin, Adrian 16, 51
Martín Patino, Basilio:
    Canciones para después de una Guerra/Songs for After the War 103–04
Martín Peña, Fernando 40–42, 52–54, 70–72
mass culture 120
McArthur, Colin 164
Medem, Julio:
    La pelota vasca. La piel contra la piedra/The Basque Ball. Skin Against Stone 118
memory, *see* cultural memory
Message2Man International Film Festival 196
Mexico City International Contemporary Film Festival (FICCO) 64, 73
micro-festivals 20
Miró, Pilar 110–11, 124
    El crimen de Cuenca/The Cuenca Crime 110
Mitchum, Robert 113
Mitre, Santiago:
    El estudiante/The Student 70
    Paulina 78
Moguillanski, Alejo:
    Castro 78
    El escarabajo de oro/The Golden Beetle 78

Mollo, Andrew:
    Winstanley 153
Montreal World Film Festival 24
Moscow International Film Festival 13, 149
Mothers of the Plaza de Mayo 68
Müller, Marco 24, 195–96
Mulvey, Laura 19

Nación newspaper 49
National Film Theatre (NFT) 21, 143, 146, 148–52, 157, 159–62, 180
    see also BFI Southbank
nationalism 5, 88, 104
Nayman, Adam 3, 16
neoliberalism 51
Netflix 76
networked spaces 147
New Argentine Cinema (NAC) 41, 60–61
New British Cinema 153–54
New Media Law (*Nueva Ley de los Medios*) 77
New Spanish Cinema 99–101
nobrow 19, 164
non-places 44
Nowell-Smith, Geoffrey 143, 146, 147–48, 162, 178–79, 188 n. 16

Odeon, Leicester Square 162
Olaciregui, Mikel 95, 111, 115, 117, 118, 121–23, 125, 128–30
orientalism 21
Ostrowska, Dorota 2

Página/12 magazine 47, 67
El País newspaper 124–25
Panozzo, Marcelo 52, 54–56, 70, 75, 79
Pena, Jaime 120, 124
Pérez Villar, Dionisio 89–90
Picazo, Miguel:
    La tía Tula/Aunt Tula 101
Picturehouse 162
Piñeiro, Matías:
    Hermia & Helena 78
    La princesa de Francia/The Princess of France 78
    Todos mienten/They All Lie 78
    Viola 78
Plakhov, Andrei 17, 116
Portabella, Pere 22, 59, 99, 100, 120, 195
    El Sopar/The Dinner 105
Porta-Fouz, Javier 41, 56, 75
Porton, Richard 14, 16, 19, 177–78, 183
postcolonialism 21
postmodernism 44, 60
Prouse, Derek 152, 160, 172
Puenzo, Luis:
    La historia oficial/The Official Story 36
Pusan International Film Festival 21, 72–73, 185

Quandt, James 22, 178
Querejeta, Elías 98, 101, 106
Quinn, James 142
Quintín (Antín, Eduardo) 16, 22, 23, 48, 49–53, 54, 58–59, 61–62, 69, 73–75, 116

Ray, Satyajit:
   The Unvanquished 148
Rayns, Tony 146, 165–67, 176, 180, 185–86, 188 n. 18
Re, Valentina 15
realism 60
Rebollo, Javier:
   La mujer sin piano/A Woman Without A Piano 125
Rebordinos, José Luis 111, 117, 120, 131–33, 197
Rejtman, Martín:
   Copacabana 68
   Rapado 41
remembrance 67–70
Renoir, Jean:
   La grande illusion / The Grand Illusion 12–13
rites, *see* ritual acts
ritual acts 9–12
Robinson, David 141
Rosell, Ulises:
   El etnógrafo/The Ethnographer 68
Rosenbaum, Jonathan 16
Rotterdam International Film Festival 19–20, 177
Roud, Richard 152, 166, 182–83
RTVE (National Spanish Television) 110–11

Said, Edward W. 67
Salamanca Conversations 92–93
San Sebastián Film Festival 3–8, 25, 87–92, 95–114, 116–33, 143–44, 151, 180, 197–98, 201
   audience 7–8, 101, 113–14, 121–23
   Conference of Film Schools 99
   economic impact on city of San Sebastián 131–33
   elitism 101, 113
   film preservation 114
   internationalism 128–30
   marketing 198
   programming 95, 120, 124–25
   sponsorship of 111
Santiago International Film Festival (SANFIC) 73
Sapir, Esteban:
   Picado Fino/Fine Powder 41
Saura, Carlos:
   Cría Cuervos/Raise Ravens 105–06
Schnitt magazine 194–95
Second World War:
   impact on film industry 13, 21–22, 100, 152
Semana Internacional de Cine de Valladolid (International Cinema Week of Valladolid), *see* Seminci
Seminci 15, 90–91, 126
Seville European Film Festival 126

shopping centres 44–47
Sight & Sound magazine 143, 147, 148
Slamdance Film Festival 76
Solaas, Eloísa 69
Solanas, Fernando:
   Tangos: El exilio de Gardel/ Tangos: The Exile of Gardel 36
Sontag, Susan 16
spectacle 197–98
St Andrew's University 2, 14
Stewart, Clare 159, 167, 174, 180, 200
Stier, Oren Baruch 67–68
Stringer, Julian 18, 20–21
Subiela, Eliseo:
   Hombre mirando al sudeste/Man Facing Southeast 36
subsidies, *see* film subsidies
Sundance Film Festival 76
Sundance Lab 129

Talent Campus Buenos Aires 64
Taylor, Diana 70
Tercer Cine/Third Cinema 35
Time Out magazine 168–69
Toronto International Film Festival 24, 177–78
Torre Nilsson, Leopoldo:
   La casa del ángel/The House of the Angel 148
tourism 6, 14, 21, 35, 88–89, 92, 100, 131, 164
transnationalism 20, 38
   see also globalization
Trapero, Pablo:
   Mundo grúa/Crane World 48, 53
   Nacido y criado/Born and Bred 68
Trueba, Fernando:
   El artista y la modelo/The Artist and the Model 108
   Ópera Prima 108
Truffaut, Francois:
   The 400 Blows 90
Tuttle, Tricia 156, 159, 162, 167, 176

UK Film Council (UKFC) 169, 174
Universidad de Buenos Aires 42
Universidad de Cine (FUC) 62–64
Universidad de Valladolid 104
   UPA! una película argentina/UPA! An Argentinian Movie (Santiago Giralt, Camila Toker, Tamae Garateguy) 79
Uribe, Imanol:
   Bwana 110
   Días contados/Running Out of Time 110
   El proceso de Burgos/The Burgos Trial 118
   La fuga de Segovia/Escape from Segovia 110
utopia 14, 40, 72–73

Valdivia International Film Festival 73
Valladolid International Film Festival, *see* Seminci
Variety magazine 24, 76
Venice International Film Festival 12, 102–03

Vermut, Carlos:
   Diamond Flash 121
   Magical Girl 130
Victoria Eugenia Theatre 99, 101
Viennale 9, 177
Villamediana, Daniel V.:
   La vida sublime/ The Life Sublime 121
Villaronga, Agustí:
   Pa Negre/ Black Bread 125
VUE 162

Whitaker, Sheila 18, 151, 154, 156–57, 159, 168
Willemen, Paul 16
Wlaschin, Ken 7, 144, 152–54, 157, 164–65, 166, 172
Wolf, Sergio 54, 65, 68, 73
Wong, Cindy Hing-Yuk 2–3, 11, 21
Wootton, Adrian 18, 155–56, 157, 168

Zero Latitude Film Festival 73
Zulueta y Besson, Antonio de 98–99, 108

Milton Keynes UK
Ingram Content Group UK Ltd.
UKHW051053220424
441551UK00012B/975

9 781781 883990